THE COMPLETE POETICAL
WORKS OF
PERCY BYSSHE SHELLEY

The Retrospect.
Cwm Elan 1812

To trace Duration's lone career
To check the chariot of the year
Whose burning wheels forever sweep
The boundaries of oblivion's deep....
To snatch from Time the monsters jaw
The children which she just had borne
And ere entombed within her maw
To drag them to the light of morn
And mark each feature with an eye
Of cold & pearless scrutiny....
It asks a soul not formed to feel
An eye of glass, a hand of steel
Thoughts that have passed thoughts that
With truth and feeling to compare;
A scene which widened fancy viewed
In the souls coldest solitude,
With that same scene when peaceful love
Flings raptures colour on the grove
When mountain meadow wood & stream

Shelley's transcript of Esdaile Poem no. 50, 1–19

THE
COMPLETE POETICAL
WORKS OF
PERCY BYSSHE
SHELLEY

EDITED BY

NEVILLE ROGERS

In four volumes

VOLUME I
1802–1813

OXFORD
AT THE CLARENDON PRESS
1972

Oxford University Press, Ely House, London W.1

GLASGOW NEW YORK TORONTO MELBOURNE WELLINGTON
CAPE TOWN IBADAN NAIROBI DAR ES SALAAM LUSAKA ADDIS ABABA
DELHI BOMBAY CALCUTTA MADRAS KARACHI LAHORE DACCA
KUALA LUMPUR SINGAPORE HONG KONG TOKYO

PRINTED IN GREAT BRITAIN
AT THE UNIVERSITY PRESS, OXFORD
BY VIVIAN RIDLER
PRINTER TO THE UNIVERSITY

ARTHURO A HOUGHTON SECUNDO

QUI IPSE MUSIS DEDITUS

MUSARUM MINISTROS OPE CONSILIOQUE

HORTATUR ADIUVAT ERIGIT

EDITOR'S PREFACE

THE aim of this edition of the Poetical Works of Shelley is to present as complete a text as possible, to give it in a form approximating as closely as possible to what the poet intended, and to supply the necessary textual commentary and explanatory notes. The four volumes correspond to the main stages in Shelley's development. The first two cover the poetry written in England: Volume I the Godwinian phase, down to 1812–13, culminating in *Queen Mab*, and Volume II the Platonic liberation of 1814–17, culminating in *Laon and Cythna* (usually known as *The Revolt of Islam*); the third and fourth cover the poetic fulfilment of Shelley's Italian years, 1818–22.

Textual criticism is a subject in which not one person in ten million has had occasion to look either for general principles or for principles which must govern the editing of a particular author. In Shelley's case, fortunately, they have been worked out, and tested, by the generations of accomplished workers, from Mary Shelley to Thomas Hutchinson, whom it is my privilege and my responsibility to succeed. A brief history of the continuous editorial struggle to ascertain and fulfil Shelley's intentions is given in the first part of my General Introduction. Such a summary seemed desirable in view of certain assertions, more knowing than knowledgeable, which, latterly, have sometimes obscured both the quality of the old text and the requirements of the new.

No effort has been spared to make this edition as complete as possible, though I should be neither surprised nor saddened by the subsequent emergence of an occasional new piece or passage. The general design is outlined in this volume in the second part of the General Introduction. Of the manifold difficulty of my labours no introductory summary would be practicable. The new material which has enlarged their scope has in no way diminished their intensity, and their demands in terms of time and technical study have seemed infinite. No editor, not even Mary Shelley, I think, has worked over a greater quantity of Shelley's manuscripts—to mention Shelley's Notebooks alone, their hard core: twenty-eight of these are today available for study, in comparison with the six available to Hutchinson. With the exception of a few tangential

ones in the Pforzheimer Library, for which I have been able to
rely on the careful transcripts printed in *Shelley and his Circle*,
I have examined all available manuscripts of Shelley's poetry and
possess photocopies of the crucial ones, not to speak of innumerable
cognate manuscripts. Omissions, verbal slips, and worse inaccur-
acies, must inevitably have occurred, and with these I can only
hope that my readers will be as patient as I believe that Shelley
would have been. Perhaps some comparative measure of my labours
might be found in terms of time alone: the best part of twenty
years was spent by my friend Lawrence J. Zillman on the editing
and re-editing of one poem, *Prometheus Unbound*, while seven years
were not too many for my friend Donald H. Reiman to spend on the
transcription and presentation of the 547 lines of 'The Triumph of
Life'. It was Wellington, I think, who described the Peninsula as
a country where large armies starve and small armies get beaten.
How easily the vast tracts of the Shelley material might beat any
single editor can be understood only by those who have explored it.
Nor would attempts to divide the labour among a team fare better
than attempts to systematize a large army for guerrilla warfare in
wild, uncharted country. Imagine attempts to win such a war by
the application of parade-ground drill and you complete the analogy,
for such is the worth of the bibliographer's drill-book in the Shelley
jungle.

From that part of my Introduction which relates to the first
volume it will be seen that the manuscripts involved are, by com-
parison, fewer and simpler than in the later volumes; manuscript
problems will be examined more closely, and conveniently, in the
latter. Each of the first three volumes contains its own index of titles
and first lines and a list of textual sources. The fourth is supplied
with a complete bibliography and indexes to cover the whole edition.

In my twenty years of labour I have necessarily incurred a formid-
able debt of gratitude to both institutions and individuals. Detailed
acknowledgement must, for practical reasons, be postponed to my
fourth, and final, volume. Meanwhile there are certain acknowledge-
ments which cannot wait. I must first of all offer commemorative
gratitude to four Oxford friends whose wisdom and experience,
alas, are no longer with us: Professor H. W. Garrod, Miss Helen
Darbishire, Mr. Percy Simpson, and Mr. J. B. Leishman. In the
original planning of this edition their kindly counsel was of crucial
value. Professor Edmund Blunden, without whose help and en-

couragement it could never have been undertaken, has allowed me, at all times, to draw freely on his unrivalled understanding of Shelley's poetry and Shelley's period. To Mr. H. W. White, the Dr. Lind of generations of Rossall Sixth Formers, a special debt must be acknowledged. He it was who, in a lesson on the Greek pastoral poets, first brought *Adonais*, Shelley, and the marvels of the Shelleyan-Platonic amalgam into the life of a games-bored schoolboy of the 1920s; and he it is to whom Shelley's editor still gratefully turns for an occasional new glimpse into that world of classical wit and learning in which Shelley and his circle lived and moved and had their being. And I must record without delay what the more recent stages of my work have owed to those who have latterly given their time and their skill to sharing with me the study and the perils of Shelley's manuscripts: my colleague Dr. James R. Thompson of the Department of English at Ohio University, and my former students Dr. Claude A. Brew, of Gustavus Adolphus College, St. Peter, Minnesota, and Dr. William J. McTaggart, of Carnegie-Mellon University. I was particularly fortunate in having Dr. McTaggart's co-operation during his year as a Fulbright Scholar in England: his patient study, percipient criticism, and kindly encouragement have smoothed many of my rougher paths. In this first volume—see Notes, p. 351—I have incurred a special debt to Dr. Thompson and to my colleague Dr. Frank B. Fieler for the last-minute researches they kindly carried out for me in the Bodleian and in the British Museum.

For the care with which they have checked proofs I am deeply grateful to Mr. Desmond King-Hele, Professor Frederick L. Jones, Dr. William J. McTaggart, Dr. Timothy Webb, my colleague Dr. Duane B. Schneider, and my graduate student Mr. R. Stanley Dicks. Valuable help in checking the manuscript has been afforded both by Mr. Dicks and by my former student Mr. Robert E. Schweid. It has to be added, of course, that the responsibility for errors is mine alone.

NEVILLE ROGERS

Ohio University,
Athens, Ohio, U.S.A.

CONTENTS

POSTHUMOUS FRAGMENTS OF MARGARET NICHOLSON, 1810

THE ESDAILE POEMS, 1805–1814

CONTENTS

GENERAL INTRODUCTION

I. HISTORY OF THE TEXT

1. *Shelley's Editions; the Manuscripts, 1802–1822*

THOUGH Shelley was as concerned about his text as any poet, he was not destined to be helpful with its presentation. Time and temperament, equally, were against him. In contrast with, say, Browning, who carefully prepared edition after edition, or Wordsworth, his long-lived contemporary, who gave infinite care to revision and rearrangement, he was always far too busy loading every rift of his short life with the ore of poetry itself to spare much time or thought for its final minting. He was, as he admitted to Stockdale on 14 November 1810,[1] 'by no means a good hand at correction' and, having 'obviated' as best he could that publisher's 'principal objections', looked to him to correct 'any error of flagrant incoherency'. As the years passed he grew more and more conscious of the shortcomings in his printed text. From the complaints he made to Ollier, and about Ollier,[2] it has been commonly assumed that the trouble, aggravated by his absence abroad, arose, quite simply, from Ollier's lack of care in following his manuscripts. If more of Shelley's actual 'copy' had survived, together with Ollier's comments on it, this ingenuous supposition could hardly have circulated. To look to Ollier, as he had looked to Stockdale, not merely to reproduce a manuscript in print but to correct it where necessary, was in accordance with a time-honoured custom of the day: Keats's reliance on John Taylor, for example, is well attested,[3] and had Shelley enjoyed a like co-operation the texts printed in his lifetime might have been better. But to make a scapegoat out of Ollier simply will not do: Shelley's manuscripts in general will acquit him. Nor will it do to treat Shelley's absence from England as having any serious textual consequences: of this belief the disproof may be found in his earlier publications. He was not abroad during the printing of *Laon and Cythna* (*The Revolt of Islam*) and must himself

---

[1] F. L. Jones, *The Letters of Percy Bysshe Shelley*, i. 20.
[2] Ibid. ii. 117, 178, 196, 244, 246, 257, 297, 410–11.
[3] H. W. Garrod, *The Poetical Works of John Keats*, xx, xxvii–xxxii, xxxv–xxxvi.

bear the responsibility for *flower-invowen* (1860), *Thee calm* (1914), *were* (3587), *tho' mighty* (4361), to look no further. Similarly with *Queen Mab* where, in 1813, he printed *Secures* (IV. 176), *offsprings* (V. 116), *reillumined* (VII. 180), and the asyntactical *extend/Their* (VIII. 232–3). When he noticed a need, and had a chance (as with this last example, when he was revising for *The Daemon of the World*), he made improvements; so too in 'Hymn to Intellectual Beauty', 2, the sibilant *amongst* of 1817 was changed in 1819 to *among*, and in line 13 the asyntactical *dost* to *doth*. His errata slips show not only what he noticed but what he missed—see too my Textual Commentary, *passim*. And Shelley's death, a disaster in all other respects, was by no means the textual disaster it has been assumed to be; all the errors just mentioned, for example, were afterwards corrected by editors. But he bequeathed far worse troubles than these.

One matter in which, as was customary, he looked to his publisher for help was the regularization of 'accidentals'[1]—to use that somewhat unfortunate bibliographical term which lumps together spelling and capitalization, mere ornaments, very often, of meaning, with punctuation which is so often its very life. Something of the burden thrown on Ollier can be deduced from the experience of Robert Bridges who, when he wished to include in *The Spirit of Man* the lines from *Prometheus Unbound* beginning at III. iii. 44, found editions and the Bodleian manuscript alike 'useless', and was obliged to set about a complete repunctuation of his own.[2] Until he brought his peculiar gifts and experience to bear upon the involved Platonic syntax of this passage, its meaning, clear enough in Shelley's head, had defied all the efforts to bring it out, made first by the poet himself and then by the generations of editors from Mary Shelley to Hutchinson. The simple truth is that Shelley not only lacked expertise in the presentation of a text, but he also lacked consciousness of the difficulty his language could present to others. His *naïveté* in believing that having heard *Prometheus*[3] recited would qualify Gisborne to 'seize any error' may be significantly measured by the passage to which I have just referred. Very few people, very few poets—with the possible exception of such an expert reader as the present Laureate—could make it

[1] See below, pp. xxxviii–xli.

[2] See Rogers, *Shelley at Work*, pp. 134 ff., and 'The Punctuation of Shelley's Syntax' *Keats–Shelley Memorial Bulletin*, xvii, 1966. Bridges's text of the passages is used by Lawrence J. Zillman in his edition of *Prometheus Unbound*, pp. 167–9.

[3] Jones, *Letters*, ii. 196.

aurally intelligible, even with the assistance of Bridges's punctuation; and the man has yet to be born whose punctuation of it could seriously benefit from the memory of hearing it read. And the Bodleian manuscript, found useless by Bridges, though not actually printer's copy, is one of Shelley's neatest. As it happens we do possess one example of a manuscript intended by Shelley for the printer: the very beautiful Pierpont Morgan manuscript of *Julian and Maddalo*. When H. Buxton Forman turned to it for 'authority' he fared no better than Bridges—the punctuation, he found, needed no fewer than ninety-four adjustments.[1] All but five had been supplied by Mary Shelley who first printed it. Shelley had sent it, originally, to Hunt, for transmission to Ollier, and, in doing so, cheerfully left him,[2] or, failing him, Peacock, to correct the proofs. Which meant, of course, that with the responsibility for proofs went the responsibility for the pointing usually done upon them. How far even one of Shelley's 'good' manuscripts can fall short of a copy-text may be seen by comparing the frontispiece of this volume with the text on p. 169 and the notes on pp. 371–2.

When Shelley died, in 1822, he had, excluding fugitive juvenilia, the following printed books to his credit:

1. *Queen Mab; A Philosophical Poem:* with Notes, privately printed and circulated, 1813;
2. *Alastor; or, The Spirit of Solitude:* and Other Poems, 1816;
3. *Laon and Cythna; or, The Revolution of the Golden City,* 1818 (revised and reissued in the same year as *The Revolt of Islam*);
4. *Rosalind and Helen,* A Modern Eclogue; With Other Poems, 1819;
5. *The Cenci,* A Tragedy, In Five Acts, 1819 (2nd edn., 1821);
6. *Prometheus Unbound,* A Lyrical Drama In Four Acts, With Other Poems, 1820;
7. *Oedipus Tyrannus; or, Swellfoot the Tyrant,* A Tragedy, In Two Acts, 1820;
8. *Epipsychidion,* Verses Addressed to the Noble and Unfortunate Lady, Emilia V——, 1821;
9. *Adonais,* An Elegy on the Death of John Keats, 1821;
10. *Hellas,* A Lyrical Drama, 1822.

[1] Forman, *Poetical Works of Percy Bysshe Shelley,* 1876, iii. 106.
[2] Jones, *Letters,* ii. 108.

Together with a mass of manuscripts, mainly unpublished, they were to provide his widow with some two decades of textual labour.

Out of the two accidental facts of Shelley's residence in Italy and the posthumous publication of much of his poetry has grown the bibliographical myth of a text corrupted by an incompetent publisher during his lifetime and by editors after his death, and needing to be 'corrected' by 'accurate' reproduction of his manuscripts. The truth, as shown by history, is the exact opposite—his editors have provided correction of the error of which his manuscripts are usually the source. It is the task of a new editor to continue their labour.

2. Mary Shelley's Editions; the Pirates; Leigh Hunt, 1824–1839

Posthumous Poems, the first fruit of Mary's labour, appeared in 1824, and immediately incurred the anger of Sir Timothy Shelley who, after some 300 copies had been sold, forced her to suppress the rest of the edition. The pirating of Shelley's work had begun in 1821, when one William Clark annoyed him by reviving Queen Mab. In 1826 William Benbow, taking advantage of the suppression of Posthumous Poems, incorporated its material in two collections of Shelley's verse. In 1829 A. and W. Galignani published in Paris a one-volume edition of The Poetical Works of Coleridge, Shelley, and Keats. Unable to prevent this and anxious, above all, to keep her husband's fame alive, Mary Shelley gave what help she could. Three other unauthorized editions soon followed: Stephen Hunt's The Beauties of Percy Bysshe Shelley in 1830, John Ascham's Works of Percy Bysshe Shelley in 1834, and Charles Daly's miniature volume of selected poems, also entitled Works, in 1836. In the meanwhile a new and important addition to the Shelley canon had been made in 1832 when Leigh Hunt published The Mask of Anarchy, with a Preface; in the year of the Reform Act it seemed to him safe to make use of the manuscript which he had thought it wise to withhold when he received it from Shelley in 1819.

By 1839 Mary Shelley had so far overcome the opposition of Sir Timothy that he consented to permit her to bring out a collected edition, provided no biography were attached. This condition she cleverly circumvented by interspersing among the poems those Notes which are such an invaluable commentary on their background. Her four-volume Poetical Works, published that year, was followed by a second, single-volume, edition which appeared before

the year was out, though it was given an 1840 imprint. With the
exception of a handful of poems not available to Mary Shelley, all
subsequent texts derive from her text of 1839. Its validity was
unconsciously demonstrated in 1958 by Charles H. Taylor, Jr., in
a remarkable piece of bibliographical research: *The Early Collected
Editions of Shelley's Poems.* Mr. Taylor made two discoveries. One
was that, when preparing her 1839 edition, Mary Shelley had dif-
ficulty, owing to Sir Timothy's suppression of her 1824 volume,
in obtaining printer's copy of its contents and consequently made
use, both for these poems and for others printed by Shelley himself,
of the more easily obtainable piratical texts brought out by Galignani
in 1829 and Ascham in 1834. She corrected errors as carefully as she
could but, not unnaturally, there were some which escaped her.
Mr. Taylor's other discovery was of the existence of an errata leaf,
tipped into some of the 1824 copies but not used in the preparation
of the 1839 edition. With great thoroughness he sets out in his book,
chronologically and in columns, all the textual changes that occurred
between the first printing of a poem, whether by Shelley in his
lifetime or by Mary in 1824, and the four-volume edition of 1839:
every error derived from the piratical editions is meticulously pin-
pointed. Like all his readers I was both impressed by this perfor-
mance and disturbed by an accompanying innuendo of 'worthless
variants . . . preserved in the best modern editions'. In my copy
I pencilled an additional column-heading '1904' and prepared to
enter in it the 'worthless variants' preserved by Hutchinson in
what hitherto has been the *textus receptus.* The result was both
surprising and illuminating. Out of all the variants detected by
Mr. Taylor not one had resulted in an uncorrected error. Some
corrections had been made by Hutchinson himself, some taken over
from H. Buxton Forman. But by far the greater number had been
made by Mary Shelley herself. What her changes reveal is that,
so far from careless copying, she used her intelligence to correct,
where rhyme and metre permitted, some such solecism, whether
due to Shelley or to herself, as a singular verb with a plural subject
or vice versa. How easily major textual issues can be obscured by
today's small bibliographical values was further illustrated by the
errata slip. On examination its practical value proved to be of the
slightest, since it relates only to poems printed in 1824 and, of the
two dozen or so changes it contains, a number represent unsatis-
factory afterthoughts which Mary Shelley did well to reject in 1839.

3. Richard Garnett to Thomas Hutchinson, 1862–1904

Mary Shelley died in 1851. Apart from juvenilia not yet traced or available, the extant textual material then consisted of:

1. Shelley's editions and her own;
2. Manuscripts preserved at Boscombe Manor, home of her son, Sir Percy Florence Shelley, and his wife;
3. Manuscripts owned by Leigh Hunt, Claire Clairmont, and other friends of the poet;
4. A Manuscript Notebook, containing early poems, owned by Ianthe Esdaile, Shelley's daughter by Harriet.

Shelley was lucky in the Victorian editors who continued Mary's work. One and all they brought to their task a considerable degree of learning, linguistic competence and care, and a capacity for reasoned judgement.

The second category of material was by far the biggest and most important. Its chief riches lay buried in Shelley's working Note-books. Lady Shelley has been criticized for the careful control she exercised. But, as the later history of these Notebooks was to show, the difficulty of piecing together and deciphering Shelley's illegible and confused scraps of writing is immense, and it is not easy to find people who can combine the time and the capacity for study which are necessary for exploring the infinitely greater problems that lie beyond mere deciphering.

In 1862 Richard Garnett brought out *Relics of Shelley*, 'a salvage', as Hutchinson comments, 'second only to *Posthumous Poems*'; not least of the fragments salvaged was the Prologue to *Hellas*. Working on visits to Boscombe, in such time as could be spared from his arduous labours at the British Museum, he could do no more than take soundings and periodical dives into the then uncharted depths of the Notebooks. Modern divers, better provided, can fault him for missed points and mistakes of deciphering; nevertheless the wonder is that he managed to fish up so much. For the rest of Lady Shelley's life he was a trusted adviser, and he was generous in helping others with clues and material. Among those helped was William Michael Rossetti, whose edition of the *Poetical Works* came out in 1870. Working, as he had to, with limited access to material, Rossetti brought to his task the *Sprachgefühl* of a family of poets, and that application of brains which, as Housman observed, is regarded by many workers upon texts as the equivalent of using hands in Association Football. Many of his conjectures were inspired; the unluckier ones were corrected by Miss Mathilde Blind, aided by material furnished by Garnett, by H. Buxton Forman in his edition of 1876, and by Rossetti himself in his revised edition of 1878.

The three editions of H. Buxton Forman (1876, 1882, 1892) constitute a landmark. They were based chiefly on a collation of Shelley's and Mary's printings with material he had himself collected, notably with manuscripts he had acquired from sources outside Shelley's family. His research was tireless, his bibliographical knowledge and experience immense, and he had a Civil Servant's passion for method and accuracy. To eke out his linguistic equipment he had the assistance of his able brother Alfred, translator of Aeschylus and of Wagner. He expanded the text, vindicated parts of it, emended other parts, and furnished a useful textual commentary and annotation. Where his judgements failed this was usually due to the handicap of having to base them on a piecemeal examination of material. In the first of his 1876 volumes, for instance, he committed himself to certain conclusions about Shelley's spelling which a wider examination of material was later to prove absurd; unfortunately he felt obliged to rationalize them. It is fair to add that he has since deceived many besides himself by the display of linguistic sciolism with which, in successive appendices, he made the attempt.

In 1886 Edward Dowden, the accomplished Dublin scholar to whom Lady Shelley entrusted the necessary papers, brought out his *Life of Shelley*, and in it he was permitted to include extracts from the poems in the Notebook owned by the Esdailes. In 1890 he followed this with an edition of the poetry. George E. Woodberry's Centenary Edition, 1893, included gleanings from one of the manuscript Notebooks presented to Harvard by Captain Silsbee, who had acquited them from Claire Clairmont, and other gleanings from manuscripts in the possession of Mr. Frederickson of Brooklyn.

Following the death of Sir Percy Florence Shelley in 1889, Lady Shelley divided the Boscombe Collection into three parts. One part remained in the family, and eventually became the property of Sir John Shelley-Rolls. A second part went to Lady Shelley's niece and adopted daughter, who married into the Abinger family. In 1893, in honour of the centenary in the previous year, the third part was presented to the Bodleian Library. For the first time a specimen was publicly available of the hard-core material out of which Mary Shelley had evolved her editions. It came, fortunately, under the discriminating eye of C. D. Locock. Ten years later the results of his patient study were published by the Clarendon Press in *An Examination of the Shelley Manuscripts in the Bodleian Library*. Within seventy-five pages he collated manuscripts with printed texts, transcribed several large, hitherto unknown fragments, and gave a number of improved readings from *Prometheus Unbound*, *Epipsychidion*, *The Witch of Atlas*, *Laon and Cythna*, and 'Prince Athanase', besides some of the translations and smaller pieces. Still more valuable than these gleanings was his patient search for what editorial principles the material might yield. A manuscript, he concluded, should have authority, roughly speaking, when it (1) gives sense instead of nonsense, or (2) is metrically more correct, or (3) is manifestly superior in sense and sound, or (4) is likely to be *misread*, or (5) is likely to be *misprinted*. That 'roughly speaking' is typical of his careful discrimination. He formed no conclusions which could be belied by a wider examination of material, and he wisely emphasized that the advancement of textual studies would depend on 'patience and additional experience'.[1] Like Shelley he realized that what mattered were 'errors in the sense', and that this meant, usually, in the syntax. In the punctuating of Shelley's involved syntax he was not afraid to admit uncertainty; for example, about the problems arising from *Prometheus Unbound* he invited correspondence—no doubt, like Bridges, he was shocked by Shelley's unhelpfulness in that neatly penned manuscript. The great principle established by *An Examination* is that Shelley's manuscripts, while important as a guide to editorial judgement, can never be more than a guide to it. The day had yet to come when they would be offered as a substitute.

Thomas Hutchinson's edition of 1904 was less an original contribution to the advancement of Shelley's text than a consolidation of the labours of his predecessors. Its main basis is the text and apparatus of Forman, enriched by the fruits of Locock's research. *An Examination* had been scrupulously limited to transcription and a search for principles. Hutchinson supplied the judgement that was needed for translating principles into a text. His text is accurately based on his materials, and his apparatus, though somewhat

[1] *An Examination*, p. 2.

clumsily distributed between footnotes and a kind of appendix, is economically presented and, on the whole, sufficient for authenticating the text. It seems a pity that he did not allow himself more time than a year for studying Locock's results. In the text of *The Cyclops*, for example, he neglected quite a number of valuable points. His linguistic sense frequently enables him to remove 'errors in the sense' by repunctuation, but such reforms might have been taken further; not least, as Professor Zillman has noted, in the text of *Prometheus Unbound*. The arrangement of the poems is not very satisfactory, being a compromise between the bibliographical principle of printing works in order of publication and the principle, more helpful for study, of an order based on date of composition. This is further complicated by the relegation of *Queen Mab* and other juvenilia to a double-column arrangement at the end of the volume. Forman's exclusion of *The Wandering Jew*, on inadequately reasoned grounds, is uncritically followed, though two other spurious pieces accepted by Forman are wisely dropped. Perhaps the most serious defect is the want of the explanatory notes demanded by a learned, allusive poetry of ideas. It may be that Hutchinson was both hastened and circumscribed by his publisher's policy, besides being influenced by contemporary notions of what befitted Shelley. Be it said, nevertheless, of both policy and performance, that this accessible, single-volume edition which so ably consolidated the textual advances of its predecessors has been a convenient and worthy basis for more than half a century of study.

4. Shelley's Text since 1904

The Locock–Hutchinson combination of 1903–4 had been a happy one. In 1911 Locock published a two-volume edition of his own. Its chief advance on Hutchinson's lay in the explanatory notes, though these left something to be desired and, to make room for them, he omitted Mary Shelley's commentaries, Shelley's Notes on *Queen Mab*, and the whole of the rest of the juvenilia. In verbal niceties and in the punctuating of Shelley's syntax he showed sensitivity, but his experience was limited by the manuscript material he had examined, and, despite the well-reasoned conclusions of *An Examination*, his judgement, as is liable to happen to those who have laboured too long at the mechanical skill of transcribing, was sometimes dulled into an undue reverence for minutiae, even, as Professor Zillman has noted, Shelley's inconsistent capitals and disastrous, all-purpose dashes. He was unfortunate in not being permitted to make use of three more Notebooks, which had been given to Garnett by Lady Shelley, and appeared in the saleroom after his death. They were bought by W. K. Bixby of St. Louis, and subsequently acquired by the Henry Huntington Library in California.

As usual the acquisition of these Notebooks was followed by the problem of how a saleroom treasure and a decipherer's nightmare could best be translated into a printed reality. With considerable wisdom the new owners enlisted H. Buxton Forman. For him there arose problems of a personal kind. He was no longer young and to produce an equivalent of Locock's *Examination*, subsequently collating their combined results in a fourth edition of his own which would displace Hutchinson's, was hardly a hopeful prospect.[1] His solution was eminently practical. In three volumes, privately printed in 1911 for the Boston Bibliophile Society, he embodied admirable transcriptions, together with a running commentary calculated not only to impress with its minutiae but also to amuse and disarm, by occasional touches of whimsy, a privileged bibliophile public to whom unusualness might appeal more than the essentials of textual criticism. His simple titular description '*Note Books of Percy Bysshe Shelley* / Deciphered, transcribed and edited by . . .' was nicely calculated to satisfy this limited public without drawing too much attention from a wider public to the somewhat anomalous use of the word 'edited'. How successfully his valuable emendations and new transcriptions lay hidden away in the *Note Books* may be partly judged by the fact that the pages of the British Museum copy remained uncut till 1951, when the present editor was permitted to cut them.

Robert Bridges's valuable investigation into the textual significance of Shelley's manuscripts has been noted on p. xx above. In 1925 Professor W. E. Peck published in the *Boston Herald* texts of two poems drawn from the two Shelley Notebooks in the Harvard University Library: 'To Constantia Singing' and 'Young Parson Richards'. Neither text amounted to much more than an uncritical copying, and the title of the second poem was a misreading of the

---

[1] For much of the information about the *Note Books* I am indebted to a conversation with the late M. Buxton Forman.

manuscript.[1] Meanwhile the large portion of the old Boscombe Collection then owned by Sir John Shelley-Rolls remained to be explored.

In 1926–30 Roger Ingpen and Walter E. Peck brought out their ten-volume edition of *The Complete Works of Percy Bysshe Shelley*, the Julian Edition; volumes i–iv contained the poetry. The production was sumptuous, and the cost consequently prohibitive to most of the reading public. The editing was perfunctory. Certain pieces not in Hutchinson's edition were included, among them passages from the Notebooks and other papers owned by Sir John, but the canon was not greatly enlarged; Forman's *Note Books of Shelley* were not made available and, apart from the scraps used by Dowden, permission to use the poems in their Notebook was not granted by the Esdaile family. The arrangement of the text was confusing, and still more confusing was the jumble of textual commentary, bibliography, biographical matter, and exegesis contained in the Notes. There was no serious preconsideration of textual principles beyond a vague desire to give new scraps to the world. As typical of the editors' methods one might take their treatment of certain passages of juvenilia of which the usual text derives from Hogg and others, but for which other texts exist in the Esdaile Notebook. Much was made of permission given by the Esdaile family to 'correct' the received text from a 'careful transcript' (actually made by Dowden) in their possession. Since this permission covered only scraps already published its significance was minimal. Nor does it seem to have occurred to the editors that to 'correct' one version of a poem from another version in which there are considerable differences in the arrangement and numbering of lines and stanzas can produce, at best, no more than a bewildering conflation. Judgements on the Julian Edition should be tempered by a recollection of the undue labour and responsibility which fell on Roger Ingpen through the personal disasters which overtook his colleague.

In 1934 appeared a handsome little volume entitled *Verse and Prose from the Manuscripts of Percy Bysshe Shelley*, privately printed and described as 'Edited by Sir John Shelley-Rolls and Roger Ingpen'. The 'edited' verse consisted, in fact, of literal transcriptions from the Shelley-Rolls Collection, partly of unpublished passages

---

[1] See William J. McTaggart, *England in 1819: Church, State and Poverty. A Study, Textual and Historical, of 'A Ballad' by Shelley, formerly entitled 'Young Parson Richards'*, Keats–Shelley Memorial Association, 1970.

and partly of variant readings of poetry long printed and known. The selection was unsystematic, the arrangement confusing, the transcription inaccurate, and the textual apparatus negligible. Though printed without relation to cognate parts of Shelley's text, and mostly in an unpunctuated, altogether non-viable form, these passages, like other printings of the kind resulting from piecemeal endeavour, did serve in their day as an indication of the raw material that was available for a new systematized edition.

In 1946 Sir John Shelley-Rolls made over the whole of his collection to the Bodleian Library. Shortly afterwards the eighth Lord Abinger kindly permitted microfilms of his collection to be added to this material and the manuscripts which had been presented by Lady Shelley in 1893. For working purposes the 'Boscombe Collection' of the nineteenth century had now been brought together again. Meanwhile the invention of the photostat, the microfilm, and, later, the Xerox process, brought new possibilities for collating material in Oxford with material in the United States and elsewhere. Facilities of access, so vital, as Garnett had emphasized, for editing, had become greater than ever before. The difficulty of handling them had increased in proportion.

One happy result of the new availability of material was an improvement in standards of mechanical accuracy and the printing of some magnificent transcription. A less happy result was a tendency towards mechanical thinking whereby transcribed material, valuable as a basis for editing, came to be offered and accepted as editing itself. The concept of a 'copy-text', i.e. the substitution for those principles of reasoned judgement known as 'textual criticism' of a Fundamentalist faith in a manuscript as something merely requiring to be copied, was nothing new; it is, in fact, a recurrent psychological and professional phenomenon well known in the editing of classical authors[1] which I have discussed elsewhere in its relation to Shelley.[2] A Bridges could find one of Shelley's best fair copies 'useless' to elucidate a difficult piece of text until he had added his expertise to the work of earlier skilled editors—but now the meticulous reproduction of one of his wildest drafts, complete with meaningless misspellings and ruptured syntax, could be solemnly accepted from some youthful transcriber as 'scholarly modern editing', and a 'correction' of Hutchinson. But these activities have been com-

---

[1] See A. E. Housman, *Selected Prose*, ed. John Carter, pp. 34–44.
[2] In three articles in the *Keats–Shelley Memorial Bulletin*, listed below, p. xlvi.

paratively few, the manuscript material being protected against them by its multiplicity. The Fundamentalist, as Housman noted, is almost always careful to pick a text of which only a single manuscript survives: in that way he bypasses one of the most exacting editorial functions, the weighing of evidence and the assignment of authority, point by point, to variants. Letters and journals are his obvious preferences and it is not easy for him to pick a poem or a group of poems from Shelley which offer the same advantages. Of the value of some recent transcriptions, as such, acknowledgement is made in this edition, and I would gladly have said no more, were it not that the Fundamentalist will always find ready, even eager, dupes who spread his confusion—for, as demonstrated by Archilochus' hedge-hog, it is often the small, single skill that most readily impresses.

Tantum religio . . . sometimes the Fundamentalist fetters can be hard to break. In 1962 the famous Notebook owned by the Esdaile family appeared in the saleroom and was acquired by the Carl H. Pforzheimer Library. Eventually it was entrusted to Mr. Kenneth Neill Cameron, a practised decipherer, who devised a courageous compromise for bridging the time-gulf and the study necessary for turning a transcriber's nugget into a minted text. In less than two years, with the help of the staff of the Library, and of a transcript made by Dowden, he was able to produce *The Esdaile Notebook*,[1] a text accompanied by a quantity of annotated points, and with no more than some three dozen misreadings. The textual principle, described as 'a limited clean-up', may be fairly illustrated, I think, from its application to No. 46, lines 103–7:

> He dared not speak, but rushed from her caress.
>   The sunny glades; the little birds of spring
> Twittering from every garlanded recess,
>   Returning verdure's joy that seem'd to sing
> Whilst woe with stern hand smote his every mental string;

May we suppose that it is our duty to do what Shelley asked Stockdale to do with his text—to 'alter any error of flagrant incoherency'? The incoherency is plain enough; its causes are the stops. Mr. Cameron remarks of Shelley's text in general that it is 'in places, difficult enough, *even* when a minimum of punctuation has been added'; the italics are mine. The difficulty here is caused partly by the semicolon after *glades* and partly by the full stop after *caress*.

The first is Shelley's, preserved in the 'limited clean-up'. The second is Mr. Cameron's, an example of the 'minimum punctuation' which he has added. What has victimized him is the Fundamentalist faith that—so sacred is the manuscript—pointing must be *quantitatively* regulated. Now supposing we try, in pursuance of what Shelley expected of his printer, to follow the advice given by Joseph Moxon to his seventeenth-century compositors and 'punctuate the sense of the copy'—i.e. to think not of the *amount* but of the *nature* of punctuation required. All we have to do is to remove Shelley's stop and Mr. Cameron's, replace them by commas, and add another comma after *sing*. Then, instead of nonsense we get syntax; not Shelley's best, perhaps, but intelligible enough to anybody familiar with his use of 'absolute' participial constructions on the Greek model. These lines are part of a passage, extending down to line 120, which Mr. Cameron describes as 'Shelley's long sentence' though, as he prints it, it is an anacoluthon for which he, not Shelley, is responsible. If we start by replacing his second semicolon, after *string*, with a full stop, the rest (see below, p. 152) is equally remediable. In justice to Shelley, on whose 'complexity' incoherent passages have been blamed, I am most unhappily compelled to observe here that, unlike a transcription which—once it is recognized as no more than a transcription—can make a limited but valuable contribution to editing, a 'limited clean-up' of this kind can do nothing but sow textual confusion.[1] It needs, however, to be observed at the same time that Mr. Cameron's determination to offer something more than a mere transcription represented, in principle at least, a commendable advance on the confused thinking of others.

Mr. Lawrence J. Zillman's work on *Prometheus Unbound* is a happier chapter of textual history. Ten years of devoted labour went towards his variorum edition of 1959.[2] With its length, its plurality of manuscripts, and its philosophical and linguistic subtlety, he had to face as exacting an exercise in true textual criticism as any single poem of Shelley's can afford. Unfortunately he too fell a victim to the Fundamentalist faith in a 'copy-text': not, this time, a manuscript but a first edition. Rejecting the heritage of

---

[1] Since my own text is based on Shelley's holograph, and Mr. Cameron's is not therefore a witness, it has seemed to me unnecessary either to swell my Commentary by collating it or to give a list of the misreadings; as this volume goes to press I note that they have been silently corrected in the literal transcription printed in *Shelley and his Circle*, vol. iv.

[2] University of Washington Press, 1959.

correction in Hutchinson's *textus receptus* he set himself to repro-
duce, 'with verbal exactness, even to typographical errors and
obvious misreadings', the 1820 *editio princeps* so deplored by Shelley
himself. (This astonishing, but by no means unparalleled, subjuga-
tion of common sense by bibliographical dogma is technically
described, I am told, as 'the historical approach'.) But with Prome-
thean courage and magnanimity Mr. Zillman has now shaken off
the bonds of dogma and spent the best part of another ten years in
revising his book.[1] This time, instead of rejecting the labours
culminating in Hutchinson, he has seen them as his obvious starting-
point; and he has used the manuscripts, in accordance with Locock's
principle, 'as a guide to judgment' rather than as a substitute for it,
in the Fundamentalist fashion. What he has now rejected is a mass
of non-significant variorum material—wisely relegated to a Xeroxed
typescript, made available to students—and his own elaborate
collection of non-significant points ('*i* of *which* possibly at first *o*'
etc.). The extent of his contribution to Shelley's text will be apparent
in my third volume. Of wider importance is his reassertion of
reasoned judgement against reductive dogma.

II. THE PRESENT EDITION

HUTCHINSON'S edition of 1904 grew out of Lady Shelley's
Bodleian benefaction of 1893. The occasion for the present edition
was the gift made to the Bodleian in 1946 by Sir John Shelley-Rolls.
The history of Shelley's text shows the successive work of editors,
from Mary Shelley to Hutchinson, in carrying out the services for
which Shelley, in his lifetime, looked to his friends and his printer.
These services I have tried to continue. In *Shelley at Work*, designed
as a preliminary inquiry into the poet's ideas and his system of
symbolism, I described the peculiarities of his manuscripts and the
apparatus constructed for dealing with them. A further preliminary
to this edition was the series of articles in the *Keats–Shelley Memorial
Bulletin* (see p. xlvi below) in which I discussed certain special
editorial problems in more detail than is possible here. My little
volume of *The Esdaile Poems* was a trial flight for the exploration
of editorial methods in general and, more particularly, the linguistic
problem of relating punctuation to syntax.

[1] *Shelley's* Prometheus Unbound, *The Text and the Drafts*, Yale University Press,
1968.

As far as possible the poems have been arranged in a chrono-
logical sequence based on their dates of composition. For poetry
in such continuous development as Shelley's this seemed desir-
able, besides falling into line with Mary's arrangement of
minor poems and fragments and her invaluable year-by-year
commentary on their background. I have departed a little
from this principle, as, for instance, in my initial category of
'Early Shorter Poems and Translations, 1802–12', which avoids
an awkward interspersing of short poems among longer ones. Where
composition extended over a period, as with *Prometheus Unbound*,
the date given is the date at which it was finished. Conjectural dating
is shown as such. Sometimes Shelley's habits can cause a perplexing
conflict between dating and connection. Thus, on re-reading, in
1819, the lament he had written in 1816 for Fanny Godwin, he
added, on the page of the draft, some emotionally connected lines
about the recent death of his son William. Both these poems
connect with two laments which he wrote for Harriet Shelley.
To complicate matters further, the first of the Harriet-laments has
two manuscript versions, one written in 1816 and the other in
1817. By grouping, headings, and cross-references, I have tried to
make both dates and connections plain, avoiding the alternatives
of duplication and lengthy notes. Shelley constantly rewrote his
pieces, often from memory, and it is not always possible to dis-
tinguish his *ultima manus*: where distinguishable, of course, I have
preferred it. Poems of disproved or doubtful authenticity have
been placed in an Appendix at the end of each volume. But here
again I have sometimes departed from principle: e.g. I could not
bring myself to disturb Shelley's own grouping of the *Victor and
Cazire* poems.

In my text, and in the accompanying Commentary, I have done
my best to show, as far as may reasonably be ascertained, what
Shelley intended to be read. In my Commentary, over and above
what is necessary for explanation and authentication of the text, I
have illustrated Shelley's creative processes by including as many
significant variants as I could without permitting them to multiply
into a minute history of verbal change. For convenient reference
the Commentary on each poem is headed with an indication of
manuscript and printed sources, date of composition, points, where
necessary, concerning the title, and the full textual lineage. For
points requiring expansion readers are referred to the Notes. The

extent and significance of manuscript witness varies, inevitably, from poem to poem; this will be discussed, more conveniently, in Volume II. Under 'Printed' I normally give only the date and the person responsible for the first printing followed by the same details concerning the last significant one: where, however, successive printings made significant additions or corrections over a period of time the details of the intermediate ones are given. Transcriptions and modified transcriptions are not collated: where, however, they have contributed to my text their help is acknowledged.

The operation of my Commentary can be understood from a few examples. Thus, with *Queen Mab*, p. 231,

PRINTED: *PBS, 1813/MWS, 1839¹, 1839²/Hutch. 1904*

signifies that the poem was first printed by Shelley in 1813, its text corrected and improved by Mary Shelley (see above, pp. xxii–xxiii) in her first and second editions of 1839 and further improved by Hutchinson who incorporated the nineteenth-century improvements with his own; since what matters to Shelley's readers is the effect of these improvements rather than their history I have not listed them. Owing to the variety of material in this edition a system of sigla would be impracticable; the abbreviations listed on pp. xlvi–xlvii should be found self-explanatory. Then, below, I say

TEXT: *1904/1839²/1839¹/1813* . . .

thus reversing the list given under PRINTED. This means that my starting text—I carefully avoid 'copy-text', both the word and the idea—is Hutchinson's of 1904, which has been collated with the earlier texts from which it derives. Only where the results of the collation have significance do I print them. To give an example, again from my Commentary on *Queen Mab*:

IX. 67 nor *1904, 1839*] or *1813*

means that Shelley printed 'or', a grammatical slip corrected by Mary in her two editions and subsequently embodied by Hutchinson, these editors being identifiable by the dates given above under PRINTED. When I give simply '1839' this means that there is no point in mentioning both editions of that year. Sometimes an editor whose text, in the main, is not a significant witness has an occasional point which demands incorporation; in such cases the editor and the date of his edition are specifically named, thus:

I. 133 frame, *Locock, 1911*] frame. *1904, 1813 and edd.*

Similarly with the manuscript sources. A reader seeking the meaning of the note on *Queen Mab* I. 55–6 will find it in the reference BM^b, *Fn., rejected 1816*. A glance above will show that 'BM^b' refers to the second of two British Museum manuscripts and 'Fn.' to a manuscript formerly owned by H. Buxton Forman; for practical purposes these documents need to be treated as manuscripts, though, as shown, they are in fact printed copies of *Queen Mab* used by Shelley when revising the poem for publication as *The Daemon of the World* in his *Alastor* volume of 1816: '*rejected 1816*' consequently means that these lines, though written by Shelley in his autograph revision, were not, in the end, printed by him. Variants, in accordance with convention, are noted by giving, first, before a square bracket, the reading preferred; if no source is named it represents my emendation of what follows the bracket. Cancelled words or passages are, as usual, enclosed between square brackets. Both clarity and practicability have demanded a severe exclusion of inessential details. Sometimes, however, it has seemed desirable to make exceptions. Thus, with Esdaile Poem No. 50, 'The Retrospect', I give

PRINTED: *15–end, Dowd. 1886/1–end, Rog. 1966.*

TEXT: *1966/1904/1886/Esd.*

This signifies that the text is based on my 1966 edition of *The Esdaile Poems*, with which has been collated Hutchinson's 1904 edition and the printing of the poem in Dowden's 1886 *Life of Shelley*. Now since 'Esd.', identifiable under AUTOGRAPH above as the Esdaile manuscript, indicates a manuscript source for *1966* it could be held that neither *1904* nor *1886* were strictly witnesses to the text. If Shelley, like some people today, had regarded his manuscripts as printer's copy the objection would hold. But this is a poem of which the whole point hangs on syntactical structure, the syntax on punctuation, and the punctuation on the editorial technique which Shelley habitually expected others to supply. Consequently today's text must draw on the inheritance of what Dowden and Hutchinson contributed, together, I hope, with my own contribution in *1966*.

For the allegation, sometimes made, that Hutchinson's text embodies corruption due to conjectural emendation I can find no confirmation. It would seem to be a hearsay version of the facts concerning the wrong conjectures, long since corrected, in Rossetti's edition of 1870. Other conjectures of Rossetti's have been proved correct by manuscript evidence later available. Myself I have been sparing of conjecture, but make use of it occasionally not as a privilege but as a duty: e.g. in *Queen Mab*, IX. 130 where I print *rack* in place of the *wreck* inherited by editors from Shelley's printing—readers unfamiliar with Shelley's penstrokes may be familiar with his love of *The Tempest*. Sometimes the manuscript has relieved me from relying on conjecture: for example (Vol. II), in 'Mont Blanc', 79, where coherence plainly requires *In such a* in place of *But such a*; and (Vol. IV), 'We meet not as then we parted . . .'[1] where the *briny dew*, a curious phrase in relation to kisses, has been amended by the word which Mr. Edmund Blunden prophesied that I should find in the manuscript.

Shelley would have been surprised to know how much careful intent has been read into his careless spelling. Reasoning from an insufficient number of instances H. Buxton Forman[2] endeavoured to discover nuance, and even grammatical significance, in *desart*, *tyger*, and other such forms. A wider examination of instances will show that they are due entirely to indifference or haste. To preserve them has two effects. First it introduces an artificial quaintness which he did not intend. Secondly it mars the effect of the unusual words with which he did intend to give colour—e.g. his Greek forms *daedal*, *crystalline*, etc., or such Latinisms as *horrent* or *honours* (for 'blossoms'), besides his genuine English archaisms such as *blosmy*, *flamy*, or *quook* (for 'quaked'), in a Bodleian fragment. Nothing is added to our knowledge of the poet by printing or annotating such everyday misspellings as *mein* for *mien*, *thier* for *their*, *hugh* for *huge*, *it's* for *its*, etc., nor such abbreviations as *thro*, *cd*, *wd*, *shd*, etc. All these occur in *The Esdaile Poems* where they have been silently regularized in accordance with the practice of both Shelley and his previous editors. So has the use of the ampersand, the hyphen, and the possessive apostrophe. Doubtful instances are noted in the Commentary. Certain forms I have left to take care of themselves; for example past participles and past tenses such as *stamped/stampt*, *caressed/carest*, etc., *O* and *oh* (though like Shelley

---

[1] I print this line from Shelley's draft.
[2] See Rogers, 'Shelley's Spelling: Theory and Practice', *Keats–Shelley Memorial Bulletin*, xvi, 1965.

I prefer the first for a vocative), and *aye/ay* (though, again like Shelley, I prefer the first). For Shelley's indifference in such matters cf. note on *The Wandering Jew*, pp. 375–6 below.

In capitalization, too, I have followed my predecessors, regularizing where necessary according to the context. Some writers—for example Blake, Carlyle, Fitzgerald—did indeed use capitals with special effect upon the printed page. But in Shelley's manuscripts, as in most educated handwriting, even within the present century, they were often little more than a calligraphic ornament. To preserve them is, once again, to obtrude an artificial, distracting quaintness: witness, for example, from the Esdaile manuscript, the pleasing, but wholly irrelevant, Orientalism suggested by *Month of Love* (8. 19), *Sons of the Wind* (41. 1), *Sister of Snow* (44. 19). Worse can happen: punctilio has elsewhere printed (an apparently vocative adverb) *O Ever* (5. 11), and (27. 12) in mid-line and mid-sentence, the word *Its*. By way of contrast one might set the *West* (27. 8) and *Echo's* (50. 121), two near-inspired touches of personification brought out by capitalization added by Hutchinson to Shelley's text.

Spelling and capitalization lie on the level of words: punctuation is a problem on a higher level, involving the whole currency of ideas in which Shelley's poetry deals. A point too easily overlooked today is that he neither thought nor wrote as a monoglot man does. Style and meaning are fused in fluent classical syntax, the power and even the meaning of which begins to disappear as soon as an editor allows himself even a modified system of reliance on the almost always unsystematic punctuation of the manuscripts or fails to allow for the infection of this in the printed text. Early examples may be seen in the Esdaile Poems. As No. 5 appears in the Notebook its two ten-line stanzas are unpunctuated except for a dash before the vocative in line 10 and an exclamation mark at the end of that line. Here, luckily, the syntax is so simple that the meaning is hardly impaired. Less simple is the opening stanza of No. 20, where a fifteen-line sentence, having its main verb in the thirteenth line, is unpunctuated save for a final exclamation mark. Sometimes Shelley does afford a little help. The opening of No. 9 is an instance (cf. p. 92 below):

> In that strange mental wandering when to live
> To breathe, to be, is undivided joy
> When the most woe worn wretch wd. cease to grieve
> When satiation's self would fail to cloy;

When unpercipient of all other things 5
Than those that press around, the breathing Earth
The gleaming sky & the fresh seasons birth,
Sensation all it⟨s⟩ wondrous rapture brings
And to itself not once the mind recurs
Is it foretaste of Heaven? 10

As an indication that the words between them form a complete
sense-unit the commas in lines 6 and 7 have some value. But
they are not enough: what we need is a parenthesis, strongly
marked. And though the semicolon in line 4 does serve to group
the first three 'when'-clauses together we need something in line 9
which would balance it and group together the remaining clauses
before we reach the main verb. Shelley's punctuation of manu-
scripts, in short, is seldom adequate, even where it does happen to
afford some help, and may never be safely trusted. Beside this
example might be set the long sentence in No. 46. 103–20, reduced
to an anacoluthon in the manuscript by the semicolons in lines 104,
107, and 116.[1] There are many places where by a combination of
punctual inadequacy with miscopying or general lack of revision,
Shelley has hopelessly corrupted his own meaning: for example
No. 20. 45–6 and No. 46. 140–3, and here I have indicated the
corruption. But, on the whole, Shelley's syntax is clear and skilful,
for all its elaboration. It is impracticable to annotate fully all the
passages where a complicated syntactical structure depends for its
punctuation, and consequently intelligibility, on editorial *Sprach-
gefühl* alone. One such passage, in No. 50, I have, however, analysed
in some detail, showing the work done first by Dowden, then by
Hutchinson, then in the present edition. Again, in No. 24. 32–52
I have, I hope, contrived to remove an anacoluthon which seems
to have passed unnoticed in previous editions.

Two special idiosyncrasies need mention. One is Shelley's addic-
tion to the dotted suspension point. This stop, usually of three
dots, but occasionally of more or less than three, is for him an
all-purpose affair which varies in significance. Literally introduced
into a modern text it would mislead the reader by seeming to
represent an ellipsis, probably intended for a dramatic aposiopesis.
I have found, as Professor Jones does,[2] that more often than not it
merely signifies the end of a sentence and requires replacement by
a full stop, exclamation mark, or interrogation mark. In his own

---

[1] See above, pp. xxxi–xxxii.   [2] *Letters*, i. vii.

printings Shelley usually so replaced it: e.g. the 1813 printing of
6. 32. In 6. 29, however, a dramatic aposiopesis does seem wanted,
and here and in a few other places I follow his use of dots.

Another common anomaly, equally due to speed of writing, is
what may be called 'anticipatory' stopping. Thus in 39. 36–7
Shelley writes

> Sweet flower! that blooms amid the weeds
> Where the rank serpent interest feeds

although the exclamatory force governs that whole sentence, so
that the strong stop needs to be placed at its end (I insert, in passing,
a personifying capital):

> Sweet flower, that blooms amid the weeds
> Where the rank serpent Interest feeds!

Sometimes, as here, the anticipatory exclamation mark might
be thought to represent no more than the once-fashionable way
of pointing a vocative. That, however, will not explain such
instances as 40. 23–4:

> O this were joy! & such as none would fear
> To purchase by a life of passing woe

where, again, the exclamation mark of the manuscript needs to be
transferred to the end of the sentence. At times the effect of this
tendency is quite irrational, as when the manuscript of 10. 23 reads

> True! Mountain Liberty alone may heal. . . .

which could only make sense if he meant 'It is true that . . .'. Once
again Shelley's mind, being too far ahead of his pen, has anticipated
an exclamatory force in the sentence by attaching his stop to an
early word in it.

Though Shelley's printings must, of course, be preferred as
a rule, there are places where they cannot be regarded as the final
indication of his intentions. Thus in No. 6, line 74, I have followed
the manuscript italicization

> Whilst the snakes whose slime *even him* defiled

in preference to the 1813 version 'even him *defiled*', whereby the
irony is diminished—so, at least, it seems to me, though Locock
thought otherwise. Again, in lines 47 and 64 of this poem I have
omitted some unhelpful commas which had crept in in 1813.

The Wandering Jew is an interesting example of textual lineage; the best text is a Victorian one based on a collation of two near-contemporary printings derived from separate but cognate manuscripts. The difficult process of punctuating Shelley's early, somewhat loose, syntax has been well carried out; nevertheless I have ventured (see below, p. 375) what seemed to me a few improvements.

In the whole matter of accidentals I have endeavoured to consider meaning rather than to aim at consistency or to systematize details. That this was Shelley's principle may be shown from an examination of the Pisa *Adonais*, about which he took particular pains; cf., in line 2, 'O, weep for Adonais!' with lines 19 and 72 where he has 'Oh weep for Adonais'; again line 306 has 'oh that it should be so!', while in 476 he prints 'oh, hasten thither'. In punctuation, everywhere, my concern, like his, has been mainly with syntax—with the avoidance, that is to say, of what he called 'errors in the sense'. Like previous editors I have silently adjusted non-significant minutiae.

In my Notes, as in my text, I have tried to ask myself what Shelley himself would have expected of a modern editor. What his poetry requires, above all else, is to be understood in relation to the ideas which animate it. Had he lived to give us the series of metaphysical essays he had planned he would have made plain to us what those ideas are. Fortunately clues are not wanting, notably the clues to his elaborate system of Platonic symbolism which run like a stream through his poetry, letters, and prose-writings, and which had already been patiently collected by Professor Notopoulos before his Notebooks revealed the manner of its evolution. In line with these clues are the epigraphs attached by Shelley to his poems, the passages from Shelley's letters, so carefully selected by Mary, keywords such as 'mystery', 'passion', etc., too frequently misunderstood, and, of course, the symbol-words themselves, 'veil', 'cave', 'dream', etc., which are everywhere recurrent.[1] I do not think that Shelley's Notes on *Queen Mab*, highly significant for the understanding of his Godwinian period, have been previously annotated, or Mary Shelley's Prefaces, a valuable key to the married love which they subtly and beautifully reveal in its Petrarchian–Platonic relationship to his work. To some extent, too, my Notes are an extension of my Commentary, elaborating what could not be briefly indicated there and is necessary to an understanding of

[1] See Rogers, *Shelley at Work*, *passim*.

a poem. Much, naturally, had to be resisted. Little, for instance, would have been added to our knowledge of Shelley by a textual exploration of the English, Latin, Greek, and French passages quoted in his Notes on *Queen Mab*, and I have contented myself with a few silent emendations of slips; so too with the bibliography appended in his footnotes to these Notes. Into this I was much tempted to delve, but was deterred by the difficulty of finality. One example will suffice. Shelley refers to [Samuel Jackson] Pratt's poem *Bread, or the Poor*. Mr. Cameron, having, it would seem, carefully checked this, gives the title (*The Young Shelley*, p. 230) as *Cottage Pictures, or the Poor*. Both titles are correct, Shelley's for the second edition of 1802, published at Tewkesbury, and Mr. Cameron's for the London edition of 1805. I cannot persuade myself that this matters, or that either Shelley or my readers would benefit if I mentioned here yet another variant of the title, found in a London edition of 1802. Again, though I have tried to note the general nature of the 'influences' underlying Shelley's poetry I have not attempted anything like a methodical source-hunt, the possibilities of which are infinite in such a learned and allusive poet, and the attractions of which are none the less for the attendant perils of *post hoc propter hoc* reasoning.

I hope I may be forgiven for the frequent references in my Notes to writings of my own. They have enabled me considerably to reduce the bulk of this edition, and it was for this purpose (see above, p. xxxiii) that they were planned to precede and to supplement it.

INTRODUCTION TO VOLUME I

1. TEXTUAL MATERIAL

THE first volume contains no previously unpublished poems. Emendations apart, the principal additions to Hutchinson's text of 1904 are the Esdaile Poems and *The Wandering Jew*. Minor additions are the Greek Epigrams of 1811, the 'Translation of a Latin Epigram by Vincent Bourne', 'Sadak the Wanderer', the 'Letter to Edward Fergus Graham' of [?] 14 May 1811, Version I of 'The Devil's Walk', and some additional lines in 'To Ireland'.

2. MANUSCRIPT SOURCES OF THE TEXT

The most important source is the Esdaile Notebook, to which I continue to give its long-known name, though it is now owned by the Carl H. Pforzheimer Library. Several of the poems in this Notebook exist in alternative manuscript versions; these are tabulated in my Notes, on p. 360. No other Notebooks belong to the period covered by this volume. The remaining manuscript sources are, with one exception, letters of Shelley's:

Bodleian Library (Bod.)
    'Bereavement': to Graham, 14 Sept. 1810.

British Museum (BM)
    'To Mary Who Died in this Opinion': to Miss Hitchener, 23 Nov. 1811.
    'The Devil's Walk', I: to Miss Hitchener, [?] 16 Jan. 1812.
    'To Ireland': to Miss Hitchener, 14 Feb. 1812.
    Queen Mab, 1813 edition, with Shelley's holograph insertions made for converting the poem to *The Daemon of the World*, here designated 'BM[b]'.[1]

Pierpont Morgan Library (Morg.)
    'St. Irvyne's Tower': to Graham, 22 Apr. 1810.

[1] The present volume had gone to press before the publication of vols. iii and iv of *Shelley and his Circle*; from these it is now known that a second copy annotated by Shelley, and, from its former ownership by Forman, here designated 'Fn.', is now the property of the Carl H. Pforzheimer Library.

Berg Collection, New York Public Library (NYPL)

'Letter to Edward Fergus Graham', [?] 14 May 1811.

Carl H. Pforzheimer Library (Pf.)

'Love': to Hogg, 8 May 1811.
'To a Star': to Hogg, *c.* 19 June 1811.

3. PRINTED SOURCES OF THE TEXT

Publications by Shelley:

Original Poetry by Victor and Cazire (with Elizabeth Shelley), J. J. Stockdale, 1810. Facsimile reprint, ed. Richard Garnett, John Lane, 1898.

Posthumous Fragments of Margaret Nicholson, J. Munday, 1810.

St. Irvyne, or The Rosicrucian, J. J. Stockdale, 1811.

'Four Epigrams from the Greek Anthology', *Oxford University and City Herald*, 5 Jan., 12 Jan., 9 Mar. 1811.

'Translation of a Latin Epigram by Vincent Bourne', *Oxford University and City Herald*, 23 Feb. 1811.

The Devil's Walk [II], printed as a broadside, 1812.

Queen Mab, privately printed, 1813.

Posthumous publications of, or containing, poetry by Shelley:

Mary Shelley, *Posthumous Poems of Percy Bysshe Shelley*, John and Henry Hunt, 1824.

The Wandering Jew, published from Shelley's manuscripts in the *Edinburgh Literary Journal*, 1829, and *Fraser's Magazine*, 1831. The two versions collated and edited: Bertram Dobell, for the Shelley Society, Reeves and Turner, 1887.

Thomas Medwin, *The Shelley Papers*, Whittaker, Treacher, 1833.

Mary Shelley, *The Poetical Works of Percy Bysshe Shelley*, 4 vols., Moxon, 1839; 2nd edn., 1 vol., 1840. [The two edns. are referred to as 1839^1 and 1839^2; see above, pp. xxii–xxiii.]

Thomas Medwin, *The Life of Shelley*, 2 vols., T. C. Newby, 1847. Revised edn., ed. H. Buxton Forman, Oxford Univ. Press, 1913.

T. J. Hogg, *The Life of Percy Bysshe Shelley*, vols. 1 and 2, Moxon, 1858. Combined edn. with Trelawny's *Recollections* and Peacock's *Memoirs*, with Introduction by Humbert Wolfe, 2 vols., Dent, 1933.

W. M. Rossetti, *The Poetical Works of Percy Bysshe Shelley*, 2 vols., Moxon, 1870; revised edn., 3 vols., 1878.

W. M. Rossetti, 'The Devil's Walk' [II], *Fortnightly Review*, 1 Jan. 1871.

H. Buxton Forman, *The Poetical Works of Percy Bysshe Shelley*, 4 vols., Reeves and Turner, 1876; 2nd edn., 2 vols., 1882; 3rd edn., 5 vols., Bell, 1892.

Edward Dowden, *The Life of Percy Bysshe Shelley*, 2 vols., Kegan Paul, 1886.

Edward Dowden, *The Poetical Works of Percy Bysshe Shelley*, Macmillan, 1890.

T. J. Wise, *Letters to Elizabeth Hitchener*, privately printed, 1890.

George E. Woodberry, *The Complete Poetical Works of Percy Bysshe Shelley*, Centenary Edition, 4 vols., Kegan Paul, 1893.

C. D. Locock, *An Examination of the Shelley Manuscripts in the Bodleian Library*, Clarendon Press, 1903.

Thomas Hutchinson, *The Complete Poetical Works of Shelley*, Clarendon Press, 1904. Reissued, among 'Oxford Standard Authors', 1905.

A. H. Koszul, *La Jeunesse de Shelley*, Bloud et Cie, 1910.

C. D. Locock, *Poems of Percy Bysshe Shelley*, 2 vols., Methuen, 1911.

R. Ingpen and W. E. Peck, *The Complete Works of Percy Bysshe Shelley*, Julian Edition, 10 vols., Benn, 1926–30 [*Poems*, 1927].

Sir John Shelley-Rolls and Roger Ingpen, *Verse and Prose from the Manuscripts of Percy Bysshe Shelley*, privately printed, 1934.

Davidson Cook, 'Sadak the Wanderer', *Times Literary Supplement*, 16 May 1936.

Kenneth Neill Cameron, *Shelley and his Circle*, Harvard Univ. Press; London, Oxford Univ. Press, 1961– [vols. i and ii, 1961; vols. iii and iv, 1970].

Frederick L. Jones, *The Letters of Percy Bysshe Shelley*, 2 vols., Clarendon Press, 1964.

Neville Rogers, *The Esdaile Poems*, Clarendon Press, 1966.

4. OTHER PRINTED MATERIAL, USED OR QUOTED[1]

In addition to the publications listed above, the following have been much used in the apparatus to Volume I:

Kenneth Neill Cameron, *The Young Shelley*, Gollancz, 1951.

---

[1] Transcriptions and modified transcriptions are not listed here: where their help has been used it is acknowledged. Only valid editions, and those significant in the textual history of a poem, have been collated.

A. M. D. Hughes, *The Nascent Mind of Shelley*, Clarendon Press, 1947.

Desmond King-Hele, *Shelley: His Thought and Work*, Macmillan, 1960.

J. A. Notopoulos, *The Platonism of Shelley*, Duke Univ. Press, 1949.

Neville Rogers, *Shelley at Work*, 2nd edn., Clarendon Press, 1967.

Neville Rogers: Three articles published in the *Keats–Shelley Memorial Bulletin* (ed. Dorothy Hewlett):

    I. 'Shelley's Spelling: Theory and Practice', xvi, 1965.

    II. 'The Punctuation of Shelley's Syntax', xvii, 1966.

    III. 'Shelley: Texts and Pretexts. The Case of First Editions', xix, 1968.

Charles H. Taylor, Jr., *The Early Collected Editions of Shelley's Poems*, Yale Univ. Press, 1958.

Lawrence J. Zillman, *Shelley's* Prometheus Unbound. *The Text and the Drafts*, Yale Univ. Press, 1968.

One book demands special listing as a permanent source of guidance about textual principles:

A. E. Housman, *Selected Prose*, ed. John Carter, Cambridge Univ. Press, 1961.

The 'Introductory Lecture' of 1892, the Prefaces to *Manilius*, 1903 and 1930, and the paper entitled 'The Application of Thought to Textual Criticism' are the foundations both of the General Introduction to this edition and of the editing itself.

5. ABBREVIATIONS AND SIGNS USED

The Commentary on each poem begins with details of its manuscript and printed sources. These, in conjunction with the details given in the two preceding sections of this Introduction, should make such abbreviations as 'Form.', 'Ross.', '1904', '1839¹', etc., self-explanatory. In my Commentary on *The Wandering Jew* I have referred to the editions of 1829 and 1831 as '29' and '31'. In my Notes on *Queen Mab*, where a few books are constantly referred to or quoted, I have avoided both titles and 'op. cit.': the references to 'Cameron', 'King-Hele', 'Notopoulos', etc., should prove sufficiently explicit. Where '1839¹' and '1839²' do not differ it seemed enough to print '1839'.

⟨ ⟩ denotes letters or words supplied conjecturally or textually doubtful.

[ ] in the Textual Commentary denotes words or letters cancelled in the manuscript.

[ ] in titles and elsewhere denotes words or letters implicit in the manuscript and supplied for clarity.

[at the end of a passage denotes that it is uncompleted in the manuscript.

A gap in a line of poetry indicates a space in the manuscript which Shelley intended to fill later.

Words and lines from the manuscript which are not part of the text are printed in my Commentary, preceded by an indication of the lines between which they occur—e.g. '16–17', '98–9'.

MARY SHELLEY'S PREFACES

PREFACE BY MARY SHELLEY
TO FIRST COLLECTED EDITION, 1839

Lui non trov'io, ma suoi santi vestigi
Tutti rivolti alla superna strada
Veggio, lunge da' laghi averni e stigi.
PETRARCA.

[1] OBSTACLES have long existed to my presenting the public with
a perfect edition of Shelley's Poems. These being at last happily
removed, I hasten to fulfil an important duty,—that of giving the
productions of a sublime genius to the world, with all the correctness
possible, and of, at the same time, detailing the history of those
productions, as they sprang, living and warm, from his heart and
brain. I abstain from any remark on the occurrences of his private
life, except inasmuch as the passions which they engendered inspired
his poetry. This is not the time to relate the truth; and I should
reject any colouring of the truth. No account of these events has
ever been given at all approaching reality in their details, either as
regards himself or others; nor shall I further allude to them than to
remark that the errors of action committed by a man as noble and
generous as Shelley, may, as far as he only is concerned, be fearlessly
avowed by those who loved him, in the firm conviction that, were
they judged impartially, his character would stand in fairer and
brighter light than that of any contemporary. Whatever faults he had
ought to find extenuation among his fellows, since they prove him to
be human; without them, the exalted nature of his soul would have
raised him into something divine.
[2] The qualities that struck any one newly introduced to Shelley
were,—First, a gentle and cordial goodness that animated his inter-
course with warm affection and helpful sympathy. The other, the
eagerness and ardour with which he was attached to the cause of
human happiness and improvement; and the fervent eloquence with
which he discussed such subjects. His conversation was marked by
its happy abundance, and the beautiful language in which he clothed

his poetic ideas and philosophical notions. To defecate life of its misery and its evil was the ruling passion of his soul; he dedicated to it every power of his mind, every pulsation of his heart. He looked on political freedom as the direct agent to effect the happiness of mankind; and thus any new-sprung hope of liberty inspired a joy and an exultation more intense and wild than he could have felt for any personal advantage. Those who have never experienced the workings of passion on general and unselfish subjects cannot understand this; and it must be difficult of comprehension to the younger generation rising around, since they cannot remember the scorn and hatred with which the partisans of reform were regarded some few years ago, nor the persecutions to which they were exposed. He had been from youth the victim of the state of feeling inspired by the reaction of the French Revolution; and believing firmly in the justice and excellence of his views, it cannot be wondered that a nature as sensitive, as impetuous, and as generous as his, should put its whole force into the attempt to alleviate for others the evils of those systems from which he had himself suffered. Many advantages attended his birth; he spurned them all when balanced with what he considered his duties. He was generous to imprudence, devoted to heroism.

[3] These characteristics breathe throughout his poetry. The struggle for human weal; the resolution firm to martyrdom; the impetuous pursuit, the glad triumph in good; the determination not to despair; —such were the features that marked those of his works which he regarded with most complacency, as sustained by a lofty subject and useful aim.

[4] In addition to these, his poems may be divided into two classes,— the purely imaginative, and those which sprang from the emotions of his heart. Among the former may be classed the *Witch of Atlas*, *Adonais*, and his latest composition, left imperfect, the *Triumph of Life*. In the first of these particularly he gave the reins to his fancy, and luxuriated in every idea as it rose; in all there is that sense of mystery which formed an essential portion of his perception of life— a clinging to the subtler inner spirit, rather than to the outward form—a curious and metaphysical anatomy of human passion and perception.

[5] The second class is, of course, the more popular, as appealing at once to emotions common to us all; some of these rest on the passion of love; others on grief and despondency; others on the sentiments inspired by natural objects. Shelley's conception of love was exalted,

absorbing, allied to all that is purest and noblest in our nature, and warmed by earnest passion; such it appears when he gave it a voice in verse. Yet he was usually averse to expressing these feelings, except when highly idealized; and many of his more beautiful effusions he had cast aside unfinished, and they were never seen by me till after I had lost him. Others, as for instance *Rosalind and Helen* and *Lines written among the Euganean Hills*, I found among his papers by chance; and with some difficulty urged him to complete them. There are others, such as the *Ode to the Skylark* and *The Cloud*, which, in the opinion of many critics, bear a purer poetical stamp than any other of his productions. They were written as his mind prompted: listening to the carolling of the bird, aloft in the azure sky of Italy; or marking the cloud as it sped across the heavens, while he floated in his boat on the Thames.

[6] No poet was ever warmed by a more genuine and unforced inspiration. His extreme sensibility gave the intensity of passion to his intellectual pursuits; and rendered his mind keenly alive to every perception of outward objects, as well as to his internal sensations. Such a gift is, among the sad vicissitudes of human life, the disappointments we meet, and the galling sense of our own mistakes and errors, fraught with pain; to escape from such, he delivered up his soul to poetry, and felt happy when he sheltered himself, from the influence of human sympathies, in the wildest regions of fancy. His imagination has been termed too brilliant, his thoughts too subtle. He loved to idealize reality; and this is a taste shared by few. We are willing to have our passing whims exalted into passions, for this gratifies our vanity; but few of us understand or sympathize with the endeavour to ally the love of abstract beauty, and adoration of abstract good, the τὸ ἀγαθὸν καὶ τὸ καλόν of the Socratic philosophers, with our sympathies with our kind. In this, Shelley resembled Plato; both taking more delight in the abstract and the ideal than in the special and tangible. This did not result from imitation; for it was not till Shelley resided in Italy that he made Plato his study. He then translated his *Symposium* and his *Ion*; and the English language boasts of no more brilliant composition than Plato's Praise of Love translated by Shelley. To return to his own poetry. The luxury of imagination, which sought nothing beyond itself (as a child burdens itself with spring flowers, thinking of no use beyond the enjoyment of gathering them), often showed itself in his verses: they will be only appreciated by minds which have

resemblance to his own; and the mystic subtlety of many of his thoughts will share the same fate. The metaphysical strain that characterizes much of what he has written was, indeed, the portion of his works to which, apart from those whose scope was to awaken mankind to aspirations for what he considered the true and good, he was himself particularly attached. There is much, however, that speaks to the many. When he would consent to dismiss these huntings after the obscure (which, entwined with his nature as they were, he did with difficulty), no poet ever expressed in sweeter, more heart-reaching, or more passionate verse, the gentler or more forcible emotions of the soul.

[7] A wise friend once wrote to Shelley: 'You are still very young, and in certain essential respects you do not yet sufficiently perceive that you are so.' It is seldom that the young know what youth is, till they have got beyond its period; and time was not given him to attain this knowledge. It must be remembered that there is the stamp of such inexperience on all he wrote; he had not completed his nine-and-twentieth year when he died. The calm of middle life did not add the seal of the virtues which adorn maturity to those generated by the vehement spirit of youth. Through life also he was a martyr to ill-health, and constant pain wound up his nerves to a pitch of susceptibility that rendered his views of life different from those of a man in the enjoyment of healthy sensations. Perfectly gentle and forbearing in manner, he suffered a good deal of internal irritability, or rather excitement, and his fortitude to bear was almost always on the stretch; and thus, during a short life, he had gone through more experience of sensation than many whose existence is protracted. 'If I die to-morrow', he said, on the eve of his unanticipated death, 'I have lived to be older than my father.' The weight of thought and feeling burdened him heavily; you read his sufferings in his attenuated frame, while you perceived the mastery he held over them in his animated countenance and brilliant eyes.

[8] He died, and the world showed no outward sign. But his influence over mankind, though slow in growth, is fast augmenting; and, in the ameliorations that have taken place in the political state of his country, we may trace in part the operation of his arduous struggles. His spirit gathers peace in its new state from the sense that, though late, his exertions were not made in vain, and in the progress of the liberty he so fondly loved.

[9] He died, and his place, among those who knew him intimately, has never been filled up. He walked beside them like a spirit of good to comfort and benefit—to enlighten the darkness of life with irradiations of genius, to cheer it with his sympathy and love. Any one, once attached to Shelley, must feel all other affections, however true and fond, as wasted on barren soil in comparison. It is our best consolation to know that such a pure-minded and exalted being was once among us, and now exists where we hope one day to join him;—although the intolerant, in their blindness, poured down anathemas, the Spirit of Good, who can judge the heart, never rejected him.

[10] In the notes appended to the poems I have endeavoured to narrate the origin and history of each. The loss of nearly all letters and papers which refer to his early life renders the execution more imperfect than it would otherwise have been. I have, however, the liveliest recollection of all that was done and said during the period of my knowing him. Every impression is as clear as if stamped yesterday, and I have no apprehension of any mistake in my statements as far as they go. In other respects I am indeed incompetent: but I feel the importance of the task, and regard it as my most sacred duty. I endeavour to fulfil it in a manner he would himself approve; and hope, in this publication, to lay the first stone of a monument due to Shelley's genius, his sufferings, and his virtues:

> Se al seguir son tarda,
> Forse avverrà che'l bel nome gentile
> Consacrerò con questa stanca penna.

POSTSCRIPT IN SECOND EDITION OF 1839

[1] In revising this new edition, and carefully consulting Shelley's scattered and confused papers, I found a few fragments which had hitherto escaped me, and was enabled to complete a few poems hitherto left unfinished. What at one time escapes the searching eye, dimmed by its own earnestness, becomes clear at a future period. By the aid of a friend, I also present some poems complete and correct which hitherto have been defaced by various mistakes and omissions. It was suggested that the poem *To the Queen of my Heart* was falsely attributed to Shelley. I certainly find no trace of it among

his papers; and, as those of his intimate friends whom I have consulted never heard of it, I omit it.

[2] Two poems are added of some length, *Swellfoot the Tyrant* and *Peter Bell the Third*. I have mentioned the circumstances under which they were written in the notes; and need only add that they are conceived in a very different spirit from Shelley's usual compositions. They are specimens of the burlesque and fanciful; but, although they adopt a familiar style and homely imagery, there shine through the radiance of the poet's imagination the earnest views and opinions of the politician and the moralist.

[3] At my request the publisher has restored the omitted passages of *Queen Mab*. I now present this edition as a complete collection of my husband's poetical works, and I do not foresee that I can hereafter add to or take away a word or line.

PUTNEY, *November* 6, 1839.

PREFACE BY MARY SHELLEY

TO THE VOLUME OF POSTHUMOUS POEMS PUBLISHED IN 1824

> In nobil sangue vita umile e queta,
> Ed in alto intelletto un puro core;
> Frutto senile in sul giovenil fiore,
> E in aspetto pensoso anima lieta.
>
> PETRARCA.

I T had been my wish, on presenting the public with the Posthumous Poems of Mr. Shelley, to have accompanied them by a biographical notice; as it appeared to me that at this moment a narration of the events of my husband's life would come more gracefully from other hands than mine, I applied to Mr. Leigh Hunt. The distinguished friendship that Mr. Shelley felt for him, and the enthusiastic affection with which Mr. Leigh Hunt clings to his friend's memory, seemed to point him out as the person best calculated for such an undertaking. His absence from this country, which prevented our mutual explanation, has unfortunately rendered my scheme abortive. I do not doubt but that on some other occasion he will pay this tribute to his lost friend, and sincerely regret that the volume which I edit has not been honoured by its insertion.

The comparative solitude in which Mr. Shelley lived was the occasion that he was personally known to few; and his fearless enthusiasm in the cause which he considered the most sacred upon earth, the improvement of the moral and physical state of mankind, was the chief reason why he, like other illustrious reformers, was pursued by hatred and calumny. No man was ever more devoted than he to the endeavour of making those around him happy; no man ever possessed friends more unfeignedly attached to him. The ungrateful world did not feel his loss, and the gap it made seemed to close as quickly over his memory as the murderous sea above his living frame. Hereafter men will lament that his transcendent powers of intellect were extinguished before they had bestowed on them their choicest treasures. To his friends his loss is irremediable: the wise, the brave, the gentle, is gone for ever! He is to them as a bright vision, whose radiant track, left behind in the memory, is worth all the realities that society can afford. Before the critics contradict me, let them appeal to any one who had ever known him. To see him was to love him: and his presence, like Ithuriel's spear, was alone sufficient to disclose the falsehood of the tale which his enemies whispered in the ear of the ignorant world.

His life was spent in the contemplation of Nature, in arduous study, or in acts of kindness and affection. He was an elegant scholar and a profound metaphysician; without possessing much scientific knowledge, he was unrivalled in the justness and extent of his observations on natural objects; he knew every plant by its name, and was familiar with the history and habits of every production of the earth; he could interpret without a fault each appearance in the sky; and the varied phenomena of heaven and earth filled him with deep emotion. He made his study and reading-room of the shadowed copse, the stream, the lake, and the waterfall. Ill health and continual pain preyed upon his powers; and the solitude in which we lived, particularly on our first arrival in Italy, although congenial to his feelings, must frequently have weighed upon his spirits; those beautiful and affecting *Lines written in Dejection near Naples* were composed at such an interval; but, when in health, his spirits were buoyant and youthful to an extraordinary degree.

Such was his love for Nature that every page of his poetry is associated, in the minds of his friends, with the loveliest scenes of the countries which he inhabited. In early life he visited the most beautiful parts of this country and Ireland. Afterwards the Alps of

Switzerland became his inspirers. *Prometheus Unbound* was written among the deserted and flower-grown ruins of Rome; and, when he made his home under the Pisan hills, their roofless recesses harboured him as he composed the *Witch of Atlas, Adonais,* and *Hellas.* In the wild but beautiful Bay of Spezzia, the winds and waves which he loved became his playmates. His days were chiefly spent on the water; the management of his boat, its alterations and improvements, were his principal occupation. At night, when the unclouded moon shone on the calm sea, he often went alone in his little shallop to the rocky caves that bordered it, and, sitting beneath their shelter, wrote the *Triumph of Life,* the last of his productions. The beauty but strangeness of this lonely place, the refined pleasure which he felt in the companionship of a few selected friends, our entire sequestration from the rest of the world, all contributed to render this period of his life one of continued enjoyment. I am convinced that the two months we passed there were the happiest which he had ever known: his health even rapidly improved, and he was never better than when I last saw him, full of spirits and joy, embark for Leghorn, that he might there welcome Leigh Hunt to Italy. I was to have accompanied him; but illness confined me to my room, and thus put the seal on my misfortune. His vessel bore out of sight with a favourable wind, and I remained awaiting his return by the breakers of that sea which was about to engulf him.

He spent a week at Pisa, employed in kind offices toward his friend, and enjoying with keen delight the renewal of their intercourse. He then embarked with Mr. Williams, the chosen and beloved sharer of his pleasures and of his fate, to return to us. We waited for them in vain; the sea by its restless moaning seemed to desire to inform us of what we would not learn:—but a veil may well be drawn over such misery. The real anguish of those moments transcended all the fictions that the most glowing imagination ever portrayed; our seclusion, the savage nature of the inhabitants of the surrounding villages, and our immediate vicinity to the troubled sea, combined to imbue with strange horror our days of uncertainty. The truth was at last known,—a truth that made our loved and lovely Italy appear a tomb, its sky a pall. Every heart echoed the deep lament, and my only consolation was in the praise and earnest love that each voice bestowed and each countenance demonstrated for him we had lost,—not, I fondly hope, for ever; his unearthly and elevated nature is a pledge of the continuation of his being, although in an altered form. Rome received his ashes; they are deposited beneath its weed-grown wall, and 'the world's sole monument' is enriched by his remains.

I must add a few words concerning the contents of this volume. *Julian and Maddalo*, the *Witch of Atlas*, and most of the *Translations*, were written some years ago; and, with the exception of the *Cyclops*, and the Scenes from the *Magico Prodigioso*, may be considered as having received the author's ultimate corrections. The *Triumph of Life* was his last work, and was left in so unfinished a state that I arranged it in its present form with great difficulty. All his poems which were scattered in periodical works are collected in this volume, and I have added a reprint of *Alastor, or the Spirit of Solitude*: the difficulty with which a copy can be obtained is the cause of its republication. Many of the Miscellaneous Poems, written on the spur of the occasion, and never retouched, I found among his manuscript books, and have carefully copied. I have subjoined, whenever I have been able, the date of their composition.

I do not know whether the critics will reprehend the insertion of some of the most imperfect among them; but I frankly own that I have been more actuated by the fear lest any monument of his genius should escape me than the wish of presenting nothing but what was complete to the fastidious reader. I feel secure that the lovers of Shelley's poetry (who know how, more than any poet of the present day, every line and word he wrote is instinct with peculiar beauty) will pardon and thank me: I consecrate this volume to them.

The size of this collection has prevented the insertion of any prose pieces. They will hereafter appear in a separate publication.

MARY W. SHELLEY

LONDON, *June* 1, 1824

EARLY
SHORTER POEMS AND
TRANSLATIONS

1802–1812

EARLY SHORTER POEMS
AND TRANSLATIONS
1802–1812

Verses on a Cat

1802

I

A CAT in distress,
Nothing more, or less;
Good folks, I must faithfully tell ye,
As I am a sinner,
It wants for some dinner   5
To stuff out its own little belly.

II

You'd not easily guess
All the modes of distress
Which torture the tenants of earth;
And the various evils,   10
Which like many devils,
Attend the poor dogs from their birth.

III

Some a living require,
And others desire
An old fellow out of the way;   15
And which is the best
I leave to be guessed,
For I cannot pretend to say.

AUTOGRAPH: *None traced.*   TRANSCRIPT: *Elizabeth Shelley; Pforzheimer Library, see
n., p. xlv.* PRINTED: *Hogg, 1858/Hutch. 1904/I and P, 1927, who collated the tran-
script.* DATE: *See n., p. 349.* TEXT: *1927, Pf., collated with 1904.*
    2 or] nor *1904, 1858*   5 wants *Pf.*] waits *1927, 1904, 1858*   7 You'd not]
You would not *1904, 1858* you mightn't *1927, Pf.*   11 like] like so *1904, 1858*
12 dogs] souls *1904, 1858*   14 others *Pf., 1858*] some others *1927*

IV

One wants society,
    Tother variety,
Others a tranquil life;   20
    Some want food,
    Others, as good,
Only require a wife.

V

But this poor little cat   25
    Only wanted a rat,
To stuff out its own little maw;
    And 'twere as good
    Had some people such food,
To make them hold their jaw!   30

Fragment: Omens

1807

HARK! the owlet flaps his wings
    In the pathless dell beneath;
Hark! 'tis the night-raven sings
    Tidings of approaching death.

Epitaphium

1808–9

[A Latin version of the Epitaph in Gray's 'Elegy'.]

I

HIC sinu fessum caput hospitali
Cespitis dormit juvenis, nec illi
Fata ridebant, popularis ille
            Nescius aurae.

∧ 20 Tother] Another *1904*, *1858*   24 require] want *1904*, *1858*   28 'twere] it
were *1904*, *1858*   29 Had some people] Some (*italicized*) people had *1904*, *1858*
30 hold their jaw!] *italicized*, *1904*, *1858*

MS.: *Untraced*. PRINTED: *Med. 1833*/*Hutch. 1904*. DATE: *See n., p. 349*. TITLE,
TEXT: *1904*/*1833*.

∨ MS: *Untraced*. PRINTED: *Med. 1847*/*Hutch. 1904*. DATE: *See n., p. 349*. TEXT:
1904/*1847*.

II

Musa non vultu genus arroganti   5
Rustica natum grege despicata,
Et suum tristis puerum notavit
                Sollicitudo.

III

Indoles illi bene larga, pectus
Veritas sedem sibi vindicavit,   10
Et pari tantis meritis beavit
                Munere coelum.

IV

Omne quod moestis habuit miserto
Corde largivit lacrimam, recepit
Omne quod coelo voluit, fidelis   15
                Pectus amici.

V

Longius sed tu fuge curiosus
Caeteras laudes fuge suspicari,
Caeteras culpas fuge velle tractas
                Sede tremenda.   20

VI

Spe tremescentes recubant in illa
Sede virtutes pariterque culpae,
In sui Patris gremio, tremenda
                Sede Deique.

17–24 *Forman found in Medwin's* Nugae, Heidelberg 1856, *a rendering of the whole poem, all in elegiacs except this Sapphic version of the Epitaph, where these lines read thus:*

Cæteris donis, fuge suspicari,
Debitas laudes meritis negare.
Cæteras culpas, fuge, velle tractas
            Sede verendâ.

Spes, metus, sacrâ, recubant in illâ
Sede, virtutes, pariterque culpæ,
In patris cari gremio, Deique,
            Pace beatâ.

In Horologium

1808–9

[For the original see n.]

INTER marmoreos Leonoræ pendula colles
Fortunata nimis Machina dicit horas.
Quas *manibus* premit illa duas insensa papillas
Cur mihi sit *digito* tangere, amata, nefas?

FOUR EPIGRAMS FROM THE GREEK ANTHOLOGY

1811

1. *The Grape*

THIS grape, of future wine the store,
Who from the tree unripened bore?
And, loathing its yet acid taste,
Thus on the ground half-eaten cast?
To every footstep passing by   5
The spurned remains obnoxious lie;—
To him, the foe of mirth and love
May Bacchus ever hostile prove,
As to the barbarous prince of yore
Who Thracia's blooming vines uptore!—   10
This grape, thus wantonly abused,
When in the sparkling glass infused,
This might have warmed some poet's lay,
Or chased corroding care away!

∧ MS.: *Untraced.*   PRINTED: *Med. 1847/Hutch. 1904.*   DATE: *See n., pp. 349–50.*
TEXT: *1904/1847.*   1 marmoreos] marmoreas *edd.*

∨ MS.: *Untraced.*   PRINTED: Oxford University and City Herald, 1. *5 Jan. 1811,* 2.
12 Jan. 1811, 3. *and* 4. *9 Mar. 1811.*   TEXT: *1811.*

2. *Supposed to be spoken by some Roses*

on the Birthday of a Beautiful Girl
who was on the Point of Marriage

WE that were wont in Spring's soft lap to bloom,
Now early blush, mid Winter's dreary gloom,
And on this day we smiling hail thy charms,
That soon a sweet maid shall bless a husband's arms;
More pleased thy lovely temples to adorn   5
Than wait the rising of the vernal morn.

3. *On Old Age*

MORTALS for age, when distant, pray;
Age, when at hand, they wish away;
The thing of which we're not possest
We constantly esteem the best.

4. *Venus and the Muses*

THE Queen of love once threatening vowed
Unless the Nine her sway allowed,
That Cupid's never-erring dart
Should quickly pierce them to the heart;
Then they: 'On Mars your menace try,   5
The little urchin WE defy.'

Translation of a Latin Epigram by Vincent Bourne

DOWN the river's gentle tide,
As to London bridge we glide,
Hark! the bells of Mary's tower
Sweetly warbled music pour!

MS.: *Untraced.*   PRINTED: Oxford University and City Herald, *23 Feb. 1811.*
TEXT: *1811.*

With what harmony and grace   5
Each preserves its stated place!
While the air, above, around,
Trembles with the various sound!

Merry changes ceaseless glide
To old Thames's willow'd side: 10
Still recede; and sweeter still,
Through the raptured breast they thrill.
Such the pleasure to our hearts,
Distant melody imparts—
Enter once within the tower   15
All the harmony is o'er.

To Mary Who Died in this Opinion

c. 1810–11

I

MAIDEN, quench the glare of sorrow
Struggling in thine haggard eye:
Firmness dare to borrow
From the wreck of destiny;
For the ray morn's bloom revealing   5
Can never boast so bright an hue
As that which mocks concealing,
And sheds its loveliest light on you.

II

Yet is the tie departed
Which bound thy lovely soul to bliss?   10
Has it left thee broken-hearted
In a world so cold as this?
Yet, though, fainting fair one,
Sorrow's self thy cup has given,
Dream thou'lt meet thy dear one,   15
Never more to part, in Heaven.

AUTOGRAPH, TITLE, DATE: *BM, letter to E. Hitchener, 23 Nov. 1811.*   PRINTED: *Ross.*
1870/Hutch. 1904.   TEXT: *1904/1870/BM.*

III

    Existence would I barter
For a dream so dear as thine,
    And smile to die a martyr
On affection's bloodless shrine.
    Nor would I change for *pleasure*   20
That withered hand and ashy cheek,
    If my heart enshrined a treasure
Such as forces thine to break.

Love

1811

Why is it said thou canst but live
    In a youthful breast and fair,
Since thou eternal life canst give,
    Canst bloom for ever there?
Since withering pain no power possesses,   5
    Nor age, to blanch thy vermeil hue,
Nor time's dread victor, death, confesses,
    Though bathed with his poison dew,
Still thou retain'st unchanging bloom,
Fixed tranquil, even in the tomb.   10
And oh! when on the blest, reviving,
    The day-star dawns of love,
Each energy of soul surviving
    More vivid, soars above,
Hast thou ne'er felt a rapturous thrill,   15
    Like June's warm breath, athwart thee fly,
O'er each idea then to steal,
    When other passions die?
Felt it in some wild noonday dream,
When sitting by the lonely stream,   20

/\ 21 *pleasure BM*] pleasure *edd.*

V AUTOGRAPH, DATE: *Pf.*, *letter to Hogg, 8 May 1811.*   PRINTED: *Hogg, 1858/Hutch.*
1904. TITLE: *Ross. 1870.* TEXT: *1904/1858/Pf.*
    1 but *Pf.*] not *edd.*   5 possesses *Pf.*] possessed *edd.*   6 age *edd.*] Age *Pf.*
7 confesses *Pf.*] confessed *edd.*

Where Silence says, 'Mine is the dell';
And not a murmur from the plain,
And not an echo from the fell,
Disputes her silent reign.

Fragment
On a Fête at Carlton House

June 1811

By the mossy brink,
With me the Prince shall sit and think;
Shall muse in visioned Regency,
Rapt in bright dreams of dawning Royalty.

Letter to Edward Fergus Graham

[?] 14 May 1811

As you will see, I wrote to you
As is most fitting right and due,
With Killjoy's frank; old Killjoy he
Is eaten up with jealousy.—
His brows so dark, his ears so blue—   5
And all this fury is for you!
Yes, Graham, thine is sure the name,
On Spanish fields so dear to fame,
Which sickening Killjoy scarce can hear
Without a mingled pang of fear!   10
Fear, hatred, cowards always have,
But Gratitude usurps the brave;
And, therefore, Graham, I will tell
You, if you don't as yet know well
Before I tell this tale to you,   15
That Killjoy, hot with envy blue,
Can neither bear, Graeme, me, or you!

∧ SOURCE: *Recollections of the Revd. C. H. Grove.*   DATE: *See n., p. 352.*   PRINTED: *Ross. 1870/Hutch. 1904.*   TEXT: *1904/1870.*

∨ AUTOGRAPH, DATE: *NYPL, letter to Graham,* [?] *14 May 1811.*   PRINTED, TITLE: *I and P,* 1927.   TEXT: *NYPL, punctuation supplied, Shelley's being negligible.*
     1 wrote *NYPL*] write *1927*   5 brows *NYPL*] brow *1927*   6 this *NYPL*] his *1927*   9 Which *NYPL*] With *1927*

A good man bears his heaven about him;
An idiot's pride won't move without him,
And pride may justly be called Hell,   20
Since 'twas from pride that Satan fell.
From pride the mighty conquerors strode
O'er half the globe, from pride the abode
Of peace becomes the poisoned cell
Where the fiends of hatred dwell—   25
Suspicion always tracks its way.
Around the wretch, what horrors play
And on his poisoned vitals prey!
Hence you, my Fargy, when we know
That you are never used to go   30
In courtship to the ancient dames
Who reverence claim instead of flames,—
Since but once in an age is seen
Of forty-eight a peerless queen,
Like Ninon famed, that girl of France   35
Who at ninety-two could dance
With such a grace as did impart
Improper flames to grandson's heart,—
We fairly may acquit your soul,
Though your life's pulses fiercely roll,   40
Of having let one wild wish glow
Of cornuting old Killjoy's brow;
Heaven knows 'twere a courageous horn
That would this frowning brow adorn!
Oh! not the fiercest antler dare   45
To stretch its fell luxuriance there!
Safe mayst thou sin; although there's none
Of what is called temptation,
And I should think 'twere no mistake
To say you sinned for sinning's sake!   50
Yet, as this place no news affords
But secret damns and glossy words
Before your face, I bid adieu,
And wish, my Graeme, good night to you.

22 conquerors *NYPL*] conqueror *1927*   29 Fargy *NYPL*] Fergy *1927*
39 We *NYPL*] All *1927*   46 fell *NYPL*] full *1927*   51 this *NYPL*] the
1927

P.S.

The wind is high, and I have been   55
With little Jack upon the green,
A dear, delightful red-faced brute;
And setting up a parachute
The wind beneath its bosom played.
Oh! Fargy, wondrous sport we made.   60

Below the last line Shelley added

Are not human minds just like this little poem?

To a Star

1811

SWEET star, which gleaming o'er the darksome scene
Through fleecy clouds of silvery radiance flingst
Spanglets of light on evening's shadowy veil,
Which shrouds the day-beam from the waveless lake,
Lighting the hour of sacred love; more sweet   5
Than the expiring morn-star's paly fires:—
Sweet star! When wearied Nature sinks to sleep,
And all is hushed,—all, save the voice of Love,
Whose broken murmurings swell the balmy blast
Of soft Favonius, which at intervals   10
Sighs in the ear of stillness,—art thou aught but Love
Lulling the slaves of interest to repose
With that mild, pitying gaze? Oh, I could look
On thy dear beam till every bond of sense
Became unnerved.   15

∧ 60 Fargy] fargy *NYPL* Fergy *1927*

∨ AUTOGRAPH, DATE: *Pf., letter to Hogg,* c. *19 June 1811.*   PRINTED: *Hogg, 1858/Hutch.*
1904.   TITLE: *Ross. 1870.*   TEXT: *1904/1858/Pf.*
   2 flingst *Pf.*] fliest *1904* flyest *1858*   3 Spanglets *Pf.*] Spanglet *1904, 1858*
11 stillness,—] stillness, *1904* stillness.—*Pf.*   but love *Pf.*] but *1904, 1858*
13 could] would *1904, 1858* cd. *Pf.*   14 On *Pf.*] In *1904*   15 unnerved *Pf.*]
enamoured *1904, 1858*

The Devil's Walk

1812

[Two versions]

I

THE Devil went out a-walking one day,
  Being tired of staying in Hell.
He dressed himself in his Sunday array;
And the reason that he was dressed so gay
    Was to cunningly pry whether under the sky   5
The affairs of earth went well.

He poked his hot nose into corners so small
  One would think that the innocents there,
Poor creatures, were just doing nothing at all
But settling some dress, or arranging some ball: 10
  The Devil saw deeper there.

He peeped in each hole, to each chamber stole,
  His promising live-stock to view.
    Grinning applause
    He just shows his claws: 15
And Satan laughed in the mirth of his soul
    That they started with fright from *his* ugly sight
Whose works they delighted to do.

A Parson with whom, in the house of prayer,
  The Devil sate side by side,   20
Bawled out that, if the Devil were [there],
  His presence he couldn't abide.
    'Ha ha!' thought Old Nick, 'That's a very stale
      trick:
    For, without the Devil, O favourite of evil,
  In thy carriage thou wouldst not ride!'   25

AUTOGRAPH: *I, BM, letter to E. Hitchener,* [?] *16 Jan. 1812. II, untraced.*   DATE:
See n., p. 353.   PRINTED: *I, T. J. Wise,* Letters to Elizabeth Hitchener, *1890/I and P,*
1927. II, PBS, as a broadside, 1812/Ross., Fortnightly Review, *1 Jan. 1871/Hutch.*
1904.   TITLE: *1812.*   TEXT: *I, 1927/BM. II, 1904/1812.*

He saw a Lawyer a viper slay
    Under his brief-covered table:
It reminded the Devil marvellously
    Of the story of Cain and Abel.

Satan next saw a Brainless King;   30
    In a house as hot as his own.
Many imps he saw near there on the wing:
They flapped the black pennon, and twisted the sting,
    Close to the very throne.

'Ah ah!' cried Satan, 'the pasture is good!   35
    My cattle will *here* thrive better than others!
        They will have for their food news of human
            blood:
They will drink the groans of the dying and dead,
And supperless never will go to bed,
    Which will make 'em as fat as their brothers.'   40

The Devil was walking in the Park,
    Dressed like a Bond Street beau:
Nor, tho' his visage was rather dark,
And his mouth was wide, his chin came out,
And something like Castlereagh was his snout,   45
    He might be called so-so.

Why does the Devil grin so wide,
    And show the horse teeth within?—
Nine and ninety on each side,
    By the clearest reckoning!   50

II

ONCE, early in the morning,
    Beelzebub arose,
With care his sweet person adorning,
    He put on his Sunday clothes.

I. 26 He saw the Devil [a Lawyer] a viper slay *BM. But cf. II. 84.*

He drew on a boot to hide his hoof,   5
   He drew on a glove to hide his claw,
His horns were concealed by a *Bras Chapeau*,
And the Devil went forth as natty a *Beau*
   As Bond-street ever saw.

He sate him down, in London town,   10
   Before earth's morning ray;
With a favourite imp he began to chat,
On religion, and scandal, this and that,
   Until the dawn of day.

And then to St. James's Court he went,   15
   And St. Paul's Church he took on his way;
He was mighty thick with every Saint,
   Though they were formal and he was gay.

The Devil was an agriculturist,
   And as bad weeds quickly grow,   20
In looking over his farm, I wist,
   He wouldn't find cause for woe.

He peeped in each hole, to each chamber stole,
   His promising live-stock to view;
Grinning applause, he just showed them his claws, 25
And they shrunk with affright from his ugly sight,
   Whose work they delighted to do.

Satan poked his red nose into crannies so small
   One would think that the innocents fair,
Poor lambkins, were just doing nothing at all   30
But settling some dress or arranging some ball,
   But the Devil saw deeper there.

A Priest, at whose elbow the Devil during prayer
   Sate familiarly, side by side,
Declared that, if the Tempter were there,   35
   His presence he would not abide.
Ah! ah! thought Old Nick, that's a very stale trick,
For without the Devil, O favourite of Evil,
   In your carriage you would not ride.

Satan next saw a brainless King,   40
    Whose house was as hot as his own;
Many Imps in attendance were there on the wing,
They flapped the pennon and twisted the sting,
    Close by the very Throne.

Ah! ah! thought Satan, the pasture is good,   45
    My Cattle will here thrive better than others;
They dine on news of human blood,
They sup on the groans of the dying and dead,
And supperless never will go to bed;
    Which will make them fat as their brothers.   50

Fat as the Fiends that feed on blood,
    Fresh and warm from the fields of Spain,
      Where Ruin ploughs her gory way,
Where the shoots of earth are nipped in the bud,
      Where Hell is the Victor's prey,   55
    Its glory the meed of the slain.

Fat—as the Death-birds on Erin's shore,
That glutted themselves in her dearest gore,
    And flitted round Castlereagh,
When they snatched the Patriot's heart, that *his*
      grasp   60
Had torn from its widow's maniac clasp,
    And fled at the dawn of day.

Fat—as the Reptiles of the tomb,
    That riot in corruption's spoil,
That fret their little hour in gloom,   65
    And creep, and live the while.

Fat as that Prince's maudlin brain,
    Which, addled by some gilded toy,
Tired, gives his sweetmeat, and again
    Cries for it, like a humoured boy.   70

For he is fat,—his waistcoat gay,
When strained upon a levee day,

II. 54 Where *1904, cj. Ross.*] When *1812*

Scarce meets across his princely paunch;
And pantaloons are like half-moons
    Upon each brawny haunch.   75

How vast his stock of calf! when plenty
    Had filled his empty head and heart,
Enough to satiate foplings twenty,
    Could make his pantaloon seams start.

The Devil (who sometimes is called Nature),   80
    For men of power provides thus well,
Whilst every change and every feature,
    Their great original can tell.

Satan saw a lawyer a viper slay,
    That crawled up the leg of his table,   85
It reminded him most marvellously
    Of the story of Cain and Abel.

The wealthy yeoman, as he wanders
    His fertile fields among,
And on his thriving cattle ponders,   90
    Counts his sure gains, and hums a song;
Thus did the Devil, through earth walking,
    Hum low a hellish song.

For they thrive well whose garb of gore
    Is Satan's choicest livery,   95
And they thrive well who from the poor
    Have snatched the bread of penury,
And heap the houseless wanderer's store
    On the rank pile of luxury.

The Bishops thrive, though they are big;   100
    The Lawyers thrive, though they are thin;
For every gown, and every wig,
    Hides the safe thrift of Hell within.

Thus pigs were never counted clean,
    Although they dine on finest corn;   105
And cormorants are sin-like lean,
    Although they eat from night to morn.

Oh! why is the Father of Hell in such glee,
 As he grins from ear to ear?
Why does he doff his clothes joyfully,   110
 As he skips, and prances, and flaps his wing,
 As he sidles, leers, and twirls his sting,
  And dares, as he is, to appear?

A statesman passed—alone to him,
 The Devil dare his whole shape uncover,   115
To show each feature, every limb,
 Secure of an unchanging lover.

At this known sign, a welcome sight,
 The watchful demons sought their King,
And every Fiend of the Stygian night,   120
 Was in an instant on the wing.

Pale Loyalty, his guilt-steeled brow,
 With wreaths of gory laurel crowned:
The hell-hounds, Murder, Want and Woe,
 Forever hungering, flocked around;   125
From Spain had Satan sought their food,
'Twas human woe and human blood!

Hark! the earthquake's crash I hear,—
 Kings turn pale, and Conquerors start,
Ruffians tremble in their fear,   130
 For their Satan doth depart.

This day Fiends give to revelry
 To celebrate their King's return,
And with delight its Sire to see
 Hell's adamantine limits burn.   135

But were the Devil's sight as keen
 As Reason's penetrating eye,
His sulphurous Majesty I ween,
 Would find but little cause for joy.

For the sons of Reason see   140
 That, ere fate consume the Pole,
The false Tyrant's cheek shall be
 Bloodless as his coward soul.

To Ireland

1812

I

THE ocean rolls between us. O thou ocean,
Whose multitudinous billows ever lash
Erin's green isle, on whose shores this venturous arm
Would plant the flag of liberty, roll on!
And with each wave whose echoings die amid   5
Thy melancholy silentness shall die
A moment too—one of those moments which
Part my friend and me!
                          I could stand
Upon thy shores, O Erin, and could count
The billows that, in their unceasing swell,   10
Dash on thy beach, and every wave might seem
An instrument in Time the giant's grasp,
To burst the barriers of Eternity.
Proceed, thou giant, conquering and to conquer!
March on thy lonely way.—The nations fall   15
Beneath thy noiseless footstep; pyramids
That for millenniums have defied the blast,
And laughed at lightnings, thou dost crush to nought.
Yon monarch, in his solitary pomp,
Is but the fungus of a winter day   20
That thy light footstep presses into dust.
Thou art a conqueror, Time! All things give way
Before thee but the 'fixed and virtuous will';
The sacred sympathy of soul which was   24
When thou wert not, which *shall be* when thou perishest.

II

Bear witness, Erin! when thine injured isle
Sees summer on its verdant pastures smile,
Its cornfields waving in the winds that sweep

AUTOGRAPH: *BM, letter to E. Hitchener, 14 Feb. 1812. See n., pp. 353-4.* DATE: *See n.*
PRINTED: *19-25, with variants, in* Q. Mab, *IX, 26-33, PBS, 1813. 26-end, Ross.
1870. 8-14, 22-25, Dowd. 1886. 15-21, Kingsland,* Poet-Lore, *July 1892. 1-end, I
and P, 1927.*   TEXT, TITLE: *1927/BM.*

6 silentness *BM*] silentless *1927*

The billowy surface of thy circling deep!
Thou tree whose shadow o'er the Atlantic gave   30
Peace, wealth and beauty to its friendly wave,
                                its blossoms fade,
And blighted are the leaves that cast its shade;
Whilst the cold hand gathers its scanty fruit
Whose chillness struck a canker to its root.   35

Sadak the Wanderer

A Fragment

? 1810–12

*   *   *

HE through storm and cloud has gone,
To the mountain's topmost stone;
He has climb'd to tear the food
From the eagle's screaming brood;
By the turbid jungle tide,   5
For his meal the wolf has died;
He has brav'd the tiger's lair,
In his bleeding prey to share.
Hark! the wounded panther's yell,
Flying from the torn gazelle!   10
By the food, wild, weary, wan,
Stands a thing that once was man!

Look upon that wither'd brow,
See the glance that burns below!
See the lank and scatter'd hair!   15
See the limb, swart, wither'd, bare!
See the feet, that leave their mark
On the soil in bloodstains dark!
Who thus o'er the world doth roam,
With the desert for his home?   20
Hath he wander'd with the brand

AUTOGRAPH: *Once owned by Dawson Turner.*   PRINTED, TITLE: *Harrison Ainsworth,* The
Keepsake, *1828/Davidson Cook,* Times Literary Supplement, *16 May 1936.*   DATE:
See n., p. 354.   TEXT: *1936.*

Of the robber in his hand?
Hath his soul been steep'd in crime
That hath smote him in his prime?
Stainless as the newborn child,   25
Strays this wanderer through the wild;
Day by day, and year by year,
Must the pilgrim wander there;
Through the mountain's rocky pile,
Through the ocean, through the isle,   30
Through the sunshine, through the snow,
Still in weariness, and woe;
Pacing still the world's huge round,
Till the mystic Fount is found,
Till the waters of the Spring   35
Round the roofs their splendours fling,
Round the pearl-embroider'd path,
Where the tyrant, Amurath,
Leaves the haram for the throne:—
Then shall all his woe be done.   40

Onward, Sadak, to thy prize!
But what night has hid the skies?
Like a dying star the sun
Struggles on through cloud-wreaths dun;
From yon mountain's shelter'd brow   45
Bursts the lava's burning flow:
Warrior! wilt thou dare the tomb
In the red volcano's womb!

In he plunges: spire on spire
Round him shoots the living fire;   50
Rivers round his footsteps pour,
Where the wave is molten ore;
Like the metal in the mould
Springs the cataract of gold;
O'er the warrior's scorching head   55
Sweeps the arch of burning lead;
O'er the warrior's dazzled glance
Eddying flames of silver dance;
By a thousand fountains fed
Roars the iron torrent red;   60

Still, beneath a mighty hand,
Treads he o'er the fiery land.
O'er his head thy purple wing,
Angel spirit of the Spring!
Through the flood, and through the field,   65
Long has been the warrior's shield.

Never fell the shepherd's tread
Softer on the blossom'd mead,
Than, thou man of anguish! thine,
Guided through this burning mine.   70

Hanging now upon the ledge,
That the precipice doth edge;
Warrior! take the fearful leap,
Though 't were as the ocean deep:
Through the realm of death and night   75
Shall that pinion scatter light,
Till the Fount before thee lies.
Onward, warrior, to the prize!
Till thy woes are all repaid:
Thine, all thine, young Kalasrade!   80

POEMS FROM ST. IRVYNE
OR
THE ROSICRUCIAN

probably 1808–1810

POEMS FROM ST. IRVYNE

OR

THE ROSICRUCIAN

probably 1808–1810

I.—*Victoria*

[Another version of *The Triumph of Conscience* below, p. 63.]

I

'Twas dead of the night, when I sat in my dwelling;
  One glimmering lamp was expiring and low;
Around, the dark tide of the tempest was swelling,
Along the wild mountains night-ravens were yelling,—
  They bodingly presaged destruction and woe.   5

II

'Twas then that I started!—the wild storm was howling,
  Nought was seen, save the lightning, which danced in
     the sky;
Above me, the crash of the thunder was rolling,
  And low, chilling murmurs, the blast wafted by.

III

My heart sank within me—unheeded the war   10
  Of the battling clouds, on the mountain-tops, broke;—
Unheeded the thunder-peal crashed in mine ear—
This heart, hard as iron, is stranger to fear;
  But conscience in low, noiseless whispering spoke.

AUTOGRAPH: *I, II, III, VI untraced. IV, a. untraced MS.; b. MS. described by Form.
See n., pp. 354-5. c. Morg., letter to Graham, 22 Apr. 1810. See n. V, Bod. MS. Shelley
adds. b. 2, letter to Graham, 14 Sept. 1810.*   DATE: *See n.*   PRINTED: *PBS, 1811/
Garnett, 1898/Hutch. 1904.*   TITLES: *I, III–V, Ross. 1870; II, VI, Dowd. 1890.*
TEXT: *1904/1811, Nos. IV and V collated with MSS.*
  I. Victoria *without title, 1811.*

IV

'Twas then that her form on the whirlwind upholding,   15
  The ghost of the murdered Victoria strode;
In her right hand, a shadowy shroud she was holding,
  She swiftly advanced to my lonesome abode.

V

I wildly then called on the tempest to bear me—

.   .   .   .

II.—'*On the Dark Height of Jura*'

I

GHOSTS of the dead! have I not heard your yelling
  Rise on the night-rolling breath of the blast,
When o'er the dark aether the tempest is swelling,
  And on eddying whirlwind the thunder-peal passed?

II

For oft have I stood on the dark height of Jura,   5
  Which frowns on the valley that opens beneath;
Oft have I braved the chill night-tempest's fury,
  Whilst around me, I thought, echoed murmurs of death.

III

And now, whilst the winds of the mountain are howling,
  O father! thy voice seems to strike on mine ear;   10
In air whilst the tide of the night-storm is rolling,
  It breaks on the pause of the elements' jar.

IV

On the wing of the whirlwind which roars o'er the moun-
    tain
  Perhaps rides the ghost of my sire who is dead: 14
On the mist of the tempest which hangs o'er the fountain,
  Whilst a wreath of dark vapour encircles his head.

II. 'On the Dark', etc., *without title 1811*; The Father's Spectre, *1870*.

III.—*Sister Rosa: A Ballad*

I

THE death-bell beats!—
The mountain repeats
The echoing sound of the knell;
  And the dark Monk now,
  Wraps the cowl round his brow,   5
As he sits in his lonely cell.

II

And the cold hand of death
Chills his shuddering breath,
As he lists to the fearful lay
  Which the ghosts of the sky,   10
  As they sweep wildly by,
Sing to departed day.
  And they sing of the hour
  When the stern fates had power
To resolve Rosa's form to its clay.   15

III

But that hour is past;
And that hour was the last
Of peace to the dark Monk's brain.
  Bitter tears, from his eyes, gushed silent and fast;
And he strove to suppress them in vain.   20

IV

Then his fair cross of gold he dashed on the floor,
When the death-knell struck on his ear.—
  'Delight is in store
  For her evermore;
But for me is fate, horror, and fear.'   25

V

Then his eyes wildly rolled,
When the death-bell tolled,

III. Sister Rosa: Ballad *1811*.

And he raged in terrific woe.
　And he stamped on the ground,—
　But when ceased the sound,   30
Tears again began to flow.

V

And the ice of despair
Chilled the wild throb of care,
And he sate in mute agony still;
　Till the night-stars shone through the cloudless air,   35
And the pale moonbeam slept on the hill.

VII

Then he knelt in his cell:—
And the horrors of hell
Were delights to his agonized pain,
　And he prayed to God to dissolve the spell,   40
Which else must for ever remain.

VIII

And in fervent pray'r he knelt on the ground,
　Till the abbey bell struck One:
His feverish blood ran chill at the sound:
A voice hollow and horrible murmured around—   45
　'The term of thy penance is done!'

IX

Grew dark the night;
The moonbeam bright
Waxed faint on the mountain high;
　And, from the black hill,   50
　Went a voice cold and still,—
'Monk! thou art free to die.'

X

Then he rose on his feet,
And his heart loud did beat,

And his limbs they were palsied with dread;   55
   Whilst the grave's clammy dew
   O'er his pale forehead grew;
And he shuddered to sleep with the dead.

XI

   And the wild midnight storm
   Raved around his tall form,   60
As he sought the chapel's gloom:
   And the sunk grass did sigh
   To the wind, bleak and high,
As he searched for the new-made tomb.

XII

   And forms, dark and high,   65
   Seemed around him to fly,
And mingle their yells with the blast:
   And on the dark wall
   Half-seen shadows did fall,
As enhorrored he onward passed.   70

XIII

   And the storm-fiends wild rave
   O'er the new-made grave,
And dread shadows linger around.
   The Monk called on God his soul to save,
And, in horror, sank on the ground.   75

XIV

   Then despair nerved his arm
   To dispel the charm,
And he burst Rosa's coffin asunder.
   And the fierce storm did swell
   More terrific and fell,   80
And louder pealed the thunder.

XV

And laughed, in joy, the fiendish throng,
  Mixed with ghosts of the mouldering dead:
And their grisly wings, as they floated along,
  Whistled in murmurs dread.   85

XVI

And her skeleton form the dead Nun reared
  Which dripped with the chill dew of hell.
In her half-eaten eyeballs two pale flames appeared,
And triumphant their gleam on the dark Monk glared,
  As he stood within the cell.   90

XVII

And her lank hand lay on his shuddering brain;
  But each power was nerved by fear.—
'I never, henceforth, may breathe again;
Death now ends mine anguished pain.—
  The grave yawns,—we meet there.'   95

XVIII

And her skeleton lungs did utter the sound,
  So deadly, so lone, and so fell,
That in long vibrations shuddered the ground;
And as the stern notes floated around,
  A deep groan was answered from hell.   100

IV.—*St. Irvyne's Tower*

I

How swiftly through Heaven's wide expanse
  Bright day's resplendent colours fade!
How sweetly does the moonbeam's glance
  With silver tint St. Irvyne's glade!

IV. St. Irvyne's Tower: Song *1811*.

II

No cloud along the spangled air 5
  Is borne upon the evening breeze;
How solemn is the scene! how fair
  The moonbeams rest upon the trees!

III

Yon dark gray turret glimmers white,
  Upon it sits the mournful owl; 10
Along the stillness of the night,
  Her melancholy shriekings roll.

IV

But not alone on Irvyne's tower,
  The silver moonbeam pours her ray;
It gleams upon the ivied bower, 15
  It dances in the cascade's spray.

V

'Ah! why do dark'ning shades conceal
  The hour, when man must cease to be?
Why may not human minds unveil
  The dim mists of futurity? 20

VI

'The keenness of the world hath torn
  The heart which opens to its blast;
Despised, neglected, and forlorn,
  Sinks the wretch in death at last.'

Additional Stanzas

For there a youth with darkened brow
  His long lost love is heard to mourn,—
He vents his swelling bosom's woe:
  'Ah! when will hours like those return?

5 air] air, *edd.*   14 silver moonbeam pours her *1811*] moonbeam pours its silver
Form., Morg.   16 in *1811*] on *Form., Morg.*   20 dim mists *1811*] dark shade
Form., Morg.

Additional Stanzas.—*In Form. and Morg. these follow V and replace VI.*

'O'er this torn soul, o'er this frail form,   5
   Let feast the fiends of tortured love!—
Let lower dire fate's terrific storm!—
   I would the pangs of death to prove!

'Ah! why do prating priests suppose
   That God can give the wretch relief?—   10
Can stop the bosom's bursting woes,
   Or calm the tide of frantic grief?

'Within me burns a raging Hell—
   Fate, I defy thy farther power!
Fate! I defy thy fiercer spell,   15
   And long for stern death's welcome hour!

'No power of Earth, of Hell or Heaven
   Can still the tumult of my brain:
The power to none save [Harriet's] given
   To calm my bosom's frantic pain.'   20

V.—*Bereavement*

I

How stern are the woes of the desolate mourner,
   As he bends in still grief o'er the hallowèd bier,
As enanguished he turns from the laugh of the scorner,
   And drops, to Perfection's remembrance, a tear;
When floods of despair down his pale cheek are streaming,
When no blissful hope on his bosom is beaming,   6
Or, if lulled for awhile, soon he starts from his dreaming,
   And finds torn the soft ties to affection so dear.

II

Ah! when shall day dawn on the night of the grave,
   Or summer succeed to the winter of death?   10
Rest awhile, hapless victim, and Heaven will save
   The spirit, that faded away with the breath.

∧ 12 calm *above* [stop] *Form., Morg.*   14 'cut away with foot of leaf', *Form.*
20 calm *above* [take] *Form., Morg.*

∨ V. Bereavement: Song *1811.*
  6 on *1811*] oer *Bod.*   7 awhile *1811*] a time *Bod.*   9 Ah! *1811*] Oh!
Bod.   10 death *1811*] Death *Bod.*

Eternity points in its amaranth bower,
Where no clouds of fate o'er the sweet prospect lower,
Unspeakable pleasure, of goodness the dower,   15
   When woe fades away like the mist of the heath.

VI.—*The Drowned Lover*

I

Ah! faint are her limbs, and her footstep is weary,
   Yet far must the desolate wanderer roam;
Though the tempest is stern, and the mountain is dreary,
   She must quit at deep midnight her pitiless home.
I see her swift foot dash the dew from the whortle,   5
As she rapidly hastes to the green grove of myrtle;
And I hear, as she wraps round her figure the kirtle,
   'Stay thy boat on the lake,—dearest Henry, I come.'

II

High swelled in her bosom the throb of affection,
   As lightly her form bounded over the lea,   10
And arose in her mind every dear recollection;
   'I come, dearest Henry, and wait but for thee.'
How sad, when dear hope every sorrow is soothing,
When sympathy's swell the soft bosom is moving,
And the mind the mild joys of affection is proving,   15
   Is the stern voice of fate that bids happiness flee!

III

Oh! dark lowered the clouds on that horrible eve,
   And the moon dimly gleamed through the tempested air;
Oh! how could fond visions such softness deceive?
   Oh! how could false hope rend a bosom so fair?   20
Thy love's pallid corse the wild surges are laving,
O'er his form the fierce swell of the tempest is raving;
But, fear not, parting spirit; thy goodness is saving,
   In eternity's bowers, a seat for thee there.

/\ 16 of *1811*] on *Bod.*

\/ VI. The Drowned Lover: Song *1811*; The Lake-Storm *Ross. 1870.*

ORIGINAL POETRY
BY VICTOR AND CAZIRE

1809–1810

ORIGINAL POETRY
BY VICTOR AND CAZIRE

1809–1810

> Call it not vain:—they do not err,
> Who say, that, when the Poet dies
> Mute Nature mourns her worshipper.
> *Lay of the Last Minstrel.*

I

A Person complained that whenever he began to write, he never could arrange his ideas in grammatical order. Which occasion suggested the idea of the following lines:

HERE I sit with my paper, my pen and my ink,
First of this thing, and that thing, and t'other thing think;
Then my thoughts come so pell-mell all into my mind,
That the sense or the subject I never can find:
This word is wrong placed,—no regard to the sense,   5
The present and future, instead of past tense,
Then my grammar I want; O dear! what a bore,
I think I shall never attempt to write more,
With patience I then my thoughts must arraign,
Have them all in due order like mutes in a train,   10
Like them too must wait in due patience and thought,
Or else my fine works will all come to nought.
My wit too's so copious, it flows like a river,
But disperses its waters on black and white never;
Like smoke it appears independent and free,   15
But ah luckless smoke! it all passes like thee—
Then at length all my patience entirely lost,
My paper and pens in the fire are tossed;

AUTHORSHIP: *I–III, Elizabeth Shelley ('Cazire'); XIV, M. G. Lewis; IV–XIII, XV–XVII, Shelley ('Victor'). See n., p. 355.* AUTOGRAPH: *III, with variants, Esd., Pf., see below, App., p. 344. Remainder untraced.* PRINTED: *PBS, autumn 1810/R. Garnett (facsimile reprint), 1898/Hutch. 1904.* DATES: *See n.* TEXT: *1904/1898.*

But come, try again—you must never despair,
Our Murray's or Entick's are not all so rare,   20
Implore their assistance—they'll come to your aid,
Perform all your business without being paid,
They'll tell you the present tense, future and past,
Which should come first, and which should come last,
This Murray will do—then to Entick repair,   25
To find out the meaning of any word rare.
This they friendly will tell, and ne'er make you blush,
With a jeering look, taunt, or an O fie! tush!
Then straight all your thoughts in black and white put,
Not minding the if's, the be's, and the but,   30
Then read it all over, see how it will run,
How answers the wit, the retort, and the pun,
Your writings may then with old Socrates vie,
May on the same shelf with Demosthenes lie,
May as Junius be sharp, or as Plato be sage,   35
The pattern or satire to all of the age;
But stop—a mad author I mean not to turn,
Nor with thirst of applause does my heated brain burn,
Sufficient that sense, wit, and grammar combined,
My letters may make some slight food for the mind;   40
That my thoughts to my friends I may freely impart,
In all the warm language that flows from the heart,
Hark! futurity calls! it loudly complains,
It bids me step forward and just hold the reins,
My excuse shall be humble, and faithful, and true,   45
Such as I fear can be made but by few—
Of writers this age has abundance and plenty,
Three score and a thousand, two millions and twenty,
Three score of them wits who all sharply vie,
To try what odd creature they best can belie,   50
A thousand are prudes who for *Charity* write,
And fill up their sheets with spleen, envy, and spite,
One million are bards, who to Heaven aspire,
And stuff their works full of bombast, rant, and fire,
T'other million are wags who in Grub-street attend,   55
And just like a cobbler the old writings mend,
The twenty are those who for pulpits indite,
And pore over sermons all Saturday night.

And now my good friends—who come after I mean,
As I ne'er wore a cassock, or dined with a dean,   60
Or like cobblers at mending I never did try,
Nor with poets in lyrics attempted to vie;
As for prudes these good souls I both hate and detest,
So here I believe the matter must rest.—
I've heard your complaint—my answer I've made,   65
And since to your calls all the tribute I've paid,
Adieu my good friend; pray never despair,
But grammar and sense and everything dare,
Attempt but to write dashing, easy, and free,
Then take out your grammar and pay him his fee,   70
Be not a coward, shrink not to a tense,
But read it all over and make it out sense.
What a tiresome girl!—pray soon make an end,
Else my limited patience you'll quickly expend.
Well adieu, I no longer your patience will try—   75
So swift to the post now the letter shall fly.

JANUARY, 1810.

II

To Miss [Harriet Grove]
from Miss [Elizabeth Shelley]

FOR your letter, dear [Hattie], accept my best thanks,
Rendered long and amusing by virtue of franks,
Though concise they would please, yet the longer the better,
The more news that's crammed in, more amusing the letter.
All excuses of etiquette nonsense I hate,   5
Which only are fit for the tardy and late,
As when converse grows flat, of the weather they talk,
How fair the sun shines—a fine day for a walk,
Then to politics turn, of Burdett's reformation,
One declares it would hurt, t'other better the nation,   10
Will ministers keep? sure they've acted quite wrong,
The burden this is of each morning-call song.
So [Charlotte] is going to [Cuckfield] you say,
I hope that success her great efforts will pay,

That [the Colonel] will see her, be dazzled outright,   15
And declare he can't bear to be out of her sight,
Write flaming epistles with love's pointed dart,
Whose sharp little arrow struck right on his heart,
Scold poor innocent Cupid for mischievous ways,
He knows not how much to laud forth her praise,   20
That he neither eats, drinks or sleeps for her sake,
And hopes her hard heart some compassion will take,
A refusal would kill him, so desperate his flame,
But he fears, for he knows she is not common game,
Then praises her sense, wit, discernment and grace,   25
He's not one that's caught by a sly looking face,
Yet that's *too* divine—such a black sparkling eye,
At the bare glance of which near a thousand will die;
Thus runs he on meaning but one word in ten,
More than is meant by most such kind of men,   30
For they're all alike, take them one with another,
Begging pardon—with the exception of my brother.
Of the drawings you mention much praise I have heard,
Most opinion's the same, with the difference of word,
Some get a good name by the voice of the crowd,   35
Whilst to poor humble merit small praise is allowed,
As in parliament votes, so in pictures a name,
Oft determines a fate at the altar of fame.—
So on Friday this City's gay vortex you quit,
And no longer with Doctors and Johnny cats sit—   40
Now your parcel's arrived [Bysshe's] letter shall go,
I hope all your joy mayn't be turned into woe,
Experience will tell you that pleasure is vain,
When it promises sunshine how often comes rain.
So when to fond hope every blessing is nigh,   45
How oft when we smile it is checked with a sigh,
When Hope, gay deceiver, in pleasure is dressed,
How oft comes a stroke that may rob us of rest.
When we think ourselves safe, and the goal near at hand,
Like a vessel just landing, we're wrecked near the strand,
And though memory forever the sharp pang must feel,   51
'Tis our duty to bear, and our hardship to steel—
May misfortunes dear Girl, ne'er thy happiness cloy,
May thy days glide in peace, love, comfort and joy,

May thy tears with soft pity for other woes flow,   55
Woes, which thy tender heart never may know,
For hardships our own, God has taught us to bear,
Though sympathy's soul to a friend drops a tear.
Oh dear! what sentimental stuff have I written,
Only fit to tear up and play with a kitten.   60
What sober reflections in the midst of this letter!
Jocularity sure would have suited much better;
But there are exceptions to all common rules,
For this is a truth by all boys learned at schools.
Now adieu my dear [Hattie] I'm sure I must tire,   65
For if I do, you may throw it into the fire,
So accept the best love of your cousin and friend,
Which brings this nonsensical rhyme to an end.

APRIL 30, 1810.

III. Song

COLD, cold is the blast when December is howling,
   Cold are the damps on a dying man's brow,—
Stern are the seas when the wild waves are rolling,
   And sad is the grave where a loved one lies low;
But colder is scorn from the being who loved thee,   5
More stern is the sneer from the friend who has proved thee,
More sad are the tears when their sorrows have moved thee,
   Which mixed with groans anguish and wild madness
      flow—

And ah! poor [Louisa] has felt all this horror,
   Full long the fallen victim contended with fate: 10
'Till a destitute outcast abandoned to sorrow,
   She sought her babe's food at her ruiner's gate—
Another had charmed the remorseless betrayer,
He turned laughing aside from her moans and her prayer,
She said nothing, but wringing the wet from her hair,   15
Crossed the dark mountain side, though the hour it was
     late.
'Twas on the wild height of the dark Penmanmawr,

That the form of the wasted [Louisa] reclined;
She shrieked to the ravens that croaked from afar,
   And she sighed to the gusts of the wild sweeping wind.—
'I call not yon rocks where the thunder peals rattle,   21
I call not yon clouds where the elements battle,
   But thee, cruel [Henry] I call thee unkind!'—

Then she wreathed in her hair the wild flowers of the
      mountain,
   And deliriously laughing, a garland entwined,   25
She bedewed it with tears, then she hung o'er the fountain,
   And leaving it, cast it a prey to the wind.
'Ah! go,' she exclaimed, 'when the tempest is yelling,
'Tis unkind to be cast on the sea that is swelling,
But I left, a pitiless outcast, my dwelling,   30
   My garments are torn, so they say is my mind—'

Not long lived [Louisa], but over her grave
   Waved the desolate form of a storm-blasted yew,
Around it no demons or ghosts dare to rave,
   But spirits of peace steep her slumbers in dew.   35
Then stay thy swift steps mid the dark mountain heather,
Though chill blow the wind and severe is the weather,
For perfidy, traveller! cannot bereave her,
   Of the tears, to the tombs of the innocent due.—

JULY, 1810.

IV. Song

COME [Harriet]! sweet is the hour,
   Soft Zephyrs breathe gently around,
The anemone's night-boding flower,
   Has sunk its pale head on the ground.

'Tis thus the world's keenness hath torn,   5
   Some mild heart that expands to its blast,
'Tis thus that the wretched forlorn,
   Sinks poor and neglected at last.—

The world with its keenness and woe,
　　Has no charms or attraction for me,　　10
Its unkindness with grief has laid low,
　　The heart which is faithful to thee.

The high trees that wave past the moon,
　　As I walk in their umbrage with you,
All declare I must part with you soon,　　15
　　All bid you a tender adieu!—

Then [Harriet]! dearest farewell,
　　You and I love, may ne'er meet again;
These woods and these meadows can tell
　　How soft and how sweet was the strain.—　　20
　　　　　　　　　　　　APRIL, 1810.

V. Song

Despair

ASK not the pallid stranger's woe,
　　With beating heart and throbbing breast,
Whose step is faltering, weak, and slow,
　　As though the body needed rest.—

Whose 'wildered eye no object meets,　　5
　　Nor cares to ken a friendly glance,
With silent grief his bosom beats,—
　　Now fixed, as in a deathlike trance.

Who looks around with fearful eye,
　　And shuns all converse with mankind,　　10
As though some one his griefs might spy,
　　And soothe them with a kindred mind.

A friend or foe to him the same,
　　He looks on each with equal eye;
The difference lies but in the name,　　15
　　To none for comfort can he fly.—

'Twas deep despair, and sorrow's trace,
  To him too keenly given,
Whose memory, time could not efface—
  His peace was lodged in Heaven.—   20

He looks on all this world bestows,
  The pride and pomp of power,
As trifles best for pageant shows
  Which vanish in an hour.

When torn is dear affection's tie,   25
  Sinks the soft heart full low;
It leaves without a parting sigh,
  All that these realms bestow.

JUNE, 1810.

VI. Song

Sorrow

To me this world's a dreary blank,
  All hopes in life are gone and fled,
My high strung energies are sank,
  And all my blissful hopes lie dead.—

The world once smiling to my view,   5
  Showed scenes of endless bliss and joy;
The world I then but little knew,
  Ah! little knew how pleasures cloy;

All then was jocund, all was gay,
  No thought beyond the present hour,   10
I danced in pleasure's fading ray,
  Fading alas! as drooping flower.

Nor do the heedless in the throng,
  One thought beyond the morrow give,
They court the feast, the dance, the song,   15
  Nor think how short their time to live.

The heart that bears deep sorrow's trace,
   What earthly comfort can console,
It drags a dull and lengthened pace,
   Till friendly death its woes enroll.—   20

The sunken cheek, the humid eyes,
   E'en better than the tongue can tell;
In whose sad breast deep sorrow lies,
   Where memory's rankling traces dwell.—

The rising tear, the stifled sigh,   25
   A mind but ill at ease display,
Like blackening clouds in stormy sky,
   Where fiercely vivid lightnings play.

Thus when souls' energy is dead,
   When sorrow dims each earthly view,   30
When every fairy hope is fled,
   We bid ungrateful world adieu.

                 AUGUST, 1810.

VII. Song

Hope

AND said I that all hope was fled,
   That sorrow and despair were mine,
That each enthusiast wish was dead,
   Had sank beneath pale Misery's shrine.—

Seest thou the sunbeam's yellow glow,   5
   That robes with liquid streams of light;
Yon distant Mountain's craggy brow.
   And shows the rocks so fair,—so bright——

'Tis thus sweet expectation's ray,
   In softer view shows distant hours,   10
And portrays each succeeding day,
   As dressed in fairer, brighter flowers,—

The vermeil tinted flowers that blossom;
  Are frozen but to bud anew,
Then sweet deceiver calm my bosom,   15
  Although thy visions be not true,—

Yet true they are,—and I'll believe,
  Thy whisperings soft of love and peace,
God never made thee to deceive,
  'Tis sin that bade thy empire cease.   20

Yet though despair my life should gloom,
  Though horror should around me close,
With those I love, beyond the tomb,
  Hope shows a balm for all my woes.

                      AUGUST, 1810.

VIII. Song

Translated from the Italian

OH! what is the gain of restless care,
  And what is ambitious treasure?
And what are the joys that the modish share,
  In their sickly haunts of pleasure?

My husband's repast with delight I spread,   5
  What though 'tis but rustic fare,
May each guardian angel protect his shed,
  May contentment and quiet be there.

And may I support my husband's years,
  May I soothe his dying pain,   10
And then may I dry my fast-falling tears,
  And meet him in Heaven again.

                      JULY, 1810.

IX. Song

Translated from the German

AH! grasp the dire dagger and couch the fell spear,
If vengeance and death to thy bosom be dear,
The dastard shall perish, death's torment shall prove,
For fate and revenge are decreed from above.

Ah! where is the hero, whose nerves strung by youth,   5
Will defend the firm cause of justice and truth;
With insatiate desire whose bosom shall swell,
To give up the oppressor to judgement and Hell—

For him shall the fair one twine chaplets of bays,
To him shall each warrior give merited praise,   10
And triumphant returned from the clangour of arms,
He shall find his reward in his loved maiden's charms.

In ecstatic confusion the warrior shall sip,
The kisses that glow on his love's dewy lip,
And mutual, eternal, embraces shall prove,   15
The rewards of the brave are the transports of love.

OCTOBER, 1809.

X. The Irishman's Song

THE stars may dissolve, and the fountain of light
May sink into ne'er ending chaos and night,
Our mansions must fall, and earth vanish away,
But thy courage O Erin! may never decay.

See! the wide wasting ruin extends all around,   5
Our ancestors' dwellings lie sunk on the ground,
Our foes ride in triumph throughout our domains,
And our mightiest heroes lie stretched on the plains.

Ah! dead is the harp which was wont to give pleasure,
Ah! sunk is our sweet country's rapturous measure,   10
But the war note is waked, and the clangour of spears,
The dread yell of Sloghan yet sounds in our ears.

Ah! where are the heroes? Triumphant in death,
Convulsed they recline on the blood-sprinkled heath,
Or the yelling ghosts ride on the blast that sweeps by,   15
And 'my countrymen! vengeance!' incessantly cry.

OCTOBER, 1809.

XI. Song

FIERCE roars the midnight storm
    O'er the wild mountain,
Dark clouds the night deform,
    Swift rolls the fountain—

See! o'er yon rocky height,   5
    Dim mists are flying—
See by the moon's pale light,
    Poor Laura's dying!

Shame and remorse shall howl,
    By her false pillow—   10
Fiercer than storms that roll,
    O'er the white billow;

No hand her eyes to close,
    When life is flying,
But she will find repose,   15
    For Laura's dying!

Then will I seek my love,
    Then will I cheer her,
Then my esteem will prove,
    When no friend is near her.   20

On her grave I will lie,
    When life is parted,
On her grave I will die,
    For the false hearted.

DECEMBER, 1809.

XII. Song

To [Harriet Grove]

AH! sweet is the moonbeam that sleeps on yon fountain,
  And sweet the mild rush of the soft-sighing breeze,
And sweet is the glimpse of yon dimly-seen mountain,
  'Neath the verdant arcades of yon shadowy trees.

But sweeter than all was thy tone of affection,   5
  Which scarce seemed to break on the stillness of eve,
Though the time it is past!—yet the dear recollection,
  For aye in the heart of thy [Percy] must live.

Yet he hears thy dear voice in the summer winds sighing,
  Mild accents of happiness lisp in his ear,   10
When the hope-wingèd moments athwart him are flying,
  And he thinks of the friend to his bosom so dear.—

And thou dearest friend in his bosom for ever
  Must reign unalloyed by the fast rolling year,
He loves thee, and dearest one never, Oh! never   15
  Canst thou cease to be loved by a heart so sincere.

AUGUST, 1810.

XIII. Song

To [Harriet Grove]

STERN, stern is the voice of fate's fearful command,
  When accents of horror it breathes in our ear,
Or compels us for aye bid adieu to the land,
  Where exists that loved friend to our bosom so dear,
'Tis sterner than death o'er the shuddering wretch bending,
And in skeleton grasp his fell sceptre extending,   6
Like the heart-stricken deer to that loved covert wending,
  Which never again to his eyes may appear—

And ah! he may envy the heart-stricken quarry,
    Who bids to the friend of affection farewell,   10
He may envy the bosom so bleeding and gory,
    He may envy the sound of the drear passing knell—
Not so deep is his grief on his death couch reposing,
When on the last vision his dim eyes are closing!
As the outcast whose love-raptured senses are losing,   15
    The last tones of thy voice on the wild breeze that swell!

Those tones were so soft, and so sad, that ah! never,
    Can the sound cease to vibrate on Memory's ear,
In the stern wreck of Nature for ever and ever,
    The remembrance must live of a friend so sincere.   20

                      AUGUST, 1810.

XIV. Saint Edmond's Eve

OH! did you observe the Black Canon pass,
    And did you observe his frown?
He goeth to say the midnight mass,
    In holy St. Edmond's town.

He goeth to sing the burial chaunt,   5
    And to lay the wandering sprite,
Whose shadowy, restless form doth haunt,
    The Abbey's drear aisle this night.

It saith it will not its wailing cease,
    'Till that holy man come near,   10
'Till he pour o'er its grave the prayer of peace,
    And sprinkle the hallowed tear.

The Canon's horse is stout and strong
    The road is plain and fair,
But the Canon slowly wends along,   15
    And his brow is gloomed with care.

Who is it thus late at the Abbey-gate?
  Sullen echoes the portal bell,
It sounds like the whispering voice of fate,
  It sounds like a funeral knell.   20

The Canon his faltering knee thrice bowed,
  And his frame was convulsed with fear,
When a voice was heard distinct and loud,
  'Prepare! for thy hour is near.'

He crosses his breast, he mutters a prayer,   25
  To Heaven he lifts his eye,
He heeds not the Abbot's gazing stare,
  Nor the dark Monks who murmured by.

Bare-headed he worships the sculptured saints
  That frown on the sacred walls,   30
His face it grows pale,—he trembles, he faints,
  At the Abbot's feet he falls.

And straight the father's robe he kissed,
  Who cried, 'Grace dwells with thee,
The spirit will fade like the morning mist,   35
  At your benedicite.

'Now haste within! the board is spread,
  Keen blows the air, and cold,
The spectre sleeps in its earthy bed,
  'Till St. Edmond's bell hath tolled,—   40

'Yet rest your wearied limbs to-night,
  You've journeyed many a mile,
To-morrow lay the wailing sprite,
  That shrieks in the moonlight aisle.'

'Oh! faint are my limbs and my bosom is cold,   45
  Yet to-night must the sprite be laid,
Yet to-night when the hour of horror's told,
  Must I meet the wandering shade.

'Nor food, nor rest may now delay,
   For hark! the echoing pile,   50
A bell loud shakes!—Oh haste away,
   O lead to the haunted aisle.'

The torches slowly move before,
   The cross is raised on high,
A smile of peace the Canon wore,   55
   But horror dimmed his eye—

And now they climb the footworn stair,
   The chapel gates unclose,
Now each breathed low a fervent prayer,
   And fear each bosom froze——   60

Now paused awhile the doubtful band
   And viewed the solemn scene,—
Full dark the clustered columns stand,
   The moon gleams pale between—

'Say father, say, what cloisters' gloom   65
   Conceals the unquiet shade,
Within what dark unhallowed tomb,
   The corse unblessed was laid.'

'Through yonder drear aisle alone it walks,
   And murmurs a mournful plaint,   70
Of thee! Black Canon, it wildly talks,
   And call on thy patron saint—

The pilgrim this night with wondering eyes,
   As he prayed at St. Edmond's shrine,
From a black marble tomb hath seen it rise,   75
   And under yon arch recline.'—

'Oh! say upon that black marble tomb,
   What memorial sad appears.'—
'Undistinguished it lies in the chancel's gloom,
   No memorial sad it bears.'   80

The Canon his paternoster reads,
  His rosary hung by his side,
Now swift to the chancel doors he leads,
  And untouched they open wide,

Resistless, strange sounds his steps impel,   85
  To approach to the black marble tomb,
'Oh! enter, Black Canon,' a whisper fell,
  'Oh! enter, thy hour is come.'

He paused, told his beads, and the threshold passed,
  Oh! horror, the chancel doors close,   90
A loud yell was borne on the rising blast,
  And a deep, dying groan arose.

The Monks in amazement shuddering stand,
  They burst through the chancel's gloom,
From St. Edmond's shrine, lo! a skeleton's hand, 95
  Points to the black marble tomb.

Lo! deeply engraved, an inscription blood red,
  In characters fresh and clear—
'The guilty Black Canon of Elmham's dead,
  And his wife lies buried here!'   100

In Elmham's tower he wedded a Nun,
  To St. Edmond's his bride he bore,
On this eve her noviciate here was begun,
  And a Monk's gray weeds she wore;—

O! deep was her conscience dyed with guilt,   105
  Remorse she full oft revealed,
Her blood by the ruthless Black Canon was spilt,
  And in death her lips he sealed;

Her spirit to penance this night was doomed,
  'Till the Canon atoned the deed,   110
Here together they now shall rest entombed,
  'Till their bodies from dust are freed—

Hark! a loud peal of thunder shakes the roof,
  Round the altar bright lightnings play,
Speechless with horror the Monks stand aloof,   115
  And the storm dies sudden away—

The inscription was gone! a cross on the ground,
  And a rosary shone through the gloom,
But never again was the Canon there found,
  Or the Ghost on the black marble tomb.   120

XV. Revenge

'AH! quit me not yet, for the wind whistles shrill,
Its blast wanders mournfully over the hill,
The thunder's wild voice rattles madly above,
You will not then, cannot then, leave me, my love.—'

'I must dearest Agnes, the night is far gone—   5
I must wander this evening to Strasburg alone,
I must seek the drear tomb of my ancestor's bones,
And must dig their remains from beneath the cold stones.

'For the spirit of Conrad there meets me this night,
And we quit not the tomb 'till dawn of the light,   10
And Conrad's been dead just a month and a day!
So farewell dearest Agnes for I must away,—

'He bid me bring with me what most I held dear,
Or a month from that time should I lie on my bier,
And I'd sooner resign this false fluttering breath,   15
Than my Agnes should dread either danger or death;

'And I love you to madness my Agnes I love,
My constant affection this night will I prove,
This night will I go to the sepulchre's jaw,
Alone will I glut its all conquering maw.'—   20

'No! no loved Adolphus—thy Agnes will share
In the tomb all the dangers that wait for you there;
I fear not the spirit, I fear not the grave,
My dearest Adolphus I'd perish to save!'—

'Nay seek not to say that thy love shall not go,   25
But spare me those ages of horror and woe,
For I swear to thee here that I'll perish ere day,
If you go unattended by Agnes away.'

The night it was bleak the fierce storm raged around,
The lightning's blue fire-light flashed on the ground,   30
Strange forms seemed to flit and howl tidings of fate,
As Agnes advanced to the sepulchre gate.

The youth struck the portal,—the echoing sound
Was fearfully rolled midst the tombstones around,
The blue lightning gleamed o'er the dark chapel spire,   35
And tinged were the storm clouds with sulphurous fire.

Still they gazed on the tombstone where Conrad reclined,
Yet they shrank at the cold chilling blast of the wind,
When a strange silver brilliance pervaded the scene,
And a figure advanced, tall in form, fierce in mien.   40

A mantle encircled his shadowy form,
As light as a gossamer borne on the storm,
Celestial terror sat throned in his gaze,
Like the midnight pestiferous meteor's blaze.—

Spirit

Thy father, Adolphus! was false, false as hell,   45
And Conrad has cause to remember it well,
He ruined my Mother, despised me his son,
I quitted the world ere my vengeance was done.

I was nearly expiring—'twas close of the day,—
A demon advanced to the bed where I lay,   50
He gave me the power from whence I was hurled,
To return to revenge, to return to the world,—

Now Adolphus I'll seize thy best loved in my arms,
I'll drag her to Hades all blooming in charms,
On the black whirlwind's thundering pinion I'll ride,   55
And fierce yelling fiends shall exult o'er thy bride.

He spoke, and extending his ghastly arms wide,
Majestic advanced with a swift noiseless stride,
He clasped the fair Agnes, he raised her on high,
And cleaving the roof sped his way to the sky.   60

All was now silent, and over the tomb,
Thicker, deeper, was swiftly extended a gloom,—
Adolphus in horror sank down on the stone,
And his fleeting soul fled with a harrowing groan.

DECEMBER, 1809.

XVI. Ghasta

or, The Avenging Demon!!!

*The idea of the following tale was taken from a few unconnected German Stanzas.
—The principal Character is evidently the Wandering Jew, and although not
mentioned by name, the burning Cross on his forehead undoubtedly alludes to that
superstition, so prevalent in the part of Germany called the Black Forest, where this
scene is supposed to lie.*

HARK! the owlet flaps her wing,
    In the pathless dell beneath,
Hark! night ravens loudly sing,
    Tidings of despair and death.—

Horror covers all the sky,   5
    Clouds of darkness blot the moon,
Prepare! for mortal thou must die,
    Prepare to yield thy soul up soon—

Fierce the tempest raves around,
    Fierce the volleyed lightnings fly,   10
Crashing thunder shakes the ground,
    Fire and tumult fill the sky.—

Hark! the tolling village bell,
    Tells the hour of midnight come,
Now can blast the powers of Hell,   15
    Fiend-like goblins now can roam—

XVI. 1–4 *Cf. 'Omens' above, p. 4, and n., p. 349.*

See! his crest all stained with rain,
  A warrior hastening speeds his way,
He starts, looks round him, starts again,
  And sighs for the approach of day.   20

See! his frantic steed he reins,
  See! he lifts his hands on high,
Implores a respite to his pains,
  From the powers of the sky.—

He seeks an Inn, for faint from toil,   25
  Fatigue had bent his lofty form,
To rest his wearied limbs awhile,
  Fatigued with wandering and the storm.

.   .   .   .

.   .   .   .   .   .

Slow the door is opened wide—
  With trackless tread a stranger came,   30
His form Majestic, slow his stride,
  He sate, nor spake,—nor told his name—

Terror blanched the warrior's cheek,
  Cold sweat from his forehead ran,
In vain his tongue essayed to speak,—   35
  At last the stranger thus began:

'Mortal! thou that saw'st the sprite,
  Tell me what I wish to know,
Or come with me before 'tis light,
  Where cypress trees and mandrakes grow.   40

'Fierce the avenging Demon's ire,
  Fiercer than the wintry blast,
Fiercer than the lightning's fire,
  When the hour of twilight's past'—

The warrior raised his sunken eye,   45
  It met the stranger's sullen scowl,
'Mortal! Mortal! thou must die,'
  In burning letters chilled his soul.

Warrior

Stranger! whoso'er you are,
   I feel impelled my tale to tell—   50
Horrors stranger shalt thou hear,
   Horrors drear as those of Hell.

O'er my Castle silence reigned,
   Late the night and drear the hour,
When on the terrace I observed,   55
   A fleeting shadowy mist to lower.—

Light the cloud as summer fog,
   Which transient shuns the morning beam;
Fleeting as the cloud on bog
   That hangs, or on the mountain stream.—   60

Horror seized my shuddering brain,
   Horror dimmed my starting eye.
In vain I tried to speak,—In vain
   My limbs essayed the spot to fly—

At last the thin and shadowy form,   65
   With noiseless, trackless footsteps came,—
Its light robe floated on the storm,
   Its head was bound with lambent flame.

In chilling voice drear as the breeze
   Which sweeps along th' autumnal ground,   70
Which wanders through the leafless trees,
   Or the mandrake's groan which floats around.

'Thou art mine and I am thine,
   'Till the sinking of the world,
I am thine and thou art mine,   75
   'Till in ruin death is hurled——

'Strong the power and dire the fate,
   Which drags me from the depths of Hell,
Breaks the tomb's eternal gate,
   Where fiendish shapes and dead men yell,   80

'Haply I might ne'er have shrank
   From flames that rack the guilty dead,
Haply I might ne'er have sank
   On pleasure's flow'ry, thorny bed—

—'But stay! no more I dare disclose,   85
   Of the tale I wish to tell,
On Earth relentless were my woes,
   But fiercer are my pangs in Hell—

'Now I claim thee as my love,
   Lay aside all chilling fear,   90
My affection will I prove,
   Where sheeted ghosts and spectres are!

'For thou art mine, and I am thine,
   'Till the dreaded judgement day,
I am thine, and thou art mine—   95
   Night is past—I must away.'

Still I gazed, and still the form
   Pressed upon my aching sight,
Still I braved the howling storm,
   When the ghost dissolved in night.—   100

Restless, sleepless fled the night,
   Sleepless as a sick man's bed,
When he sighs for morning light,
   When he turns his aching head,—

Slow and painful passed the day,   105
   Melancholy seized my brain,
Lingering fled the hours away,
   Lingering to a wretch in pain.—

At last came night, ah! horrid hour,
   Ah! chilling time that wakes the dead,   110
When demons ride the clouds that lower,
   —The phantom sat upon my bed.

In hollow voice, low as the sound
    Which in some charnel makes its moan,
That floats along the burying ground,   115
    The phantom claimed me as her own.

Her chilling finger on my head,
    With coldest touch congealed my soul—
Cold as the finger of the dead,
    Or damps which round a tombstone roll—   120

Months are passed in lingering round,
    Every night the spectre comes,
With thrilling step it shakes the ground,
    With thrilling step it round me roams—

Stranger! I have told to thee,   125
    All the tale I have to tell—
Stranger! canst thou tell to me,
    How to 'scape the powers of Hell?—

Stranger

Warrior! I can ease thy woes,
    Wilt thou, wilt thou, come with me—   130
Warrior! I can all disclose,
    Follow, follow, follow me.

Yet the tempest's duskiest wing,
    Its mantle stretches o'er the sky,
Yet the midnight ravens sing,   135
    'Mortal! Mortal! thou must die.'

At last they saw a river clear,
    That crossed the heathy path they trod,
The Stranger's look was wild and drear,
    The firm Earth shook beneath his nod—   140

He raised a wand above his head,
    He traced a circle on the plain,
In a wild verse he called the dead,
    The dead with silent footsteps came.

114 its] it *1810*   115 That] What *1810 and edd.*

A burning brilliance on his head,   145
   Flaming filled the stormy air,
In a wild verse he called the dead,
   The dead in motley crowd were there.—

'Ghasta! Ghasta! come along,
   Bring thy fiendish crowd with thee,   150
Quickly raise th' avenging Song,
   Ghasta! Ghasta! come to me.'

Horrid shapes in mantles gray,
   Flit athwart the stormy night,
'Ghasta! Ghasta! come away,   155
   Come away before 'tis light.'

See! the sheeted Ghost they bring,
   Yelling dreadful o'er the heath,
Hark! the deadly verse they sing,
   Tidings of despair and death!   160

The yelling Ghost before him stands,
   See! she rolls her eyes around,
Now she lifts her bony hands,
   Now her footsteps shake the ground.

Stranger

Phantom of Theresa say,   165
   Why to earth again you came,
Quickly speak, I must away!
   Or you must bleach for aye in flame,—

Phantom

Mighty one I know thee now,
   Mightiest power of the sky,   170
Know thee by thy flaming brow,
   Know thee by thy sparkling eye.

That fire is scorching! Oh! I came,
   From the caverned depth of Hell,
My fleeting false Rodolph to claim,   175
   Mighty one! I know thee well.—

Stranger

Ghasta! seize yon wandering sprite,
   Drag her to the depth beneath,
Take her swift, before 'tis light,
   Take her to the cells of death!   180

Thou that heardst the trackless dead,
   In the mouldering tomb must lie,
Mortal! look upon my head,
   Mortal! Mortal! thou must die.

Of glowing flame a cross was there,   185
   Which threw a light around his form,
Whilst his lank and raven hair,
   Floated wild upon the storm.—

The warrior upwards turned his eyes,
   Gazed upon the cross of fire,   190
There sat horror and surprise,
   There sat God's eternal ire.—

A shivering through the Warrior flew,
   Colder than the nightly blast,
Colder than the evening dew,   195
   When the hour of twilight's past.—

Thunder shakes th' expansive sky,
   Shakes the bosom of the heath,
'Mortal! Mortal! thou must die'—
   The warrior sank convulsed in death.   200

JANUARY, 1810.

XVII. Fragment

or the Triumph of Conscience

'TWAS dead of the night when I sate in my dwelling,
  One glimmering lamp was expiring and low,—
Around the dark tide of the tempest was swelling,
Along the wild mountains night-ravens were yelling,
  They bodingly presaged destruction and woe!   5

'Twas then that I started, the wild storm was howling,
  Nought was seen, save the lightning that danced on the sky,
Above me the crash of the thunder was rolling,
  And low, chilling murmurs the blast wafted by.—

My heart sank within me, unheeded the jar   10
  Of the battling clouds on the mountain-tops broke,
Unheeded the thunder-peal crashed in mine ear,
This heart hard as iron was stranger to fear,
  But conscience in low noiseless whispering spoke.

'Twas then that her form on the whirlwind uprearing,   15
  The dark ghost of the murdered Victoria strode,
Her right hand a blood-reeking dagger was bearing,
  She swiftly advanced to my lonesome abode.—

I wildly then called on the tempest to bear me!
  .   .   .   .
  .   .   .   .

POSTHUMOUS FRAGMENTS
OF MARGARET NICHOLSON

Being Poems found among the Papers
of that noted Female who attempted the life
of the King in 1786

Edited by John Fitzvictor

1810

POSTHUMOUS FRAGMENTS
OF MARGARET NICHOLSON

Being Poems found among the Papers of that noted Female
who attempted the life of the King in 1786.

Edited by John Fitzvictor

1810

ADVERTISEMENT

THE energy and native genius of these Fragments must be the only apology
which the Editor can make for thus intruding them on the public notice.
The first I found with no title, and have left it so. It is intimately con-
nected with the dearest interests of universal happiness; and much as we
may deplore the fatal and enthusiastic tendency which the ideas of this
poor female had acquired, we cannot fail to pay the tribute of unequivocal
regret to the departed memory of genius, which, had it been rightly
organized, would have made that intellect, which has since become the
victim of frenzy and despair, a most brilliant ornament to society.

In case the sale of these Fragments evinces that the public have any
curiosity to be presented with a more copious collection of my unfortunate
Aunt's poems, I have other papers in my possession which shall, in that
case, be subjected to their notice. It may be supposed they require much
arrangement; but I send the following to the press in the same state in
which they came into my possession.

J. F.

War

AMBITION, power, and avarice, now have hurled
Death, fate, and ruin, on a bleeding world.
See! on yon heath what countless victims lie,
Hark! what loud shrieks ascend through yonder sky;

AUTHORSHIP: 'Epithalamium' possibly not Shelley's. See n., pp. 356–8. MS.: Untraced.
DATE: See n. PRINTED: PBS, Nov. 1810/Hutch. 1904. TITLES: 'War', Woodberry,
1893; others 1810. TEXT: 1904/1810.

Tell then the cause, 'tis sure the avenger's rage   5
Has swept these myriads from life's crowded stage:
Hark to that groan, an anguished hero dies,
He shudders in death's latest agonies;
Yet does a fleeting hectic flush his cheek,
Yet does his parting breath essay to speak—   10
   'Oh God! my wife, my children—Monarch thou
For whose support this fainting frame lies low,
For whose support in distant lands I bleed,
Let his friends' welfare be the warrior's meed.
He hears me not—ah! no—kings cannot hear,   15
For passion's voice has dulled their listless ear.
To thee, then, mighty God, I lift my moan,
Thou wilt not scorn a suppliant's anguished groan.
Oh! now I die—but still is death's fierce pain—
God hears my prayer—we meet, we meet again.'   20
He spake, reclined him on death's bloody bed,
And with a parting groan his spirit fled.
   Oppressors of mankind to *you* we owe
The baleful streams from whence these miseries flow;
For you how many a mother weeps her son,   25
Snatched from life's course ere half his race was run!
For you how many a widow drops a tear,
In silent anguish, on her husband's bier!
   'Is it then Thine, Almighty Power,' she cries,
'Whence tears of endless sorrow dim these eyes?   30
Is this the system which Thy powerful sway,
Which else in shapeless chaos sleeping lay,
Formed and approved?—it cannot be—but oh!
Forgive me, Heaven, my brain is warped by woe.'
   'Tis not—He never bade the war-note swell,   35
He never triumphed in the work of hell—
Monarchs of earth! thine is the baleful deed,
Thine are the crimes for which thy subjects bleed.
Ah! when will come the sacred fated time,
When man unsullied by his leaders' crime,   40
Despising wealth, ambition, pomp, and pride,
Will stretch him fearless by his foemen's side?
Ah! when will come the time, when o'er the plain
No more shall death and desolation reign?

When will the sun smile on the bloodless field,   45
And the stern warrior's arm the sickle wield?
Not whilst some King, in cold ambition's dreams,
Plans for the field of death his plodding schemes;
Not whilst for private pique the public fall,
And one frail mortal's mandate governs all,   50
Swelled with command and mad with dizzying sway;
Who sees unmoved his myriads fade away.
Careless who lives or dies—so that he gains
Some trivial point for which he took the pains.
What then are Kings?—I see the trembling crowd,   55
I hear their fulsome clamours echoed loud;
Their stern oppressor pleased appears awhile,
But April's sunshine is a Monarch's smile—
Kings are but dust—the last eventful day
Will level all and make them lose their sway;   60
Will dash the sceptre from the Monarch's hand,
And from the warrior's grasp wrest the ensanguined brand.
    Oh! Peace, soft Peace, art thou for ever gone,
Is thy fair form indeed for ever flown?
And love and concord hast thou swept away,   65
As if incongruous with thy parted sway?
Alas, I fear thou hast, for none appear.
Now o'er the palsied earth stalks giant Fear,
With War, and Woe, and Terror, in his train;
List'ning he pauses on the embattled plain,   70
Then speeding swiftly o'er the ensanguined heath,
Has left the frightful work to Hell and Death.
See! gory Ruin yokes his blood-stained car,
He scents the battle's carnage from afar;
Hell and Destruction mark his mad career,   75
He tracks the rapid step of hurrying Fear;
Whilst ruined towns and smoking cities tell,
That thy work, Monarch, is the work of Hell.
'It is thy work!' I hear a voice repeat,
Shakes the broad basis of thy blood-stained seat;   80
And at the orphan's sigh, the widow's moan,
Totters the fabric of thy guilt-stained throne—
'It is thy work, O Monarch;' now the sound
Fainter and fainter, yet is borne around,

Yet to enthusiast ears the murmurs tell   85
That Heaven, indignant at the work of Hell,
Will soon the cause, the hated cause remove,
Which tears from earth peace, innocence, and love.

Fragment

Supposed to be an Epithalamium of Francis Ravaillac and Charlotte Corday

'Tis midnight now—athwart the murky air,
   Dank lurid meteors shoot a livid gleam;
From the dark storm-clouds flashes a fearful glare,
   It shows the bending oak, the roaring stream.

I pondered on the woes of lost mankind,   5
   I pondered on the ceaseless rage of Kings;
My rapt soul dwelt upon the ties that bind
   The mazy volume of commingling things,
When fell and wild misrule to man stern sorrow brings.

I heard a yell—it was not the knell,   10
   When the blasts on the wild lake sleep,
That floats on the pause of the summer gale's swell,
   O'er the breast of the waveless deep.

I thought it had been death's accents cold
   That bade me recline on the shore;   15
I laid mine hot head on the surge-beaten mould,
   And thought to breathe no more.

      But a heavenly sleep
      That did suddenly steep
      In balm my bosom's pain,   20
   Pervaded my soul,
   And free from control,
      Did mine intellect range again.

Methought, enthroned upon a silvery cloud,
   Which floated mid a strange and brilliant light,   25
My form upborne by viewless aether rode,
   And spurned the lessening realms of earthly night.

What heavenly notes burst on my ravished ears,
    What beauteous spirits met my dazzled eye!
Hark! louder swells the music of the spheres,   30
    More clear the forms of speechless bliss float by,
And heavenly gestures suit aethereal melody.

But fairer than the spirits of the air,
    More graceful than the Sylph of symmetry,
Than the enthusiast's fancied love more fair,   35
    Were the bright forms that swept the azure sky.
Enthroned in roseate light, a heavenly band
    Strewed flowers of bliss that never fade away;
They welcome virtue to its native land,
    And songs of triumph greet the joyous day   40
When endless bliss the woes of fleeting life repay.

Congenial minds will seek their kindred soul,
    E'en though the tide of time has rolled between;
They mock weak matter's impotent control,
    And seek of endless life the eternal scene.   45
At death's vain summons *this* will never die,
    In Nature's chaos *this* will not decay—
These are the bands which closely, warmly, tie,
    Thy soul, O Charlotte, 'yond this chain of clay,
To him who thine must be till time shall fade away.   50

Yes, Francis! thine was the dear knife that tore
    A tyrant's heart-strings from his guilty breast,
Thine was the daring at a tyrant's gore,
    To smile in triumph, to contemn the rest;
And thine, loved glory of thy sex! to tear   55
    From its base shrine a despot's haughty soul,
To laugh at sorrow in secure despair,
    To mock, with smiles, life's lingering control,
And triumph mid the griefs that round thy fate did roll.

Yes! the fierce spirits of the avenging deep   60
    With endless tortures goad their guilty shades.
I see the lank and ghastly spectres sweep
    Along the burning length of yon arcades;

And I see Satan stalk athwart the plain;
   He hastes along the burning soil of Hell.   65
'Welcome, ye despots, to my dark domain,
   With maddening joy mine anguished senses swell
To welcome to their home the friends I love so well.'

     .   .   .   .

Hark! to those notes, how sweet, how thrilling sweet
They echo to the sound of angels' feet.   70

     .   .   .   .

Oh haste to the bower where roses are spread,
For there is prepared thy nuptial bed.
Oh haste—hark! hark!—they're gone.

     .   .   .   .

Chorus of Spirits

Stay, ye days of contentment and joy,
   Whilst love every care is erasing,   75
Stay ye pleasures that never can cloy,
   And ye spirits that can never cease pleasing.
And if any soft passion be near,
   Which mortals, frail mortals, can know,
Let love shed on the bosom a tear,   80
   And dissolve the chill ice-drop of woe.

SYMPHONY

Francis

'Soft, my dearest angel, stay,
Oh! you suck my soul away;
Suck on, suck on, I glow, I glow!
Tides of maddening passion roll,   85
And streams of rapture drown my soul.
Now give me one more billing kiss,
Let your lips now repeat the bliss,
Endless kisses steal my breath,
No life can equal such a death.'   90

66 ye *1904*] thou *1810*

Charlotte

'Oh! yes I will kiss thine eyes so fair,
  And I will clasp thy form;
Serene is the breath of the balmy air,
  But I think, love, thou feelest me warm
And I will recline on thy marble neck   95
  Till I mingle into thee;
And I will kiss the rose on thy cheek,
  And thou shalt give kisses to me.
For here is no morn to flout our delight,
  Oh! dost thou not joy at this?   100
And here we may lie an endless night,
  A long, long night of bliss.'

Spirits! when raptures move,
Say what it is to love,
When passion's tear stands on the cheek,   105
  When bursts the unconscious sigh;
And the tremulous lips dare not speak
  What is told by the soul-felt eye.
But what is sweeter to revenge's ear
  Than the fell tyrant's last expiring yell?   110
Yes! than love's sweetest blisses 'tis more dear
  To drink the floatings of a despot's knell.
I wake—'tis done—'tis over.

                .   .   .   .   .

Despair

AND canst thou mock mine agony, thus calm
  In cloudless radiance, Queen of silver night?
Can you, ye flow'rets, spread your perfumed balm
  Mid pearly gems of dew that shine so bright?
And you wild winds, thus can you sleep so still   5
  Whilst throbs the tempest of my breast so high?
Can the fierce night-fiends rest on yonder hill,
  And, in the eternal mansions of the sky,
Can the directors of the storm in powerless silence lie?

Hark! I hear music on the zephyr's wing,   10
  Louder it floats along the unruffled sky;
Some fairy sure has touched the viewless string—
  Now faint in distant air the murmurs die.
Awhile it stills the tide of agony.
  Now—now it loftier swells—again stern woe   15
Arises with the awakening melody.
  Again fierce torments, such as demons know,
In bitterer, feller tide, on this torn bosom flow.

Arise ye sightless spirits of the storm,
  Ye unseen minstrels of the aëreal song,   20
Pour the fierce tide around this lonely form,
  And roll the tempest's wildest swell along.
Dart the red lightning, wing the forkèd flash,
  Pour from thy cloud-formed hills the thunder's roar;
Arouse the whirlwind—and let ocean dash   25
  In fiercest tumult on the rocking shore,—
Destroy this life or let earth's fabric be no more.

Yes! every tie that links me here is dead;
  Mysterious Fate, thy mandate I obey,
Since hope and peace, and joy, for aye are fled,   30
  I come, terrific power, I come away.
Then o'er this ruined soul let spirits of Hell,
  In triumph, laughing wildly, mock its pain;
And though with direst pangs mine heart-strings swell,
  I'll echo back their deadly yells again,   35
Cursing the power that ne'er made aught in vain.

Fragment

YES! all is past—swift time has fled away,
  Yet its swell pauses on my sickening mind;
How long will horror nerve this frame of clay?
  I'm dead, and lingers yet my soul behind.

Oh! powerful Fate, revoke thy deadly spell,   5
  And yet that may not ever, ever be,
Heaven will not smile upon the work of Hell;
  Ah! no, for Heaven cannot smile on me;
Fate, envious Fate, has sealed my wayward destiny.

I sought the cold brink of the midnight surge,   10
  I sighed beneath its wave to hide my woes,
The rising tempest sung a funeral dirge,
  And on the blast a frightful yell arose.
Wild flew the meteors o'er the maddened main,
  Wilder did grief athwart my bosom glare;   15
Stilled was the unearthly howling, and a strain,
  Swelled mid the tumult of the battling air,
'Twas like a spirit's song, but yet more soft and fair.

I met a maniac—like he was to me,
  I said—'Poor victim, wherefore dost thou roam?   20
And canst thou not contend with agony,
  That thus at midnight thou dost quit thine home?'
'Ah there she sleeps: cold is her bloodless form,
  And I will go to slumber in her grave;
And then our ghosts, whilst raves the maddened storm, 25
  Will sweep at midnight o'er the wildered wave;
Wilt thou our lowly beds with tears of pity lave?'

'Ah! no, I cannot shed the pitying tear,
  This breast is cold, this heart can feel no more;
But I can rest me on thy chilling bier,   30
  Can shriek in horror to the tempest's roar.'

.   .   .   .   .

The Spectral Horseman

WHAT was the shriek that struck Fancy's ear
As it sate on the ruins of time that is past?
Hark! it floats on the fitful blast of the wind,
And breathes to the pale moon a funeral sigh.

It is the Benshie's moan on the storm,   5
Or a shivering fiend that thirsting for sin,
Seeks murder and guilt when virtue sleeps,
Winged with the power of some ruthless king,
And sweeps o'er the breast of the prostrate plain.
It was not a fiend from the regions of Hell   10
That poured its low moan on the stillness of night:
It was not a ghost of the guilty dead,
Nor a yelling vampire reeking with gore;
But aye at the close of seven years' end,
That voice is mixed with the swell of the storm,   15
And aye at the close of seven years' end,
A shapeless shadow that sleeps on the hill
Awakens and floats on the mist of the heath.
It is not the shade of a murdered man,
Who has rushed uncalled to the throne of his God,   20
And howls in the pause of the eddying storm.
This voice is low, cold, hollow, and chill,
'Tis not heard by the ear, but is felt in the soul.
'Tis more frightful far than the death-daemon's scream,
Or the laughter of fiends when they howl o'er the corpse   25
Of a man who has sold his soul to Hell.
It tells the approach of a mystic form,
A white courser bears the shadowy sprite;
More thin they are than the mists of the mountain,
When the clear moonlight sleeps on the waveless lake.   30
More pale *his* cheek than the snows of Nithona,
When winter rides on the northern blast,
And howls in the midst of the leafless wood.
Yet when the fierce swell of the tempest is raving,
And the whirlwinds howl in the caves of Inisfallen,   35
Still secure mid the wildest war of the sky,
The phantom courser scours the waste,
And his rider howls in the thunder's roar.
O'er him the fierce bolts of avenging Heaven
Pause, as in fear, to strike his head.   40
The meteors of midnight recoil from his figure,
Yet the 'wildered peasant, that oft passes by,
With wonder beholds the blue flash through his form:
And his voice, though faint as the sighs of the dead,

The startled passenger shudders to hear,   45
More distinct than the thunder's wildest roar.
Then does the dragon, who, chained in the caverns
To eternity, curses the champion of Erin,
Moan and yell loud at the lone hour of midnight,
And twine his vast wreaths round the forms of the daemons;   50
Then in agony roll his death-swimming eyeballs,
Though 'wildered by death, yet never to die!
Then he shakes from his skeleton folds the nightmares,
Who, shrieking in agony, seek the couch
Of some fevered wretch who courts sleep in vain;   55
Then the tombless ghosts of the guilty dead
In horror pause on the fitful gale.
They float on the swell of the eddying tempest,
And scared seek the caves of gigantic . . .
Where their thin forms pour unearthly sounds   60
On the blast that sweeps the breast of the lake,
And mingles its swell with the moonlight air.

Melody to a Scene of Former Times

ART thou indeed forever gone,
    Forever, ever, lost to me?
Must this poor bosom beat alone,
    Or beat at all, if not for thee?
Ah! why was love to mortals given,   5
To lift them to the height of Heaven,
Or dash them to the depths of Hell?
    Yet I do not reproach thee, dear!
Ah, no! the agonies that swell
        This panting breast, this frenzied brain,   10
    Might wake my ——'s slumb'ring tear.
    Oh! Heaven is witness I did love,
And Heaven does know I love thee still,
Does know the fruitless sick'ning thrill,
    When reason's judgement vainly strove   15
To blot thee from my memory;
But which might never, never be.
Oh! I appeal to that blest day

When passion's wildest ecstasy
Was coldness to the joys I knew   20
When every sorrow sunk away.
Oh! I had never lived before,
But now those blisses are no more.
    And now I cease to live again,
I do not blame thee, love; ah, no!   25
The breast that feels this anguished woe
Throbs for thy happiness alone.
Two years of speechless bliss are gone,
I thank thee, dearest, for the dream.
'Tis night—what faint and distant scream   30
Comes on the wild and fitful blast?
It moans for pleasures that are past,
It moans for days that are gone by.
Oh! lagging hours, how slow you fly!
    I see a dark and lengthened vale,   35
The black view closes with the tomb;
But darker is the lowering gloom
    That shades the intervening dale.
In visioned slumber for awhile
I seem again to share thy smile,   40
I seem to hang upon thy tone.
    Again you say, 'Confide in me,
For I am thine, and thine alone,
    And thine must ever, ever be.'
But oh! awak'ning still anew,   45
Athwart my enanguished senses flew
    A fiercer, deadlier agony!

THE ESDAILE POEMS

1805–1814

THE ESDAILE POEMS

1. *To Harriet* [*Shelley*]

1811-12

VERSION I

For Version II see below, p. 231.

WHOSE is the love that, gleaming through the world,
Wards off the poisonous arrow of its scorn?
    Whose is the warm and partial praise,
    Virtue's most sweet reward?

Whose looks gave grace to the majestic theme,   5
The sacred, free and fearless theme of truth?
    Whose form did I gaze fondly on,
    And love mankind the more?

Harriet! on thine:—thou wert my purer soul;
Thou wert the inspiration to my song;   10
    Thine are these early wilding flowers,
    Though garlanded by me.

Then twine the withering wreath-buds round thy brow:
Its bloom may deck their pale and faded prime,—
    Can they survive without thy love   15
    Their wild and moody birth?

2. *A Sabbath Walk*

Probably late 1811 or early 1812

SWEET are the stilly forest glades:
Imbued with holiest feelings there
I love to linger pensively
    And court seclusion's smile;

∧ TITLE: *Esd., in Harriet Shelley's handwriting.* AUTOGRAPH: *Esd.* PRINTED: *Rog. 1966.*
[*Version II, with* Queen Mab, *PBS, 1813.*] DATE: *See nn., p. 361.* TEXT: *1966/Esd.*
∨ TITLE, AUTOGRAPH: *Esd.* DATE: *See n., p. 362.* PRINTED: *Rog. 1966.* TEXT: *1966/Esd.*
The title is preceded by the word 'Poems', which suggests that No. 1 was a later addition.

This mountain labyrinth of loveliness   5
Is sweet to me even when the frost has torn
All save the ivy clinging to the rocks
Like friendship to a friend's adversity!
   Yes! in my soul's devotedness
   I love to linger in the wilds: 10
   I have my God and worship him,
   O vulgar souls, more ardently
     Than ye the Almighty fiend
     Before whose throne ye kneel.

'Tis not the soul pervading all,   15
'Tis not the fabled cause that framed
The everlasting orbs of Heaven
   And this eternal earth,
Nor the cold Christians' bloodstained King of Kings
Whose shrine is in the temple of my heart,—   20
'Tis that Divinity whose work and self
Is harmony and wisdom, truth and love;
   Who, in the forests' rayless depth,
   And in the cities' wearying glare,
   In sorrow, solitude and death,   25
     Accompanies the soul
     Of him who dares be free.

It is a lovely winter's day;
Its brightness speaks of Deity,
Such as the good man venerates,   30
   Such as the Poet loves;
Ah! softly o'er the quiet of the scene
A pealing harmony is felt to rise.—
The village bells are sweet, but they denote
That spirits love by the clock, and are devout   35
   All at a stated hour; the sound
   Is sweet to sense, but to the heart
   It tells of worship insincere,
   Creeds half-believed,—the ear that bends
   To custom, prejudice and fear,   40
     The tongue that's bought to speak,
     The heart that's hired to feel.

19 Christians'] Christians *Esd.*   20 shrine] shine *Esd.*   23 forests'] forests *Esd.*

But to the man sincerely good
Each day will be a Sabbath day,
Consigned to thoughts of holiness,   45
    And deeds of living love:
The God he serves requires no cringing creed,
No idle prayers, no senseless mummeries,
No gold, no temples and no hireling priests,—
The winds, the pine-boughs and the waters make   50
    Its melody. The hearts of all
    The beings it pervadeth form
    A temple for its purity;—
The wills of those that love the right
    Are offerings beyond   55
    Thanksgivings, prayers and gold.

3. *The Crisis*

? 1810–11

WHEN we see Despots prosper in their weakness,
When we see Falsehood triumph in its folly,
When we see Evil, Tyranny, Corruption,
    Grin, grow and fatten,—

When Virtue toileth through a world of sorrow,   5
When Freedom dwelleth in the deepest dungeon,
When Truth in chains and infamy bewaileth
    O'er a world's ruin,—

When Monarchs laugh upon their thrones securely,
Mocking the woes which are to them a treasure,   10
Hear the deep curse, and quench the mother's hunger
    In her child's murder;—

Then may we hope the consummating hour
Dreadfully, sweetly, swiftly is arriving
When light from darkness, peace from desolation   15
    Bursts unresisted,—

AUTOGRAPH, TITLE: *Esd.*   DATE: *See n., p. 362.*   PRINTED: *13–16, Dowd. 1886/1–end,*
Rog. 1966.   TEXT: *1966/Esd.*

Then, 'mid the gloom of doubt and fear and anguish,
The votaries of Virtue may raise their eyes to heaven,
And confident watch till the renovating day-star
    Gild the horizon.   20

4. *Passion*

To the [   ]

? Early 1812

FAIR are thy berries to the dazzled sight,
Fair is thy chequered stalk of mingling hues,
    And yet thou dost conceal
    A deadly poison there
        Uniting good and ill.   5

Art thou not like a lawyer whose smooth face
Doth promise good, while hiding so much ill?
    Ah, no! The semblance even
    Of goodness lingereth not
        Within that hollow eye.   10

Art thou the tyrant, whose unlovely brow
With rare and glittering gems is contrasted?
    No,—thou may'st kill the body:
    He withers up the soul,—
        Sweet thou when he is nigh!   15

Art thou the wretch whose cold and sensual soul
His hard-earned mite tears from the famished hind,
    Then says that God hath willed
    Many to toil and groan
        That few may boast at ease?   20

Art thou the slave whose mercenary sword,
Stained with an unoffending brother's blood,
    Deeper yet shows the spot
    Of cowardice, whilst he
        Who wears it talks of courage?   25

AUTOGRAPH: *Esd.*   TITLE, DATE: *See nn., pp. 361–2 and 362–3.*   PRINTED: *Rog. 1966.*
TEXT: *1966/Esd.*
  7 Doth] Dost *Esd.*

Ah, no! Else, while I gaze upon thy bane,
I should not feel unmingled with contempt
   This awful feeling rise:
     As if I stood at night
       In some weird ruin's shade.   30

Thou art like youthful passion's quenchless fire,
Which in some unsuspecting bosom glows:
   So wild, so beautiful,
     Possessing wondrous power
       To wither or to warm.   35

Essence of Virtue blasting Virtue's prime,
Bright bud of Truth producing Falsehood's fruit,
   Freedom's own soul, that binds
     The human will in chains
       Indissolubly fast,—   40

Prime source of all that's lovely, good and great,
Debasing man below the meanest brute,
   Spring of all healing streams,
     Yet deadlier than the gall
       Blackening a monarch's heart,—   45

Why art thou thus, O Passion? Custom's chains
Have bound thee from thine heaven-directed flight,
   Or thou would'st never thus
     Bring misery to man,
       Uniting good and ill.   50

5. *To Harriet* [*Shelley*]

1811–12

NEVER, oh, never, shall yonder sun
   Through my frame its warmth diffuse,
When the heart that beats in its faithful breast
   Is untrue, fair girl, to thee!—
     Nor the beaming moon   5
     On its nightly voyage

∧ 30 weird] wierd *above* [grey] *in Esd.*

∨ TITLE, AUTOGRAPH: *Esd.*   DATE: *See nn., p. 361.*   PRINTED: *Rog. 1966.*   TEXT:
1966/Esd.

Shall visit this spirit with softness again,
　　When its soaring hopes
　　And its fluttering fears
　Are untrue, fair girl, to thee!　　　　　　　　　10

Oh! ever, while this frail brain has life,
　Will it thrill to thy love-beaming gaze,
And whilst thine eyes with affection gleam,
　It will worship the spirit within,
　　And when death comes　　　　　　　　　15
　　To quench their fire,
A sorrowful rapture their dimness will shed,
　　As I bind me tight
　　With thine auburn hair
And die, as I lived, with thee.　　　　　　　　20

6. *Falsehood and Vice*

A DIALOGUE

? 1809–10

WHILST monarchs laughed upon their thrones
To hear a famished nation's groans,
And hugged the wealth wrung from the woe
That makes its eyes and veins o'erflow,—
Those thrones, high built upon the heaps　　　5
Of bones where frenzied Famine sleeps,
Where Slavery wields her scourge of iron,
Red with mankind's unheeded gore,
And War's mad fiends the scene environ,
Mingling with shrieks a drunken roar,—　　　10
There Vice and Falsehood took their stand,
High raised above the unhappy land.

AUTOGRAPH: *Esd.*　DATE: *See n., p. 363.*　PRINTED: *with* Q. Mab (*n. on IV. 178–9*)
PBS, 1813/Rog. 1966.　TITLE: *Esd. and 1813.*　TEXT: *1966 (1813, collated with Esd.).*
　4 its *1813*] thier *Esd.*　　　7 wields *1813*] with *Esd.*　　　8 Red with *1813*]
Stained in *Esd.*　　　10 roar,—] roar, *1813* roar *Esd.*

Falsehood

Brother! arise from the dainty fare,
Which thousands have toiled and bled to bestow;
A finer feast for thy hungry ear   15
Is the news that I bring of human woe.

Vice

And, secret one, what hast thou done,
To compare, in thy tumid pride, with me—
Me, whose career, through the blasted year,
Has been tracked by despair and agony?   20

Falsehood

What have I done!—I have torn the robe
From baby Truth's unsheltered form,
And round the desolated globe
Borne safely the bewildering charm:
My tyrant-slaves to a dungeon-floor   25
Have bound the fearless innocent,
And streams of fertilizing gore
Flow from her bosom's hideous rent,
Which this unfailing dagger gave. . . .
I dread that blood!—No more!—this day   30
Is ours, though her eternal ray
Must shine upon our grave.
Yet know, proud Vice, had I not given
To thee the robe I stole from Heaven,
Thy shape of ugliness and fear   35
Had never gained admission here.

Vice

And know, that had I disdained to toil,
But sate in my loathsome cave the while,
And ne'er to these hateful sons of Heaven,
GOLD, MONARCHY, and MURDER, given;   40

18 me—] me? *1813* me *Esd.*   19 Me, whose] I whose *1813 and Esd.*   20 Has
been tracked by despair and agony? *1813*] Has been marked by ruin and misery *Esd.*
21 I have torn *1813*] I've torn *Esd.*   24 Borne *1813*] Worn *Esd.*   26 fearless
1813] dauntless *Esd.*   30 No more!] no more— *1813* no more. *Esd.*   32 grave.
1813] grave . . . *Esd.*   34 robe *1813*] mask *Esd.*   38 loathsome *1813*] noisome
Esd.   40 and *1813*] or *Esd.*

Hadst thou with all thine art essayed
One of thy games then to have played,
With all thine overweening boast,
Falsehood! I tell thee thou hadst lost!—
Yet wherefore this dispute?—we tend,   45
Fraternal, to one common end;
In this cold grave beneath my feet
Will our hopes, our fears, and our labours, meet.

Falsehood

I brought my daughter, RELIGION, on earth:
She smothered Reason's babes in their birth;   50
But dreaded their mother's eye severe,—
So the crocodile slunk off slily in fear,
And loosed her bloodhounds from the den. . . .
They started from dreams of slaughtered men,
And, by the light of her poison eye,   55
Did her work o'er the wide earth frightfully:
The dreadful stench of her torches' flare,
Fed with human fat, polluted the air:
The curses, the shrieks, the ceaseless cries
Of the many-mingling miseries,   60
As on she trod, ascended high
And trumpeted my victory!—
Brother, tell what thou hast done.

Vice

I have extinguished the noon-day sun
In the carnage-smoke of battles won: 65
Famine, Murder, Hell and Power
Were glutted in that glorious hour
Which searchless Fate had stamped for me
With the seal of her security. . . .
For the bloated wretch on yonder throne   70
Commanded the bloody fray to rise.

44 hadst *1813*] had *Esd.*   45 Yet *1813*] But *Esd.*   47 feet *Esd.*] feet, *1813*
50 Reason's babes *1813*] its sweetest buds *Esd.*   51 their mother's *1813*] Reasons
Esd.   57 dreadful *1813*] deathy *Esd.*   64 sun *Esd.*] sun, *1813*   67 glutted
1813] sated *Esd.*   glorious *1813*] joyous *Esd.*

Like me he joyed at the stifled moan
Wrung from a nation's miseries;
While the snakes, whose slime *even him* defiled,
In ecstasies of malice smiled: 75
They thought 'twas theirs,—but mine the deed!
Theirs is the toil, but mine the meed—
Ten thousand victims madly bleed.
They dream that tyrants goad them there
With poisonous war to taint the air: 80
These tyrants, on their beds of thorn,
Swell with the thoughts of murderous fame,
And with their gains to lift my name
Restless they plan from night to morn:
I—I do all; without my aid   85
Thy daughter, that relentless maid,
Could never o'er a death-bed urge
The fury of her venomed scourge.

Falsehood

Brother, well:—the world is ours;
And whether thou or I have won,   90
The pestilence expectant lowers
On all beneath yon blasted sun.
Our joys, our toils, our honours meet
In the milk-white and wormy winding-sheet:
A short-lived hope, unceasing care,   95
Some heartless scraps of godly prayer,
A moody curse, and a frenzied sleep
Ere gapes the grave's unclosing deep,
A tyrant's dream, a coward's start,
The ice that clings to a priestly heart,   100
A judge's frown, a courtier's smile,
Make the great whole for which we toil;

74 While *1813*] Whilst *Esd.*   *even him* defiled *Esd.*] even him *defiled 1813*; *see Intr.,
p. xl*   79 dream *1813*] think *Esd.*   80–81 *Esd. has*
                    [But hired assassins! tis not vice
                    Tis her sweet sister Cowardice . . .]
82 with the thoughts *1813*] in *above* [with] thier dreams *Esd.*   83 name *Esd.*]
name. *1813*

And, brother, whether thou or I
Have done the work of misery,
It little boots: thy toil and pain,   105
Without my aid, were more than vain;
And but for thee I ne'er had sate
The guardian of Heaven's palace gate.

7. *To the Emperors of Russia and Austria who eyed the battle of Austerlitz from the Heights whilst Buonaparte was active in the thickest of the fight*

? 1805–10

COWARD Chiefs! who, while the fight
    Rages in the plain below,
Hide the shame of your affright
    On yon distant mountain's brow,—
Does one human feeling creep   5
Through your hearts' remorseless sleep?
On that silence cold and deep
    Does one impulse flow
Such as fires the Patriot's breast,
Such as breaks the Hero's rest?   10

No, cowards! Ye are calm and still—
    Keen frosts that blight the human bud,
Each opening petal blight and kill,
    And bathe its tenderness in blood.
Ye hear the groans of those who die,   15
Ye hear the whistling death-shots fly
And, when the yells of victory
    Float o'er the murdered good,
Ye smile secure.—On yonder plain
The game, if lost, begins again.   20

Think ye the restless fiend who haunts
    The tumult of yon gory field,
Whom neither shame nor danger daunts,
    Who dares not fear, who cannot yield,

AUTOGRAPH, TITLE: *Esd.* DATE: *See n., p. 363.* PRINTED: *Rog. 1966.* TEXT: *1966/Esd.*

Will not with equalizing blow 25
Exalt the high, abase the low
And, in one mighty shock, o'erthrow
    The slaves that sceptres wield,—
Till from the ruin of the storm
Ariseth Freedom's awful form? 30

Hushed below the battle's jar
    Night rests silent on the heath,
Silent save when vultures soar
    Above the wounded warrior's death.
How sleep ye now, unfeeling Kings? 35
Peace seldom folds her snowy wings
On poisoned memory's conscience-stings
    Which lurk bad hearts beneath,
Nor downy beds procure repose
Where crime and terror mingle throes. 40

Yet may your terrors rest secure,—
    Thou, northern chief, why startest thou?
Pale Austria,—calm those fears! Be sure
    The tyrant needs such slaves as you!
Think ye the world would bear his sway 45
Were dastards such as you away?
No! they would pluck his plumage gay,
    Torn from a nation's woe,
And lay him in the oblivious gloom
Where Freedom now prepares your tomb. 50

8. *To November*

1811–12

O MONTH of gloom, whose sullen brow
    Bears stamp of storms that lurk beneath,—
No care or horror bringest thou
    To one who draws his breath

∧ 33 when *possibly* where *Esd.*   34 warrior's] warriors *Esd.*

∨ AUTOGRAPH, TITLE: *Esd.*   DATE: *See nn., p. 361.*   PRINTED: *Rog. 1966.*   TEXT:
1966/Esd.
    There is a cross in Esd. against the title. Perhaps Shelley intended a footnote.

Where Zephyrs play and sunbeams shine   5
Unstained by any fog of thine!

Whilst thou obscure'st the face of day
   Her radiant eyes can gild the gloom,
Darting a soft and vernal ray
   On Nature's leafless tomb,—   10
Yes, though the landscape's beauties flee,
My Harriet makes it spring to me!

Then raise thy fogs, invoke thy storms;
   Thy malice still my soul shall mar,
And, whilst thy rage the Heaven deforms,   15
   Shall laugh at every care;
And each pure feeling shall combine
To tell its Harriet 'I am thine!'

It once was May; the month of love
   Did all it could to yield me pleasure,   20
Waking each green and vocal grove
   To a many-mingling measure;
But warmth and peace could not impart
To such a cold and shuddering heart.

Now thou art here—come, do thy worst   25
   To chill the breast that Harriet warms!
I fear me, sullen month, thou'lt burst
   With envy of her charms
And, finding nothing's to be done,
Turn to December ere thou'st won!   30

9. *Written on a Beautiful Day in Spring*

? Spring 1812

In that strange mental wandering when to live,
   To breathe, to be, is undivided joy,
When the most woe-worn wretch would cease to grieve,
   When Satiation's self would fail to cloy;

∧ 15 thy] the *Esd.*   28 of *over* at *apparently,* but *possibly* at *over* of
∨ AUTOGRAPH, TITLE: *Esd.*   DATE: *See n., p. 364.*   PRINTED: *Rog. 1966.*   TEXT: *1966/Esd.*
1–10 *For punctuation see Intr., pp. xxxviii–xxxix.*

When, unpercipient of all other things   5
    Than those that press around—the breathing Earth,
    The gleaming sky and the fresh season's birth—
Sensation all it⟨s⟩ wondrous rapture brings,
    And to itself not once the mind recurs;—
      Is it foretaste of Heaven?   10
    So sweet as this the nerves it stirs
And, mingling in the vital tide
      With gentle motion driven,
    Cheers the sunk spirits, lifts the languid eye
And, scattering through the frame its influence wide,   15
    Revives the spirits when they droop and die,
The frozen blood with genial beaming warms,
And to a gorgeous fly the sluggish worm transforms.

10. *On leaving London for Wales*

Autumn 1812

THOU miserable city!—where the gloom
    Of penury mingles with the tyrant's pride,
And virtue bends in sorrow o'er the tomb
    Where Freedom's hope and Truth's high courage died!
    May floods and vales and mountains me divide   5
From all the taints thy wretched walls contain!—
    That life's extremes, in desolation wide,
No more heap horrors on my beating brain
Nor sting my shuddering heart to sympathy with pain!

With joy I breathe the last and full farewell   10
    That long has quivered on my burdened heart;
My natural sympathies to rapture swell
    As from its day thy cheerless glooms depart;
    Nor all the glare thy gayest scenes impart
Could lure one sigh, could steal one tear from me,   15
    Or lull to languishment the wakeful smart
Which virtue feels for all 'tis forced to see,
Or quench the eternal flame of generous Liberty.

AUTOGRAPH, TITLE: *Esd.*   DATE: *See n., p. 364.*   PRINTED: *19–45, 53–63, Dowd.*
1886/1–end, Rog. 1966.   TEXT: *1966/1886/Esd.*
  2 tyrant's] tyrants *Esd.*   10 full *possibly* free *Esd.*

Hail to thee, Cambria, for the unfettered wind
   Which from thy wilds even now methinks I feel,   20
Chasing the clouds that roll in wrath behind,
   And tightening the soul's laxest nerves to steel!—
   True mountain Liberty alone may heal
The pain which Custom's obduracies bring!—
   And he who dares in fancy even to steal   25
One draught from Snowdon's ever sacred spring
Blots out the unholiest rede of wordly witnessing!

And shall that soul, to selfish peace resigned,
   So soon forget the woe its fellows share?
Can Snowdon's Lethe from the free-born mind   30
   So soon the page of injured penury tear?
   Does this fine mass of human passion dare
To sleep, unhonouring the patriot's fall,
   Or life's sweet load in quietude to bear
While millions famish even in Luxury's hall,   35
And Tyranny, high raised, stern lowers over all?

No, Cambria, never may thy matchless vales
   A heart so false to hope and virtue shield!—
Nor ever may thy spirit-breathing gales
   Waft freshness to the slaves who dare to yield!   40
   For me . . . the weapon that I burn to wield
I seek amid thy rocks to ruin hurled—
   That Reason's flag may over Freedom's field,
Symbol of bloodless victory, wave unfurled,
A meteor-sign of love effulgent o'er the world!   45

Hark to that shriek! My hand had almost clasped
   The dagger that my heart had cast away,
When the pert slaves whose wanton power had grasped
   All hope that springs beneath the eye of day,
   Pass before Memory's gaze in long array.   50
The storm fleets by and calmer thoughts succeed,
   Feelings once more mild Reason's voice obey:
Woe be the tyrant's and the murderer's meed,—
But Nature's wound alone should make their conscience bleed.

36 lowers *possibly* towers *Esd.*   over *Esd.*] on *1886*   53 tyrant's . . . murderer's]
tyrants . . . murderers *Esd.*

Do thou, wild Cambria, calm each struggling thought;   55
   Cast thy sweet veil of rocks and woods between,
That by the soul to indignation wrought
   Mountains and dells be mingled with the scene;
   Let me forever be what I have been,
But not forever at my needy door   60
   Let Misery linger, speechless, pale and lean;
I am the friend of the unfriended poor,—
Let me not madly stain their righteous cause in gore.

No more! The visions fade before my sight
   Which Fancy pictures in the waste of air,   65
Like lovely dreams ere morning's chilling light;
   And sad realities alone are there.
   Ah! neither woe nor fear nor pain can tear
Their image from the tablet of my soul
   Nor the mad floods of despotism, where   70
Lashed into desperate furiousness they roll,
Nor Passion's soothing voice, nor Interest's cold control.

11. *A Winter's Day*

Probably 1811–12

O WINTRY day, that mockest Spring
   With hopes of the reviving year,
That sheddest softness from thy wing
And, near the cascades murmuring,
   Awakenest sounds so clear   5
That peals of vernal music swing
   Through the balm atmosphere!—

Why hast thou given, O year, to May
   A birth so premature,—
To live one uncompleted day?   10
That the mad whirlwind's sullen sway

AUTOGRAPH, TITLE: *Esd.* DATE: *See n., p. 364.* PRINTED: *Rog. 1966.* TEXT: *1966/Esd.*
  4 cascades *thus Esd., but possibly for* cascade's   10 uncompleted] incompleted
Esd.   11 whirlwind's] whirlwinds *Esd.*

May sweep it from the moor,
And winter reassume the sway
     That shall so long endure?

Art thou like Genius' matin-bloom,—   15
     Unwelcome promise of its prime,
That scattereth its rich perfume
Around the portals of the tomb,
     Decking the scar of Time
In mockery of the early doom?   20

Art thou like Passion's rapturous dream,
     That o'er life's stormy dawn
Doth dart its wild and flamy beam,
Yet like a fleeting flash doth seem
     When many chequered years are gone,   25
⟨And tell the illusion of its gleam
     Life's blasted springs alone⟩?

Whate'er thou emblemest, I'll breathe
     Thy transitory sweetness now,
And whether Health with roseate wreath   30
May bind mine head, or creeping Death
     Steal o'er my pulse's flow,
Struggling the wintry winds beneath
     I'll love thy vernal glow.

12. *To Liberty*

? 1811–12

OH, let not Liberty
     Silently perish!—
May the groan and the sigh
     Yet the flame cherish!

∧ 15 Genius'] Genius's *Esd.*   26–7 *See n. p. 364.*   32 pulse's] pulses *Esd.*

∨ AUTOGRAPH, TITLE: *Esd.*   DATE: *See n., p. 364.*   PRINTED: *26–30, Dowd. 1886/1-end,*
Rog. 1966.   TEXT: *1966/Esd.*

Till the voice to Nature's bursting heart given,   5
 Ascending loud and high,
 A world's indignant cry
  And, startling on his throne
  The tyrant grim and lone,
Shall beat the deaf vault of Heaven.   10

 Say, can the Tyrant's frown
  Daunt those who fear not?
 Or break the spirits down
  His badge that wear not?
Can chains or death or infamy subdue   15
 The free and fearless soul
 That dreads not their control,
  Sees Paradise and Hell,
  Sees the palace and the cell,
Yet bravely dares prefer the good and true?   20

 Regal pomp and pride
  The Patriot falls in scorning:
 The spot whereon he died
  Should be the despot's warning,—
The voice of blood shall on his crimes call down revenge! 25
 And the spirits of the brave
 Shall start from every grave,
  Whilst, from her Atlantic throne,
  Freedom sanctifies the groan
That fans the glorious fires of its change!   30

 Monarch!—sure employer
  Of vice and want and woe,
 Thou conscienceless destroyer,
  Who and what art thou?—
The dark prison-house that in the dust shall lie,   35
 The pyramid which guilt
 First planned, which Man has built,—
  At whose footstone want and woe
  With a ceaseless murmur flow,
And whose peak attracts the tempests of the sky!   40

11 Tyrant's] Tyrants *Esd.*   18 Sees] Yet Sees *Esd.*   24 despot's] despots
Esd.   25 shall *over* in *Esd.*

The pyramids shall fall—
  And, Monarchs, so shall ye!
Thrones shall rust in the hall
  Of forgotten royalty!
Whilst Virtue, Truth and Peace shall arise,   45
  And a Paradise on Earth
From your fall shall date its birth,
  And human life shall seem
  Like a short and happy dream,
Ere we wake in the daybeam of the skies.   50

13. *On Robert Emmet's Tomb*

February–March 1812

MAY the tempests of winter that sweep o'er thy tomb
  Disturb not a slumber so sacred as thine!
May the breezes of summer that breathe of perfume
  Waft their balmiest dews to so hallowed a shrine!

May the foot of the tyrant, the coward, the slave,   5
  Be palsied with dread where thine ashes repose!—
Where that undying shamrock still blooms on thy grave
  Which sprung when the dawnlight of Erin arose.

There oft have I marked, the grey gravestones among,
  Where thy relics distinguished in lowliness lay,   10
The peasant boy pensively lingering long,
  〈And silently weep as he passed away.〉

And how could he not pause if the blood of his sires
  Ever wakened one generous throb in his heart?—
How could he inherit a spark of their fires   15
  If tearless and frigid he dared to depart?

Not the scrolls of a court could emblazon thy fame
  Like the silence that reigns in the palace of thee,
Like the whispers that pass of thy dearly-loved name,
  Like the tears of the good, like the groans of the free. 20

AUTOGRAPH: *Esd.*   TITLE: *Esd. See n., p. 365.*   DATE: *See n.*   PRINTED: *21–28, Dowd.
1886/1–end, Rog. 1966.*   TEXT: *1966/Esd.*
  18 *There is a cross against this line. Perhaps a footnote was intended.*

No trump tells thy virtues—the grave where they rest
   With thy dust shall remain unpolluted by fame,
Till thy foes, by the world and by fortune caressed,
   Shall pass like a mist from the light of thy name.

When the storm-cloud that lowers o'er the daybeam is gone, 25
   Unchanged, unextinguished its life-spring will shine;
When Erin has ceased with their memory to groan
   She will smile through the tears of revival on thine.

14. *A Tale of Society as it is*

From Facts, 1811

1811–12

SHE was an agèd woman, and the years
   Which she had numbered on her toilsome way
   Had bowed her natural powers to decay.
   She was an agèd woman; yet the ray
Which faintly glimmered through the starting tears,   5
   Pressed from their beds by silent misery,
   Hath soul's imperishable energy.
She was a cripple, and incapable
   To add one mite to golden luxury;
And therefore did her spirit clearly feel   10
   That Poverty, the crime of tainting stain,
Would merge her in its depths never to rise again.

One only son's love had supported her.
   She long had struggled with infirmity
   Lingering from human life-scenes; for to die,   15
   When Fate has spared to rend some mental tie,
Not many wish and surely fewer dare.
   But when the tyrant's bloodhounds forced her child

AUTOGRAPH: *1–end, Esd., 1–79, BM, letter to E. Hitchener, 7 Jan. 1812.* TITLE: *Esd.*
DATE: *See n., p. 365.* PRINTED: *1–79, from BM, Ross. 1870/1–79, from a transcript of Esd. (see Intr., p. xxix), I and P, 1927/1–end, from Esd., Rog. 1966.* TEXT: *1966/1870/ Esd./BM.*
  5 the *Esd.*] her *BM*   6 from their beds *Esd.*] into light *BM* from their lids *1927*
9 golden *Esd.*] gold-fed *BM*   10 clearly *Esd.*] dimly *BM*   12 the *Esd.*] its *BM*
15 from *Esd.*] to *BM, 1927*   17 Not *Esd.*] *BM MS. torn* Would *1870*   18 her *Esd.*] the *BM*

For his curst power unhallowed arms to wield,
Bend to another's will, become a thing   20
    More senseless than the sword of battlefield,
Then did she feel keen sorrow's keenest sting,
And many years had passed ere comfort they would bring.

For seven years did this poor woman live
    In unparticipated solitude.   25
    Thou might'st have seen her in the forest rude
    Picking the scattered remnants of its wood;
If human thou might'st then have learned to grieve.
    The gleanings of precarious charity
    Her scantiness of food did scarce supply,   30
The proofs of an unspeaking sorrow dwelt
    Within her ghastly hollowness of eye;
Each arrow of the season's change she felt;
    Yet still she yearned, ere her sad course were run—
One only hope it was—once more to see her son.   35

It was an eve of June, when every star
    Spoke peace from Heaven to those on Earth that live.
    She rested on the moor. 'Twas such an eve
    When first her soul began indeed to grieve:
Then he was here—now he is very far.   40
    The freshness of the balmy evening
    A sorrow o'er her weary soul did fling,
Yet not devoid of rapture's mingled tear;
    A balm was in the poison of the sting.
This agèd sufferer for many a year   45
    Had never felt such comfort. She suppressed
A sigh and, turning round . . . clasped William to her breast!

And though his form was wasted by the woe
    Which despots on their victims love to wreak,

---

19 his curst *BM*] tyrants *Esd. See n.*   23 would] wd. *Esd.* cd. *BM*   26 forest
BM] desart *Esd. See n.*   28 grieve *Esd.*] feel *BM*   34 yearned *Esd.*] groans
BM   her sad course *Esd.*] yet her race *BM*   37 to those on Earth that live]
omitted in BM where the line is filled out by a row of crosses. See n.   41 freshness
Esd.] sweetness *BM*   42 weary *Esd.*] aged *BM*   45 This *Esd.*] The *BM*
49 despots *Esd.*] tyrants *BM*

Though his sunk eyeball and his faded cheek 50
  Of slavery, violence and scorn did speak,
Yet did the agèd woman's bosom glow:
  The vital fire seemed re-illumed within
  By this sweet unexpected welcoming.
O consummation of the fondest hope 55
  That ever soared on Fancy's dauntless wing!
O tenderness that foundst so sweet a scope!
  Prince, who dost swell upon thy mighty sway,—
When thou canst feel such love thou shalt be great as they!

Her son, compelled, the tyrant's foes had fought, 60
  Had bled in battle, and the stern control
  That ruled his sinews and coerced his soul
  Utterly poisoned life's unmingled bowl,
And unsubduable evils on him wrought.
  He was the shadow of the lusty child 65
  Who, when the time of summer season smiled,
For her did earn a meal of honesty,
  And with affectionate discourse beguiled
The keen attacks of pain and poverty,—
  Till Power, as envying this her only joy, 70
From her maternal bosom tore the unhappy boy.

And now cold Charity's unwelcome dole
  Was insufficient to support the pair;
  And they would perish rather than would bear
  The law's stern slavery and the insolent stare 75
With which law loves to rend the poor man's soul—
  The bitter scorn, the spirit-sinking noise
  Of heartless mirth which women, men and boys
Wake in this scene of legal misery.
  Oh, William's spirit rather would rejoice 80
On some wild heath with his dear charge to die,—
  The death that keenest penury might give
Were sweeter far than cramped by slavery to live!

50 eyeball *Esd.*, *BM*] eyeballs *1870*   51 slavery *Esd.*, *BM*] slavery's *1870*
56 dauntless *Esd.*] wildest *BM*   58 swell upon *Esd.*] pride thee on *BM*   59 thou
Esd., *BM*] italicized, *1927*, *1870*   60 tyrant's] tyrants *Esd.* country's *BM*
62 That *Esd.*] Which *BM*   64 wrought *Esd.*] brought *BM*   67 For her did
earn *Esd.*] Did earn for her *BM*   70 this her *Esd.*] her this *BM*   74–5 perish . . .
stare *underlined in BM*

And they have borne thus long the winter's cold,
 The driving sleet, the penetrating rain;   85
 It seemeth that their element is pain,
 And that they never will feel life again.
For is it life to be so deathlike old?—
 The sun's kind light feeds every living thing
 That spreads its blossoms to the breath of spring, 90
But who feeds thee, unhappy wanderer?
 With the fat slaves who from the rich man's board
Lick the fallen crumbs thou scantily dost share,
And mutterest for the gift a heartless prayer;
 The flow'rs fade not thus—thou must poorly die: 95
The changeful year feeds them, the tyrant man feeds thee.

And is it life that in youth's blasted morn
 Not one of youth's dear raptures is enjoyed,—
 All natural bliss with servitude alloyed,
 The beating heart, the sparkling eye destroyed 100
And manhood of its brightest glories shorn?—
 Debased by rapine, drunkenness and woe,
 The foeman's sword, the vulgar tyrant's blow,—
Ruined in body and soul, till heaven arrive,
 His health and peace insultingly laid low?— 105
Without a fear to die or wish to live,
 Withered and sapless, miserably poor,
Relinquished for his wounds to beg from door to door?

See'st thou yon humble sod where osiers bind
 The pillow of the monumentless dead?   110
 There, since her thorny pilgrimage is sped,
 The agèd sufferer rests on the cold bed
Which all who seek or who avoid must find.
 O let her sleep! And there, at close of eve,
 'Twere holiness in solitude to grieve   115
And ponder on the wretchedness of Earth.
 With joy of melancholy I would leave
A spot that to such deep-felt thoughts gives birth,
 And, though I could not pour the useless prayer,
Would weep upon the grave and leave a blessing there. 120

15. *The Solitary*

1810

DARE'ST thou amid this varied multitude
  To live alone, an isolated thing?
  To see the busy beings round thee spring,
And care for none?—in thy calm solitude
A flower that scarce breathes in the desert rude   5
  To Zephyr's passing wing?

Not the swarth Pariah in some Indian grove,
  Lone, lean, and hunted by his brothers' hate,
  Hath drunk so deep the cup of bitter fate
As that poor wretch who cannot, cannot love: 10
He bears a load which nothing can remove,
  A killing, withering weight.

He smiles—'tis sorrow's deadliest mockery;
  He speaks—the cold words flow not from his soul;
  He acts like others, drains the genial bowl,—   15
Yet, yet he longs, although he fears, to die;
He pants to reach what yet he seems to fly,
  Dull life's extremest goal.

16. *The Monarch's Funeral*

AN ANTICIPATION

1810

THE growing gloom of eventide
  Has quenched the sunbeam's latest glow,
And lowers upon the woe and pride
  That blasts the city's peace below.

∧ AUTOGRAPH, TITLE, DATE: *Esd.*   PRINTED: *from a transcript, probably, of Esd. (see n.,
p. 365), Ross. 1870/from Esd., Rog. 1966.*   TEXT: *1966/Esd.*

∨ AUTOGRAPH, TITLE, DATE: *Esd.*   PRINTED: *Rog. 1966.*   TEXT: *1966/Esd.*
  1 growing *possibly* glowing *in Esd., though the uncertain second letter might be an
anticipation of* glow *in the next line.*   2 sunbeam's] sunbeams *Esd., possibly for*
sunbeams'

At such an hour how sad the sight,—   5
   To mark a Monarch's funeral,
When the dim shades of awful night
   Rest on the coffin's velvet pall!—

To see the Gothic arches show
   A varied mass of light and shade,   10
While to the torches' crimson glow
   A vast cathedral is displayed!—

To see with what a silence deep
   The thousands o'er this death-scene brood,—
As though some wizard's charm did creep   15
   Upon the countless multitude!—

To see this awful pomp of death
   For one frail mass of mouldering clay,
When nobler men the tomb beneath
   Have sunk unwept, unseen away!   20

For who was he, the uncoffined slain
   That fell in Erin's injured isle,
Because his spirit dared disdain
   To light his country's funeral pile?

Shall he not ever live in lays   25
   The warmest that a Muse may sing,
Whilst monumental marbles raise
   The fame of a departed King?

May not the Muse's darling theme
   Gather its glorious garland thence,   30
Whilst some frail tombstone's dotard dream
   Fades with a Monarch's impotence?

—Yet 'tis a scene of wondrous awe
   To see a coffined Monarch lay,
That the wide grave's insatiate maw   35
   Be glutted with a regal prey!

Who *now* shall public councils guide?
   Who rack the poor, on gold to dine?
Who waste the means of regal pride
   For which a million wretches pine?   40

It is a child of earthly breath,
   A being perishing as he,
Who, throned in yonder pomp of death,
   Hath now fulfilled his destiny.

Now dust to dust restore, O Pride!—   45
   Unmindful of thy fleeting power,
Whose empty confidence has vied
   With human life's most treacherous hour,

One moment feel that in the breast
   With regal crimes and troubles vext   50
The pampered earthworms soon will rest,—
   One moment feel—and die the next!

Yet deem not in the tomb's control
   The vital lamp of life can fail,—
Deem not that e'er the Patriot's soul   55
   Is wasted by the withering gale!

The dross which forms the *King* is gone
   And reproductive earth supplies,—
As senseless as the clay and stone
   In which the kindred body lies;   60

The soul which makes the *Man* doth soar,
   And love alone survives to shed
All that its tide of bliss can pour
   Of Heaven upon the blessed dead.

So shall the sun for ever burn,   65
   So shall the midnight lightnings die,
And joy that glows at Nature's bourne
   Outlive terrestrial misery.

45 restore, O Pride!—] restore! . . . O Pride *Esd. See n., p. 366*

And will the crowd who silent stoop
  Around the lifeless Monarch's bier,   70
A mournful and dejected group,
  Breathe not one sigh, or shed one tear?

Ah, no! 'Tis wonder, 'tis not woe,—
  Even royalists might groan to see
The *Father of the People* so   75
  Lost in the Sacred Majesty!

17. *To the Republicans of North America*

February 1812

BROTHERS! between you and me
  Whirlwinds sweep and billows roar,
Yet in spirit oft I see
  On the wild and winding shore
Freedom's bloodless banner wave,—   5
Feel the pulses of the brave
Unextinguished by the grave,—
  See them drenched in sacred gore,—
Catch the patriot's gasping breath
Murmuring 'Liberty in death!'   10

Shout aloud! Let every slave
  Crouching at Corruption's throne
Start into a man, and brave
  Racks and chains without a groan!—
Let the castle's heartless glow   15
And the hovel's vice and woe

AUTOGRAPH: *1–end, Esd.; 1–30, 41–50, BM, letter to E. Hitchener, 14 Feb. 1812.*
TITLE, DATE: *See n., p. 366.*   PRINTED: *1–30, 41–50, Ross. 1870/1–30, 41–50, from a transcript of Esd. (see Intr., p. xxix), 1 and P, 1927/1–end, from Esd., Rog. 1966.*
TEXT: *1966/Esd.*

  4 the *Esd.*] thy *BM*   **5** banner *Esd.*] banners *BM, 1927*   **7** by *Esd.*] in *BM*   **9** patriot's *1870*] patriots *Esd.* warriors *BM*   **10** 'Liberty *1870*] Liberty *Esd., BM, 1927* in *Esd.*] or *BM, 1927* death!'] death *Esd., BM* 'death!' *1927*
15 castle's *BM*] castles *Esd.*   **16** hovel's] hovels *Esd., BM*

Fade like gaudy flowers that blow,
   Weeds that peep and then are gone!—
Whilst, from misery's ashes risen,
Love shall burst the captive's prison.   20

Cotopaxi! bid the sound
   Through thy sister mountains ring,
Till each valley smile around
   At the blissful welcoming!
And, O thou stern Ocean-deep,   25
Whose eternal billows sweep
Shores where thousands wake to weep
   Whilst they curse some villain king,
On the winds that fan thy breast
   Bear thou news of Freedom's rest!   30

Earth's remotest bounds shall start,
   Every despot's bloated cheek,
Pallid as his bloodless heart,
   Frenzy woe and dread shall speak;
Blood may fertilise the tree   35
Of new-bursting Liberty,—
Let the guiltiness then be
   On the slaves that ruin wreak,
On the unnatural tyrant-brood,
Slow to peace and swift to blood.   40

Can the daystar dawn of love
   Where the flag of war unfurled
Floats with crimson stain above
   Such a desolated world?—
Never! but, to vengeance driven,   45
When the patriot's spirit shriven
Seeks in death its native Heaven,
   Then, to speechless horror hurled,
Widowed Earth may balm the bier
Of its memory with a tear.   50

20 captive's] Captives *Esd.*, *BM* Captive *1927*   26 Whose eternal *Esd.*] Thou whose foamy *BM*   28 some *Esd.*] a *BM*   44 The fabric of a ruined world *BM*   48 There to desolation hurled *BM*   49 Earth may balm *Esd.*] love may watch *BM* earth may watch *1927*   50 Balm thee with its dying tear *BM, 1927*

18. *Written at Cwm Elan*
[July–August] 1811

WHEN the peasant hies him home and the day-planet reposes,
  Pillowed on the azure peaks that bound the western sight,
When each mountain flower its modest petal tremulously closes,
  And sombre, shrouded Twilight comes to lead her sister Night,—
Vestal dark! how dear to me are then thy dews of lightness,   5
That bathe my brow so withering, scorched beneath the daybeam's
    brightness,—
More dear to me, though Day be robed in vest of dazzling whiteness,
  Is one folding of the garment dusk that wraps thy form, O Night!

With thee I still delight to sit where dizzy Danger slumbers,
  Where 'mid the rocks the fitful blast hath waked its wildest lay,
Till beneath the yellow moonbeam decay the dying numbers,   11
  And Silence, even in Fancy's throne, hath seized again the sway.
Again she must resign it—hark! For wildest cadence pouring,
Far, far amid the viewless glen beneath the Elan roaring,
'Mid tangèd woods and shapeless rocks with moonlight summits
    soaring,   15
  It mingles its magic murmuring with the blast that floats away.

19. *To Death*
1810

DEATH! where is thy victory?
  To triumph whilst I die?—
To triumph whilst thine ebon wing
  Enfolds my shuddering soul?
O Death! where is thy sting?   5
  Not when the tides of murder roll,

∧ AUTOGRAPH, TITLE: *Esd.*   DATE: *See n., p. 366.*   PRINTED: *Rog.1966.*   TEXT: *1966/Esd.*
  6 daybeam's] daybeams *Esd.*   14 glen *above* [rocks] *Esd.*   15 tangèd]
tangued *Esd. See n.*

∨ AUTOGRAPH: *1–end, Esd.; 1–48, Pf., loose sheet, given to Hogg.*   TITLE: *Esd.*   DATE: *See n.,*
p. 366 PRINTED: *1–48, from Pf., Hogg, 1858/1–48, from a transcript of Esd. (see Intr.,*
p. xxix), I and P, 1927/1–end, from Esd., Rog. 1966.   TEXT: *1966/1858/Esd.*
  3 ebon wing *Esd.*] ebon wing *above* [hand of fate] *Pf.*   6 when *Esd., Pf.*] where
1927

When Nations groan that Kings may bask in bliss,
Death, couldst thou boast a victory such as this!—
       When, in his hour
       Of pomp and power,   10
    Thy slave, the mightiest murderer, gave
      'Mid Nature's cries,
      The sacrifice
Of myriads to glut the grave,—
When sunk the tyrant, sensualism's slave,   15
Or Freedom's life-blood streamed upon thy shrine,—
Stern despot, couldst thou boast a victory such as mine?

    To know in dissolution's void
      That earthly hopes and fears decay,
That every sense but Love, destroyed   20
      Must perish with its kindred clay—
      Perish Ambition's crown,
      Perish its sceptred sway,—
From Death's pale front fade Pride's fastidious frown,
In Death's damp vault the lurid fires decay   25
Which Envy lights at heaven-born Virtue's beam—
      That all the cares subside
      Which lurk beneath the tide
      Of life's unquiet stream,—
      Yes! this were victory!   30
And on some rock whose dark form glooms the sky
   To stretch these pale limbs when the soul is fled,—
To baffle the lean passions of their prey,
   To sleep within the chambers of the dead!—
     Oh, not the wretch, around whose dazzling throne   35
His countless courtiers mock the words they say,
    Triumphs amid the bud of glory blown
As I on Death's last pang and faint expiring groan!

---

8 couldst *Esd.*] canst *Pf.*   9–10 *a single line in Pf.*   11 Thy slave *Esd.*] Thy
blow *Pf.* His blow *1858*   12–13 *a single line in Pf.*   14 myriads *Esd.*] millions
Pf.   15 sensualism's *Esd.*] desolation's *Pf.*   17 despot *Esd.*] tyrant *Pf.*
19 That earthly *Esd.*] That mortals *Pf.* hopes and fears *Esd.*] bubbles sank *above*
[hopes and fears] *Pf.* decay *Esd.*] away *Pf.*   20 sense *Esd.*] thing *Pf.*   23 its
Esd.] her *Pf.*   26 Which *Esd.*] That *Pf.*   30 were *Esd.*] is *Pf., 1927*   31 some
Esd.] yon *Pf.*   32 when *Esd., Pf.*] where *1927*   34 chambers *Esd.*] palace
Pf., 1927   35 wretch *Esd.*] King *Pf.*   38 on Death's last pang *Esd.*] in this
cold bed *Pf., 1927*

Tremble, ye Kings, whose luxury mocks the woe
That props the column of unnatural state!—   40
    Ye the curses, deep though low,
    From Misery's tortured breast that flow,
      Shall usher to your fate.
Tremble, ye conquerors, at whose fell command
  The War-Fiend riots o'er an happy land!   45
    Ye Desolation's gory throng
    Shall bear from victory along
      To Death's mysterious strand.
'Twere well that Vice no pain should know
  But every scene that Memory gives,   50
Though from the self-same fount might flow
  The joy which Virtue aye receives.
It is the grave,—no conqueror triumphs now;
  The wreaths of bay that bound his head
Wither around his fleshless brow,—   55
    Where is the mockery fled
    That fired the tyrant's gaze?
'Tis like the fitful glare that plays
On some dark-rolling thunder-cloud,—
    Plays whilst the thunders roar   60
    But, when the storm is past,
    Fades like the warrior's name.
Death! in thy vault when Kings and peasants lie,
Not Power's stern rod nor Fame's most thrilling blasts
Can liberate thy captives from decay,—   65
My triumph their defeat, my joy their shame,
  Welcome then, peaceful Death! I'll sleep with thee,—
  Mine be thy quiet home, and thine my Victory!

---

39 Kings *Esd.*] proud *Pf.*   luxury *Esd.*] grandeur *over* [bosoms] *Pf.*   40 That *Esd.*] Which *Pf.*   the] Thy *Esd., Pf.*   41 curses, deep though low *Esd.*] plainings faint & low *Pf.*   42 breast *Esd.*] soul *above* [breast] *Pf.*   45 happy *Esd.*] peaceful *Pf.*   47 from victory *Esd.*] victorious *Pf.*   48 Death's *Esd.*] that *Pf.*   49 well *possibly* Hell   64 Not *over* [Can] *Esd.*   nor] or *Esd.*   65 Can liberate *Thus, apparently, Esd., though ink is smudged.*

20. '*Dark Spirit of the Desert Rude . . .*'

July–August 1811

DARK Spirit of the desert rude,
That o'er this awful solitude,
Each tangled and untrodden wood,
  Each dark and silent glen below,
  Where sunlight's gleamings never glow,   5
Whilst, jetty, musical and still
In darkness speeds the mountain rill,—
  That o'er yon broken peaks sublime,
  Wild shapes that mock the scythe of Time,
And the pure Elan's foamy course   10
Wavest thy wand of magic force,—
  Art thou yon sooty and fearful fowl
That flaps its wing o'er the leafless oak—
  That o'er the dismal scene doth scowl
And mocketh music with ⟨its⟩ croak?   15

I've sought thee where day's beams decay
  On the peak of the lonely hill;
I've sought thee where they melt away
  By the wave of the pebbly rill;
I've strained to catch thy murky form   20
Bestride the rapid and gloomy storm,—
  Thy red and sullen eyeball's glare
  Has shot in a dream through the midnight air,
But never did thy shape express
Such an emphatic gloominess.   25

And where art thou, O thing of gloom?—
On Nature's unreviving tomb,
  Where sapless, blasted and alone
  She mourns her blooming centuries gone!
From the fresh sod the violets peep,   30
The buds have burst their frozen sleep,
  Whilst every green and peopled tree
  Is alive with Earth's sweet melody.

AUTOGRAPH: *Esd.*   DATE: *See n., p. 367.*   PRINTED: *Rog. 1966.*   TEXT: *1966/Esd.*
  15 ⟨its⟩ *conjectural: tangled over-writing in Esd.*

But thou alone art here
Thou, desolate oak, whose scathèd head 35
For ages has never tremblèd,
Whose giant trunk dead lichens bind,
Moaningly sighing in the wind,
With huge loose rocks beneath thee spread,
Thou, thou alone art here! 40
Remote from every living thing,
Tree, shrub or grass or flower,
Thou seemest of this spot the King,
And, with a regal power,
⟨Suck⟩, like that race, all sap away, 45
And yet upon the spoil ⟨decay⟩.

21. *Reality*

1812–13

There is no work, nor device, nor knowledge, nor
wisdom, in the grave, whither thou goest.
Ecclesiastes ix. 10

THE pale, the cold, and the moony smile
Which the meteor beam of a starless night
Sheds on a lonely and sea-girt isle,
Ere the dawning of morn's undoubted light,
Is the flame of life so fickle and wan 5
That flits round our steps till their strength is gone.

O man! hold thee on in courage of soul
Through the stormy shades of thy worldly way,
And the billows of cloud that around thee roll
Shall sleep in the light of a wondrous day, 10

∧ 44 And *above* [that] *Esd.*   45–6 *See n.*

∨ AUTOGRAPH: *Esd.*   DATE: *See n., p. 367.*   PRINTED: *PBS, with* Alastor, *1816/*
Rog. 1966.   TITLE: *1966; see n.; none in 1816; 'On Death' 1839 and edd.*   TEXT:
1966 (1816 collated with Esd.).
    2 starless *1816*] stormy *Esd.*   4 Ere *1816*] Till *Esd.*   5 flame *1816*] taper *Esd.*
7 in *1816*] with *Esd.*   8 Thro the long long night of thy doubtful way *Esd.*
10–12   Shall subside in the calm of eternal day
                         For all in this world we can surely know
                         Is a little delight and a little woe   *Esd.*

Where hell and heaven shall leave thee free
To the universe of destiny.

This world is the nurse of all we know,
   This world is the mother of all we feel,
And the coming of death is a fearful blow   15
   To a brain unencompassed with nerves of steel;
When all that we know, or feel, or see,
Shall pass like an unreal mystery.

The secret things of the grave are there,
   Where all but this frame must surely be,   20
Though the fine-wrought eye and the wondrous ear
   No longer will live to hear or to see
All that is great and all that is strange
In the boundless realm of unending change.

Who telleth a tale of unspeaking death?   25
   Who lifteth the veil of what is to come?
Who painteth the shadows that are beneath
   The wide-winding caves of the peopled tomb?
Or uniteth the hopes of what shall be
With the fears and the love for that which we see?   30

22. 'Death-spurning Rocks . . .'

? July–August 1811
? June–July 1812

DEATH-spurning rocks! Here have ye towered since Time
   Sprung from Tradition's mist-encircled height,
Which Memory's palsied pinion dreads to climb
   Awed by the phantoms of its beamless night,—
      Death-spurning rocks! Each jagged form   5
      Shall still arrest the passing storm,

∧ 13–14   All we behold we feel that we know
                      All we percieve we know that we feel   *Esd.*
16 with nerves *1816*] by nervestrings *Esd.*   17 or feel, or see *1816*] we feel &
we see *Esd.*   18 pass *1816*] fleet by *Esd.*   20 frame *1816*] body *Esd.*
23 great *1816*] bright *Esd.*   24 boundless realm *1816*] gradual path *Esd.*
25 a tale *1816*] the tales *Esd.*   27 shadows *1816*] beings *Esd.*   28 wide-
winding caves *1816*] wide stretching realms *Esd.*   29 Or *1816*] And *Esd.*

∨ AUTOGRAPH: *Esd.*   DATE: *See n., p. 367.*   PRINTED: *Rog. 1966.*   TEXT: *1966/Esd.*

Whilst, rooted there, the agèd oak
Is shivered by the lightning's stroke;
Years shall fade fast and centuries roll away,—
Ye shall spurn death no more but like your oak decay!   10

A maniac-sufferer soared with wild intent
Where Nature formed these wonders. On the way
There is a little spot . . . Fiends would relent
Knew they the snares that there for Memory lay,—
How many a hope and many a fear,   15
And many a vain and bitter tear;
Whilst each prophetic feeling wakes
A brood of mad and venomed snakes
To make the lifesprings of his soul their food,
To twine around his veins and fatten on his blood!   20

To quench his pangs he fled to the wild moor.
One fleeting beam flashed but its gloom to show,—
Turned was the way-worn wanderer from the door
Where Pity's self promised to soothe his woe.
Shall he ⟨turn⟩ back? The tempest there   25
Sweeps fiercely through the turbid air,
Beyond a gulf before that yawns,
The day-star shines, the daybeam dawns,—
God! Nature! Chance!—Remit this misery,—
It burns!—Why need he live to weep who does not fear to
die?   30

23. *The Tombs*

February–March 1812

THESE are the tombs. O cold and silent Death,
Thy kingdom and thy subjects here I see!—
The record of thy victories
Is graven on every speaking stone
That marks what once was man.   5

∧ 11 A *over* The *apparently in Esd.*   14 snares *above* [pangs] *Esd.*   [veins] viens
above [nerves] *Esd.*   25 turn *Shelley seems to have written* fal, *converted the first two
letters to* tu, *and added* n, *though failing to convert the third letter very well.*

∨ AUTOGRAPH, TITLE: *Esd.* DATE: *See n., p. 367.* PRINTED: *14–15, Dowd. 1886/1–end,
Rog. 1966.* TEXT: *1966/Esd.*
   3 thy] the *Esd.*

These are the tombs. Am I, who sadly gaze
On the corruption and the skulls around,
  To sum the mass of loathsomeness,
  And to a mound of mouldering flesh,
    Say: 'Thou wert human life'?   10

In thee once throbbed the Patriot's beating heart,
In thee once lived the Poet's soaring soul,
  The pulse of love, the calm of thought,
  Courage and charity and truth,
    And high devotedness;   15

All that could sanctify the meanest deeds,
All that might give a manner and a form
  To matter's speechless elements,
  To every brute and morbid shape
    Of this phantasmal world,—   20

⟨That the high sense which from the stern rebuke
Of Erin's victim patriot's death-soul shone
  When blood and chains defiled the land
  Lives in the torn uprooted heart
    His savage murderers burn.⟩   25

Ah, no! Else, while these tombs before me stand,
My soul would hate the coming of its hour,
  Nor would the hopes of life and love
  Be mingled with those fears of death
    That chill the warmest heart.   30

24. *To Harriet* [*Shelley*]

1811–12

IT is not blasphemy to hope that Heaven
More perfectly will give those nameless joys
Which throb within the pulses of the blood
And sweeten all that bitterness which Earth

∧ 19 every *above* [all the] *Esd.*   22 patriot's] patriots *Esd.*   21–5 *See n.*

∨ AUTOGRAPH, TITLE: *Esd.*   DATE: *See nn., p. 361.*   PRINTED: *5–13, from a transcript by Garnett (see n. on No. 15), Ross. 1870/58–69, PBS, 1813 (see nn., p. 360)/1–end, Dowd. 1886, Rog. 1966.*   TEXT: *1966/1886/1813/Esd.*

Infuses in the heaven-born soul. O thou   5
Whose dear love gleamed upon the gloomy path
Which this lone spirit travelled, drear and cold,
Yet swiftly leading to those awful limits
Which mark the bounds of Time and of the space
When Time shall be no more; wilt thou not turn   10
Those spirit-beaming eyes and look on me,
Until I be assured that Earth is Heaven,
And Heaven is Earth?—will not thy glowing cheek,
Glowing with soft suffusion, rest on mine,
And breathe magnetic sweetness through the frame   15
Of my corporeal nature, through the soul
Now knit with these fine fibres? I would give
The longest and the happiest day that fate
Has marked on my existence but to feel
One soul-reviving kiss . . . O thou most dear,   20
'Tis an assurance that this Earth is Heaven,
And Heaven the flower of that untainted seed
Which springeth here beneath such love as ours.
Harriet! let death all mortal ties dissolve,
But ours shall not be mortal! The cold hand   25
Of Time may chill the love of earthly minds
Half frozen now; the frigid intercourse
Of common souls lives but a summer's day;
It dies, where it arose, upon this earth.
But ours! oh, 'tis the stretch of Fancy's hope   30
To portray its continuance as now,
Warm, tranquil, spirit-healing. Nor when age
Has tempered these wild ecstasies, and given
A soberer tinge to the luxurious glow
Which blazing on devotion's pinnacle   35
Makes virtuous passion supersede the power
Of reason; nor when life's aestival sun
To deeper manhood shall have ripened me;
Nor when some years have added judgement's store
To all thy woman sweetness—all the fire   40
Which throbs in thine enthusiast heart,—not then
Shall holy friendship (for what other name

32–52 *See n., p. 367.*   32 spirit-healing. Nor *Esd.*] spirit-healing; nor *1886 and edd.*
40 sweetness—] sweetness, *Esd.*   41 heart,—] heart, *Esd.* heart; *1886 and edd.*

May love like ours assume?),—not even then
Shall Custom so corrupt, or the cold forms
Of this desolate world so harden us   45
That, when we think of the dear love that binds
Our souls in soft communion while we know
Each other's thoughts and feelings, we can say
Unblushingly a heartless compliment,
Praise, hate, or love with the unthinking world,   50
Or dare to cut the unrelaxing nerve
That knits our love to virtue. Can those eyes,
Beaming with mildest radiance on my heart
To purify its purity, e'er bend
To soothe its vice or consecrate its fears?   55
Never, thou second Self! Is confidence
So vain in virtue that I learn to doubt
The mirror even of Truth? Dark flood of Time!
Roll as it listeth thee—I measure not
By months or moments thy ambiguous course.   60
Another may stand by me on thy brink,
And watch the bubble whirled beyond his ken
That pauses at my feet. The sense of love,
The thirst for action, and the impassioned thought
Prolong my being: if I wake no more,   65
My life more actual living will contain
Than some gray veteran's of the world's cold school,
Whose listless hours unprofitably roll
By one enthusiast feeling unredeemed.
Virtue and Love! unbending Fortitude,   70
Freedom, Devotedness and Purity—
That life my Spirit consecrates to you!

43 assume?),—] assume?) *Esd.* assume?), *1886 and edd.*   46, 48 That, . . . we
can] As . . . can we *Esd., 1886 and edd.*   47 communion] communion, *Esd., 1886
and edd.*   58 Time! *1813*] Time *Esd.* Time, *1886 and edd.*   59 thee—*1813*]
thee. *Esd.* thee; *1886 and edd.*   60 months *1813, Esd.*] month *1886 and edd.*
61 thy *Esd., 1886 and edd.*] the *1813*   62 ken *1813, Esd.*] ken, *1886 and edd.*
63 That *1813*] Which *Esd., 1886 and edd.*   65 being: *1813*] being. *Esd.* being;
1886 and edd.   67 gray *1813, 1886 and edd.*] grey *Esd.*   68 roll *Esd., 1886 and
edd.*] roll, *1813*

25. *Sonnet*

To Harriet [Shelley] on her Birthday

1 August 1812

O THOU whose radiant eyes and beamy smile,
    Yet even a sweeter somewhat indexing,
Have known full many an hour of mine to guile,
    Which else would only bitter memories bring:
O ever thus, thus, as on this natal day,   5
    Though Age's frost may blight those tender eyes,
    Destroy that kindling cheek's transparent dyes,
And those luxuriant tresses change to grey—
    Ever as now with Love and Virtue's glow
May thine unwithering soul not cease to burn,—   10
    Still may thine heart with those pure thoughts o'erflow
Which force from mine such quick and warm return!
    And I must love thee even more than this,
Nor doubt that thou and I part but to meet in bliss.

26. *Sonnet*

To a Balloon laden with Knowledge

August 1812

BRIGHT ball of flame that through the gloom of even
    Silently takest thine aethereal way,
    And with surpassing glory dimm'st each ray
Twinkling amid the dark blue depths of Heaven,—
    Unlike the fire thou bearest, soon shalt thou   5
Fade like a meteor in surrounding gloom,
    Whilst that, unquenchable, is doomed to glow
A watch-light by the patriot's lonely tomb;
    A ray of courage to the oppressed and poor;

∧ AUTOGRAPH, TITLE, DATE: *Esd.*   PRINTED: *9–12, Dowd. 1886/1–end, Rog. 1966.*
TEXT: *1966/1886/Esd.*

∨ AUTOGRAPH: *Esd.*   TITLE: *Esd. See n., p. 368.*   DATE: *See n.*   PRINTED: *Dowd.*
1886/Rog. 1966.   TEXT: *1966/1886/Esd.*

A spark, though gleaming on the hovel's hearth,   10
   Which through the tyrant's gilded domes shall roar;
A beacon in the darkness of the Earth;
   A sun which, o'er the renovated scene,
   Shall dart like Truth where Falsehood yet has been.

27. *Sonnet*

On Launching some Bottles filled with Knowledge
into the Bristol Channel

August 1812

VESSELS of heavenly medicine! May the breeze
   Auspicious waft your dark green forms to shore;
   Safe may ye stem the wide surrounding roar
Of the wild whirlwinds and the raging seas;
   And oh! if Liberty e'er deigned to stoop   5
From yonder lowly throne her crownless brow,
   Sure she will breathe around your emerald group
The fairest breezes of her West that blow,
   Yes! she will waft ye to some freeborn soul
Whose eye-beam, kindling as it meets your freight,   10
   Her heaven-born flame on suffering Earth will light,
Until its radiance gleams from pole to pole,
   And tyrant-hearts with powerless envy burst
   To see their night of ignorance dispersed.

∧ 11 tyrant's] tyrants *Esd.*

∨ AUTOGRAPH: *Esd.*   TITLE: *Esd. See n. on No. 26, p. 368.*   DATE: *See n.*   PRINTED:
Dowd. 1886/Rog. 1966.   TEXT: *1966/1886/Esd.*
   3 stem *thus 1886, and preferred here, though Esd. might read* stern   8 West *1904*]
west *Esd., 1886*   11 on] in *1886*

28. *Sonnet*

*On Waiting for a Wind to cross the Bristol Channel
from Devonshire to Wales*

August 1812

OH, for the South's benign and balmy breeze!
   Come, gentle Spirit! Through the wide Heaven sweep:
Chase inauspicious Boreas from the seas,
   That gloomy tyrant of the unwilling deep!
These wilds, where Man's profane and tainting hand   5
   Nature's primaeval loveliness has marred
   And some few souls of the high bliss debarred
Which else obey her powerful command,
   I leave without a sigh; ye mountain piles
That load in grandeur Cambria's emerald vales,   10
   Whose sides are fair in cultivation's smiles,
Around whose jagged heads the storm-cloud sails,—
   A heart that's all thine own receive in me
With Nature's fervour ⟨fraught⟩ and calm in ⟨purity⟩!

29. *To Harriet* [*Shelley*]

1811–12

HARRIET! thy kiss to my soul is dear,—
   At evil or pain I would never repine
If to every sigh and to every tear
   Were added a look and a kiss of thine.
Nor is it the look when it glances fire,   5
   Nor the kiss when bathed in the dew of delight,
Nor the throb of the heart when it pants desire
   From the shadows of eve to the morning light,

⋀ AUTOGRAPH, TITLE: *Esd.* DATE: *See n., p. 368.*   PRINTED: *5–10, partially, Dowd.
1886/1–end, Rog. 1966.*   TEXT: *1966/1886/Esd.*
  13 receive] recieves *Esd.*   14 ⟨fraught⟩ *conjectural: the last four letters seem
clear*   ⟨purity⟩ *conjectural: possibly* piety—*the last two letters seem clear.*

⋁ AUTOGRAPH, TITLE: *Esd.*   DATE: *See nn., p. 361.*   PRINTED: *Rog. 1966.*   TEXT:
1966/Esd.

But the look when a lustre of joy-mingled woe
    Has faintly obscured all its bliss-beaming Heaven—   10
Such a lovely, benign and enrapturing glow
    As sunset can paint on the clouds of even—
And a kiss, which the languish of silent love,
    Though eloquent, faints with the toil of expressing,
Yet so light that thou canst not refuse, my dove,   15
    To add this one to the debt of caressing.

Harriet! adieu to all vice and care,—
    Thy love is my heaven, thy arms are my world!
While thy kiss and thy look to my soul remain dear
    I should smile though Earth from its base be hurled: 20
For a heart as pure and a mind as free
    As ever gave lover to thee I give,
And all that I ask in return from thee
    Is to love like me and with me to live.

This heart that beats for thy love and bliss,   25
    Harriet, beats for its country too;
And it never would thrill with thy look or kiss
    If it dared to that country's cause be untrue.
Honour and wealth and life it spurns,
    But thy love is a prize it is sure to gain,   30
And the heart that with love and virtue burns
    Will never repine at evil or pain.

30. *Mary to the Sea-Wind*

? 1812–13

I IMPLORE thee, I implore thee, softly-swelling breeze,
    Waft swift the sail of my lover to the shore,
That under the shadow of yon darkly-woven trees
    I may meet him, I may meet him, to part with him no more.

For this boon, for this boon, sweet Sea-Wind, will I weave   5
    A garland wild of heath flowers to breathe to thee perfume;

AUTOGRAPH, TITLE: *Esd.*   DATE: *See n., p. 368.*   PRINTED: *Rog. 1966.*   TEXT: *1966/Esd.*

Thou will kiss them yet, like Henry's, thy kisses will but leave
   A more heaven-breathing fragrance and sense-enchanting bloom.

And then on summer evens I will hasten to inhale,
   Remembering that thou wert so kind, thy balmy, balmy breath,
And when thy tender pinions in the gloom begin to fail,   11
   I will catch thee to my bosom ere thou diest on the heath.

I will catch thee to my bosom—and, if Henry's oaths are true,
   A softer, sweeter grave thou wilt never find than there;
Nor is it lovely Sea-Wind, nor is it to undo   15
   That my arms are so inviting, that my bosom is so fair.

31. *A Retrospect of Times of Old*

August 1812

THE mansions of the Kings are tenantless,—
   Low lie in dust their glory and their shame!
No tongue survives their virtuous deeds to bless,—
   No tongue with execration blasts their fame!
But on some ruined pile, where yet the gold[1]   5
   Casts purple brilliance o'er colossal snow,
   Where sapphire eyes in breathing statues glow,
   And the tainted blast sighs 'mid the reeds below,
Where grim effigies of the Gods of old
   In mockery stand of ever-changing men   10
   (Their ever-changing worship, ah, how vain!
Yet baubles aye must please the multitude!)—
There Desolation dwells. . . . Where are the Kings?
   Why sleep they now if sleep be not eternal?
   Cannot Oblivion's silent tauntings call   15
The Kings and Heroes from their quietude
   Of Death, to snatch the scrolls from her palsying hand
To tell the world how mighty once they were? . . .
They dare not wake . . . thy victory is here

[1] Gilding yet remains on the cornices of the ruined palaces of Persepolis. [*Shelley's footnote*.]

AUTOGRAPH, TITLE: *Esd*. DATE: *See n., p. 368*. PRINTED: *Rog. 1966*. TEXT: *1966/Esd*.

11–12   Thier ever changing worship ah how vain!
         (Yet baubles aye must please the multitude)   *Esd. See n.*

O Death! . . . yet I hear unearthly voices cry   20
'Death, thou'lt be swallowed up in victory!'

Yes, dream of fame! The halls are desolate
   Where whitened skeletons of thine heroes lie;
Stillness keeps watch before each grass-grown gate,
   Save where, amid thy towers, the simoon's sigh   25
Wakes the lone lyre whose mistress sleeps below,
And bids it thrill to notes of awfulness and woe.

Here, ages since, some royal bloodhound crept,
   When on these pillared piles a midnight lay
   Which but from visioned memories long has fled,   30
To work ambition whilst his brother slept
   And, reckless of the peaceful smile that played
   Around his dream-fraught features when, betrayed,
   They told each innocent secret of the day,
Wakened the thoughtless victim, bade him stare   35
Upon the murderous steel . . . The chaste, pale glare
   Of the midnight moonbeam kissed its glittering blade
   A moment and, its brightness quenched in blood,
   Distained with murder the moon's silver flood!
The blushing moon wide-gathering vapours shrouded;   40
   One moment did he triumph,—but remorse,
Suspicion, anguish, fear all triumph clouded—
   Destruction, suicide, his last resource!—
Wide yawned the torrent,—the moon's stormy flash
Disclosed its black tumultuousness—the crash   45
   Of rocks and boughs mixed with its roarings hoarse:
A moment, and he dies! Hark to the awful dash!

Such were thy works, Ambition, even amid
   The darksome times of generations gone
Which the dark veil of viewless hours has hid,   50
   The veil of hours for ever onward flown.[1]

[1] I believe it was only in those early times when Monarchy was in its apprenticeship that its compunction for evil deeds was unendurable. There is no instance upon record parallel to that related above, but I know that neither men nor sets of men become vicious but slowly, and step by step, each less difficult than the former. [*Shelley's footnote.*]

22 dream of fame! *over* [?] brilliant piles   44 Wide] *Shelley seems to have written, unmetrically,* wider *and attempted to delete the last letter.*

Swift roll the waves of Time's eternal tide,
  The peasant's grave, marked by no tribute stone,
Not less remembered than the gilded bed
    In which the hero slept,—now ever gone   55
    Passion and will and power, flesh, heart and brain and bone!

Each trophied bust, where gore-emblazoned Victory
  In breathing marble shook the ensanguined spear,
Flinging its heavy purple canopy
    In cold expanse o'er martyred Freedom's bier,—   60
Each gorgeous altar where the victims bled
    And grim gods frowned above their human prey,—
Where the high temple echoing to the yell
    Of death-pangs, to the long and shuddering groan,
Whilst sacred hymns along the aisles did swell   65
    And pitiless priests drowned each discordant moan,—
All, all have faded in past time away!
    New gods, like men, changing in ceaseless flow,
Ever at hand as ancient ones decay,
    Heroes and kings and laws have plunged the world in woe!   70

Sesostris, Caesar, and Pizarro,—come!
Thou, Moses, and Mahommed,[1]—leave that gloom!
  Destroyers, never shall your memory die!
Approach, pale Phantom, to yon mouldering tomb
    Where all thy bones, hopes, crimes, and passions lie!   75
And thou, poor peasant, when thou pass'st the grave
  Where, deep enthroned in monumental pride,
Sleep low in dust the mighty and the brave,
    Where the mad conqueror, whose gigantic stride
    The Earth was too confined for, doth abide,   80
    Housing his bones amid a little clay,—
In gratitude to Nature's Spirit bend,
And wait in still hope for thy better end.

---

[1] To this innumerable list of legal murderers our own age affords numerous addenda. Frederic of Prussia, Buonaparte, Suvoroff, Wellington and Nelson are the most skilful and notorious scourges of their species of the present day. [*Shelley's footnote.*]

32. *The Voyage*

A Fragment

Devonshire, August 1812

QUENCHED is old Ocean's rage:
  Each horrent wave, that flung
Its neck that writhed beneath the tempest's scourge
  Indignant up to Heaven,
  Now breathes in its sweet slumber   5
  To mingle with the day
  A spirit of tranquillity.
  Beneath the cloudless sun
  The gently swelling main
  Scatters a thousand colourings;   10
And the wind, that wanders vaguely through the void,
With the flapping of the sail, and the dashing at the prow,
And the whistle of the sailor in that shadow of a calm
  A ravishing harmony makes.
Oh, why is a rapt soul e'er recalled   15
  From the palaces of visioned bliss
  To the cells of real sorrow?

  That little vessel's company
  Beheld the sight of loveliness:
  The dark grey rocks that towered   20
  Above the slumbering sea,
  And their reflected forms
Deep in its faintly-waving mirror given;
  They heard the low breeze sighing
  The listless sails and ropes among,   25
  They heard the music at the prow,
  And the hoarse, distant clash
  Sent from yon gloomy caves
Where Earth and Ocean strive for mastery.

  A mingled mass of feeling   30
  Those human spirits pressed,

AUTOGRAPH, TITLE, DATE: *Esd.*   PRINTED: *Rog. 1966.*   TEXT: *1966/Esd.*

As they heard, and saw, and felt
Some fancied fear, and some real woe
Mixed with those glimpses of heavenly joy
    That dawned on each passive soul.   35
Where is the woe that never sees
One joybeam illumine the night of the mind?
    Where is the bliss that never feels
One dart from the quiver of earthly pain?

The young and happy spirits now   40
Along the world are voyaging;
Love, friendship, virtue, truth,
Simplicity of sentiment and speech,
    And other sensibilities
Known by no outward name—   45
Some faults that Love forgives,
Some flaws that Friendship shares;
Hearts passionate and benevolent,
Alive, and urgent to repair
The errors of their brother heads—   50
    All voyage with them too.
They look to land, they look to sea,—
Bounded one is, and palpable
Even as a noonday scene,
The other indistinct and dim,   55
Spangled with dizzying sunbeams,
Boundless, untrod by human step,
Like the vague blisses of a midnight dream,
    Or Death's immeasurable main,
Whose lovely islands gleam at intervals   60
Upon the Spirit's visioned solitude
Through Earth's wide-woven and many-coloured veil.

It is a moveless calm.
    The sailor's whistle shrill
Speeds clearly through the sleeping atmosphere,—   65
As country curates pray for rain
When drought has frustrated full long,
He whistles for a wind
With just the same success.

Two honest souls were they,   70
And oft had braved in fellowship the storm,
   Till, from that fellowship, had sprung
   A sense of right and liberty
Unbending, undismayed,—aye, they had seen
   Where danger, death and terror played   75
   With human lives in the boiling deep;
   And they had seen the scattered spray
   Of the green and jagged mountain-wave,
   Hid in the lurid tempest-cloud
With lightnings tingeing all its fleeting form,   80
   Rolled o'er their fragile bark.
   A dread and hopeless month
   Had they participated once
   In that diminutive bark,—
Their tearless eyes uplifted unto Heaven   85
   So fruitlessly for aid,
Their parchèd mouths oped eager to the shower
So thin and sleety in that arctic clime,
   Their last hard crust was shared
   Impartial in equality;   90
   And, in the dreadful night
   When all had failed, even hope,
  Together they had shared the gleam
   Shot from yon lighthouse tower
   Across the waste of waves.   95
And therefore are they brave, free, generous,—
For who that had so long fought hand to hand
With famine, toil and hazard, smiled at Death
When, leaning from the bursting billow's height,
He stares so ghastly terrible, would waste   100
One needless word for life's contested toys?
Who that had shared his last and nauseous crust
With Famine and a friend would not divide
A landsman's meal with one who needed it?
Who that could rule the elements and spurn   105
Their fiercest rage would bow before a slave
Decked in the fleetingness of earthly power?
Who that had seen the soul of Nature work,
Blind, changeless, and eternal in her paths,

Would shut his eyes and ears, quaking before　　　110
The bubble of a Bigot's blasphemy?[1]

　　The faintly moving prow
Divided Ocean's smoothness languidly.
　　A landsman there reclined,
　　With lowering, close-contracted brow,　　　115
　　And mouth updrawn at intervals
As fearful of his fluctuating bent,
　　His eyes wide-wandering round
　　In insecure malignity,
Rapacious, mean, cruel and cowardly,　　　120
Casting upon the loveliness of day
　　The murkiness of villainy.
By other nurses than the battling storm,
Friendship, Equality and Sufferance,
　　His manhood had been cradled,—　　　125
Inheritor to all the vice and fear
Which kings and laws and priests and conquerors spread
　　On the woe-fertilized world.
　　Yes, in the dawn of life,
When guileless confidence and unthinking love　　　130
　　Dilate all hearts but those
Which servitude or power has cased in steel,
He bound himself to an unhappy woman,
Not of those pure and heavenly links that Love
　　Twines round a feeling to Freedom dear,　　　135
But of vile gold, cank'ring the breast it binds,
　　Corroding and inflaming every thought,
　　Till vain desire, remorse and fear
　　Envenom all the being.
Yet did this chain, though rankling in the soul　　　140

---

[1] It is remarkable that few are more experimentally convinced of the doctrine of Necessity than old sailors, who have seen much and various service. The peculiarly engaging and frank generosity of seafaring men probably is an effect of this cause. Those employed in small and ill-equipped trading-vessels seem to possess this generosity in a purer degree than those of a King's ship. The habits of subjection and coercion imbued into the latter may suffice to explain the cause of the difference. [*Shelley's footnote.*]

　111 blasphemy?[1] *conjectural reference for Shelley's Note, written at the foot of the pages covering 95–127.*

Not bind the grosser body; he was wont
   All means to try of thriving;
To those above him the most servile cringe
That ignorance e'er gave to titled Vice
   Was simperingly yielded;   145
To those beneath the frown which Commerce darts
On cast-off friends unprofitably poor
   Was less severe than his.

   There was another too,—
   One of another mould   150
He had been cradled in the wildest storm
   Of Passion and, though now
The feebler light of worn-out energies
Shone on his soul, yet ever and anon
   A flash of tempests long passed by   155
   Would wake to pristine visions.
Now he was wrapt in a wild, woeful dream—
   Deeply his soul could love—
And, as he gazèd on the boundless sea
Chequered with sunbeams and with shade   160
Alternate to infinity,
   He fell into a dream.

   He dreamed that all he loved
Across the shoreless wastes were voyaging
By that unpitying landsman piloted,   165
   And that at length they came
   To a black and ⟨sullen⟩ island rock.
   Barren the isle—no egg,
Which sea-mews leave upon the wildest shore;
   Barren the isle—no blade   170
Of grass, no seaweed, not the vilest thing
   For human nutriment.

He struggled with the pitiless landsman there
   But, nerved though his frame with love,
   Quenchless, despairing love,   175
   It nought availed; strong Power

167 ⟨sullen⟩ *over* barren *written, apparently, in anticipation of 168, 170. Despite smudging the last three letters seem clear. An underlying word has been erased of which the last four letters seem to be* less.

Truth, love and courage vanquished;
A rock was piled upon his feeble breast,—
All was subdued but that
Which is immortal, unsubduable.   180

He still continued dreaming;
The rock upon his bosom quenched not
The frenzy and defiance of his eye.
But the strong and coward landsman laughed to scorn
His unprevailing fortitude,   185
And, in security of malice, stabbed
One who accompanied his voyagings.
The blood gushed forth, the eye grew dim,
The nerve relaxed, the life was gone;
His smile of dastardly revenge   190
Glared upon [the] dead frame;
Then back the victim flung his head;
In horror insupportable,
Upon the jagged rock whereon he lay,—
And human nature paused awhile   195
In pity to his woe.

When he awaked to life
She whom he loved was bending over him,
Haggard her sunken eye,
Bloodless her quivering lips.—   200
She bended to bestow
The burning moisture from her feverish tongue
To lengthen out his life
Perhaps till succour came!—
But more her dear soft eyes in languid love,   205
When life's last gleam was flickering in decay,
The waning spark rekindled,
And the faint lingering kiss of her withered lips
Mingled a rapture with his misery.
A bleeding sister lay   210
Beside this wretched pair
And he, the dastard of relentless soul,
In moody malice lowered over all.

And this is but a dream!
For yonder—see! The port in sight   215
The vessel makes towards it!
The sight of their safety then,
And the hum of the populous town,
Awakened them from a night of horror
To a day of secure delights.   220

Lo! here, a populous town;
Two dark rocks either side defend,
The quiet water sleeps within,
Reflecting every roof and every mast.
A populous town?—It is a den   225
Where wolves keep lambs to fatten on their blood,—
'Tis a distempered spot: should there be one
Just, dauntless, rational, he would appear
A madman to the rest.
Yes! smooth-faced tyrants, chartered by a Power   230
Called King, who in the castellated keep
Of a far-distant land wears out his days
Of miserable dotage, pace the quay,
And by the magic of that dreadful word,
Hated though dreadful, shield their impotence,   235
Their lies, their murders and their robberies.
See, where the sailor, absent many years,
With Heaven in his rapture-speaking eyes,
Seeks the low cot where all his wealth reposes,
To bring himself for joy and his small store,   240
Hard-earned by years of peril and of toil,
For comfort to his famine-wasted babes.
Deep in the dark blue sea the unmoving moon
Gleams beautifully quiet,—such a night
When the last kiss from Mary's quivering lips   245
Unmanned him. To the well-known door he speeds;
His faint hand pauses on the latch.—His heart
Beats eagerly,—when suddenly the gang
Dissolves his dream of rapture. No delay!
No pity!—Unexpostulating Power   250
Deals not in human feelings. He is stript

237 sailor] sailors *Esd.*

By those low slaves whose masters' names inflict
Curses more fell than even themselves would give!
The Indian muslins and the Chinese toys
(These for small gain and those for boundless love   255
Thus carefully concealed) are torn away,—
The very handkerchief his Mary gave,
Which in unchanging faithfulness he wore,
Rent from his manly neck! His kindling eye
Beamed vengeance, and the tyrants' manacles   260
Shook on his struggling arm: 'Where is my wife?
'Where are my children?' Close beside him stood
A sleek and pampered townsman: 'Oh! your wife
'Died last year in the House of Industry;
'Your young ones all are dead, except one brat   265
'Stubborn as you—parish apprentice now.'

They have appropriated human life
And human happiness,—but these weigh nought
In the nice-balanced Politician's scale,
Who finds that murder is expedient,   270
And that vile means can answer glorious ends.
Wide Nature has outstretched her fertile earth
In commonage to all,—but they have torn
Her dearest offspring from her bleeding breast,
Have disunited liberty and life,   275
Severed all right from duty, and confused
Virtue with selfishness,—the grass-green hills
The fertile valleys and the limpid streams,
The beach on the sea-shore, the sea itself,
The very snow-clad mountain-peaks, whose height   280
Forbids all human footstep, the ravines,
Where cataracts have roared ere Monarchs were,—
Nature, fair Earth, and Heaven's untainted air
Are all apportioned out.—Some bloated Lord,
Some priestly pilferer or some Snake of Law,   285
Some miserable mockery of a man,
Some slave without a heart looks over these
And calls them *Mine*, in self-approving pride!

252 masters'] masters *Esd*.   264 last year] this time year *Esd*.

The millionth of the produce of the vale
He sets apart for *charity*. Vain fool!   290
He gives in mercy, while stern Justice cries:
'Be thou as one of them,—resign thine hall
'Brilliant with murder's trophies, and the board
'Loaded with surfeiting viands, and the gems
'Which millions toil to buy thee.—Get thee hence   295
'And dub thyself a man,—then dare to throw
'One act of usefulness, one thought of love
'Into the balance of thy past misdeeds!'

33. *A Dialogue*

1809

Death

YES! my dagger is drenched with the blood of the brave,
I have sped with Love's wings from the battlefield grave,
   Where Ambition is hushed 'neath the peace-giving sod,
   And slaves cease to tremble at Tyranny's nod;
I offer a calm habitation to thee,—   5
Victim of grief, wilt thou slumber with me?
   Drear and damp is my hall, but a mild Judge is there,
   Who steeps in oblivion the brands of Despair;
Nor a groan of regret, nor a sigh, nor a breath
Dares dispute with grim Silence the empire of Death,   10
   Nor the howlings of envy resound through the gloom
   That shrouds in its mantle the slaves of the tomb;
I offer a calm habitation to thee,—
Say, victim c {grief, wilt thou slumber with me?

AUTOGRAPH: *Esd., Trin. Coll., Camb.* (*loose sheets given to Hogg*).   TITLE, DATE:
Esd.   PRINTED: *from Camb. MS., Hogg, 1858/from Esd., Rog. 1966/from a transcript
of Esd., I and P, 1927. See Intr., p. xxix.*   TEXT: *1966/Esd.*
   1 Yes *Esd.*] For *Camb.*   drenched with *Esd.*] bathed in *Camb.*   2 battlefield
Esd.] battlefield's *1927*   I come, care-worn tenant of life, from the grave *Camb.*
3 Ambition is hushed *Esd.*] Innocence sleeps *Camb.*   4 slaves *Esd.*] the good
Camb.   6 Victim *Esd.*] Say, victim *Camb.*   7 My mansion is damp, cold
silence is there, *Camb.*   8 But it lulls in oblivion the fiends of despair, *Camb.*
9 Nor . . . nor . . . nor *Esd.*] not . . . not . . . not *Camb.*   11–12 *not in Camb.*

Mortal

Mine eyelids are heavy, my soul seeks repose,   15
It longs in thy arms to embosom its woes,
It longs in that realm to deposit its load,
Where no longer the scorpions of Perfidy goad,—
Where the phantoms of Prejudice vanish away,
And Bigotry's bloodhounds lose scent of their prey;   20
Yet tell me, dark Death: when thine empire is o'er,
What awaits on Futurity's mist-circled shore?

Death

Cease, cease, wayward Mortal! I dare not unveil
The shadows that float o'er Eternity's vale;
What think'st thou will wait thee? A Spirit of Love[1]   25
That will hail thy blest advent to mansions above;
For Love, Mortal, gleams through the gloom of my sway,
And the clouds that surround me fly fast at its ray.

Hast thou *loved*?—Then depart from these regions of
            hate,
And in slumber with me quench the arrows of fate,   30
That canker and burn in the wounds of a heart
That urges its sorrows with me to depart;
I offer a calm habitation to thee,—
Say, victim of grief, wilt thou slumber with me?

[1] The author begs to be understood by this expression neither to mean the Creator of the Universe nor the Christian Deity. When this little poem was written the line stood thus: 'What waits for the good?' but he has altered it on transcription because, however his feelings may love to linger on a future state of happiness, neither justice, reason nor passion can reconcile to his belief that the crimes of this life, equally necessary and inevitable as its virtues, should be punished in another.

> . . . earth in itself
> Contains at once the evil and the cure;
> And all-sufficing Nature can chastise
> Those who transgress her law . . . [*Shelley's footnote.*]

16 arms *Esd.*] cells *Camb.*   17 that realm *Esd.*] thy cells *Camb.*   22 mist-circled *Esd.*] mist-covered *1927*   24 o'er *Esd.*] on *Camb.*   25 What think'st thou will wait thee? *Esd.*] Nought waits for the good but *Camb.*   26 thy *Esd.*] their *Camb.*   mansions *Esd.*] regions *Camb.*   28 And the clouds that *Esd.*] And the shades which *Camb.*   29 *loved*? *Esd.*] loved? *Camb.*   30 quench *Esd.*] blunt *Camb.*   31-2 *not in Camb. or 1927*

Mortal

Oh, sweet is thy slumber! and sweeter the ray   35
Which after thy night introduces the day;
  How soft, how persuasive, Self-interest's breath,
  Though it floats to mine ear from the bosom of Death!
I hoped that I quite was forgotten by all,
Yet a lingering friend may be grieved at my fall,   40
  And Virtue forbids, though I languish, to die,
  When departure might heave Virtue's breast with a sigh.
Yet, Death!—oh, my friend! snatch this form to thy shrine,
And I fear, dear destroyer, I shall not repine.

34. *Eyes*

1810

How eloquent are eyes!
Not the rapt Poet's frenzied lay
When the soul's wildest feelings stray
  Can speak so well as they.

How eloquent are eyes!   5
Not music's most impassioned note
On which Love's warmest fervours float
  Like them bids rapture rise.

Love, look thus again!—
That your look may light a waste of years,   10
Darting the beam that conquers cares
  Through the cold shower of tears!

∧ 35 sweeter *Esd.*] sweet is *Camb.*   37 soft *Esd.*] concealed *Camb.*   40 may
Esd.] might *Camb.*   41 Virtue *Esd.*] duty *Camb.*   43 Yet *Esd.*] O *Camb.*

∨ AUTOGRAPH, DATE: *Esd.*   PRINTED: *1–13, from a transcript by Garnett, apparently from
Esd.* (*see n. on No. 15, p. 365*), Ross. *1870/1–end*, Rog. *1966.*   TITLE: *1870, I and
P, 1927.*   TEXT: *1966/Esd.*
  2 Poet's *1870*] Poets *Esd.*   8 Like them *1870*] Like they *Esd.*   bids *1870*] bid *Esd.*

Love, look thus again!—
That Time the victor, as he flies,
May pause to gaze upon thine eyes,—   15
   A victor then in vain!

Yet no!—Arrest not Time!
For Time, to others dear, we spurn;
When Time shall *be* no more we burn,
   When Love meets full return.   20
   Ah, no!—Arrest not Time!—
Fast let him fly on eagle wing,
Nor pause till Heaven's unfading spring
   Breathes round its holy clime.

   Yet quench that thrilling gaze   25
Which passionate Friendship arms with fire!
For what will eloquent eyes inspire
   But feverish, false desire?
   Quench then that thrilling gaze!—
For age may freeze the tremulous joy,   30
But age can never *love* destroy,—
   It lives to better days.

   Age cannot love destroy!—
Can perfidy then blight its flower,
Even when, in most unwary hour,   35
   It blooms in Fancy's bower?

   Age cannot love destroy!—
Can slighted vows then rend the shrine
On which its chastened splendours shine
   Around a dream of joy?   40

35. *'Hopes that Bud . . .'*

1810

HOPES that bud in youthful breasts
  Live not through the lapse of time;
Love's rose a host of thorns invests,
  And ungenial is the clime
    Where its blossoms blow.   5
Youth says, 'The purple flowers are mine,'
  That fade the while they glow.

Dear the boon to Fancy given,
  Retracted while 'tis granted;
Sweet the rose that breathes in Heaven,   10
  Although on Earth 'tis planted
    Where its blossoms blow,
Where by the frosts its leaves are riven
  That fade the while they glow.

The pure soul lives that heart within   15
  Which age cannot remove
If undefiled by tainting sin,—
  A sanctuary of love,
    Where its blossoms blow,—
Where, in this unsullied shrine,   20
  They fade not while they glow.

AUTOGRAPH: *Esd., Pf., letter to Hogg, c. 19 June 1811.*   DATE: *Esd.*   PRINTED: *1–14,
from Pf., Hogg, 1858/1–14, from a transcript of Esd., I and P, 1927/1–end, from Esd.,
Rog. 1966.*   TEXT: *1966/Esd.*
  1 bud *Esd.*] swell *Pf.*   2 not through *Esd.*] they thro *Pf.* they this *1858*   lapse
Esd.] waste *Pf., 1927*   3 a *Esd.*] an *Pf.*   invests *Pf.*] invest *Esd.*   4 And
Esd.] Cold *Pf.*   5 blossoms *Esd.*] honours *Pf.*   6–7 *alternatively* mine . . .
glow'   7 That fade *Esd.*] Which die *Pf.*   9 while 'tis *Esd.*] whilst it's *Pf.*
10 that breathes *Esd.*] which lives *Pf.*   11 planted *Pf.*] planten *Esd.*
12 blossoms *Esd.*] honours *Pf., 1927*
In place of 15–20, following a row of crosses, Pf. has

            Age cannot love destroy
              But perfidy can blast the flower
              E'en when in most unwary hour
              It blooms in Fancy's bower
            Age cannot love destroy
              But Perfidy can rend the shrine
              In which its vermeil splendours shine

See n., p. 369.

36. *To the Moonbeam*

23 September 1809

MOONBEAM, leave the shadowy dale,
  To cool this burning brow!
Moonbeam, why art thou so pale,
As thou glidest along the midnight vale,
    Where dewy flowrets grow?   5
      Is it to mimic me?
      Ah, that can never be;
        For thy path is bright,
        And the clouds are light,
That at intervals shadow the star-studded night.   10

Now all is deathy still on earth;
  Nature's tired frame reposes;
Yet, ere the golden morning's birth
  Its radiant gates uncloses,
    Flies forth her balmy breath.   15
    But mine is the midnight of death,
    And Nature's morn
    To my bosom forlorn
Brings but a gloomier night, implants a deadlier thorn.

Wretch, suppress the glare of madness   20
  Struggling in thine haggard eye!
For the keenest throb of sadness,
  Pale despair's most sickening sigh,
    Is but to mimic me.
    But that can never be,   25
    When the darkness of care
    And the death of despair
Seem in my breast but joys to the pangs that rankle there.

AUTOGRAPH: *Esd., Pf., letter to Hogg, 17 May. 1811.*   TITLE: *Pf.*   DATE: *Esd.*   PRINTED:
*From Pf., Hogg, 1858/from a transcript of Esd. (see Intr., p. xxix), I and P, 1927/from
Esd., Rog. 1966.*   TEXT: *1966/Esd.*
  1 dale *Esd.*] vale *Pf.*   2 cool *Esd.*] bathe *Pf.*   3 Moonbeam *Esd., Pf.*]
Moonbeam cool *1927*   4 as thou walkest oer the dewy dale *Pf.*   5 dewy
flowrets *Esd.*] humble wild flowers *Pf.*   7 Ah *Esd.*] But *Pf.*   8 thy
path *Esd.*] Thine orb *Pf.*   13 Yet *over* And ere *Esd.*] And ere *Pf.* Yet in *1927*
14 gates *Esd.*] hues *Pf., 1927*   15 her *Esd.*] its *Pf.*   25 But that can never
be *Esd.*] And this must ever be *Pf.*   26 darkness *Esd.*] twilight *Pf.*   27 death
Esd.] night *Pf.*   28 rankle *Esd.*] walk *Pf.* wake *1858*

37–40. *Four Poems to Mary*

November 1810

[SHELLEY'S] ADVERTISEMENT

The few poems immediately following are selected from many written during three weeks of an entrancement caused by hearing Mary's story. I hope that the delicate and discriminating genius of the friend who related it to me will allow the publication of the heart-breaking facts under the title of 'Leonora'. For myself, at that time, 'nondum amabam, et amare amabam, quaerebam quid amarem, amans amare'.

Mary died three months before I heard her tale.

37. *To Mary I*

DEAR girl, thou art wildered by madness!
    Yet do not look so, sweet,—
I could share in the sigh of thy sadness;
    Thy woe my soul could meet.

I loved a heart sincerely,   5
    Yes, dear it was to mine—
Yet, Mary, I love more dearly
    One tender look of thine.

Oh, do not say that Heaven
    Will frown on errors past,—   10
Thy faults are all forgiven,
    Thy virtues ever last.[1]

[1] This opinion is, of all others, the most deeply rooted in my conviction. The enquirer will laugh at it as a dream, the Christian will abhor it as a blasphemy—Mary who repeatedly attempted suicide, yet was unwilling to die alone.—Nor is it probable that she would, had I instead of my friend been subjected to the trial of sitting a summer's night by her side, whilst two glasses of poison stood on the table and she folded me to her tremulous bosom in ecstasies of friendship and despair! [*Shelley's footnote.*]

AUTOGRAPH: *Esd.*   TITLES: *See nn., p. 361.*   DATE: *Esd., with No. 37.*   PRINTED: *Rog. 1966.*   TEXT: *1966/Esd.*

12 *conjectural reference for Shelley's note, written at the foot of pages covering 7–28 and extending to the next page.*

SHELLEY'S FOOTNOTE.—*Cancelled at end*: What are the Romances of Leadenhall Str. to this of real life?

The cup with death o'erflowing
　　I'll drink, fair girl, to thee;
For when the storm is blowing   15
　　To shelter we may flee.

Thou canst not bear to languish
　　In this frail chain of clay,
And I am tired of anguish,—
　　Love, let us haste away!   20

Like thee I fear to weather
　　Death's darksome wave alone,—
We'll take the voyage together,
　　Come, Mary, let's begone!

Strange mists my woe efface, love,   25
　　And thou art pale in Death,—
Give one, one last embrace, love,
　　And we resign our breath.

38. *To Mary II*

FAIR one, calm that bursting heart!
　　Dares then fate to frown on thee,
Lovely, spotless as thou art—
　　Though its worst poison lights on me?
　　　　Then dry that tear,—   5
　　　　Thou needest not fear
These woes when thy limbs are cold on the bier.

Start not from winter's breathing, dearest,
　　Though bleak is yonder hill,—
As perjured love the blast thou fearest   10
　　Is not half so deadly chill!
　　　　Like these winds that blow
　　　　No remorse does it know
And colder it strikes than the driving snow.

The tomb is damp and dark and low,   15
    Yet with thee the tomb I do not dread,—
There is not a place of frightful woe
    Where with thee I'd refuse to lay my head.
        But our souls shall not sleep
        In the grave damp and deep   20
But in love and devotion[1] their holy-day keep.

39. *To Mary III*

MARY, Mary, art thou gone
    To sleep in thine earthy cell?
Presses thy breast the death-cold stone,
Pours none the tear, the sob, the groan,
Where murdered virtue sleeps alone,   5
    Where its first glory fell?

Mary, Mary, past is past!
    I submit in silence to fate's decree,
Though the tear of distraction gushes fast
And, at night when the lank reeds hiss in the blast,   10
    My spirit mourns in sympathy.

Thou wert more fair in mind than are
    The fabled heavenly train,
But thine was the pang of corroding care,
Thine cold contempt and lone despair,   15
And thwarted love, more hard to bear.
And I, wretch, weep that such they were,
    And I—still drag my chain.

Thou wert but born to weep, to die,
To feel dissolved the dearest tie,   20
    Its fragments by the pitiless world
    Adown the blast of fortune hurled,
To strive with envy's wreckful storm,—
    Thou wert but born to weep and die,

---

[1] The expression *devotion* is not used in a religious sense; for which abuse of this lovely word few have a greater horror than the Author. [*Shelley's footnote.*]

Nor could thy ceaseless misery   25
   Nor heavenly virtues aught avail,
   Nor taintless innocence prevail
With the world's slaves thy love to spare,
Nor the magic, unearthly atmosphere
That wrapt thine ethereal form.   30

Such, loveliest Mary, was thy fate,
   And such is Virtue's doom:
Contempt, neglect and hatred wait,
Where yawns a wide and dreary gate,
   To drag its votaries to the tomb,—   35
Sweet flower, that blooms amid the weeds
Where the rank serpent Interest feeds!

40. *To the Lover of Mary*

DRINK the exhaustless moonbeam, where its glare
   Wanly lights murdered virtue's funeral
   And tremulous sheds on the corpse-shrouding pall
     A languid, languid flare!—
Hide thee, poor wretch, where yonder baleful yew   5
   Sheds o'er the clay that now is tenantless,
   Whose spirit once thrilled to thy warm caress,
     Its deadly, deadly dew!
The moonray will not quench thy misery,
But the yew's death-drops will bring peace to thee, 10
And yonder clay-cold grave thy bridal bed shall be.

And since the spirit dear that breathes of Heaven
   Has burst the powerless bondage of its clay
   And soars an angel to eternal day,
     Purged of its earthly leaven,   15
Thy yearnings now shall bend thee to the tomb,
   Oblivion blot a life without a stain,
   And death's cold hand round thy heart's ceaseless pain
     Enfold its veil of gloom.

30 ethereal] etherial *over* heavenly *in Esd.*

The wounds shall close of Misery's scorpion goad   20
When Mary greets thee in her blest abode
And worships holy Love in purity, thy God.

Oh, this were joy, and such as none would fear
    To purchase by a life of passing woe!—
    For on this earth the sickly flowers that glow   25
        Breathe of perfection there.
Yet live,—for others barter thine own bliss,
    And living show what towering virtue dares
    To accomplish even in this vale of tears!
        Turn Hell to Paradise   30
And, spurning selfish joy, soar high above
The Heaven of Heavens, let even eternal Love,
Despised awhile, thy sense of holier Virtue[1] prove!

41. *Bigotry's Victim*

1810

DARES the llama, most fleet of the sons of the wind,
    The lion to rouse from his lair?
When the tiger awakes can the fast-fleeting hind
    Repose trust in his footsteps of air?
No! abandoned it sinks in helpless despair,   5
    The monster transfixes his prey,
    On the sand flows its life-blood away;
And the rocks and the woods to the death-yells reply,
Protracting the horrible harmony.

[1] As if they were not synonymous! [*Shelley's footnote.*]

AUTOGRAPH: *Esd., TCU, letter to Hogg, 28 Apr. 1811.*   TITLE: *See nn., p. 361.*   DATE:
Esd.   PRINTED: *From TCU, Hogg, 1858/from a transcript of Esd. (see Intr.,
p. xxix), I and P, 1927/from Esd., Rog. 1966.*   TEXT: *1966/Esd.*
  2 lair *Esd.*] scull covered lair *TCU*   3 awakes *Esd., TCU*] approaches *1858*
5 it *Esd.*] he *TCU*   helpless despair *Esd.*] a trance of despair *TCU*   7 its *Esd.*]
his *TCU, 1927*   8 And the rocks and the woods *Esd.*] Whilst India's rocks *TCU*
the *Esd.*] his *TCU*

Yet the fowl of the desert, when danger encroaches,   10
   Dares dreadless to perish, defending her brood,
Though the fiercest of cloud-piercing tyrants approaches,
   Thirsting—aye, thirsting for blood,
And demands, like mankind, his brother for food;
     Yet more lenient, more gentle than they;   15
     For hunger, not glory, the prey
Must perish. Revenge does not howl o'er the dead,
Nor ambition with fame bind the murderer's head.

Though weak as the llama that bounds on the mountains,
   And endued not with fast-fleeting footsteps of air,   20
Yet, yet will I draw from the purest of fountains,
   Though a fiercer than tigers is there.
Though, more frightful than death, it scatters despair,
   And its shadow, eclipsing the day,
     Spreads the darkness of deepest dismay   25
O'er the withered and withering nations around,
And the war-mangled corpses that rot on the ground.

They came to the fountain to draw from its stream
   Waves too poisonously lovely for mortals to see;
They basked for a while in the love-darting beam,   30
   Then perished,—and perished like me.
For in vain from the grasp of Religion I flee;
     The most tenderly loved of my soul
     Are slaves to its chilling control.
It pursues me, it blasts me! Oh, where shall I fly?   35
What remains but to curse it, to curse it and die?

---

10 desert *TCU*] desart *Esd. See n.*, *p. 369.*   11 dreadless *Esd.*] fearless *TCU*
16 hunger *Esd.*] *italicized TCU*   17 o'er *Esd.*] in *TCU*   18 bind *Esd.*]
crown *TCU*   23 frightful *Esd.*] dreadful *TCU*   24 And *Esd.*] Tho *TCU*
eclipsing *Esd.*] eclipses *TCU*   25 Spreads *Esd.*] And *TCU*   26 Spreads the
influence of soul-chilling terror around *TCU*   27 war-mangled *Esd.*] lowers on
the *TCU*   29 poisonously lovely *Esd.*] pure too celestial *TCU*   30 basked
Esd.] bathed *TCU*   the *Esd.*] its *TCU*, *1927*   love-darting *Esd.*] silvery *TCU*
32 Religion *Esd.*, *TCU*] the Bigot *1858*   34 its *Esd.*, *TCU*] his *1858*   chilling
Esd.] hated *TCU*   35 It . . . it *Esd.*, *TCU*] He . . . he *1858*   Oh, where shall
Esd., *TCU*] 'Tis vain that *1858*   36 it . . . it *Esd.*, *TCU*] him . . . him *1858*

42. *Love and Tyranny*

1809

I WILL kneel at thine altar, will crown thee with bays,
  Whether God, Love or Virtue thou art!
Thou shalt live,—aye, more long than these perishing lays:
  Thou shalt live in this high-beating heart!
Dear Love! from its life-springs thou never shalt part,   5
    Though Prejudice, clanking her chain,
    Though Interest, groaning in gain,
May tell me thou closest to Heaven the door,
May tell me that thine is the way to be poor.

The victim of merciless tyranny's power   10
  May smile at his chains if with thee;
The most sense-enslaved loiterer in Passion's sweet bower
  Is a wretch if unhallowed by thee;
Thine, thine is the bond that alone binds the free,—
    Can the free worship bondage? Nay more,   15
    What they feel not, believe not? Adore
What, if felt, if believed, if existing, must give
To thee to create, to eternize, to live?—

For Religion, more keen than the blasts of the North,
  Darts its frost through the self-palsied soul;   20
Its slaves on the work of destruction go forth,—
    The divinest emotions that roll
Submit to the rod of its impious control;
    At the venomous blast of its breath
    Love, concord, lies gasping in death,   25
Philanthropy utters a war-drownèd cry,
And selfishness conquering cries 'Victory'!

Can we then, thus tame, thus impassive, behold
  That alone whence our life springs destroyed?
Shall Prejudice, Priestcraft, Opinion and Gold,   30
  Every Passion with interest alloyed,
Where Love ought to reign, fill the desolate void?

AUTOGRAPH, DATE: *Esd.*   TITLE: *1966. See nn., p. 361.*   PRINTED: *Rog. 1966.*
TEXT: *1966/Esd.*
  5 shalt] shall *Esd.*

But the Avenger arises, the throne
Of selfishness totters,—its groan
Shakes the nations—it falls, Love seizes the sway; 35
The sceptre it bears unresisted away.

43. *Fragment of a Poem, &c.—*

[See Appendix]

44. *On an Icicle that clung to the Grass of a Grave*

1809

OH! take the pure gem to where southernly breezes
   Waft repose to some bosom as faithful as fair,
In which the warm current of love never freezes,
   As it circulates freely and shamelessly there,
     Which, untainted by crime, unpolluted by care, 5
Might dissolve this dim icedrop, might bid it arise,
Too pure for these regions, to gleam in the skies.

For I found the pure gem, when the daybeam returning,
   Ineffectual gleams on the snow-spangled plain,
When to others the longed-for arrival of morning 10
   Brings relief to long night-dreams of soul-racking pain;
     But regret is an insult—to grieve is in vain:
And why should we grieve that a spirit so fair
Sought Heaven to meet with its kindred there?

AUTOGRAPH: *Esd., Pf., letter to Hogg, 6 Jan. 1811.* TITLE, DATE: *Esd.* PRINTED: *From Pf., Hogg, 1858/from a transcript of Esd. (see Intr., p. xxix), I and P, 1927/from Esd., Rog. 1966.* TEXT: *1966/Esd.*
  1 southernly *Esd., Pf.*] southerly *1858, 1927* 4 As it circulates *Esd.*] As it rises *Pf.* Circulates *1927* freely and shamelessly *Esd.*] unmingled with selfishness *Pf.*
5 crime *Esd.*] Pride *Pf.* 6 this *Esd., Pf.*] the *1927*
Between 7 and 8 Pf. has this stanza
        Or where the stern warrior his country defending
          Dares fearless the dark-rolling battle to pour
        Or o'er the fell corpse of a dread Tyrant bending
          Where Patriotism red with his guilt-reeking gore
          Plants Liberty's flag on the slave-peopled shore,
        With Victory's cry, with the shout of the free,
        Let it fly taintless Spirit to mingle with thee.

9 snow-spangled *Esd.*] snow-covered *Pf.* 10 longed-for *Esd.*] wished for *Pf.*
11 night-dreams *Esd.*] visions *Pf.* 13 And *Esd.*] Say *above* And *underlined Pf.*
14 Sought *Esd.*] Seeks *Pf.* meet *Esd.*] mix *Pf.* its *Esd., Pf.*] its own *1858, 1927*

Yet 'twas some angel of kindness, descending   15
    To share in the load of mortality's woe,
Who, over thy lowly-built sepulchre bending,
    Bade sympathy's tenderest teardrops to flow,
    And consigned the rich gift to the sister of snow;
And if angels can weep, sure I may repine,   20
And shed teardrops, though frozen to ice, on thy shrine.

45. 'Cold are the Blasts . . .'
[See Appendix]

46. Henry and Louisa[1]
1809

A POEM IN TWO PARTS
She died for love—and he for glory

PART THE FIRST
The Parting
Scene: England

I

WHERE are the heroes? Sunk in death they lie.
    What toiled they for? Titles and wealth and fame.
But the wide heaven is now their canopy,
    And 'legal murderers' their loftiest name.

---

[1] The stanza of this poem is radically that of Spenser although I suffered myself at the time of writing it to be led into occasional deviations. These defects I do not alter now, being unwilling to offer any outrage to the living portraiture of my own mind, bad as it may be pronounced. [*Shelley's footnote.*]

∧ 15 Yet *Esd.*] But still *Pf.*   angel *Esd.*] spirit *Pf.*   18 teardrops *Esd.*] tear drop *Pf.*
19 Not for *thee* soft compassion celestials did know *Pf.*   20 And *Esd.*] But *Pf.*
angels *Esd.*] angels *italicized Pf., 1927*   I *Esd.*] Man *italicized Pf.*   21 May weep
in mute grief o'er thy low-laid shrine. *Pf.*
After 21 Pf. has this stanza
          And did I then say for the Altar of Glory
            That the earliest the loveliest flowers I'd entwine
        Tho' with millions of blood-reeking victims 'tis gory
           Tho' the tears of the widow polluted its shine
           Tho' around the orphans, the fatherless pine.
         Oh! fame all thy glories I'd yield for a tear
           To shed on the grave of an heart so sincere.

∨ AUTOGRAPH, TITLE, DATE: *Esd.*   PRINTED: *Rog. 1966.*   TEXT: *1966/Esd.*
   3 canopy *over* canopies

Enshrined on brass their glory and their shame   5
What though torn Peace and martyred Freedom see?—
What though to most remote posterity
   Their names, their selfishness, for aye enscrolled,
   A shuddering world's blood-boltered eyes behold,
Mocking mankind's unbettered misery?—   10
   Can this perfection give? Can valour prove
One wish for others' bliss, one throb of love? . . .

II

Yet darest thou boast thyself superior thou,
   Vile worm, whom lovely woman deigns to bless?—
And, meanly selfish, bask in glory's glow,   15
   Rending the soul-spun ties of tenderness
   Where all desires rise for thine happiness?
Canst thou boast thus and hope to be forgiven?
   Oh, when thou started'st from her last caress,
From purest love by vulgar glory driven,   20
Couldst thou have e'er deserved, if thou resigned'st, Heaven?

III

---

21 *the stanza-headings III, IV, and V are followed in Esd. by blank spaces down to the
line here numbered as 22. See n., p. 370.*

IV

V

⟨And, shadowed by Affection's purple wing,   22
  Bid thee forget how Time's fast footstep sped:
Would die in peace when thou wert mingled with the dead.⟩

VI

Had glory's fire consumed each tender tie   25
  That links to love the heaven-aspiring soul?
Could not that voice, quivering in agony,
  That struggling pale resolve, that dared control
Passion's wild flood when wildest it did roll,—
Could not impassioned tenderness that burst   30
  Cold prudery's bondage, owning all it felt,—
Could not these, warrior, quench thy battle-thirst?
  Nought this availed thine iron-bound breast to melt,—
To make thy footsteps pause where love and freedom dwelt?

VII

Yes, every soul-nerve vibrated. A space   35
    Enchained in speechless awe the warrior stood;
Superior reason, virtue, manner, grace
    Claimed for a space their rights,—in varying mood
    Before her lovely eyes in thought he stood,
Whilst glory's train flashed on his mental eye,   40
    Which wandered wildly where the fight's red flood,
The crash of death, the storm of victory
Roll round the hopes of love that only breathe to die.

VIII

Then she exclaimed, as love-nerved sense returned,
    'Go!—Mingle in thy country's battle-tide!   45
Forget that love's pale torch hath ever burned
    Until thou meet'st me clothed in victor-pride;
May guardian spirits keep thee! Far and wide
O'er the red regions of the day-scorched zone
    For glory seek!—But here thou wilt abide   50
Here in this breast thou wilt abide alone,—
I will thine empire be. My heart shall be thy throne.'

IX

When princes at fair Reason's bidding bend,
    Resigning power for virtue's fadeless meed,
Or spirits of Heaven to man submission lend,   55
    The debt of gratitude is great indeed;
In vain the heart its thankfulness to prove
    Aye might attempt to do the debt away.
Yet what is this compared to Woman's love,—
    Dear Woman's love, the dawn of Virtue's day,—   60
The bliss-inspiring beam, the soul-illuming ray?

52 My heart *possibly, in error,* thy heart

X

Then Henry spoke, as he checked the rising tear:
  'That I have loved thee, and must love for ever,
Heaven is a witness—Heaven to whom are dear
    The hearts that earthly chances cannot sever,   65
    Where bloom the flowers that cease to blossom never.
Religion sanctifies the cause: I go
  To execute its vengeance. Heaven will give
To me (so whispers hope) to quell the foe:
    Heaven gives the good to conquer and to live,   70
And thou shalt next to God his votive heart receive.

XI

'Say, is not he the Tyrant of the World?
  And are not we the injured and the brave?
Unmoved shall we behold his flag unfurled,
    Flouting with impious wing Religion's grave,   75
    Triumphant gleaming o'er the passive wave?—
Nor raise an arm nor one short pleasure yield
  The boon of immortality to save?
Hope is our tempered lance, faith is our shield;
Conquest or death for these wait on the gory field.   80

XII

'Even at that hour when hostile myriads clash
  And terrible death shakes his resistless dart,
Mingling wild wailings with the battle crash,
    Then thou and Heaven shall share this votive heart;
    When from pale dissolution's grasp I start,   85
(If Heaven so wills) even then will I be thine,
  Nor can the whelming tomb have power to part
From all it loves a heart that loves like mine—
From thee round whom its hopes, its joys, its fears entwine.'

XIII

A sicklier tint crept o'er Louisa's cheek: 90
   'But thou art dearer far to me than all
That fancy's visions feign, or tongue can speak,—
   Yes! May I die, and be that death eternal,
   When other thoughts but thee my soul enthral!
The joys of heaven I prize thee far above: 95
   Thee, dearest, will my soul its saviour call,—
My faith is thine—my faith-gained heaven thy love,
My hell when cruel Fates thee from these arms remove.

XIV

'Farewell.' She spoke. The warrior's war-steeled breast,
   Quivering in feeling's agonised excess,   100
Scarce drew its breath, to sickliness oppressed
   By mingled self-reproach and tenderness;
   He dared not speak, but rushed from her caress,
The sunny glades, the little birds of spring,
   Twittering from every garlanded recess,   105
Returning verdure's joy that seemed to sing,
Whilst Woe with stern hand smote his every mental string.

XV

The fragrant dew-mists from the ivied thorn,
   Whose form o'ershadowed love's most blissful bower,
Where oft would fly the tranquil time of morn,   110
   Or swifter urge its flight dear evening's hour,
   When purple twilight in the east would lower
And the amorous starbeam kiss the loveliest form
   That ever bruised a pleasure-fainting flower,
Whose emanative eyebeam, thrilling warm,   115
Around her sacred presence shed a rapturing charm,—

104 glades,] glades; *Esd.*   107 string.] string; *Esd.*   111 hour,] hower *Esd.*
116 charm,—] charm; *Esd.*

XVI

Each object so beloved, each varied tone
  Of heavenly feeling that can never die,
Each little throb his heart had ever known
  Impetuous rushed on fainting memory.   120
  Yet not alone for parted ecstasy
To which he now must bid a long adieu
  Started the bitter tear or burst the sigh:
No, all the pangs that, spite concealment, grew
O'er his Louisa's peace, a deeper soul-pang drew.   125

XVII

The balmy breath of soul-reviving dawn
  That kissed the bosom of the waveless lake,
Scented with spring-flowers o'er the level lawn,
  Struck on his sense, to woe scarce yet awake;
  He felt its still reproach; the upland brake   130
Rustled beneath his war-steed's eager prance;
  Hastening to Egypt's shore his way to take
But swifter hastening to dispel the trance
Of grief, he hurried on, smothering the last sad glance.

XVIII

Sweet flower! in dereliction's solitude   135
  That scatterest perfume to the unheeding gale,
And in the grove's unconscious quietude
  Murmurest (thyself scarce conscious) thy sad tale!—
  Sure it is subject for the Poet's wail,
  Though faint, that one so worthy to be prized   140
  The fairest flower of the loveliest vale,
To withering Glory should be sacrificed,
That hides his hateful form in Virtue's garb disguised.

140–3 Though] That *1966* Tho *probably intended to correct* That *Esd. See n., p. 370.*

XIX

Religion, hated cause of all the woe
   That makes the world this wilderness! Thou spring   145
Whence terror, pride, revenge and perfidy flow!—
   The curses which thy pampered minions bring
   On thee shall Virtue's votary fear to fling?
And thou, dear Love,—thy tender ties to sever,
   To drown in shouts thy bliss-fraught murmuring,   150
Ceaseless shall selfish Prejudice endeavour?
Shall she succeed? Oh, no! Whilst I live, never, never!

XX

For, by the wrongs that flaming deep
   Within this bosom's agony . . .
That dry the source whence others weep,—   155
   I swear that thou shalt die.

PART THE SECOND

The Meeting

Scene: Africa

I

'Tis night.—No planet's brilliance dares to light
   The dim and battle-blushing scenery;
Friends mixed with foes urge unremitting fight
   Beneath war's suffocating canopy,   160
   And, as sulphureous meteors fire the sky,
Fast flash the deathful thunderbolts of war,
   Whilst groans unite in frightful harmony,
And wakened vultures, shrieking from afar,
Scent their half-murdered prey amid the battle's jar.   165

153 deep *not, I think,* sleep *in Esd.*   154 agony . . .] agony *Esd. See n.*

II

Now had the Genius of the South, sublime
  On mighty Atlas' tempest-cinctured throne,
Looked over Afric's desolated clime,
  Deep wept at slavery's everlasting moan
  And his most dear-belovèd nation's groan.   170
The Boreal whirlwind's shadowy wings that sweep
  The varied bosom of the northern world
That hears contending thunders on the deep
  Sees hostile flags on Egypt's strand unfurled,
Brings Egypt's faintest groan to waste and ruin hurled.   175

III

Is ⟨this⟩ then all that sweeps the midnight sand?
  Tells the wild blast no tales of deeper woe?
Does war alone pollute the unhappy land?
  No,—the low fluttering and the hectic glow
  Of hope, whose sickly flowret scarce can blow,   180
Chilled by the ice-blast of intense despair,
  Anguish that dries the big tear ere it flow,
And maniac love that sits by the beacon's glare,
With eyes on nothing fixed, dim like a mist-clothed star!

IV

No fear save one could daunt her. Ocean's wave,   185
  Bearing Britannia's hired assassins on
To victory's shame or an unhonoured grave,
  Beheld Louisa 'mid an host alone;
  The womanly dress that veiled her fair form is gone,
Gone is the timid wandering of her eye,   190
  Pale firmness nerved her anguished heart to stone:
The sense of shame, the flush of modesty
By stern resolve were quenched or only glowed to die.

166–75 *See n.* 170 groan.] groan *1966, Esd.*   183 beacon's] beacons *Esd.*
185 her.] her— *Esd.*   187 victory's shame *corrected by Shelley from* victory stern,

V

'Where is my love, my Henry—is he dead?'
   Half drowned in smothered anguish wildly burst   195
From her parched lips—'Is my adored one dead?
   Knows none my Henry? War! thou source accurst
   In whose red flood I see these sands immersed,
Hast thou quite whelmed compassion's tearful spring
   Where thy fierce tide rolls to slake Glory's thirst?   200
Perhaps thou, warrior, some kind word dost bring
From my poor Henry's lips when death its shade did fling.'

VI

A tear of pity dimmed the warrior's gaze;
   'I know him not, sweet maiden, yet the fight
That casts on Britain's fame a brighter blaze   205
   Should spare all yours, if aught I guess aright.
   But ah! by yonder flash of sulphurous light
The dear-loved work of battle has begun—
   Fame calls her votaries.' He fled. The night
Had far advanced before the fray was done;   210
Scarce sunk the roar of war before the rising sun.

VII

But sight of wilder grief where slept the dead
   Was witnessed by the morn's returning glow,
When frantic o'er the waste Louisa sped
   To drink her dying lover's latest vow.   215
   Sighed 'mid her locks the sea-gales as they blew,
Bearing along faint shrieks of dying men,
   As if they sympathised with her deep woe;
   Silent she paused a space, and then again
New-nerved by fear and hope, sprang wild across the plain.   220

   199 whelmed *above* [dried] *Esd.*   208 begun—] begun. *Esd.*   220 fear
possibly fears *Esd.*

VIII

See where she stops again!—A ruin's shade
  Darkens his fading lineaments; his cheek,
On which remorseful pain is deep portrayed,
    Glares death-convulsed and ghastly; utterings break,
    Shuddering, unformed, his tongue essays to speak.   225
There low he lies, poor Henry! Where is now
    Thy dear, devoted love? Is there no friend
To bathe with tears that anguish-burning brow—
    None comfort in this fearful hour to lend,
When to remorseful grief thy parting spirits bend?   230

IX

Yes, pain had steeped each dying limb in flame
  When, mad with mingled hope and pale dismay,
Fleet as the wild deer, his Louisa came,
    Nerved by distraction. A pale tremulous ray
    Flashed on her eyes from the expiring day;   235
Life for a space rushed to his fainting breast,
    The breathing form of love-enlivened clay
In motionless rapture pale Louisa pressed
And, stung by maddening hope, in tears her bliss expressed.

X

Yet was the transport wavering: the dew   240
  Of bodily pain that bathed his pallid brow,
The pangs that through his anguished members flew,
    Though half subdued by Love's returning glow,
    Doubt mixed with lingering hope must needs bestow.
Then she exclaimed, 'Love, I have sought thee far,   245
    Whence our own Albion's milder sea-gales blow
To this stern scene of fame-aspiring war,—
Through waves of danger past thou wert my polar star.

226 There *possibly* thus   227 devoted *possibly* deserted

XI

'Live then, dear source of life! And let the ray
  Which lights thy kindling eyebeam softly speak   250
That thou hast loved when I was far away.
  Yet thou art pale; death's hectic lights thy cheek!—
Oh, if one moment Fate the chain should break
Which binds thy soul unchangeably to mine!
  Another moment's pain fate dare not wreak;   255
Another moment—I am ever thine,—
Love, turn those eyes on me! Ah, death has dimmed their shine!'

XII

  Ceased her voice; the accents mild
    In frightful stillness died away;
  More sweet than Memnon's plainings wild   260
    That float upon the morning ray
      Died every sound,—save when,
      At distance o'er the plain,
  Britannia's legions, swiftly sweeping
  Glory's ensanguined harvest reaping,   265
      Mowed down the field of men,
  And the silent ruins, crumbling nigh,
  With echoes low prolonged the cry
    Of mingled defeat and victory.

XIII

  More low, more faint, yet far more dread   270
    Arose the expiring warrior's groan;
  Stretched on the sand, his bloody bed,
  In agonised death was Henry laid,
    But he did not fall alone.
  Why then that anguished sigh   275
  Which seems to tear the vital tie,
    Fiercer than death, more fell
  Than tyranny, contempt or hate?
    Why does that breast with horror swell
  Which ought to triumph over fate?   280

Why?—Ask the pallid grief-worn mien
Of poor Louisa, let it speak.
But her firm heart would sooner break
    Than doubt the soul where love had been.

XIV

Now, now he dies!—his parting breath 285
    The sulphurous gust of battle bears;
The shriek, the groan, the gasp of death
    Unmoved Louisa hears,
And a smile of triumph lights her eye
With more than mortal radiancy.— 290
    Sacred to Love a deed is done,
    Gleams through battle-clouds the sun!
Gleams it on all that's good and fair,
Stretched on the earth to moulder there!
      Shall virtue perish? No! 295
    Superior to Religion's tie,
    Emancipate from misery,
Despising self, their souls can know
All the delight love can bestow
    When Glory's phantom fades away 300
    Before Affection's purer ray,—
When tyrants cease to wield the rod,
And slaves to tremble at their nod!

XV

There, near the stunted palms that shroud
    The spot from which their spirits fled, 305
Shall pause the human hounds of blood,
    And own a secret dread;
There shall the victor's steel-clad brow,
Though flushed by conquest's crimson glow,
    Be changed with inward fear; 310
There stern and steady by long command,
The pomp-fed despot's sceptred hand
    Shall shake as if death were near,
Whilst the lone captive in his train
Feels comfort as he shakes his chain. 315

300 When *possibly* Where   311 steady *above* [bronzed]

47. *A Translation of the Marseillaise Hymn*

c. 19 June 1811

I

HASTE to battle, Patriot-Band,
  A day of glory dawns on thee!
Against thy rights is raised an hand,
  The blood-red hand of tyranny!
See, the ferocious slaves of power   5
Across the wasted country scour,
And in thy very arms destroy
The pledges of thy nuptial joy,
  Thine unresisting family!

Chorus

Then citizens form in battle array,
For this is the dawn of a glorious day!—
  March, march, fearless of danger and toil,
  And the rank gore of tyrants shall water your soil!

2

What wills the coward, traitorous train
  Of Kings, whose trade is perfidy?
For whom is forged this hateful chain,
  For whom prepared this slavery?
For you!—On you their vengeance rests,—   5
What transports ought to thrill your breasts!
  Frenchmen! this unhallowed train
  To ancient woe would bind again
    Those souls whom valour has made free!

Chorus

Then citizens etc. . . .

AUTOGRAPH: *Esd. NYPL, stanza 4 only, letter to E. F. Graham, c. 19 June 1811.* TITLE: *Esd.* DATE: *See n., p. 370.* PRINTED: *From a transcript of Esd., Koszul,* La Jeunesse de Shelley, *1910/from Esd., Rog. 1966.* TEXT: *1966/Esd.*

3

What! Shall foreign bands compel
   Us to the laws of tyranny?
Shall hired soldiers hope to quell
   The arm upraised for liberty?
Great God!—By these united arms   5
Shall despots [in] their own alarms
Pass 'neath the yoke made for our head!
Yea, pomp-fed Kings shall quake with dread,
   These masters of Earth's destiny!

Chorus

Then citizens etc. . . .

4

Tremble Kings, despised of Man,
   Ye traitors to your country!
Tremble! Your parricidal plan
   At length shall meet its destiny!
We are all soldiers fit for fight,   5
But if we sink in glory's night
Our Mother Earth will give ye new
The brilliant pathway to pursue
   That leads to death or victory!

Chorus

Then citizens etc. . . .

5

Frenchmen! On the guilty brave
   Pour your vengeful energy!—
Yet, in your triumph pitying, save
   The unwilling slaves of tyranny;

Stanza 3, line 6 despots in their *Koszul*] despots their *Esd.*

But let the gore-stained despots bleed,   5
Be death fell Bouillé's bloodhound-meed,
Chase those unnatural fiends away
Who on their mother's vitals prey
    With more than tiger cruelty!

Chorus

Then citizens etc. . . .

6

Sacred Patriotism! Uphold
    The avenging bands who fight with thee!
And thou, more dear than meaner gold,
    Smile on our efforts, Liberty!
Where Conquest's crimson streamers wave   5
Haste thou to the happy brave,
Where at our feet thy dying foes
See, as their failing eyes unclose,
    Our glory and thy victory!

Chorus

Then citizens etc. . . .

48. *Written in Very Early Youth*

? 1807–9

I'LL lay me down by the churchyard tree
And resign me to my destiny;
    I'll bathe my brow with the poison dew
    That falls from yonder deadly yew;
And, if it steal my soul away,   5
To bid it wake in realms of day,
    Spring's sweetest flowers shall never be
    So dear to gratitude and me!

∧ *Stanza 5, line* 6 Bouillé's] Bouillie's *Esd.*

∨ AUTOGRAPH, TITLE: *Esd.*   DATE: *See n., p. 371.*   PRINTED: *Rog. 1966.*   TEXT:
1966/Esd.

Earthborn glory cannot breathe
Within the damp recess of death: 10
  Avarice, Envy, Lust, Revenge
  Suffer there a fearful change,—
All that grandeur ever gave
Moulders in the silent grave;
  Oh, that I slept near yonder yew,   15
  That this tired frame might moulder too!

Yet Pleasure's folly is not mine,
No votarist I at Glory's shrine;
  The sacred gift for which I sigh
Is not to live, to feel alone;   20
  I only ask to calmly die,
That the tomb might melt this heart of stone
  To love beyond the grave.

49. *Zeinab and Kathema*

Summer 1811

UPON the lonely beach Kathema lay,
  Against his folded arm his heart beat fast;
Through gathering tears the sun's departing ray
  In coldness o'er his shuddering spirit passed,
And, all unfelt, the breeze of evening came   5
That fanned with quivering wing his wan cheek's feeble flame.

'Oh', cried the mourner, 'could this widowed soul
  But fly where yonder sun now speeds to dawn!'
He paused—a thousand thoughts began to roll;
  Like waves they swept in restless tumult on,—   10
Like those fast waves that quick-succeeding beat
Without one lasting shape the beach beneath his feet.

∧ 18 shrine] shine *Esd.*

∨ AUTOGRAPH, TITLE: *Esd.*   DATE: *See n., p. 371.*   PRINTED: *79–84,* Dowd. *1886/1–*
end, Rog. *1966.*   TEXT: *1966/Esd.*

And, now the beamless, broad and yellow sphere
    Half sinking lingered on the crimson sea,
A shape of darksome distance does appear   15
    Within its semi-circled radiancy.
All sense was gone to his betrothèd one—
His eye fell on the form that dimmed the setting sun,—

He thought on his betrothèd. For his youth
    With her that was its charm to ripeness grew;   20
All that was dear in love or fair in truth
    With her was shared as childhood's moments flew,
And mingled with sweet memories of her
Was life's unveiling morn with all its bliss and care.

A wild and lovely superstition's spell,   25
    Love for the friend that life and freedom gave,
Youth's growing hopes that watch themselves so well,
    Passion so prompt to blight, so strong to save,
And childhood's host of memories combine
Her life and love around his being to entwine.   30

And to their wishes with its joy-mixed pain
    Just as the veil of hope began to fall,
The Christian murderers over-ran the plain
    Ravaging, burning, and polluting all.—
Zeinab was reft to grace the robbers' land;   35
Each drop of kindred blood stained the invaders' brand.

Yes! they had come their holy book to bring,
    Which God's own son's apostles had compiled
That charity and peace and love might spring
    Within a world by God's blind ire defiled.   40
But rapine, war and treachery rushed before
Their hosts, and murder dyed Kathema's bower in gore.

    13–24 *See n.*   14 sea,] sea *Esd.*   16 radiancy.] radiancy *Esd.*
19 betrothèd. For] betrothed . . . for *Esd.*   24 care.] care *Esd.*   25 spell,]
spell *Esd.*   26 gave,] gave; *Esd.*

Therefore his soul was widowed, and alone
 He stood in the world's wide and drear expanse;
No human ear could shudder at his groan,   45
 No heart could thrill with his unspeaking glance,—
One only hope yet lingering dared to burn,
Urging to high emprize and deeds that danger spurn.

The glow has failed on Ocean's western line,
 Faded from every moveless cloud above;   50
The moon is up—she that was wont to shine
 And bless thy childish nights of guileless love,
Unhappy one, ere Christian rapine tore
All ties and stained thy hopes in a dear mother's gore.

The form that in the setting sun was seen   55
 Now in the moonlight slowly nears the shore,
The white sails gleaming o'er the billows green
 That sparkle into foam its prow before,—
A wanderer of the deep it seems to be,
On high adventures bent and feats of chivalry.   60

Then hope and wonder filled the mourner's mind;
 He gazed till vision even began to fail;
When, to the pulses of the evening wind,
 A little boat approaching gave its sail,
Rode on the slow-raised surges near the strand,   65
Ran up the beach and gave some stranger men to land.

'If thou wilt bear me to far England's shore,
 Thine is this heap—the Christian's God.'
The chief with gloating rapture viewed the ore,
 And his pleased avarice gave the willing nod;   70
They reach the ship, the freshening breezes rise,
And smooth and fast they speed beneath the moonlight skies.

54 dear *possibly* dead 65 on] *possibly* oer *in Esd.*

What heart e'er felt more ardent longings now?
    What eye than his e'er beamed with riper hope,
As curbed impatience on his open brow   75
    There painted fancy's unsuspected scope?
As all that's fair the foreign land appeared,
By ever-present love, wonder and hope endeared.

Meanwhile through calm and storm, through night and day,
    Unvarying in her aim the vessel went,   80
As if some inward spirit ruled her way
    And her tense sails were conscious of intent,
Till Albion's cliffs gleamed o'er her plunging bow,
And Albion's river-floods bright sparkled round her prow.

Then on the land in joy Kathema leaped,   85
    And kissed the soil in which his hopes were sown—
These even now in thought his heart has reaped.
    Elate of body and soul he journeyed on,
And the strange things of a strange land passed by
Like motes and shadows pressed upon his charmèd eye.   90

Yet Albion's changeful skies and chilling wind
    The change from Cashmire's vale might well denote:
There Heaven and Earth are ever bright and kind,
    Here blights and storms and damp for ever float,
Whilst hearts are more ungenial than the zone,—   95
Gross, spiritless, alive to no pangs but their own.

There flowers and fruits are ever fair and ripe,
    Autumn there mingles with the bloom of spring,
And forms unpinched by frost or hunger's gripe
    A natural veil o'er natural spirits fling,—   100
Here woe on all but wealth has set its foot,
Famine, disease and crime even Wealth's proud gates pollute.

Unquiet death and premature decay,
    Youth tottering on the crutches of old age,
And, ere the noon of manhood's riper day,   105
    Pangs that no art of medicine can assuage,
Madness and passion, ever mingling flames,
And souls that well become such miserable frames—

These are the bribes which Art to man has given,
 To yield his taintless nature to her sway: 110
So might dark night with meteors tempt fair Heaven
 To blot the sunbeam and forswear the day,
Till gleams of baleful light alone might show
The pestilential mists, the darkness and the woe.

Kathema little felt the sleet and wind,   115
 He little heeded the wide-altered scene;
The flame that lived within his eager mind
 There kindled all the thoughts that once had been;
He stood alone in England's varied woe,
Safe, 'mid the flood of crime that round his steps did flow. 120

It was an evening when the bitterest breath
 Of dark December swept the mists along
That the lone wanderer ⟨came to⟩ a wild heath.
 Courage and hope had stayed his nature long;
Now cold and unappeasèd hunger spent   125
His strength; sensation failed in total languishment.

When he awaked to life cold horrors crept
 Even to his heart, for a damp deathy smell
Had slowly come around him while he slept.
 He started—lo, the fitful moonbeams fell   130
Upon a dead and naked female form
That from a gibbet high swung to the sullen storm!

And wildly in the wind her dark hair swung,
 Low mingling with the clangour of the chain,
Whilst ravenous birds of prey that on it clung   135
 In the dull ear of night poured their sad strain,
And ghastlily her shapeless visage shone
In the unsteady light, half mouldered to the bone.

Then madness seized Kathema, and his mind
 A prophecy of horror filled; he scaled   140
The gibbet which swung slowly in the wind
 High o'er the heath.—Scarcely his strength availed
To grasp the chain when, by the moonlight's gleam,
His palsied gaze was fixed on Zeinab's altered frame.

---

123 ⟨came to⟩ *conjecture for smudged words* 127 horrors] *possibly* horror *in Esd.*
133 her *apparently,* over its 138 to *possibly* thro *in Esd.*

Yes!—in those orbs once bright with life and love   145
  Now full-fed worms bask in unnatural light;
That neck on which his eyes were wont to rove
  In rapture, changed by putrefaction's blight,
Now rusts the ponderous links that creak beneath
Its weight, and turns to life the frightful sport of death.   150

Then in the moonlight played Kathema's smile
  Calmly—in peace his spirit seemed to be.
He paused, even like a man at ease awhile,
  Then spoke: 'My love! I will be like to thee,—
A mouldering carcase or a spirit blest,—   155
With thee corruption's prey or Heaven's happy guest!'

He twined the chain around his neck, then leapt
  Forward,—in haste to meet the life to come . . .
An iron-souled son of Europe might have wept
  To witness such a noble being's doom,   160
As on the death-scene Heaven indignant frowned,
And night in horror drew her veil the deed around.

For they had torn his Zeinab from her home,—
  Her innocent habits were all rudely riven
And, dragged to live in love's untimely tomb,   165
  To prostitution, crime and woe was driven;
The human race seemed leagued against her weal
And indignation cased her naked heart in steel.

Therefore against them she waged ruthless war
  With their own arms of bold and bloody crime;   170
Even like a mild and sweetly-beaming star
  Whose rays were wont to grace the matin-prime
Changed to a comet, horrible and bright,
Which wild careers awhile then sinks in dark-red night.

Thus, like its God, unjust and pitiless,   175
  Crimes first are made and then avenged by Man.
For where's the tender heart whose hope can bless
  Or Man's or God's unprofitable plan,—
A universe of horror and decay,
Gibbets, disease and wars and hearts as hard as they?   180

164–6 *See n.*   164 riven] shriven *Esd.*   172 rays *above* [beams]   grace
above [mark]   173 changed to *above* [Even like]   177 hope *above* [heart]

50. *The Retrospect*

Cwm Elan, 1812

To trace Duration's lone career,
To check the chariot of the year,
Whose burning wheels forever sweep
The boundaries of oblivion's deep,—
To snatch from Time the monster's jaw   5
   The children which she just had borne
And, ere entombed within her maw,
   To drag them to the light of morn,
And mark each feature with an eye
Of cold and fearless scrutiny! . . .   10
It asks a soul not formed to feel,
An eye of glass, a hand of steel,
Thoughts that have passed and thoughts that are
With truth and feeling, to compare
A scene which wildered fancy viewed   15
In the soul's coldest solitude,
With that same scene when peaceful love
Flings rapture's colour o'er the grove,
When mountain, meadow, wood and stream
With unalloying glory gleam,   20
And to the spirit's ear and eye
Are unison and harmony.

The moonlight was my dearer day;
Then would I wander far away,
And, lingering on the wild brook's shore   25
To hear its unremitting roar,
Would lose in the ideal flow
All sense of overwhelming woe;
Or at the noiseless noon of night
Would climb some heathy mountain's height,   30

AUTOGRAPH, TITLE: *Esd.*   DATE: *See n., p. 371.*   PRINTED: *15–end, Dowd. 1886/1–end,
Rog. 1966.*   TEXT: *1966/1904/1886/Esd.*
   4 deep,—] deep . . . *Esd.*   10 scrutiny! . . .] scrutiny . . . *Esd.*   14 feeling,]
feeling *Esd.*   compare] compare; *Esd.*   22–3 *Esd. has a space between these lines.
No space in 1886*

And listen to the mystic sound
That stole in fitful gasps around.
I joyed to see the streaks of day
Above the purple peaks decay,
And watch the latest line of light   35
Just mingling with the shades of night;
For day with me was time of woe
When even tears refused to flow;
Then would I stretch my languid frame
   Beneath the wild-wood's gloomiest shade,   40
And try to quench the ceaseless flame
   That on my withered vitals preyed;
Would close mine eyes and dream I were
   On some remote and friendless plain,
And long to leave existence there,   45
   If with it I might leave the pain
That with a finger cold and lean
Wrote madness on my withering mien.

It was not unrequited love
That bade my wildered spirit rove;   50
'Twas not the pride disdaining life,
That with this mortal world at strife
Would yield to the soul's inward sense,
Then groan in human impotence,
And weep because it is not given   55
To taste on Earth the peace of Heaven.
'Twas not that in the narrow sphere
   Where Nature fixed my wayward fate
There was no friend or kindred dear
   Formed to become that spirit's mate,   60
Which, searching on tired pinion, found
Barren and cold repulse around;
Ah, no! yet each one sorrow gave
New graces to the narrow grave.

For broken vows had early quelled   65
The stainless spirit's vestal flame;
Yes! whilst the faithful bosom swelled,
Then the envenomed arrow came,

And Apathy's unaltering eye
Beamed coldness on the misery;   70
And early I had learned to scorn
   The chains of clay that bound a soul
Panting to seize the wings of morn,
And where its vital fires were born
   To soar, and spurn the cold control   75
Which the vile slaves of earthly night
Would twine around its struggling flight.
Oh, many were the friends whom fame
Had linked with the unmeaning name
Whose magic marked among mankind   80
The casket of my unknown mind,
Which hidden from the vulgar glare
Imbibed no fleeting radiance there.
My darksome spirit sought—it found
A friendless solitude around.   85
For who that might undaunted stand,
The saviour of a sinking land,
Would crawl, its ruthless tyrant's slave,
And fatten upon Freedom's grave,
Though doomed with her to perish, where   90
The captive clasps abhorred despair.

They could not share the bosom's feeling,
Which, passion's every throb revealing,
Dared force on the world's notice cold
Thoughts of unprofitable mould,   95
Who bask in Custom's fickle ray,
Fit sunshine of such wintry day!—
They could not in a twilight walk
Weave an impassioned web of talk,
Till mysteries the spirit press   100
In wild yet tender awfulness,
Then feel within our narrow sphere
How little yet how great we are!
But they might shine in courtly glare,
Attract the rabble's cheapest stare,   105

77–8 *Esd. has no space. A space in 1886*   100 spirit *Esd.*] spirits *1886*

And might command where'er they move
A thing that bears the name of love;
They might be learnèd, witty, gay,
Foremost in fashion's gilt array,
On Fame's emblazoned pages shine,   110
Be princes' friends, but never mine!

Ye jagged peaks that frown sublime,
Mocking the blunted scythe of Time,
Whence I would watch its lustre pale
Steal from the moon o'er yonder vale: 115

Thou rock, whose bosom black and vast,
    Bared to the stream's unceasing flow,
Ever its giant shade doth cast
    On the tumultuous surge below:
Woods, to whose depth retires to die   120
The wounded Echo's melody,
And whither this lone spirit bent
The footstep of a wild intent:

Meadows, whose green and spangled breast
These fevered limbs have often pressed,   125
Until the watchful fiend Despair
Slept in the soothing coolness there!—
Have not your varied beauties seen
The sunken eye, the withering mien,
Sad traces of the unuttered pain   130
That froze my heart and burned my brain?

How changed since Nature's summer form
Had last the power my grief to charm,
Since last ye soothed my spirit's sadness,
Strange chaos of a mingled madness!   135
Changed?—not the loathsome worm that fed
In the dark mansions of the dead,
Now soaring through the fields of air,
And gathering purest nectar there,

121 Echo's *1904*] echo's *Esd.*, *1886*

A butterfly, whose million hues   140
The dazzled eye of wonder views,
Long lingering on a work so strange,
Has undergone so bright a change!

How do I feel my happiness?
I cannot tell, but they may guess   145
Whose every gloomy feeling gone,
Friendship and passion feel alone;
Who see mortality's dull clouds
    Before affection's murmur fly,
    Whilst the mild glances of her eye   150
Pierce the thin veil of flesh that shrouds
    The spirit's radiant sanctuary.

O thou! whose virtues latest known,
First in this heart yet claim'st a throne,—
Whose downy sceptre still shall share   155
The gentle sway with virtue there,—
Thou fair in form, and pure in mind,
    Whose ardent friendship rivets fast
The flowery band our fates that bind,
    Which incorruptible shall last   160
When duty's hard and cold control
Had thawed around the burning soul,—
The gloomiest retrospects that bind
With crowns of thorn the bleeding mind,
The prospects of most doubtful hue   165
That rise on Fancy's shuddering view
Are gilt by the reviving ray
Which thou hast flung upon my day.

146 feeling *over* [passion]   152 radiant *Esd.*] inmost *1886*   164 crowns *above*
[coronets]   bleeding *above* the mind   *caret after* the   153–68 *For punctuation*
see n., pp. 372–3.

51. *The Wandering Jew's Soliloquy*

? 1810–11

Is it the Eternal Triune, is it He
Who dares arrest the wheels of destiny
  And plunge me in this lowest Hell of Hells?
Will not the lightning's blast destroy my frame?
  Will not steel drink the blood-life where it swells?   5
  No—let me hie where dark Destruction dwells,
To rouse her from her deeply-caverned lair,
And, taunting her curst sluggishness to ire,
  Light long Oblivion's death-torch at its flame
And calmly mount Annihilation's pyre.   10

  Tyrant of Earth! pale Misery's jackal Thou!
    Are there no stores of vengeful violent fate
    Within the magazines of Thy fierce hate?
No poison in Thy clouds to bathe a brow
    That lowers on Thee with desperate contempt?   15
Where is the noonday Pestilence that slew
    The myriad sons of Israel's favoured nation?
Where the destroying Minister that flew
    Pouring the fiery tide of desolation
Upon the leagued Assyrian's attempt?   20
Where the dark Earthquake-daemon who engorged
At thy dread word Korah's unconscious crew?
Or the Angel's two-edged sword of fire that urged
Our primal parents from their bower of bliss
  (Reared by Thine hand) for errors not their own   25
  By Thine omniscient mind foredoomed, foreknown?
Yes! I would court a ruin such as this,
  Almighty Tyrant, and give thanks to Thee!—
  Drink deeply, drain the cup of hate, remit! . . . Then I
    may die!

AUTOGRAPH, TITLE: *Esd.*   DATE: *See n., p. 373.*   PRINTED: *from a transcript of Esd., with*
The Wandering Jew, Bertram Dobell, 1887/from Esd., Rog. 1966.   TEXT: *1966/Esd.*
  3 this *Esd.*] the *1887*   10–11 *Esd. has a blank space; no space in 1887*
22 thy *Esd.*] the *1887*   27 this, *1887*] this *Esd.*   28 Tyrant,] Tyrant!
Esd., 1887   Thee!—] thee.— *Esd.* Thee— *1887*   29 deeply,] deeply— *Esd., 1887*
hate,] hate— *Esd.* hate; *1887*   remit! . . . Then I] remit then I *Esd.* remit this—I *1887*
    At the end of this poem Shelley notes the last of a series of line-counts which run through
Esd. His total is 2822.

52. *Sonnet*

To Ianthe [*Shelley*]

September 1813

I LOVE thee, baby! for thine own sweet sake;
   Those azure eyes, that faintly dimpled cheek,
   Thy tender frame so eloquently weak,
Love in the sternest heart of hate might wake;
But more when o'er thy fitful slumber bending   5
   Thy mother folds thee to her wakeful heart,
Whilst love and pity, in her glances blending,
   All that thy passive eyes can feel impart;
More, when some feeble lineaments of her
   Who bore thy weight beneath her spotless bosom,   10
As with deep love I read thy face, recur,—
   More dear art thou, O fair and fragile blossom;
Dearest when most thy tender traits express
The image of thy mother's loveliness.

53. *Sonnet*

Evening—to Harriet [*Shelley*]

September 1813

Probably composed 31 July 1813

O THOU bright Sun, beneath the dark blue line
   Of western distance that sublime descendest,
And, gleaming lovelier as thy beams decline,
   Thy million hues to every vapour lendest,
And over cobweb lawn and grove and stream   5
   Sheddest the liquid magic of thy light,
   Till calm Earth, with the parting splendour bright,
Shows like the vision of a beauteous dream!—

∧ AUTOGRAPH, TITLE, DATE: *Esd.*   PRINTED: *Dowd. 1886/Rog. 1966.*   TEXT: *1966/ 1886/Esd.*

∨ AUTOGRAPH, TITLE: *Esd.*   DATE: *Esd., but see n., p. 373.*   PRINTED: *Dowd. 1886/ Rog. 1966.*   TEXT: *1966/1886/Esd.*

What gazer now with astronomic eye
Could coldly count the spots within thy sphere?   10
    Such were thy lover, Harriet, could he fly
The thoughts of all that makes his passion dear,
    And, turning senseless from thy warm caress,
    Pick flaws in our close-woven happiness.

54. *To Harriet* [*Shelley*]

May 1814

THY look of love has power to calm
    The stormiest passion of my soul;
Thy gentle words are drops of balm
    In life's too bitter bowl;
No grief is mine, but that alone   5
These choicest blessings I have known.

Harriet! if all who long to live
    In the warm sunshine of thine eye,
That price beyond all pain must give
    Beneath thy scorn to die—   10
Then hear thy chosen own too late
His heart most worthy of thy hate.

Be thou, then, one among mankind
    Whose heart is harder not for state,
Thou only virtuous, gentle, kind   15
    Amid a world of hate;
And by a slight endurance seal
A fellow-being's lasting weal.

∧ 13 from *above* [to]

∨ TRANSCRIPT: *H. Shelley, in Esd.*   TITLE, DATE: *Esd.*   PRINTED: *Dowd. 1886/Rog. 1966.*
TEXT: *1966/1886/Esd.*

    7 Harriet] Harriett *here and in the title: not in accordance with her normal spelling or*
Shelley's
    After line 18, at the foot of the page, Harriet has added Cook's Hotel.

For pale with anguish is his cheek,
   His breath comes fast, his eyes are dim,   20
Thy name is struggling ere he speak,
   Weak is each trembling limb;
In mercy let him not endure
The misery of a fatal cure.

Oh, trust for once no erring guide!   25
   Bid the remorseless feeling flee;
'Tis malice, 'tis revenge, 'tis pride,
   'Tis anything but thee;
Oh, deign a nobler pride to prove,
And pity if thou canst not love.   30

55. *'Full Many a Mind . . .'*

[See Appendix]

56. *To Harriet* [*? Grove*]

Undated

OH, Harriet, love like mine that glows
   What rolling years can e'er destroy?
Without thee can I tell my woes?
   And with thee can I speak my grief?

Ah no,—past all the futile power   5
   Of words to tell is love like mine;
My love is not the fading flower
   That fleets ere it attain its prime:
A moment of delight with thee
   Would pay me for an age of pain.   10

\/ TRANSCRIPT: *H. Shelley, in Esd.*   TITLE, DATE: *See n., p. 373.*   PRINTED: *Rog.*
1966.   TEXT: *1966/Esd.*

I'll tell not of rapture and joy
  Which swell through the libertine's frame;
That breast must feel bliss with alloy
  That is scorched by so selfish a flame.

It were pleasure to die for my love,   15
  It were rapture to sink in the grave
My eternal affection to prove,
  My ever dear Harriet to save.

Without thee all pleasure were gloom
  And with thee all sorrow were joy;   20
Ere I knew thee, my Harriet, each year
  Passed in mournful rotation away,—
No friend to my bosom was dear,
  Slow rolled the unvarying day.

Shall I wake then those horrors anew   25
  That swelled in my desperate brain
When to Death's darkened portals I flew
  And sought misery's relief to my pain?

That hour which tears thee from me
  Leaves nothing but death and despair,   30
And that, Harriet, never could be
  Were thy mind less enchantingly fair.

'Tis not for the charms of thy form
  Which decay with the swift-rolling year,—
Ah, no! Heaven expands to my sight—   35
  For Elysium with Harriet must be!

57. *'Late was the Night . . .'*

[See Appendix]

24 unvarying] unvayraying *Esd.*   28 misery's] miseries *Esd.*
Written below line 36, still in H. Shelley's hand,
          Cwm Elan / Adieu my love good night.   *See n.*

58. *To St. Irvyne—to Harriet* [*Grove*]

28 February 1805

O'ER thy turrets, St. Irvyne, the winter winds roar,
    The long grass of thy towers streams to the blast;
Must I never, St. Irvyne, then visit thee more?
    Are those visions of transient happiness past?

When with Harriet I sat on the mouldering height,   5
    When with Harriet I gazed on the star-spangled sky,
And the August moon shone through the dimness of night,—
    How swiftly the moments of pleasure fled by!

How swift is a fleeting smile chased by a sigh
    This breast, this poor sorrow-torn breast must confess;   10
Oh Harriet, loved Harriet, though thou art not nigh,
    Think not thy lover thinks of thee less!

How oft have we roamed, through the stillness of eve,
    Through St. Irvyne's old rooms that so fast fade away!
That those pleasure-winged moments were transient I grieve:
    My soul like those turrets falls fast to decay.   16

My Harriet is fled, like a fast-fading dream,
    Which fades ere the vision is fixed on the mind,
But has left a firm love and a lasting esteem
    That my soul to her soul must eternally bind.   20

When my mouldering bones lie in the cold, chilling grave,
    When my last groans are borne o'er Strood's wide lea,
And over my tomb the chill night-tempests rave,
    Then, loved Harriet, bestow one poor thought on me.

TRANSCRIPT: *H. Shelley, in Esd.*   TITLE: *See n., p. 373.*   DATE: *Esd.*   PRINTED: *Rog.*
1966.   TEXT: *1966/Esd.*

THE WANDERING JEW

THE WANDERING JEW

1810

If I will that he tarry till I come, what is that to thee?
Follow thou me.—St. John, xxi. 22.

PREFACE

[By Shelley]

THE subject of the following Poem is an imaginary personage, noted for the various and contradictory traditions which have prevailed concerning him—The Wandering Jew. Many sage monkish writers have supported the authenticity of this fact, the reality of his existence. But as the quoting them would have led me to annotations perfectly uninteresting, although very fashionable, I decline presenting anything to the public but the bare poem, which they will agree with me not to be of sufficient consequence to authorise deep antiquarian researches on its subject. I might, indeed, have introduced, by anticipating future events, the no less grand, although equally groundless, superstitions of the battle of Armageddon, the personal reign of J[esus] C[hrist], &c.; but I preferred, improbable as the following tale may appear, retaining the old method of describing past events: it is certainly more consistent with reason, more interesting, even in works of imagination. With respect to the omission of elucidatory notes, I have followed the well-known maxim of 'Do unto others as thou wouldest they should do unto thee.'

January, 1811.

AUTOGRAPH: *Ballantyne MS.; Stockdale MS.; both now lost. See nn., p. 374.*   DATE: *See nn., p. 375.*   PRINTED: *435, 443–51, 780, 782–90, as epigraphs with* St. Irvyne, PBS, *1811| Selections from Ball.* Edinburgh Lit. Journ., *Nos. 33, 34, and 59, 1829/1–end, from Stockd.,* Fraser's Mag., *1831/780–90, 1401–8,* Medw. *1847/1–end, from 1831, collated with 1829,* Bertram Dobell, *for the Shelley Society, 1887. See nn., pp. 374–5.*   TEXT: *1887, recollated and revised: italicized passages, omitted in 1831,* are *from 1829. See nn., p. 374.*

Q

Canto I

'Me miserable, which way shall I fly?
Infinite wrath and infinite despair—
Which way I fly is hell—myself am hell;
And in this lowest deep a lower deep,
To which the hell I suffer seems a heaven.'

Paradise Lost.

THE brilliant orb of parting day
Diffused a rich and mellow ray,
Above the mountain's brow;
It tinged the hills with lustrous light,
It tinged the promontory's height,   5
Still sparkling with the snow;
And, as aslant it threw its beam,
Tipt with gold the mountain stream
That laved the vale below;
Long hung the eye of glory there,   10
And linger'd as if loth to leave
A scene so lovely and so fair.
'Twere luxury even, there to grieve;
So soft the clime, so balm the air,
So pure and genial were the skies,   15
In sooth 'twas almost Paradise,—
For ne'er did the sun's splendour close
On such a picture of repose.
All, all was tranquil, all was still,
Save when the music of the rill,   20
Or distant waterfall,
At intervals broke on the ear
Which Echo's self was charmed to hear,
And ceased her babbling call.
With every charm the landscape glow'd   25
Which partial Nature's hand bestow'd;
Nor could the mimic hand of art
Such beauties or such hues impart.

---

2 mellow *87, 31*] a mellow *29*   7 And, *29*] And *87, 31*   8 Tipt *87, 31*]
Tipp'd *29*   9 below; *87, 31*] below. *29*   13 luxury even, there to *87, 31*]
there even luxury to *29*   grieve; *29*] grieve. *87, 31*   *18 repose.*] repose;— *87, 29*
20 when *87, 31*] where *29*   21 Or *87, 31*] Or a *29*   23 Echo's *29*] echo's
87, 31   charmed *87, 31*] pleased *29*

Light clouds, in fleeting livery gay,
Hung painted in grotesque array 30
Upon the western sky:
Forgetful of the approaching dawn,
The peasants danced upon the lawn,
For the vintage time was nigh:
How jocund to the tabor's sound, 35
O'er the smooth, trembling turf they bound!—
In every measure light and free,
The very soul of harmony!
Grace in each attitude, they move,
They thrill to amorous ecstasy, 40
Light as the dewdrops of the morn,
That hang upon the blossomed thorn,
Subdued by the pow'r of resistless Love.
Ah! days of innocence, of joy,
Of rapture that knows no alloy,— 45
Haste on, ye roseate hours!
Free from the world's tumultuous cares,
From pale distrust, from hopes and fears,
Baneful concomitants of time,—
'Tis yours, beneath this favour'd clime, 50
Your pathway strewn with flowers,
Upborne on pleasure's downy wing,
To quaff a long unfading spring,
And beat with light and careless step the ground;
The fairest flowers too soon grow sere, 55
Too soon shall tempests blast the year,
And sin's eternal winter reign around!

But see, what forms are those,
Scarce seen by glimpse of dim twilight,
Wandering o'er the mountain's height? 60
They swiftly haste to the vale below:
One wraps his mantle around his brow,
As if to hide his woes;

29 clouds, *87, 31*] clouds *29* 30 Hung *29*] Hung, *87, 31* 36 O'er the smooth, trembling turf *87, 31*] The smooth turf trembling as *29* bound!—] bound, *87, 31, 29*
38 harmony! *29*] harmony; *87, 31* 42 blossomed *87, 31*] blossom'd *29*
45 *alloy,—*] alloy, *87, 29* 46 *on,*] on— *87, 29* *hours!*] hours, *87, 29*
57 *around!*] around. *87, 29*

And as his steed impetuous flies,
What strange fire flashes from his eyes!   65
The far-off city's murmuring sound
Was borne on the breeze which floated around;
Noble Padua's lofty spire
Scarce glow'd with the sunbeam's latest fire,
Yet dashed the travellers on—   70
Ere night o'er the earth was spread,
Full many a mile they must have sped,
Ere their destined course was run.
Welcome was the moonbeam's ray,
Which slept upon the towers so grey.   75
But, hark! a convent's vesper bell—
It seemed to be a very spell—
The stranger checked his courser's rein,
And listened to the mournful sound:
Listened—and paused—and paused again: 80
A thrill of pity and of pain
Through his inmost soul had passed,
While gushed the tear-drops silently and fast.

A crowd was at the convent gate,
The gate was opened wide;   85
No longer on his steed he sate,
But mingled with the tide.
He felt a solemn awe and dread,
As he the chapel entered;
Dim was the light from the pale moon beaming,   90
As it fell on the saint-cyphered panes
Or, from the western window streaming,
Tinged the pillars with varied stains.
To the eye of enthusiasm strange forms were gliding
In each dusky recess of the aisle;   95
And indefined shades in succession were striding
O'er the coignes[1] of the Gothic pile.

---

[1] Buttress nor coigne of vantage.—*Macbeth.* [*Shelley's footnote.*]

88 dread, *31*] dread. *87, 29*   91 saint-cyphered *87, 31*] saint-ciphered *29*   panes
29] panes; *87, 31*   92 Or,] Or *87, 31*   94 gliding *87, 31*] gliding, *29*
96 striding] striding, *87, 31*   97 Gothic] gothic *87, 31* pillar'd *29*   pile. *87, 31*]
pile:— *29*

The pillars to the vaulted roof
In airy lightness rose;
Now they mount to the rich Gothic ceiling aloof,   100
And exquisite tracery disclose.

The altar illumined now darts its bright rays,
The train passed in brilliant array;
On the shrine Saint Pietro's rich ornaments blaze,
And rival the brilliance of day.   105
Hark!—now the loud organ swells full on the ear—
So sweetly mellow, chaste, and clear;
Melting, kindling, raising, firing,
Delighting now, and now inspiring,
Peal upon peal the music floats—   110
Now they list still as death to the dying notes;
Whilst the soft voices of the choir,
Exalt the soul from base desire;
Till it mounts on unearthly pinions free,
Dissolved in heavenly ecstasy.   115

Now a dead stillness reigned around,
Uninterrupted by a sound;
Save when in deadened response ran,
The last faint echoes down the aisle,
Reverberated through the pile,   120
As within the pale the holy man,
With voice devout and saintly look,
Slow chaunted from the sacred book,
Or pious prayers were duly said,
For spirits of departed dead.   125
With beads and crucifix and hood,
Close by his side the abbess stood;
Now her dark penetrating eyes
Were raised in suppliance to heaven,
And now her bosom heaved with sighs,   130
As if to human weakness given.
Her stern, severe, yet beauteous brow
Frowned on all who stood below;

105 day. *31*] day *87. See nn., p. 375.*

And the fire which flashed from her steady gaze,
As it turned on the listening crowd its rays,   135
Superior virtue told,—
Virtue as pure as heaven's own dew,
But which, untainted, never knew,
To pardon weaker mould.
The heart though chaste and cold as snow—   140
'Twere faulty to be virtuous so.

Not a whisper now breathed in the pillared aisle—
The stranger advanced to the altar high—
Convulsive was heard a smothered sigh!
Lo! four fair nuns to the altar draw near,   145
With solemn footstep, as the while
A fainting novice they bear—
The roses from her cheek are fled
But there the lily reigns instead;
Light as a sylph's, her form confest,   150
Beneath the drapery of her vest,
A perfect grace and symmetry;
Her eyes, with rapture form'd to move,
To melt with tenderness and love,
Or beam with sensibility,   155
To Heaven were raised in pious prayer,
A silent eloquence of woe;
Now hung the pearly tear-drop there,
Sate on her cheek a fix'd despair;
And now she beat her bosom bare,   160
As pure as driven snow.
Nine graceful novices around
Fresh roses strew upon the ground:
In purest white arrayed,
Nine spotless vestal virgins shed   165
Sabæan incense o'er the head
Of the devoted maid.

They dragged her to the altar's pale,
The traveller leant against the rail,

162 novices *87, 31*] Novices *29*   163 strew *87, 31*] strew'd *29*   164 arrayed,
87, 31] array'd *29*   165 Nine *87, 31*] Three *29*   166 Sabæan *87, 31*]
Sabean *29*

And gazed with eager eye,—   170
His cheek was flushed with sudden glow,
On his brow sate a darker shade of woe,
As a transient expression fled by.

The sympathetic feeling flew
Through every breast, from man to man,   175
Confused and open clamours ran,
Louder and louder still they grew;
When the abbess waved her hand,
A stern resolve was in her eye,
And every wild tumultuous cry   180
Was stilled at her command.

The abbess made the well known sign—
The novice reached the fatal shrine,
And mercy implored from the power divine;
At length she shrieked aloud,   185
She dashed from the supporting nun,
Ere the fatal rite was done,
And plunged amid the crowd.
Confusion reigned throughout the throng,
Still the novice fled along,   190
Impelled by frantic fear,
When the maddened traveller's eager grasp
In firmest yet in wildest clasp
Arrested her career.
As fainting from terror she sank on the ground,   195
Her loosened locks floated her fine form around;
The zone which confined her shadowy vest
No longer her throbbing bosom prest,
Its animation dead;
No more her feverish pulse beat high,   200
Expression dwelt not in her eye,
Her wildered senses fled.

      .   .   .   .   .

Hark! Hark! the demon of the storm!
I see his vast expanding form
Blend with the strange and sulphurous glare   205
Of comets through the turbid air.

Yes, 'twas his voice, I heard its roar,
The wild waves lashed the caverned shore
In angry murmurs hoarse and loud,
Higher and higher still they rise;   210
Red lightnings gleam from every cloud
And paint wild shapes upon the skies;
The echoing thunder rolls around,
Convulsed with earthquake rocks the ground.

The traveller yet undaunted stood,   215
He heeded not the roaring flood;
Yet Rosa slept, her bosom bare,
Her cheek was deadly pale,
The ringlets of her auburn hair
Streamed in a lengthened trail,   220
And motionless her seraph form;
Unheard, unheeded raved the storm,
Whilst, borne on the wing of the gale,
Came the harrowing shriek of the white sea-mew
As o'er the midnight surge she flew;   225
The howlings of the squally blast
As o'er the beetling cliffs it passed
Mingled with the peals on high,
That, swelling louder, echoed by,
Assailed the traveller's ear.   230
He heeded not the maddened storm
As it pelted against his lofty form,
He felt no awe, no fear—
In contrast, like the courser pale[1]
That stalks along Death's pitchy vale   235
With silent, with gigantic tread,
Trampling the dying and the dead.

Rising from her death-like trance,
Fair Rosa met the stranger's glance;
She started from his chilling gaze,   240
Wild was it as the tempest's blaze,

---

[1] 'Behold a pale horse, and his name that sate upon him was Death, and Hell followed
with him.'—Revelation, vi. 8. [*Shelley's footnote.*]

222–37 *See n. p. 375.*   222 storm] storm. *87, 31*   224 Came the] The
87, 31   227 passed] passed; *87, 31*   233 fear—] fear. *87, 31*

It shot a lurid gleam of light.
A secret spell of sudden dread,
A mystic, strange, and harrowing fear,
As when the spirits of the dead,   245
Drest in ideal shapes appear,
And hideous glance on human sight—
Scarce could Rosa's frame sustain,
The chill that pressed upon her brain.

Anon, that transient spell was o'er,   250
Dark clouds deform his brow no more,
But rapid fled away;
Sweet fascination dwelt around,
Mixed with a soft, a silver sound,
As soothing to the ravished ear   255
As what enthusiast lovers hear,
Which seems to steal along the sky,
When mountain mists are seen to fly,
Before the approach of day.
He seized on wondering Rosa's hand,   260
'And, ah!' cried he, 'be this the band
Shall join us, till this earthly frame,
Sinks convulsed in bickering flame!
When around the demons yell,
And drag the sinful wretch to hell,   265
Then, Rosa, will we part—
Then fate, and only fate's decree,
Shall tear thy lovely soul from me,
And rend thee from my heart!
Long has Paulo sought in vain,   270
A friend to share his grief,—
Never will he seek again,
For the wretch has found relief,
Till the Prince of Darkness bursts his chain,
Till death and desolation reign—   275
Rosa, wilt thou then be mine?
Ever fairest, I am thine!'

He ceased, and on the howling blast,
Which wildly round the mountain passed,

255 ear] ear, *87, 31*   256 hear,] hear; *87, 31*   263 flame!] flame— *87, 31*

Died his accents low;   280
Yet fiercely howled the midnight storm,
As Paulo bent his awful form,
And leaned his lofty brow.

Rosa

'Stranger, mystic stranger, rise;
Whence do these tumults fill the skies?   285
Who conveyed me, say, this night,
To this wild and cloud-capped height?
Who art thou? and why am I
Beneath Heaven's pitiless canopy?
For the wild winds roar around my head;   290
Lightnings redden the wave;—
Was it the power of the mighty dead,
Who live beneath the grave?
Or did the Abbess drag me here,
To make yon swelling surge my bier?'   295

Paulo

'Ah, lovely Rosa! cease thy fear,
It was thy friend who bore thee here—
I, thy friend, till this fabric of earth,
Sinks in the chaos that gave it birth;
Till the meteor-bolt of the God above,   300
Shall tear its victim from his love,—
That love which must unbroken last,
Till the hour of envious fate is past;
Till the mighty basements of the sky
In bickering hell-flames heated fly: 305
E'en then will I sit on some rocky height,
Whilst around lower clouds of eternal night,
E'en then will I loved Rosa save
From the yawning abyss of the grave!
Or, into the gulf impetuous hurled,   310
If sinks with its latest tenants the world,

309 grave!] grave.— *87, 31*   310 hurled,] hurled—*87, 31*

Then will our souls in union fly
Throughout the wide and boundless sky:
Then, free from th' ills that envious fate
Has heaped upon our mortal state,   315
We'll taste ethereal pleasure;
Such as none but thou canst give,—
Such as none but I receive,
And rapture without measure!'

As thus he spoke, a sudden blaze   320
Of pleasure mingled in his gaze:
Illumined by the dazzling light,
He glows with radiant lustre bright;
His features with new glory shine,
And sparkle as with beams divine.   325
'Strange, awful being,' Rosa said,
'Whence is this superhuman dread,
That harrows up my inmost frame?
Whence does this unknown tingling flame,
Consume and penetrate my soul?   330
By turns with fear and love possessed,
Tumultuous thoughts swell high my breast;
A thousand wild emotions roll,
And mingle their resistless tide;
O'er thee some magic arts preside;   335
As by the influence of a charm
Lulled into rest my griefs subside,
And safe in thy protecting arm,
I feel no power can do me harm:
But the storm raves wildly o'er the sea,—   340
Bear me away! I confide in thee!'

319 measure!] measure. *87, 31*   340 sea,—] sea, *87, 31*

Canto II

'I could a tale unfold, whose slightest word
Would harrow up thy soul, freeze thy young blood,
Make thy two eyes, like stars, start from their spheres;
Thy knotted and combined locks to part,
And each particular hair to stand on end,
Like quills upon the fretful porcupine.'—*Hamlet.*

THE horrors of the mighty blast,
The lowering tempest-clouds were past,
Had sunk beneath the main;
Light baseless mists were all that fled,   345
Above the weary traveller's head,
As he left the spacious plain.

Fled were the vapours of the night,
Faint streaks of rosy-tinted light
Were painted on the matin grey;   350
And as the sun began to rise,
To pour his animating ray,
Glowed with his fire the eastern skies,
The distant rocks—the far-off bay,
The ocean's sweet and lovely blue,   355
The mountain's variegated breast,
Blushing with tender tints of dawn,
Or with fantastic shadows drest.
The waving wood, the opening lawn,
Rose to existence, waked anew,   360
In colours exquisite of hue;
Their mingled charms Victorio viewed,
And lost in admiration stood.

From yesternight how changed the scene,
When howled the blast o'er the dark cliff's side,   365
And mingled with the maddened roar
Of the wild surge that lashed the shore!
To-day scarce heard the whispering breeze,
And still and motionless the seas,

361 hue;] hue, *87, 31*   367 shore!] shore. *87, 31*   368 To-day] To-day—
87, 31   369 seas,] seas *87, 31*

Scarce heard the murmuring of their tide;   370
All, all is peaceful and serene!
Serenely on Victorio's breast
It breathed a soft and tranquil rest,
Which bade each wild emotion cease,
And hushed the passions into peace.   375

Along the winding Po he went,
His footsteps to the spot were bent
Where Paulo dwelt, his wandered friend,
For thither did his wishes tend.
Noble Victorio's race was proud,   380
From Cosmo's blood he came;
To him a wild untutored crowd
Of vassals in allegiance bowed,
Illustrious was his name;
Yet vassals and wealth he scorned, to go   385
Unnoticed with a man of woe:
Gay hope and expectation sate,
Throned in his eager eye,
And ere he reached the castle gate,
The sun had mounted high.   390

Wild was the spot where the castle stood,
Its towers embosomed deep in wood;
Gigantic cliffs, with craggy steeps,
Reared their proud heads on high,
Their bases were washed by the foaming deeps,   395
Their summits were hid in the sky;
From the valley below they excluded the day,
That valley ne'er cheered by the sunbeam's ray;
Nought broke on the silence drear,
Save the hungry vultures darting by,   400
Or eagles yelling fearfully,
As they bore to the rocks their prey,
Or when the fell wolf ravening prowled,
Or the gaunt wild boar fiercely howled
His hideous screams on the night's dull ear.   405

371 serene!] serene, *87, 31*   383 vassals] vassals, *87, 31*   392 wood;] wood, *87, 31*

Borne on pleasure's downy wing,
Downy as the breath of spring,
Not thus fled Paulo's hours away,
Though brightened by the cheerful day:
Friendship or wine, or softer love,   410
The sparkling eye, the foaming bowl,
Could with no lasting rapture move,
Nor still the tumults of his soul.
And yet there was in Rosa's kiss
A momentary thrill of bliss;   415
Oft the dark clouds of grief would fly,
Beneath the beams of sympathy;
And love and converse sweet bestow,
A transient requiem from woe.—

Strange business, and of import vast   420
On things which long ago were past,
Drew Paulo oft from home;
Then would a darker, deeper shade,
By sorrow traced, his brow o'erspread
And o'er his features roam.   425
Oft as they spent the midnight hour,
And heard the wintry wild winds rave
Midst the roar and spray of the dashing wave,
Was Paulo's dark brow seen to lour.
Then, as the lamp's uncertain blaze   430
Shed o'er the hall its partial rays,
And shadows strange were seen to fall,
And glide upon the dusky wall,
Would Paulo start with sudden fear.
Why then unbidden gush'd the tear,   435
As he mutter'd strange words to the ear?—
Why frequent heaved the smother'd sigh?—
Why did he gaze on vacancy,
As if some strange form was near?
Then would the fillet of his brow   440
Fierce as a fiery furnace glow,
As it burn'd with red and lambent flame,
Then would cold shuddering seize his frame,

420 vast] vast, *87, 31*   443 shuddering *87, 31*] shudderings *11*

As gasping he labour'd for breath.
The strange light of his gorgon eye,   445
As, frenzied and rolling dreadfully,
It glared with terrific gleam,
Would chill like the spectre gaze of Death,
As, conjured by feverish dream,
He seems o'er the sick man's couch to stand,   450
And shakes the dread lance in his skeleton hand.

But when the paroxysm was o'er,
And clouds deform'd his brow no more,
Would Rosa soothe his tumults dire,
Would bid him calm his grief,   455
Would quench reflection's rising fire,
And give his soul relief.
As on his form with pitying eye,
The ministering angel hung,
And wiped the drops of agony,   460
The music of her syren tongue
Lull'd forcibly his griefs to rest.
Like fleeting visions of the dead,
Or midnight dreams, his sorrows fled:
Waked to new life through all his soul   465
A soft delicious languor stole,
And lapt in heavenly ecstasy
He sank and fainted on her breast.

'Twas on an eve, the leaf was sere,
Howl'd the blast round the castle drear,   470
The boding night-bird's hideous cry
Was mingled with the warning sky;
Heard was the distant torrent's dash,
Seen was the lightning's dark red flash
As it gleamed on the stormy cloud;   475
Heard was the troubled ocean's roar,
As its wild waves lash'd the rocky shore;
The thunder mutter'd loud,

444 breath. *87, 31*] breath; *11*   445 gorgon *87, 31*] meteor *11*   446 As,
87] As *31* Which, *11*   447 It glared *87, 31*] Glar'd *11*   terrific *87, 31*] hideous
11   448 Death *11*] death *87, 31*   449 As, *87*] As *31*   461 syren *87, 31*]
siren *29*   462 rest. *29*] rest *87, 31*   474 flash] flash. *87, 31*

As wilder still the lightnings flew;
Wilder as the tempest blew,   480
More wildly strange their converse grew.

They talk'd of the ghosts of the mighty dead,—
If, when the spark of life were fled,
They visited this world of woe?
Or, were it but a phantasy,   485
Deceptive to the feverish eye,
When strange forms flashed upon the sight,
And stalk'd along at the dead of night?
Or if, in the realms above,
They still, for mortals left below,   490
Retain'd the same affection's glow,
In friendship or in love?
Debating thus, a pensive train,
Thought upon thought began to rise;
Her thrilling wild harp Rosa took;   495
What sounds in softest murmurs broke
From the seraphic strings!
Celestials borne on odorous wings
Caught the dulcet melodies;
The life-blood ebb'd in every vein,   500
As Paulo listen'd to the strain.

SONG

'What sounds are those that float upon the air,
As if to bid the fading day farewell,—
What form is that so shadowy, yet so fair,
Which glides along the rough and pathless dell?   505

Nightly those sounds swell full upon the breeze,
Which seems to sigh as if in sympathy;
They hang amid yon cliff-embosom'd trees,
Or float in dying cadence through the sky.

482 dead,—] dead *87, 31*   492 love?] love,— *87, 31*   498 wings] wings,
87, 31   499 melodies;] melodies, *87, 31*   502 'What *87*] What *31, 29*

Now rests that form upon the moonbeam pale,　　510
In piteous strains of woe its vesper sings;
Now—now it traverses the silent vale,
Borne on transparent ether's viewless wings.

Oft will it rest beside yon abbey's tower,
Which lifts its ivy-mantled mass so high,　　515
Rears its dark head to meet the storms that lour,
And braves the trackless tempests of the sky.

That form, the embodied spirit of a maid
Forced by a perjured lover to the grave;
A desperate fate the madden'd girl obey'd,　　520
And from the dark cliff plung'd into the wave.

There the deep murmurs of the restless surge,
The mournful shriekings of the white sea-mew,
The warring waves, the wild winds, sang her dirge,
And o'er her bones the dark red coral grew.　　525

Yet though that form be sunk beneath the main,
Still rests her spirit where its vows were given;
Still fondly visits each loved spot again,
And pours its sorrows on the ear of Heaven.

That spectre wanders through the abbey dale,　　530
And suffers pangs which such a fate must share;
Early her soul sank in death's darken'd vale,
And ere long all of us must meet her there.'

She ceased, and on the listening ear
Her pensive accents died;　　535
So sad they were, so softly clear,
It seemed as if some angel's sigh
Had breathed the plaintive symphony;

514 abbey's 87, 31] Abbey's 29　　515 high,] high; 87, 31　　518 maid] maid,
87, 31　　521 cliff 31] cliffs 87　　530 abbey 87, 31] Abbey's 29　　533 there.' 87]
there 31, 29

So ravishingly sweet their close,
The tones awakened Paulo's woes;   540
Oppressive recollections rose,
And poured their bitter tide.
Absorbed awhile in grief he stood;
At length he seemed as one inspired,
His burning fillet blazed with blood,   545
A lambent flame his features fired.
'The hour is come, the fated hour;
Whence is this new, this unfelt power?—
Yes, I've a secret to unfold,
And such a tale as ne'er was told,   550
A dreadful, dreadful mystery!
Scenes at whose retrospect e'en now
Cold drops of anguish on my brow,
The icy chill of death I feel:
Wrap, Rosa, bride, thy breast in steel,   555
Thy soul with nerves of iron brace,
As to your eyes I darkly trace,
My sad, my cruel destiny!—

'Victorio, lend your ears, arise,
Let us seek the battling skies,   560
Wild o'er our heads the thunder crashing,
And at our feet the wild waves dashing,
As tempest, clouds, and billows roll,
In gloomy concert with my soul!
Rosa, follow me—   565
For my soul is joined to thine,
And thy being's linked to mine—
Rosa, list to me!'

545 blood,] blood— *87, 31*   552 Scenes] Scenes, *87, 31*   now] now, *87, 31*
553-4 *See n., p. 377.*   558 destiny!] destiny. *87, 31*   562 dashing,] dashing;
87, 31   564 soul!] soul. *87, 31*   568 me!'] me.' *87, 31*

Canto III

'His form had not yet lost
All its original brightness, nor appeared
Less than archangel ruined, and the excess
Of glory obscured; but his face
Deep scars of thunder had intrenched, and care
Sate on his faded cheek.'—*Paradise Lost*.

Paulo

' 'TIS sixteen hundred years ago,
Since I came from Israel's land;   570
Sixteen hundred years of woe!—
With deep and furrowing hand,
God's mark is painted on my head;
Must there remain until the dead
Hear the last trump, and leave the tomb,   575
And earth spouts fire from her riven womb.

'*How can I paint that dreadful day,*
That time of terror and dismay,
When, for our sins, a Saviour died,
And the meek Lamb was crucified!   580
'Twas on that day, as borne along
To slaughter by the insulting throng,
Infuriate for Deicide,
I mocked our Saviour, and I cried,
"Go, go." "Ah! I will go," said he,   585
"Where scenes of endless bliss invite;
To the blest regions of the light
I go, but thou shalt here remain—
Thou diest not till I come again!"
E'en now, by horror traced, I see   590
His perforated feet and hands;

581 'Twas on *29*] As dread *87, 31*   as *29*] when *87, 31*   585 said he, *87, 31*]
he said *29*   586 invite; *87, 31*] invite, *29*   587 light *87, 31*] light; *29*
588 remain— *87, 31*] remain, *29*   589 again!"] again"— *87, 31*

Nor see thy dying day
Till I return again." *29*

The madden'd crowd around him stands,
Pierces his side the ruffian spear,
Big rolls the bitter anguish'd tear;
Hark that deep groan! He dies, he dies!   595
And breathes, in death's last agonies,
Forgiveness to his enemies!
Then was the noon-day glory clouded,
The sun in pitchy darkness shrouded;
Then were strange forms through the darkness
  gleaming,   600
And the red orb of night on Jerusalem beaming,
Which faintly, with ensanguined light,
Dispersed the thickening shades of night.
Convulsed, all nature shook with fear,
As if the very end was near;   605
Earth to her centre trembled;
Rent in twain was the temple's veil,
The graves gave up their dead;
Whilst ghosts and spirits, ghastly pale,
Glared hideous on the sight,   610
Seen through the dark and lurid air,
As fiends, array'd in light,
Threw on the scene a frightful glare,
And, howling, shriek'd with hideous yell—
They shriek'd in joy, for a Saviour fell!   615
'Twas then I felt the Almighty's ire;
Then full on my remembrance came
Those words despised, alas, too late!
The horrors of my endless fate

592 stands, *29*] stands. *87, 31* 594 tear; *29*] tear. *87, 31* 595 *Thus 29*
Hark, that deep groan!—he dies—he dies. *87, 31* 597 enemies! *29*] enemies. *87, 31*
599 shrouded; *29*] shrouded. *87, 31* 601 beaming, *29*] beaming; *87, 31*
603 night. *87, 31*] night; *29*
605–24

  Earth trembled as if the end was near.
  Rent was the Temple's veil in twain—
  The graves gave up their dead again.
  'Twas then I felt the Almighty's ire—
  Those words flashed on my soul, my frame,
  Scorched breast and brain as with a flame
  Of unextinguishable fire! *31*

612 *fiends*,] fiends *87, 29* 618 *despised, alas*,] despised alas! *87, 29*

Flashed on my soul and shook my frame;   620
They scorch'd my breast as with a flame
Of unextinguishable fire;
An exquisitely torturing pain
Of frenzying anguish fired my brain.
By keen remorse and anguish driven,   625
I called for vengeance down from Heaven;
But, ah! the all-wasting hand of Time,
Might never wear away my crime!
I scarce could draw my fluttering breath—
Was it the appalling grasp of death?   630
I lay entranced, and deemed he shed
His dews of poppy o'er my head;
But though the kindly warmth was dead,
The self-inflicted torturing pangs
Of conscience lent their scorpion fangs,   635
Still life prolonging, after life was fled.

'Methought, what glories met my sight,
As burst a sudden blaze of light—
Illumining the azure skies,
I saw the blessed Saviour rise!   640
But how unlike to him who bled!—
Where then this thorn-encircled head?
Where the big drops of agony
Which dimmed the lustre of his eye,
Or deathlike hue that overspread   645
The features of that heavenly face?
Gone now was every mortal trace;
His eyes with radiant lustre beamed—
His form confessed celestial grace,
And with a blaze of glory streamed.   650
Innumerable hosts around,
Their brows with wreaths immortal crowned,
With amaranthine chaplets bound,
As on their wings the cross they bore,
Deep dyed in the Redeemer's gore,   655

626 Heaven;] Heaven. *87, 31*   638 light—] light, *87, 31*   640 rise!] rise.
87, 31   641 bled!—] bled! *87, 31*   644 eye,] eye? *87, 31*

Attune their golden harps, and sing
Loud hallelujahs to their King!

'But, in an instant, from my sight,
Fled were the visions of delight.
Darkness had spread her raven pall;   660
Dank, lurid darkness cover'd all.
All was as silent as the dead;
I felt a petrifying dread,
Which harrowed up my frame;
When suddenly a lurid stream   665
Of dark red light, with hideous gleam,
Shot like a meteor through the night,
And painted Hell upon the skies—
The Hell from whence it came.
What clouds of sulphur seemed to rise!   670
What sounds were borne upon the air!
The breathings of intense despair—
The piteous shrieks—the wails of woe—
The screams of torment and of pain—
The red-hot rack—the clanking chain!   675
I gazed upon the gulf below,
Till, fainting from excess of fear,
My tottering knees refused to bear
My odious weight—I sink—I sink!
Already had I reached the brink.   680
The fiery waves disparted wide,
To plunge me in their sulphurous tide;
When, racked by agonizing pain,
I started into life again.

'Yet still the impression left behind   685
Was deeply graven on my mind,
In characters whose inward trace
No change or time could e'er deface;
A burning cross illumed my brow,
I hid it with a fillet grey,   690
But could not hide the wasting woe

657 King!] King. *87, 31*   672–5 *See nn., p. 375.*   679 weight—] weight. *87, 31*

That wore my wildered soul away,
And ate my heart with living fire:
I knew it was the avenger's sway,
I felt it was the avenger's ire!   695

'A burden on the face of earth,
I cursed the mother who gave me birth;
I cursed myself—my native land!
Polluted by repeated crimes,
I sought in distant foreign climes   700
If change of country could bestow
A transient respite from my woe—
Vain from myself the attempt to fly,
Sole cause of my own misery!

'Since when in death-like trance I lay,   705
Passed, slowly passed, the years away
That poured a bitter stream on me;
Then, all at once, I longed to see
Jerusalem, alas! my native place—
Jerusalem, alas! no more in name: 710
No portion of her former fame
Had left behind a single trace;
Her pomp, her splendour, was no more;
Her towers no longer seem to rise,
To lift their proud heads to the skies;   715
Fane and monumental bust
Long levelled even with the dust,
The holy pavements were stained with gore,
The place where the sacred temple stood
Was crimson-dyed with Jewish blood;   720
Long since, my parents had been dead,
All my posterity had bled
Beneath the dark Crusader's spear—
No friend was left my path to cheer,

693 fire:] fire. *87, 31*   698 land!] land *87, 31*   702 woe—] woe. *87, 31*
704 misery!] misery. *87, 31*   705 when] when, *87, 31*   708 Then, all at
once, I] When once I fondly *87, 31*   709 place—] place, *87, 31*   710 name:]
name, *87, 31*   712 trace;] trace. *87, 31*   713 more;] more. *87, 31*   715 skies;]
skies. *87, 31*   716 bust] bust, *87, 31*   717 dust,] dust. *87, 31*   718 gore,]
gore. *87, 31*   720 blood;] blood. *87, 31*   723 spear—] spear, *87, 31*

To shed a few last setting rays   725
Of sunshine on my evening days!

'*Rack'd by the tortures of the mind,*
How have I long'd to plunge beneath
The mansions of repelling death,
And strove that resting place to find   730
Where earthly sorrows cease!
Oft, when the tempest-fiends engaged,
And the warring winds tumultuous raged,
Confounding skies with seas,
Then would I rush to the towering height   735
Of the gigantic Teneriffe,
Or some precipitous cliff,
All in the dead of the silent night.

'*I have cast myself from the mountain's height,*
Above was day—below was night;   740
The substantial clouds that lower'd beneath
Bore my destested form;
They whirl'd it above the volcanic breath,

727–63   How have I longed to plunge beneath
                     The mansions of repelling death
                     Where earthly sorrows cease!
                     Oft have I rushed to the towering height
                     Of the gigantic Teneriffe,
                     Or some precipitous cliff,
                     All in the dead of the stormy night,
                     And flung me to the seas.
                     The substantial clouds that lower'd beneath,
                     Bore my detested form;
                     They whirl'd it above volcanic breath,
                     And the meteors of the storm.
                     Hark to the thunder's awful crash!
                     Hark to the midnight lightning's hiss!
                     At length was heard a sullen dash,
                     Which made the hollow rocks around
                     Rebellow to the awful sound,
                     The yawning ocean opening wide,
                     Received me in its vast abyss,
                     And whelm'd me in its foaming tide—
                     My astounded senses fled!
                     Oh! would that I had waked no more,
                     But the wild surge swept my corpse ashore—
                     I was not with the dead!   *31*

729 *death,*] death! *87, 29*   731 *cease!*] cease, *87, 29*

And the meteors of the storm;
The torrents of electric flame   745
Scorch'd to a cinder my fated frame.
Hark to the thunder's awful crash—
Hark to the midnight lightning's hiss!
At length was heard a sullen dash,
Which made the hollow rocks around   750
Rebellow to the awful sound;
The yawning ocean opening wide,
Received me in its vast abyss,
And whelm'd me in its foaming tide.
Though my astounded senses fled,   755
Yet did the spark of life remain;
Then the wild surges of the main
Dash'd and left me on the rocky shore.
Oh! would that I had waked no more!
Vain wish! I lived again to feel   760
Torments more fierce than those of hell
A tide of keener pain to roll,
And the bruises to enter my inmost soul!

'I cast myself in Etna's womb,[1]
If haply I might meet my doom,   765

[1] 'I cast myself from the overhanging summit of the gigantic Teneriffe into the wide weltering ocean. The clouds which hung upon its base below, bore up my odious weight; the foaming billows swoln by the fury of the northern blast, opened to receive me, and, burying in a vast abyss, at length dashed my almost inanimate frame against the crags. The bruises entered into my soul, but I awoke to life and all its torments. I precipitated myself into the crater of Vesuvius, the bickering flames and melted lava vomited me up again and though I felt the tortures of the damned, though the sulphureous bitumen scorched the blood within my veins, parched up my flesh and burnt it to a cinder, still did I live to drag the galling chain of existence on. Repeatedly have I exposed myself to the tempestuous battling of the elements; the clouds which burst upon my head in crash terrific and exterminating, and the flaming thunderbolt hurled headlong on me its victim, stunned but not destroyed me. The lightning, in bickering coruscation, blasted me; and like the shattered oak, which remains a monument of faded grandeur, and outlives the other monarchs of the forest, doomed me to live for ever. Nine times did this dagger enter into my heart—the ensanguined tide of existence followed the repeated plunge; at each stroke, unutterable anguish seized my frame, and every limb was convulsed by the pangs of approaching dissolution. The wounds still closed, and still I breathe the hated breath of life.'

I have endeavoured to deviate as little as possible from the extreme sublimity of idea which the *style* of the German author, of which this is a translation, so forcibly impresses. [*Shelley's footnote.*]

761 *hell*] hell! *87, 29*

In torrents of electric flame;
Thrice happy had I found a grave
'Mid fierce combustion's tumults dire,
'Mid oceans of volcanic fire
Which whirl'd me in their sulphurous wave,   770
And scorched to a cinder my hated frame,
Parch'd up the blood within my veins,
And rack'd my breast with damning pains;
Then hurl'd me from the mountain's entrails dread.
With what unutterable woe   775
Even now I feel this bosom glow—
I burn—I melt with fervent heat—
Again life's pulses wildly beat—
What endless throbbing pains I live to feel!
The elements respect their Maker's seal,—   780
That seal deep printed on my fated head!

'Still like the scathèd pine-tree's height,
Braving the tempests of the night
Have I 'scaped the bickering fire,—
Like the scathèd pine which a monument stands   785
Of faded grandeur, which the brands
Of the tempest-shaken air
Have riven on the desolate heath,
Yet it stands majestic even in death,
And rears its wild form there.   790
Thus have I 'scaped the ocean's roar,
The red-hot bolt from God's right hand,
The flaming midnight meteor brand,
And Etna's flames of bickering fire.
Thus am I doom'd by fate to stand,   795
A monument of the Eternal's ire;
Nor can this being pass away,
Till time shall be no more.

'I pierce with intellectual eye,
Into each hidden mystery;   800
I penetrate the fertile womb
Of nature; I produce to light

780 elements *87, 31*] Elements *47*   seal,— *87, 31*] seal! *47*   781 head!] head.
87, 31   783 night *87, 31*] night, *11, 47*   784 fire,—] fire. *87, 31* flame. *11*
791 roar,] roar *87, 31*

The secrets of the teeming earth,
And give air's unseen embryos birth:
The past, the present, and to come,   805
Float in review before my sight:
To me is known the magic spell,
To summon e'en the Prince of Hell;
Awed by the Cross upon my head,
His fiends would obey my mandates dread,   810
To twilight change the blaze of noon,
And stain with spots of blood the moon—
But that an interposing hand
Restrains my potent arts, my else supreme command.'

He raised his passion-quivering hand,   815
He loosed the grey encircling band,
A burning Cross was there;
Its colour was like to recent blood,
Deep marked upon his brow it stood,
And spread a lambent glare.   820
Dimmer grew the taper's blaze,
Dazzled by the brighter rays,
Whilst Paulo spoke—'twas dead of night—
Fair Rosa shuddered with affright;
Victorio, fearless, had braved death   825
Upon the blood-besprinkled heath;
Had heard, unmoved, the cannon's roar,
Echoing along the Wolga's shore,
When the thunder of battle was swelling,
When the birds for their dead prey were yelling,   830
When the ensigns of slaughter were streaming,
And falchions and bayonets were gleaming,
And almost felt death's chilling hand,
Stretched on ensanguined Wolga's strand,
And, careless, scorned for life to cry.   835
Yet now he turned aside his eye,
Scarce could his death-like terror bear,
And owned now what it was to fear.

'Once a funeral met my aching sight,
It blasted my eyes at the dead of night,   840

828 shore,] shore. *87, 31*   835 cry.] cry, *87, 31*

When the sightless fiends of the tempests rave,
And hell-birds howl o'er the storm-blacken'd wave.
Nought was seen, save at fits, but the meteor's glare
And the lightnings of God painting hell on the air;
Nought was heard save the thunder's wild voice in the
    sky,   845
And strange birds who, shrieking, fled dismally by.
'Twas then from my head my drench'd hair that I tore,
And bade my vain dagger's point drink my life's gore;
'Twas then I fell on the ensanguined earth,
And cursed the mother who gave me birth!   850
My maddened brain could bear no more—
Hark! the chilling whirlwind's roar;
The spirits of the tombless dead
Flit around my fated head,—
Howl horror and destruction round,   855
As they quaff my blood that stains the ground,
And shriek amid their deadly stave,—
"Never shalt thou find the grave!
Ever shall thy fated soul
In life's protracted torments roll,   860
Till, in latest ruin hurl'd,
And fate's destruction, sinks the world!
Till the dead arise from the yawning ground,
To meet their Maker's last decree,
Till angels of vengeance flit around,   865
And loud-yelling demons seize on thee!"

'Ah! would were come that fated hour,
When the clouds of chaos around shall lower;
When this globe calcined by the fury of God
Shall sink beneath his wrathful nod!'   870

As thus he spake, a wilder gaze
Of fiend-like horror lit his eye
With a most unearthly blaze,
As if some phantom-form passed by.
At last he stilled the maddening wail   875
Of grief, and thus pursued his tale:—

848 bade *87, 31*] bid *29*

'Oft I invoke the fiends of hell,
And summon each in dire array—
I know they dare not disobey
My stern, my powerful spell.   880
—Once on a night, when not a breeze
Ruffled the surface of the seas,
The elements were lulled to rest,
And all was calm save my sad breast—
On death resolved, intent,   885
I marked a circle round my form;
About me sacred reliques spread,
The reliques of magicians dead,
And potent incantations read—
I waited their event.   890

'All at once grew dark the night,
Mists of swarthiness hung o'er the pale moonlight.
Strange yells were heard, the boding cry
Of the night raven that flitted by,
Whilst the silver-winged mew   895
Startled with screams o'er the dark wave flew.
'Twas then I seized a magic wand,
The wand by an enchanter given,
And deep dyed in his heart's red blood.
The crashing thunder pealed aloud;   900
I saw the portentous meteor's glare
And the lightnings gleam o'er the lurid air;
I raised the wand in my trembling hand,
And pointed Hell's mark at the zenith of Heaven.

'A superhuman sound   905
Broke faintly on the listening ear,
Like to a silver harp the notes,
And yet they were more soft and clear.
I wildly strained my eyes around—
Again the unknown music floats.   910
Still stood Hell's mark above my head—
In wildest accents I summoned the dead—
And through the unsubstantial night,

884 breast—] breast, *87, 31*   885 resolved,] resolved—*87, 31*

It diffused a strange and fiendish light;
Spread its rays to the charnel-house air,   915
And marked mystic forms on the dark vapours there.
The winds had ceased—a thick dark smoke
From beneath the pavement broke;
Around ambrosial perfumes breathe
A fragrance, grateful to the sense,   920
And bliss, past utterance, dispense.
The heavy mists, encircling, wreath,
Disperse, and gradually unfold
A youthful female form;—she rode
Upon a rosy-tinted cloud;   925
Bright stream'd her flowing locks of gold;
She shone with radiant lustre bright,
And blazed with strange and dazzling light;
A diamond coronet deck'd her brow,
Bloom'd on her cheek a vermeil glow;   930
The terrors of her fiery eye
Pour'd forth insufferable day,
And shed a wildly lurid ray.
A smile upon her features play'd,
But there, too, sate portray'd   935
The inventive malice of a soul
Where wild demoniac passions roll;
Despair and torment on her brow,
Had mark'd a melancholy woe
In dark and deepen'd shade.   940
Under those hypocritic smiles,
Deceitful as the serpent's wiles,
Her hate and malice were conceal'd;
Whilst on her guilt-confessing face,
Conscience, the strongly printed trace   945
Of agony betray'd,
And all the fallen angel stood reveal'd.
She held a poniard in her hand,
The point was tinged by the lightning's brand;
In her left a scroll she bore,   950
Crimson'd deep with human gore;
And, as above my head she stood,
Bade me smear it with my blood.

She said that when it was my doom
That every earthly pang should cease,   955
The evening of my mortal woe
Would close beneath the yawning tomb;
And, lull'd into the arms of death,
I should resign my labouring breath;
And in the sightless realms below   960
Enjoy an endless reign of peace.
She ceased—oh, God, I thank thy grace,
Which bade me spurn the deadly scroll!
Uncertain for a while I stood—
The dagger's point was in my blood.   965
Even now I bleed!—I bleed!
When suddenly what horrors flew,
Quick as the lightnings, through my frame;
Flash'd on my mind the infernal deed,
The deed which would condemn my soul   970
To torments of eternal flame.
Drops colder than the cavern dew
Quick coursed each other down my face,
I labour'd for my breath;
At length I cried, "Avaunt! thou fiend of Hell,   975
Avaunt! thou minister of death!"
I cast the volume on the ground,
Loud shriek'd the fiend with piercing yell,
And more than mortal laughter peal'd around.
The scatter'd fragments of the storm   980
Floated along the Demon's form,
Dilating till it touched the sky;
The clouds that roll'd athwart his eye,
Reveal'd by its terrific ray,
Brilliant as the noontide day,   .   985
Gleam'd with a lurid fire;
Red lightnings darted around his head,
Thunders hoarse as the groans of the dead,
Pronounced their Maker's ire;
A whirlwind rush'd impetuous by,   990
Chaos of horror fill'd the sky;

954 said] said, *87, 31*   955 cease,] cease; *87, 31*   963 scroll!] scroll; *87, 31*
968 lightnings,] lightnings *87, 31*

I sunk convulsed with awe and dread.
When I waked the storm was fled,
But sounds unholy met my ear,
And fiends of hell were flitting near! 995

'Here let me pause—here end my tale,
My mental powers begin to fail;
At this short retrospect I faint:
Scarce beats my pulse—I lose my breath,
I sicken even unto death. 1000
Oh! hard would be the task to paint
And gift with life past scenes again;
To knit a long and linkless chain,
Or strive minutely to relate
The varied horrors of my fate. 1005
Rosa! I could a tale disclose,
So full of horror—full of woes,
Such as might blast a demon's ear,
Such as a fiend might shrink to hear—
But, no—' 1010

Here ceased the tale. Convulsed with fear,
The tale yet lived in Rosa's ear—
She felt a strange mysterious dread,
A chilling awe as of the dead.
Gleamed on her sight the demon's form? 1015
Heard she the fury of the storm?
The cries and hideous yells of death?
Tottered the ground her feet beneath?
Was it the fiend before her stood?
Saw she the poniard drop with blood? 1020
All seemed to her distempered eye
A true and sad reality.

.   .   .   .   .

995 near!] near. *87, 31*   1014 dead.] dead; *87, 31*   1015 form?] form. *87, 31*

Canto IV

Οὔτοι γυναῖκας, ἀλλὰ Γοργόνας λέγω·
οὐδ' αὖτε Γοργείοισιν εἰκάσω τύποις
. . . μέλαιναι δ', ἐς τὸ πᾶν βδελύκτροποι·
ῥέγκουσι, δ' οὐ πλατοῖσι φυσιάμασιν·
ἐκ δ' ὀμμάτων λείβουσι δυσφιλῆ βίαν.

Æschylus, Eumenides, 48-54.

'————What are ye
So withered and so wild in your attire,
That look not like th' inhabitants of earth,
And yet are on't?—Live you, or are you aught
That man may question?'   Macbeth.

AH! why does man, whom God has sent
As the Creation's ornament,
Who stands amid his works confest   1025
The first, the noblest, and the best—
Whose vast, whose comprehensive eye,
Is bounded only by the sky—
O'erlook the charms which Nature yields,
The garniture of woods and fields,   1030
The sun's all vivifying light,
The glory of the moon by night,
And to himself alone a foe,
Forget from whom these blessings flow?
And is there not in friendship's eye,   1035
Beaming with tender sympathy,
An antidote to every woe?
And cannot woman's love bestow
An heav'nly paradise below?
Such joys as these to man are given,   1040
And yet you dare to rail at Heaven,
Vainly oppose the Almighty Cause,
Transgress His universal laws,
Forfeit the pleasures that await
The virtuous in this mortal state,   1045

1026 The first—the noblest—and the best; *87, 31*   1027 vast,] vast—*87, 31*
1028 sky—] sky, *87, 31*   1037 woe? *87, 31*] woe *29*   1041 Heaven, *29*]
Heaven; *87, 31*   1043 laws, *29*] laws; *87, 31*   1045 state, *29*] state; *87, 31*

Question the goodness of the Power on high,
In misery live, despairing die!
What then is man, how few his days,
And heighten'd by what transient rays!—
Made up of plans of happiness,   1050
Of visionary schemes of bliss!
The varying passions of his mind
Inconstant, varying as the wind;
Now hush'd to apathetic rest,
Now tempested with storms his breast,   1055
Now with the fluctuating tide
Sunk low in meanness, swoln with pride,—
Thoughtless, or overwhelm'd with care,
Hoping, or tortured by despair!

The sun had sunk beneath the hill,   1060
Soft fell the dew, the scene was still;
All nature hailed the evening's close.
Far more did lovely Rosa bless
The twilight of her happiness;
Even Paulo blest the tranquil hour   1065
As in the aromatic bower,
Or wandering through the olive grove,
He told his plaintive tale of love;
But welcome to Victorio's soul
Did the dark clouds of evening roll!   1070
But, ah! what means his hurried pace,
Those gestures strange, that varying face,
Now pale with mingled rage and ire,
Now burning with intense desire?—
That brow where brood the imps of care,   1075
That fixed expression of despair,
That haste, that labouring for breath?—
His soul is madly bent on death:
A dark resolve is in his eye,—

1047 die!] die. *87, 29*   1049 rays!—] rays; *87, 31* rays, *29*   1051 *bliss!*]
bliss, *87, 29*   1055 breast, *29*] breast; *87, 31*   1057 pride,—] pride; *87, 31*
pride *29*   1064 happiness;] happiness. *87, 31*   1071–81 *See nn., p. 375.*
1072 face,] face; *87, 31*   1074 desire?—] desire; *87, 31*   1077 breath?—]
breath— *87, 31*   1078 death:] death. *87, 31*   1079 eye,—] eye, *87, 31*

Victorio raves—I hear him cry,   1080
'Rosa is Paulo's eternally.'

But whence is that soul-harrowing moan,
Deep drawn and half supprest—
A low and melancholy tone,
That rose upon the wind?   1085
Victorio wildly gazed around,
He cast his eyes upon the ground,
He raised them to the spangled air,
But all was still—was quiet there.
Hence, hence, this superstitious fear!   1090
'Twas but the fever of his mind
That conjured the ideal sound,
To his distempered ear!

With rapid step, with frantic haste,
He scoured the long and dreary waste;   1095
And now the gloomy cypress spread
Its darkened umbrage o'er his head;
The stately pines above him high,
Lifted their tall heads to the sky;
Whilst o'er his form the poisonous yew   1100
And melancholy nightshade threw
Their baleful deadly dew.
At intervals the moon shone clear;
Yet, passing o'er her disk, a cloud
Would now her silver beauty shroud.   1105
The autumnal leaf was parched and sere;
It rustled like a step to fear.
The precipice's battled height
Was dimly seen through the mists of night,
As Victorio moved along.   1110
At length he reach'd its summit dread,
The night-wind whistled round his head
A wild funereal song.
A dying cadence swept around
Upon the waste of air,   1115
It scarcely might be called a sound,
For stillness yet was there,

1090 fear!] fear; *87, 31*   1093 ear!] ear. *87, 31*   1100 form] form, *87, 31*

Save when the roar of the waters below
Was wafted by fits to the mountain's brow.
Here for a while Victorio stood   1120
Suspended o'er the yawning flood,
And gazed upon the gulf beneath.
No apprehension paled his cheek,
No sighs from his torn bosom break,
No terror dimm'd his eye.   1125
'Welcome, thrice welcome, friendly death.'
In desperate harrowing tone he cried,
'Receive me, ocean, to your breast,
Hush this ungovernable tide,
This troubled sea to rest.   1130
Thus do I bury all my grief—
This plunge shall give my soul relief,
This plunge into eternity!'
I see him now about to spring
Into the watery grave: 1135
Hark, the death angel flaps his wing
O'er the blacken'd wave!
Hark, the night-raven shrieks on high
To the breeze which passes on!
Clouds o'ershade the moonlight sky—   1140
The deadly work is almost done—
When a soft and silver sound,
Softer than the fairy song,
Which floats at midnight hour along
The daisy-spangled ground,   1145
Was borne upon the wind's soft swell.
Victorio started—'twas the knell
Of some departed soul;
Now on the pinion of the blast,
Which o'er the craggy mountain pass'd,   1150
The lengthen'd murmurs roll—
Till, lost in ether, dies away
The plaintive, melancholy lay.
'Tis said congenial sounds have power
To dissipate the mists that lower   1155

1121 o'er 87, 31] on 29   1136 Hark,] Hark! 87, 31   1137 wave!] wave. 87, 31
1138 Hark,] Hark! 87, 29   1139 on!] on; 87, 31   1152 Till,] Till 87, 31

Upon the wretch's brow—
To still the maddening passions' war—
To calm the mind's impetuous jar—
To turn the tide of woe.
Victorio shudder'd with affright,   1160
Swam o'er his eyes thick mists of night;
Even now he was about to sink
Into the ocean's yawning womb,
But that the branches of an oak,
Which, riven by the lightning's stroke,   1165
O'erhung the precipice's brink,
Preserved him from the billowy tomb;
Quick throbb'd his pulse with feverish heat,
He wildly started on his feet,
And rush'd from the mountain's height.   1170

The moon was down, but thro' the air
Wild meteors spread a transient glare;
Borne on the wing of the swelling gale,
Above the dark and woody dale,
Thick clouds obscured the sky.   1175
All was now wrapped in silence drear,
Not a whisper broke on the listening ear,
Not a murmur floated by.

In thought's perplexing labyrinth lost
The trackless heath he swiftly crost.   1180
Ah! why did terror blanch his cheek?
Why did his tongue attempt to speak,
And fail in the essay?
Through the dark midnight mists, an eye,
Flashing with crimson brilliancy,   1185
Poured on his face its ray.
What sighs pollute the midnight air?
What mean those breathings of despair?
Thus asked a voice, whose hollow tone
Might seem but one funereal moan.   1190
Victorio groaned, with faltering breath,
'I burn with love, I pant for death!'
Suddenly a meteor's glare,

1172 glare;] glare, *87, 31*

With brilliant flash illumed the air;
Bursting through clouds of sulphurous smoke,　　1195
As on a Witch's form it broke!
Of herculean bulk her frame
Seemed blasted by the lightning's flame;
Her eyes that flared with lurid light,
Were now with bloodshot lustre filled;　　1200
They blazed like comets through the night,
And now thick rheumy gore distilled;
Black as the raven's plume, her locks
Loose streamed upon the pointed rocks,
Wild floated on the hollow gale,　　1205
Or swept the ground in matted trail.
Vile loathsome weeds, whose pitchy fold
Was blackened by the fire of Hell,
Her shapeless limbs of giant mould
Scarce served to hide—as she the while　　1210
'Grinned horribly a ghastly smile'
And shrieked with demon yell.

Terror unmanned Victorio's mind,
His limbs, like lime-leaves in the wind,
Shook, and his brain in wild dismay　　1215
Swam. Vainly he strove to turn away.
'Follow me to the mansions of rest,'
The weird female cried;
The life-blood rushed thro' Victorio's breast
In full and swelling tide.　　1220
Attractive as the eagle's gaze,
And bright as the meridian blaze,
Led by a sanguine stream of light,
He followed through the shades of night—
Before him his conductress fled,　　1225
As swift as the ghosts of the dead,
When on some dreadful errand they fly,
In a thunderblast sweeping the sky.

They reached a rock whose beetling height
Was dimly seen thro' the clouds of night;　　1230

1196 broke!] broke, *87, 31*　　1200 filled;] filled. *87, 31*　　1204 rocks,] rocks; *87,31*
1206 trail.] trail; *87, 31*　　1208 Was] Were *87, 31*　　1216 Swam.] Swam— *87, 31*

Illumined by the meteor's blaze,
Its wild crags caught the reddened rays
And their refracted brilliance threw
Around a solitary yew,
Which stretched its blasted form on high,   1235
Braving the tempests of the sky.
As glared the flame—a caverned cell,
More pitchy than the shades of hell,
Lay open to Victorio's view.
Lost for an instant was his guide;   1240
He rushed into the mountain's side.
At length with deep and harrowing yell
She bade him quickly speed,
For that ere again had risen the moon
'Twas fated that there must be done   1245
A strange—a deadly deed.

Swift as the wind Victorio sped;
Beneath him lay the mangled dead
Around dank putrefaction's power
Had caused a dim blue mist to lower.   1250
Yet an unfixed, a wandering light
Dispersed the thickening shades of night;
Yet the weird female's features dire
Gleamed through the lurid yellow air
With a deadly livid fire,   1255
Whose wild, inconstant, dazzling light
Dispelled the tenfold shades of night;
Whilst her hideous fiendlike eye
Fixed on her victim with horrid stare
Flamed with more kindled radiancy—   1260
More frightful far than that of Death,
When exulting he stalks o'er the battle heath,
Or of the dread prophetic form,
Who rides the curled clouds in the storm,
And borne upon the tempest's wings,   1265
Death, despair, and horror brings.
Strange voices then and shrieks of death
Were borne along the trackless heath;

1254 air] air: *87, 31* 1257 night;] night *87, 31* 1260 radiancy—] radiancy;
87, 31 1262 heath,] heath; *87, 31*

Tottered the ground his steps beneath;
Rustled the blast o'er the dark cliff's side,   1270
And their works unhallowed spirits plied,
As they shed their baneful breath.

Yet Victorio hastened on—
Soon the dire deed will be done.
'Mortal', the female cried, 'this night   1275
Shall dissipate thy woe;
And, ere return of morning light
The clouds that shade thy brow,
Like fleeting summer mists shall fly
Before the sun that mounts on high.   1280
I know the wishes of thy heart—
A soothing balm I could impart:
Rosa is Paulo's—can be thine,
For the secret power is mine.'

Victorio

'Give me that secret power—Oh! give   1285
To me fair Rosa—I will live
To bow to thy command!
Rosa but mine—and I will fly
E'en to the regions of the sky,
Will traverse every land!'   1290

Witch

'Calm then those transports and attend,
Mortal, to one, who is thy friend—
The charm begins.'

                    An ancient book
Of mystic characters she took;
Her loose locks floated on the air,   1295
Her eyes were fixed in lifeless stare,

1287 command!] command. *87, 31*   1290 land!'] land.' *87, 31*   1295 air,
29] air; *87, 31*   1296 stare, *29*] stare: *87, 31*

She traced a circle on the floor;
Around dank chilling vapours lower;
A golden cross on the pavement she threw;
'Twas tinged with a flame of lambent blue,   1300
From which bright scintillations flew;—
By it she cursed her Saviour's soul!
Around strange fiendish laughs did roll,
A hollow, wild, and frightful sound,
At fits was heard to float around.   1305
She uttered then, in accents dread,
Some maddening rhyme that wakes the dead,
And forces every shivering fiend
To her their demon-forms to bend.
At length a wild and piercing shriek,   1310
As the dark mists disperse and break,
Announced the coming Prince of Hell—
His horrid form obscured the cell!
Victorio shrunk, unused to shrink,
E'en at extremest danger's brink;   1315
The witch then pointed to the ground,
Infernal shadows flitted around,
And with their prince were seen to rise;
The cavern bellows with their cries,

1298 lower; 29] lower: 87, 31   1299 threw; 29] threw, 87, 31   1300 with
87, 31] by 29   1301 flew;— 29] flew; 87, 31   1302 soul! 29] soul; 87, 31
1303-5

> Then savage laughter round did roll,
> A hollow, wild, and frightful sound,
> In air above, and under ground.   29

1308 fiend] fiend, 87, 31   1309 bend. 29] bend; 87, 31   1313 cell!] cell. 87, 31
1313-21

> But when his form obscured the cell,
> What words could paint, what tongue could tell,
> The terrors of his look!
> The witch's heart unused to shrink
> Even at extremest danger's brink,
> With deadliest terror shook!
> And with their Prince were seen to rise
> Spirits of every shape and hue,—
> A hideous and infernal crew,
> With hell-fires flashing from their eyes.
> The cavern bellows with their cries,
> Which, echoing through a thousand caves,
> Sound like as many tempest-waves.   29

Which echoing through a thousand caves,   1320
Sound like as many tempest waves.

Inspired and wrapt in bickering flame,
The strange, the awful being stood;—
Words unpremeditated came,
In unintelligible flood   1325
From her black tumid lips—array'd
In livid fiendish smiles of joy—
Lips, which now dropped with deadly dew,
And now, extending wide, displayed
Projecting teeth of mouldy blue.   1330
As with a loud and piercing cry
A mystic, harrowing lay she sang,
Along the rocks a death-peal rang;
In accents hollow, deep and drear,
They struck upon Victorio's ear;   1335
As ceased the soul-appalling verse,
Obedient to its power, grew still
The hellish shrieks;—the mists disperse;—
Satan—a shapeless, hideous beast—
In all his horrors stood confest!   1340
And as his vast proportions fill
The lofty cave, his features dire
Gleam with a pale and sulphurous fire;
From his fixed glance of deadly hate
Even she shrunk back, appalled with dread—   1345
For there contempt and malice sate,
And from his basiliskine eye
Sparks of living fury fly,
Which wanted but a being to strike dead.

A wilder, a more awful spell   1350
Now echoed through the long-drawn cell;

1323 The strange, the awful being *87, 31*] The strange and wild enchantress *29*
stood;— *29*] stood. *87, 31*   1325 flood *31*] flood. *87, 29*   1326 lips— *29*]
lips,— *87, 31*   1327 joy— *29*] joy; *87, 31*   1329 displayed] displayed, *87,
31, 29*   1330 blue. *29*] hue, *87, 31*   1331 cry] cry, *87, 31*   1333 rang;]
rang. *87, 31*
1333–5

          The rocks, as with a death-peal, rang
          And the dread accents, deep and drear,
          Struck terror on the dark night's ear!   *29*

The demon bowed to its mandates dread.
'Receive this potent drug,' he cried,
'Whoever quaffs its fatal tide,
Is mingled with the dead!'   1355
Swept by a rushing sulphurous blast,
Which wildly through the cavern pass'd,
The fatal word was borne.
The cavern trembled with the sound,[1]
Trembled beneath his feet the ground,—   1360
With strong convulsions torn,
Victorio, shuddering, fell.
But soon awakening from his trance,
He cast around a fearful glance—
Yet gloomy was the cell,   1365
Save where a lamp's uncertain flare
Cast a flickering, dying glare.

Witch

'Receive this dear-earned drug—its power
Thou, mortal, soon shalt know:
This drug shall be thy nuptial dower,   1370
This drug shall seal thy woe.
Mingle it with Rosa's wine,
Victorio—Rosa then is thine!'

She spake, and, to confirm the spell,
A strange and subterranean sound   1375
Reverberated long around,
In dismal echoes—the dark cell
Rocked as in terror—through the sky
Hoarse thunders murmured awfully,
And winged with horror, darkness spread   1380
Her mantle o'er Victorio's head.

---

[1]   'Death!
Hell trembled at the hideous name and sighed
From all its caves, and back resounded death.'—*Paradise Lost*. [*Shelley's footnote*.]

1355 dead!'] dead.' *87, 31*   1360 ground,—] ground, *87, 31*   1362 fell.]
fell; *87, 31*   1364 glance—] glance, *87, 31*   1373 thine!'] thine.' *87, 31*

He gazed around with dizzy fear,
No fiend, no witch, no cave, was near;
But the blasts of the forest were heard to roar,
The wild ocean's billows to dash on the shore.   1385
The cold winds of Heaven struck chill on his frame;
For the cave had been heated by hell's blackening flame,
And his hand grasped a casket—the philtre was there!

.   .   .   .

Sweet is the whispering of the breeze
Which scarcely sways yon summer trees;   1390
Sweet is the pale moon's pearly beam,
Which sleeps upon the silver stream,
In slumber cold and still:
Sweet those wild notes of harmony,
Which on the blast that passes by,   1395
Are wafted from yon hill;
So low, so thrilling, yet so clear,
Which strike enthusiast fancy's ear:
Which sweep along the moonlight sky,
Like notes of heavenly symphony.   1400

Song

See yon opening flower
Spreads its fragrance to the blast;
It fades within an hour,
Its decay is pale, is fast.
Paler is yon maiden;   1405
Faster is her heart's decay;
Deep with sorrow laden,
She sinks in death away.

.   .   .   .

'Tis the silent dead of night—
Hark! hark! what shriek so low yet clear,   1410
Breaks on calm rapture's pensive ear,
From Lara's castled height?

1401 flower *87, 31*] rose *47*   1402 blast; *87, 31*] gale; *47*   1404 pale, is fast.
87, 31] fast—is pale *47*

'Twas Rosa's death-shriek fell!
What sound is that which rides the blast,
As onward its fainter murmurs pass'd?   1415
'Tis Rosa's funeral knell!
What step is that the ground which shakes?
'Tis the step of a wretch, nature shrinks from his tread;
And beneath their tombs tremble the shuddering dead;
And while he speaks the churchyard quakes.   1420

Paulo

'Lies she there for the worm to devour?
Lies she there till the judgment hour?
Is then my Rosa dead?
False fiend! I curse thy futile power!
O'er her form will lightnings flash,   1425
O'er her form will thunders crash,
But harmless from my head
Will the fierce tempest's fury fly,
Rebounding to its native sky.—
Who is the God of Mercy?—where   1430
Enthroned the power to save?
Reigns he above the viewless air?
Lives he beneath the grave?
To him would I lift my suppliant moan,
That power should hear my harrowing groan;—   1435
Is it then Christ's terrific Sire?
Ah! I have felt his burning ire,
I feel,—I feel it now,—
His flaming mark is fix'd on my head,

1421 devour?] devour, *87, 31, 29*   1422 hour?] hour, *87, 31, 29*   1423 dead?]
dead! *87, 31, 29*   1431 Enthroned *87, 29*] Enthrones *31*
1437–51

                 Wild anguish glooms my brow;
                 His flaming mark is fixed on my head,
                 And must there remain in traces dread;
                 I feel—I feel it now!'
                 As thus he spoke grew dark the sky,
                 Hoarse thunders murmured awfully,
                 'O Demon! I am thine!' he cried,
                 A hollow, fiendish voice replied,
                 'Come! for thy doom is misery!'   *31*

And must there remain in traces dread!   1440
Wild anguish glooms my brow;
Oh! Griefs like mine that fiercely burn,
Where is the balm can heal?
Where is the monumental urn
Can bid to dust this frame return,   1445
Or quench the pangs I feel?'

As thus he spoke grew dark the sky,
Hoarse thunders murmured awfully,
'O Demon! I am thine!' he cried.
A hollow, fiendish voice replied,   1450
'Come! for thy doom is misery!'

1440 *dread!*] dread; *87, 29*   1443 *heal?*] heal! *87, 29*   1446 *feel?*] feel!
87, 29   1451 *misery!*] misery. *87, 29*

QUEEN MAB

A PHILOSOPHICAL POEM
WITH NOTES

1812–1813

QUEEN MAB

A PHILOSOPHICAL POEM WITH NOTES

1812–1813

ECRASEZ L'INFAME!—*Correspondance de Voltaire.*

Avia Pieridum peragro loca, nullius ante
Trita solo; juvat integros accedere fonteis;
Atque haurire: juvatque novos decerpere flores

. . . .

Unde prius nulli velarint tempora musae.
Primum quod magnis doceo de rebus; et arctis
Religionum animos nodis exsolvere pergo.—*Lucret.* lib. iv.

Δὸς ποῦ στῶ, καὶ κόσμον κινήσω.—*Archimedes.*

[DEDICATION]

To Harriet [Shelley]

VERSION II

For Version I see above, p. 81

WHOSE is the love that gleaming through the world,
Wards off the poisonous arrow of its scorn?
  Whose is the warm and partial praise,
  Virtue's most sweet reward?

Beneath whose looks did my reviving soul   5
Riper in truth and virtuous daring grow?
  Whose eyes have I gazed fondly on,
  And loved mankind the more?

DATE: *See nn., p. 380.*   PRINTED: *PBS, 1813/MWS, 1839¹, 1839²/Hutch.
1904.*   MSS.: *a. Esd., a variant version of the Dedication; see above, p. 81. b. BMᵃ,
letter to E. Hitchener, 14 Feb. 1812, a prose version, with variants, of IX. 26–33. c. BMᵇ,
a copy, formerly owned by T. J. Wise, of 1813, bearing Shelley's autograph revisions for
converting I, II, into* The Daemon of the World, *pub. with* Alastor *in 1816. d. Fn.,
another copy of 1813, formerly owned by Forman, and similarly used by Shelley; in this,
however, not only I and II but also VIII and IX are revised.*   TEXT: *1904/1839²/1839¹/
1813 collated with BMᵃ, BMᵇ, and Forman's account of Fn.*
[DEDICATION]: *omitted in 1839¹.*

Harriet! on thine:—thou wert my purer mind;
Thou wert the inspiration of my song;   10
     Thine are these early wilding flowers,
     Though garlanded by me.

Then press into thy breast this pledge of love;
And know, though time may change and years may roll,
     Each floweret gathered in my heart   15
     It consecrates to thine.

I

     How wonderful is Death,
     Death and his brother Sleep!
One, pale as yonder waning moon
     With lips of lurid blue;
The other, rosy as the morn   5
     When throned on ocean's wave
     It blushes o'er the world:
Yet both so passing wonderful!

     Hath then the gloomy Power
Whose reign is in the tainted sepulchres   10
     Seized on her sinless soul?
     Must then that peerless form
Which love and admiration cannot view
Without a beating heart, those azure veins
Which steal like streams along a field of snow,   15
     That lovely outline, which is fair
     As breathing marble, perish?
     Must putrefaction's breath
Leave nothing of this heavenly sight
     But loathsomeness and ruin?   20
     Spare nothing but a gloomy theme,
On which the lightest heart might moralize?
     Or is it only a sweet slumber
     Stealing o'er sensation,
     Which the breath of roseate morning   25
     Chaseth into darkness?

Will Ianthe wake again,
And give that faithful bosom joy
Whose sleepless spirit waits to catch
Light, life and rapture from her smile?   30

Yes! she will wake again,
Although her glowing limbs are motionless,
And silent those sweet lips,
Once breathing eloquence,
That might have soothed a tiger's rage,   35
Or thawed the cold heart of a conqueror.
Her dewy eyes are closed,
And on their lids, whose texture fine
Scarce hides the dark blue orbs beneath,
The baby Sleep is pillowed: 40
Her golden tresses shade
The bosom's stainless pride,
Curling like tendrils of the parasite
Around a marble column.

Hark! whence that rushing sound?   45
'Tis like the wondrous strain
That round a lonely ruin swells,
Which, wandering on the echoing shore,
The enthusiast hears at evening:
'Tis softer than the west wind's sigh;   50
'Tis wilder than the unmeasured notes
Of that strange lyre whose strings
The genii of the breezes sweep:
Those lines of rainbow light
Are like the moonbeams when they fall   55
Through some cathedral window, but the tints
Are such as may not find
Comparison on earth.

Behold the chariot of the Fairy Queen!
Celestial coursers paw the unyielding air;   60

I. 55-6   Are like such rays as many coloured streams
                 Throw on the roof of some impending crag—
                                       BM^b, Fn., rejected 1816

59   [Behold] the chariot of the Universal Queen
                                         Fn., rejected 1816

Their filmy pennons at her word they furl,
And stop obedient to the reins of light:
   These the Queen of Spells drew in,
   She spread a charm around the spot,
And leaning graceful from the aethereal car,   65
   Long did she gaze, and silently,
      Upon the slumbering maid.

Oh! not the visioned poet in his dreams,
When silvery clouds float through the 'wildered brain,
When every sight of lovely, wild and grand   70
   Astonishes, enraptures, elevates,
     When fancy at a glance combines
     The wondrous and the beautiful,—
   So bright, so fair, so wild a shape
     Hath ever yet beheld,   75
As that which reined the coursers of the air,
   And poured the magic of her gaze
     Upon the maiden's sleep.

   The broad and yellow moon
     Shone dimly through her form—   80
That form of faultless symmetry;
The pearly and pellucid car
   Moved not the moonlight's line:
   'Twas not an earthly pageant:
Those who had looked upon the sight,   85
   Passing all human glory,
   Saw not the yellow moon,
   Saw not the mortal scene,
   Heard not the night-wind's rush,
   Heard not an earthly sound,   90
   Saw but the fairy pageant,
   Heard but the heavenly strains
   That filled the lonely dwelling.

I. 69   When silver clouds infold his floating form
                                            Fn., rejected 1816
83   Move the still moonlight's line
                                            Fn., rejected 1816

The Fairy's frame was slight, yon fibrous cloud,
That catches but the palest tinge of even,   95
And which the straining eye can hardly seize
When melting into eastern twilight's shadow,
Were scarce so thin, so slight; but the fair star
That gems the glittering coronet of morn,
Sheds not a light so mild, so powerful,   100
As that which, bursting from the Fairy's form,
Spread a purpureal halo round the scene,
    Yet with an undulating motion,
    Swayed to her outline gracefully.

    From her celestial car   105
    The Fairy Queen descended,
    And thrice she waved her wand
Circled with wreaths of amaranth:
    Her thin and misty form
    Moved with the moving air,   110
    And the clear silver tones,
    As thus she spoke, were such
As are unheard by all but gifted ear.

Fairy

    'Stars! your balmiest influence shed!
    Elements! your wrath suspend!   115
    Sleep, Ocean, in the rocky bounds
        That circle thy domain!
    Let not a breath be seen to stir
    Around yon grass-grown ruin's height,
        Let even the restless gossamer   120
            Sleep on the moveless air!
            Soul of Ianthe! thou,
Judged alone worthy of the envied boon,
That waits the good and the sincere; that waits
Those who have struggled, and with resolute will   125
Vanquished earth's pride and meanness, burst the chains,
The icy chains of custom, and have shone
The day-stars of their age;—Soul of Ianthe!
            Awake! arise!'

I. 95 even *1904, 1813 and edd.*] day *Fn., rejected 1816*

Sudden arose 130
Ianthe's Soul; it stood
All beautiful in naked purity,
The perfect semblance of its bodily frame,
Instinct with inexpressible beauty and grace;
Each stain of earthliness 135
Had passed away, it reassumed
Its native dignity, and stood
Immortal amid ruin.

Upon the couch the body lay
Wrapped in the depth of slumber: 140
Its features were fixed and meaningless,
Yet animal life was there,
And every organ yet performed
Its natural functions: 'twas a sight
Of wonder to behold the body and soul. 145
The self-same lineaments, the same
Marks of identity were there:
Yet, oh, how different! One aspires to Heaven,
Pants for its sempiternal heritage,
And ever-changing, ever-rising still, 150
Wantons in endless being.
The other, for a time the unwilling sport
Of circumstance and passion, struggles on;
Fleets through its sad duration rapidly:
Then, like an useless and worn-out machine, 155
Rots, perishes, and passes.

Fairy

'Spirit! who hast dived so deep;
Spirit! who hast soared so high;
Thou the fearless, thou the mild,
Accept the boon thy worth hath earned, 160
Ascend the car with me.'

I. 130–1   From the mute frame a lovely ghost arose
                                    Fn., rejected 1816
133 frame, *Locock, 1911*] frame. *1904, 1813 and edd.*   134 grace; *Locock, 1911*]
grace, *1904, 1813 and edd*

Spirit

'Do I dream? Is this new feeling
But a visioned ghost of slumber?
    If indeed I am a soul,
A free, disembodied soul,   165
        Speak again to me.'

Fairy

'I am the Fairy MAB: to me 'tis given
The wonders of the human world to keep:
The secrets of the immeasurable past,
In the unfailing consciences of men,   170
Those stern, unflattering chroniclers, I find:
The future, from the causes which arise
In each event, I gather: not the sting
Which retributive memory implants
In the hard bosom of the selfish man;   175
Nor that ecstatic and exulting throb
Which virtue's votary feels when he sums up
The thoughts and actions of a well-spent day,
Are unforeseen, unregistered by me:
And it is yet permitted me, to rend   180
The veil of mortal frailty, that the spirit,
Clothed in its changeless purity, may know
How soonest to accomplish the great end
For which it hath its being, and may taste
That peace, which in the end all life will share.   185
This is the meed of virtue; happy Soul,
        Ascend the car with me!'

    The chains of earth's immurement
        Fell from Ianthe's spirit;
They shrank and brake like bandages of straw   190
    Beneath a wakened giant's strength.
        She knew her glorious change,
    And felt in apprehension uncontrolled

I. 189–90   They brake like bandages of straw beneath
                   A wakened giant's strength
                                    BM^b, Fn., rejected 1816

New raptures opening round:
Each day-dream of her mortal life,   195
Each frenzied vision of the slumbers
 That closed each well-spent day,
 Seemed now to meet reality.

The Fairy and the Soul proceeded;
 The silver clouds disparted;   200
And as the car of magic they ascended,
 Again the speechless music swelled,
 Again the coursers of the air
Unfurled their azure pennons, and the Queen
 Shaking the beamy reins   205
 Bade them pursue their way.

The magic car moved on.
The night was fair, and countless stars
Studded Heaven's dark blue vault,—
 Just o'er the eastern wave   210
Peeped the first faint smile of morn:—
 The magic car moved on—
 From the celestial hoofs
The atmosphere in flaming sparkles flew,
 And where the burning wheels   215
Eddied above the mountain's loftiest peak,
 Was traced a line of lightning.
Now it flew far above a rock,
 The utmost verge of earth,
The rival of the Andes, whose dark brow   220
 Lowered o'er the silver sea.

Far, far below the chariot's path,
 Calm as a slumbering babe,
 Tremendous Ocean lay.
The mirror of its stillness showed   225
 The pale and waning stars,
 The chariot's fiery track,
 And the gray light of morn
 Tingeing those fleecy clouds
 That canopied the dawn.   230

Seemed it, that the chariot's way
Lay through the midst of an immense concave,
Radiant with million constellations, tinged
    With shades of infinite colour,
    And semicircled with a belt   235
    Flashing incessant meteors.

    The magic car moved on.
    As they approached their goal
The coursers seemed to gather speed;
The sea no longer was distinguished; earth   240
    Appeared a vast and shadowy sphere;
    The sun's unclouded orb
    Rolled through the black concave;
    Its rays of rapid light
Parted around the chariot's swifter course,   245
    And fell, like ocean's feathery spray
    Dashed from the boiling surge
    Before a vessel's prow.

    The magic car moved on.
    Earth's distant orb appeared   250
The smallest light that twinkles in the heaven;
    Whilst round the chariot's way
    Innumerable systems rolled,
    And countless spheres diffused
    An ever-varying glory.   255
    It was a sight of wonder: some
Were hornèd like the crescent moon;
Some shed a mild and silver beam
Like Hesperus o'er the western sea;
Some dashed athwart with trains of flame,   260
Like worlds to death and ruin driven;
Some shone like suns, and, as the chariot passed,
    Eclipsed all other light.

    Spirit of Nature! here!
In this interminable wilderness   265
Of worlds, at whose immensity

I. 232 *Shelley writes* ??verse too long *then* Thro the hollow chasm of &c] *Fn.*
251 twinkles in the heaven; *1904, 1813 and edd.*] shines among the stars. *Fn., rejected
1816*

Even soaring fancy staggers,
Here is thy fitting temple.
   Yet not the lightest leaf
That quivers to the passing breeze   270
   Is less instinct with thee:
   Yet not the meanest worm
That lurks in graves and fattens on the dead
   Less shares thy eternal breath.
    Spirit of Nature! thou!   275
   Imperishable as this scene,
    Here is thy fitting temple.

II

I<small>F</small> solitude hath ever led thy steps
   To the wild Ocean's echoing shore,
    And thou hast lingered there,
    Until the sun's broad orb
   Seemed resting on the burnished wave,   5
    Thou must have marked the lines
   Of purple gold, that motionless
    Hung o'er the sinking sphere:
   Thou must have marked the billowy clouds
   Edged with intolerable radiancy   10
    Towering like rocks of jet
    Crowned with a diamond wreath.
    And yet there is a moment,
    When the sun's highest point
Peeps like a star o'er Ocean's western edge,   15
When those far clouds of feathery gold,
   Shaded with deepest purple, gleam
   Like islands on a dark blue sea;
Then has thy fancy soared above the earth,
    And furled its wearied wing   20
    Within the Fairy's fane.

    Yet not the golden islands
   Gleaming in yon flood of light,
    Nor the feathery curtains
   Stretching o'er the sun's bright couch,   25

    Nor the burnished Ocean waves
      Paving that gorgeous dome,
  So fair, so wonderful a sight
As Mab's aethereal palace could afford.
Yet likest evening's vault, that faery Hall!   30
As Heaven, low resting on the wave, it spread
     Its floors of flashing light,
     Its vast and azure dome,
     Its fertile golden islands
     Floating on a silver sea;   35
Whilst suns their mingling beamings darted
Through clouds of circumambient darkness,
   And pearly battlements around
  Looked o'er the immense of Heaven.

    The magic car no longer moved.   40
     The Fairy and the Spirit
     Entered the Hall of Spells:
      Those golden clouds
    That rolled in glittering billows
    Beneath the azure canopy   45
With the aethereal footsteps trembled not:
    The light and crimson mists,
Floating to strains of thrilling melody
   Through that unearthly dwelling,
Yielded to every movement of the will.   50
Upon their passive swell the Spirit leaned,
And, for the varied bliss that pressed around,
   Used not the glorious privilege
    Of virtue and of wisdom.

     'Spirit!' the Fairy said,   55
  And pointed to the gorgeous dome,
    'This is a wondrous sight
   And mocks all human grandeur;
But, were it virtue's only meed, to dwell
In a celestial palace, all resigned   60
To pleasurable impulses, immured
Within the prison of itself, the will
Of changeless Nature would be unfulfilled.

II. 46 With *1904*, *1813 and edd.*] To *Fn.*, *rejected 1816*

Learn to make others happy. Spirit, come!
This is thine high reward:—the past shall rise;   65
Thou shalt behold the present; I will teach
          The secrets of the future.'

          The Fairy and the Spirit
Approached the overhanging battlement.—
          Below lay stretched the universe!   70
          There, far as the remotest line
          That bounds imagination's flight,
               Countless and unending orbs
          In mazy motion intermingled,
          Yet still fulfilled immutably   75
               Eternal Nature's law.
               Above, below, around,
                    The circling systems formed
               A wilderness of harmony;
               Each with undeviating aim,   80
In eloquent silence, through the depths of space
          Pursued its wondrous way.

          There was a little light
That twinkled in the misty distance:
          None but a spirit's eye   85
          Might ken that rolling orb;
          None but a spirit's eye,
          And in no other place
But that celestial dwelling, might behold
Each action of this earth's inhabitants.   90
          But matter, space and time
In those aëreal mansions cease to act;
And all-prevailing wisdom, when it reaps
The harvest of its excellence, o'erbounds
Those obstacles, of which an earthly soul   95
          Fears to attempt the conquest.

          The Fairy pointed to the earth.
          The Spirit's intellectual eye
          Its kindred beings recognized.
The thronging thousands, to a passing view,   100
          Seemed like an ant-hill's citizens.

How wonderful! that even
The passions, prejudices, interests,
That sway the meanest being, the weak touch
  That moves the finest nerve,   105
  And in one human brain
Causes the faintest thought, becomes a link
  In the great chain of Nature.

  'Behold,' the Fairy cried,
'Palmyra's ruined palaces!—   110
  Behold! where grandeur frowned;
  Behold! where pleasure smiled;
What now remains?—the memory
  Of senselessness and shame—
  What is immortal there?   115
  Nothing—it stands to tell
  A melancholy tale, to give
  An awful warning: soon
Oblivion will steal silently
  The remnant of its fame.   120
  Monarchs and conquerors there
Proud o'er prostrate millions trod—
The earthquakes of the human race;
Like them, forgotten when the ruin
  That marks their shock is past.   125

  'Beside the eternal Nile,
  The Pyramids have risen.
Nile shall pursue his changeless way:
  Those Pyramids shall fall;
Yea! not a stone shall stand to tell   130
  The spot whereon they stood!
Their very site shall be forgotten,
  As is their builder's name!

  'Behold yon sterile spot;
Where now the wandering Arab's tent   135
  Flaps in the desert-blast.
There once old Salem's haughty fane
Reared high to Heaven its thousand golden domes,
  And in the blushing face of day
  Exposed its shameful glory.   140

Oh! many a widow, many an orphan cursed
The building of that fane; and many a father,
Worn out with toil and slavery, implored
The poor man's God to sweep it from the earth,
And spare his children the detested task   145
Of piling stone on stone, and poisoning
  The choicest days of life,
  To soothe a dotard's vanity.
There an inhuman and uncultured race
Howled hideous praises to their Demon-God;   150
They rushed to war, tore from the mother's womb
The unborn child,—old age and infancy
Promiscuous perished; their victorious arms
Left not a soul to breathe. Oh! they were fiends:
But what was he who taught them that the God   155
Of nature and benevolence hath given
A special sanction to the trade of blood?
His name and theirs are fading, and the tales
Of this barbarian nation, which imposture
Recites till terror credits, are pursuing   160
 Itself into forgetfulness.

'Where Athens, Rome, and Sparta stood,
There is a moral desert now:
The mean and miserable huts,
The yet more wretched palaces,   165
Contrasted with those ancient fanes,
Now crumbling to oblivion;
The long and lonely colonnades,
Through which the ghost of Freedom stalks,
 Seem like a well-known tune,   170
Which in some dear scene we have loved to hear,
 Remembered now in sadness.
  But, oh! how much more changed,
  How gloomier is the contrast
  Of human nature there!   175
Where Socrates expired, a tyrant's slave,
A coward and a fool, spreads death around—
 Then, shuddering, meets his own.

Where Cicero and Antoninus lived,
  A cowled and hypocritical monk   180
    Prays, curses and deceives.

    'Spirit, ten thousand years
    Have scarcely passed away,
Since, in the waste where now the savage drinks
His enemy's blood, and aping Europe's sons,   185
    Wakes the unholy song of war,
    Arose a stately city,
Metropolis of the western continent:
  There, now, the mossy column-stone,
Indented by Time's unrelaxing grasp,   190
    Which once appeared to brave
    All, save its country's ruin;
    There the wide forest scene,
Rude in the uncultivated loveliness
    Of gardens long run wild,   195
Seems, to the unwilling sojourner, whose steps
  Chance in that desert has delayed,
Thus to have stood since earth was what it is.
  Yet once it was the busiest haunt,
Whither, as to a common centre, flocked   200
  Strangers, and ships, and merchandise:
    Once peace and freedom blessed
    The cultivated plain:
    But wealth, that curse of man,
Blighted the bud of its prosperity: 205
Virtue and wisdom, truth and liberty,
Fled, to return not, until man shall know
  That they alone can give the bliss
    Worthy a soul that claims
Its kindred with eternity.   210

    'There's not one atom of yon earth
    But once was living man;
  Nor the minutest drop of rain,
  That hangeth in its thinnest cloud,
    But flowed in human veins: 215
    And from the burning plains
    Where Libyan monsters yell,

From the most gloomy glens
Of Greenland's sunless clime,
To where the golden fields   220
Of fertile England spread
Their harvest to the day,
Thou canst not find one spot
Whereon no city stood.

'How strange is human pride!   225
I tell thee that those living things,
To whom the fragile blade of grass,
That springeth in the morn
And perisheth ere noon,
Is an unbounded world;   230
I tell thee that those viewless beings,
Whose mansion is the smallest particle
Of the impassive atmosphere,
Think, feel and live like man;
That their affections and antipathies,   235
Like his, produce the laws
Ruling their moral state;
And the minutest throb
That through their frame diffuses
The slightest, faintest motion,   240
Is fixed and indispensable
As the majestic laws
That rule yon rolling orbs.'

The Fairy paused. The Spirit,
In ecstasy of admiration, felt   245
All knowledge of the past revived; the events
Of old and wondrous times,
Which dim tradition interruptedly
Teaches the credulous vulgar, were unfolded
In just perspective to the view;   250
Yet dim from their infinitude.
The Spirit seemed to stand
High on an isolated pinnacle;
The flood of ages combating below,

The depth of the unbounded universe   255
    Above, and all around
Nature's unchanging harmony.

III

'FAIRY!' the Spirit said,
And on the Queen of Spells
Fixed her aethereal eyes,
'I thank thee. Thou hast given
A boon which I will not resign, and taught   5
A lesson not to be unlearned. I know
The past, and thence I will essay to glean
A warning for the future, so that man
May profit by his errors, and derive
    Experience from his folly: 10
For, when the power of imparting joy
Is equal to the will, the human soul
    Requires no other Heaven.'

Mab

'Turn thee, surpassing Spirit!
Much yet remains unscanned.   15
Thou knowest how great is man,
Thou knowest his imbecility:
Yet learn thou what he is:
Yet learn the lofty destiny
Which restless time prepares   20
For every living soul.

'Behold a gorgeous palace, that amid
Yon populous city rears its thousand towers
And seems itself a city. Gloomy troops

II. 257 foll., *cf.* The Daemon of the World *253–86*,
      None dare relate what fearful mysteries
      The spirit was, nor the portentous [voice] groan
      Which when the flood was still, the living world
      Sent in complaint to that divinest fane.
      While from the deep a multitudinous throng
      Of motley shapes, the envious Present leads
      [Which] Who raging horribly their armed hands
      Hurl high, where inaccessibly serene
                          Fn., rejected 1816

Of sentinels, in stern and silent ranks,   25
Encompass it around: the dweller there
Cannot be free and happy; hearest thou not
The curses of the fatherless, the groans
Of those who have no friend? He passes on:
The King, the wearer of a gilded chain   30
That binds his soul to abjectness, the fool
Whom courtiers nickname monarch, whilst a slave
Even to the basest appetites—that man
Heeds not the shriek of penury; he smiles
At the deep curses which the destitute   35
Mutter in secret, and a sullen joy
Pervades his bloodless heart when thousands groan
But for those morsels which his wantonness
Wastes in unjoyous revelry, to save
All that they love from famine: when he hears   40
The tale of horror, to some ready-made face
Of hypocritical assent he turns,
Smothering the glow of shame, that, spite of him,
Flushes his bloated cheek.
                                    Now to the meal
Of silence, grandeur, and excess, he drags   45
His palled unwilling appetite. If gold,
Gleaming around, and numerous viands culled
From every clime, could force the loathing sense
To overcome satiety,—if wealth
The spring it draws from poisons not,—or vice,   50
Unfeeling, stubborn vice, converteth not
Its food to deadliest venom; then that king
Is happy; and the peasant who fulfils
His unforced task, when he returns at even,
And by the blazing faggot meets again   55
Her welcome for whom all his toil is sped,
Tastes not a sweeter meal.
                                    Behold him now
Stretched on the gorgeous couch; his fevered brain
Reels dizzily awhile: but ah! too soon
The slumber of intemperance subsides,   60
And conscience, that undying serpent, calls
Her venomous brood to their nocturnal task.

Listen! he speaks! oh! mark that frenzied eye—
Oh! mark that deadly visage.'

King

     'No cessation!
Oh! must this last for ever? Awful Death,   65
I wish, yet fear to clasp thee!—Not one moment
Of dreamless sleep! O dear and blessèd peace!
Why dost thou shroud thy vestal purity
In penury and dungeons? wherefore lurkest
With danger, death, and solitude; yet shunn'st 70
The palace I have built thee? Sacred peace!
Oh visit me but once, but pitying shed
One drop of balm upon my withered soul.'

The Fairy

'Vain man! that palace is the virtuous heart,
And Peace defileth not her snowy robes   75
In such a shed as thine. Hark! yet he mutters;
His slumbers are but varied agonies,
They prey like scorpions on the springs of life.
There needeth not the hell that bigots frame
To punish those who err: earth in itself   80
Contains at once the evil and the cure;
And all-sufficing Nature can chastise
Those who transgress her law,—she only knows
How justly to proportion to the fault
The punishment it merits.
       Is it strange   85
That this poor wretch should pride him in his woe?
Take pleasure in his abjectness, and hug
The scorpion that consumes him? Is it strange
That, placed on a conspicuous throne of thorns,
Grasping an iron sceptre, and immured   90
Within a splendid prison, whose stern bounds
Shut him from all that's good or dear on earth,
His soul asserts not its humanity?

That man's mild nature rises not in war
Against a king's employ? No—'tis not strange.   95
He, like the vulgar, thinks, feels, acts and lives
Just as his father did; the unconquered powers
Of precedent and custom interpose
Between a *king* and virtue. Stranger yet,
To those who know not Nature, nor deduce   100
The future from the present, it may seem,
That not one slave, who suffers from the crimes
Of this unnatural being; not one wretch,
Whose children famish, and whose nuptial bed
Is earth's unpitying bosom, rears an arm   105
To dash him from his throne!
        Those gilded flies
That, basking in the sunshine of a court,
Fatten on its corruption!—what are they?
—The drones of the community; they feed
On the mechanic's labour: the starved hind   110
For them compels the stubborn glebe to yield
Its unshared harvests; and yon squalid form,
Leaner than fleshless misery, that wastes
A sunless life in the unwholesome mine,
Drags out in labour a protracted death,   115
To glut their grandeur; many faint with toil,
That few may know the cares and woe of sloth.

'Whence, think'st thou, kings and parasites arose?
Whence that unnatural line of drones, who heap
Toil and unvanquishable penury   120
On those who build their palaces, and bring
Their daily bread?—From vice, black loathsome vice;
From rapine, madness, treachery, and wrong;
From all that 'genders misery, and makes
Of earth this thorny wilderness; from lust,   125
Revenge, and murder. . . . And when Reason's voice,
Loud as the voice of Nature, shall have waked
The nations; and mankind perceive that vice
Is discord, war, and misery; that virtue
Is peace, and happiness and harmony;   130
When man's maturer nature shall disdain

The playthings of its childhood;—kingly glare
Will lose its power to dazzle; its authority
Will silently pass by; the gorgeous throne
Shall stand unnoticed in the regal hall,   135
Fast falling to decay; whilst falsehood's trade
Shall be as hateful and unprofitable
As that of truth is now.
                      Where is the fame
Which the vainglorious mighty of the earth
Seek to eternize? Oh! the faintest sound   140
From Time's light footfall, the minutest wave
That swells the flood of ages, whelms in nothing
The unsubstantial bubble. Ay! to-day
Stern is the tyrant's mandate, red the gaze
That flashes desolation, strong the arm   145
That scatters multitudes. To-morrow comes!
That mandate is a thunder-peal that died
In ages past; that gaze, a transient flash
On which the midnight closed, and on that arm
The worm has made his meal.
                     The virtuous man,   150
Who, great in his humility, as kings
Are little in their grandeur; he who leads
Invincibly a life of resolute good,
And stands amid the silent dungeon-depths
More free and fearless than the trembling judge,   155
Who, clothed in venal power, vainly strove
To bind the impassive spirit;—when he falls,
His mild eye beams benevolence no more:
Withered the hand outstretched but to relieve;
Sunk Reason's simple eloquence, that rolled   160
But to appal the guilty. Yes! the grave
Hath quenched that eye, and Death's relentless frost
Withered that arm: but the unfading fame
Which Virtue hangs upon its votary's tomb;
The deathless memory of that man, whom kings   165
Call to their mind and tremble; the remembrance
With which the happy spirit contemplates
Its well-spent pilgrimage on earth,
Shall never pass away.

'Nature rejects the monarch, not the man;   170
The subject, not the citizen: for kings
And subjects, mutual foes, forever play
A losing game into each other's hands,
Whose stakes are vice and misery. The man
Of virtuous soul commands not, nor obeys.   175
Power, like a desolating pestilence,
Pollutes whate'er it touches; and obedience,
Bane of all genius, virtue, freedom, truth,
Makes slaves of men, and, of the human frame,
A mechanized automaton.
                               When Nero,   180
High over flaming Rome, with savage joy
Lowered like a fiend, drank with enraptured ear
The shrieks of agonizing death, beheld
The frightful desolation spread, and felt
A new-created sense within his soul   185
Thrill to the sight, and vibrate to the sound;
Think'st thou his grandeur had not overcome
The force of human kindness? and, when Rome,
With one stern blow, hurled not the tyrant down,
Crushed not the arm red with her dearest blood,   190
Had not submissive abjectness destroyed
Nature's suggestions?
                        Look on yonder earth:
The golden harvests spring; the unfailing sun
Sheds light and life; the fruits, the flowers, the trees,
Arise in due succession; all things speak   195
Peace, harmony, and love. The universe,
In Nature's silent eloquence, declares
That all fulfil the works of love and joy,—
All but the outcast, Man. He fabricates
The sword which stabs his peace; he cherisheth   200
The snakes that gnaw his heart; he raiseth up
The tyrant, whose delight is in his woe,
Whose sport is in his agony. Yon sun,
Lights it the great alone? Yon silver beams,
Sleep they less sweetly on the cottage thatch   205
Than on the dome of kings? Is mother Earth
A step-dame to her numerous sons, who earn

Her unshared gifts with unremitting toil;
A mother only to those puling babes
Who, nursed in ease and luxury, make men   210
The playthings of their babyhood, and mar,
In self-important childishness, that peace
Which men alone appreciate?

     'Spirit of Nature! no.
The pure diffusion of thy essence throbs   215
  Alike in every human heart.
    Thou, aye, erectest there
  Thy throne of power unappealable:
Thou art the judge beneath whose nod
Man's brief and frail authority   220
    Is powerless as the wind
    That passeth idly by.
Thine the tribunal which surpasseth
  The show of human justice,
    As God surpasses man.   225

     'Spirit of Nature! thou
Life of interminable multitudes;
  Soul of those mighty spheres
Whose changeless paths through Heaven's deep silence lie;
    Soul of that smallest being,   230
    The dwelling of whose life
  Is one faint April sun-gleam;—
    Man, like these passive things,
Thy will unconsciously fulfilleth:
  Like theirs, his age of endless peace,   235
    Which time is fast maturing,
    Will swiftly, surely come;
And the unbounded frame, which thou pervadest,
    Will be without a flaw
  Marring its perfect symmetry.   240

IV

'How beautiful this night! the balmiest sigh,
Which vernal zephyrs breathe in evening's ear,
Were discord to the speaking quietude
That wraps this moveless scene. Heaven's ebon vault,
Studded with stars unutterably bright,   5
Through which the moon's unclouded grandeur rolls,
Seems like a canopy which love had spread
To curtain her sleeping world. Yon gentle hills,
Robed in a garment of untrodden snow;
Yon darksome rocks, whence icicles depend,   10
So stainless, that their white and glittering spires
Tinge not the moon's pure beam; yon castled steep,
Whose banner hangeth o'er the time-worn tower
So idly, that rapt fancy deemeth it
A metaphor of peace;—all form a scene   15
Where musing Solitude might love to lift
Her soul above this sphere of earthliness;
Where Silence undisturbed might watch alone,
So cold, so bright, so still.
                   The orb of day,
In southern climes, o'er ocean's waveless field   20
Sinks sweetly smiling: not the faintest breath
Steals o'er the unruffled deep; the clouds of eve
Reflect unmoved the lingering beam of day;
And vesper's image on the western main
Is beautifully still. To-morrow comes: 25
Cloud upon cloud, in dark and deepening mass,
Roll o'er the blackened waters; the deep roar
Of distant thunder mutters awfully;
Tempest unfolds its pinion o'er the gloom
That shrouds the boiling surge; the pitiless fiend,   30
With all his winds and lightnings, tracks his prey;
The torn deep yawns,—the vessel finds a grave
Beneath its jaggèd gulf.
                    Ah! whence yon glare
That fires the arch of Heaven?—that dark red smoke
Blotting the silver moon? The stars are quenched   35

In darkness, and the pure and spangling snow
Gleams faintly through the gloom that gathers round!
Hark to that roar, whose swift and deaf'ning peals
In countless echoes through the mountains ring,
Startling pale Midnight on her starry throne!   40
Now swells the intermingling din; the jar
Frequent and frightful of the bursting bomb;
The falling beam, the shriek, the groan, the shout,
The ceaseless clangour, and the rush of men
Inebriate with rage:—loud, and more loud   45
The discord grows; till pale Death shuts the scene,
And o'er the conqueror and the conquered draws
His cold and bloody shroud.—Of all the men
Whom day's departing beam saw blooming there,
In proud and vigorous health; of all the hearts   50
That beat with anxious life at sunset there;
How few survive, how few are beating now!
All is deep silence, like the fearful calm
That slumbers in the storm's portentous pause;
Save when the frantic wail of widowed love   55
Comes shuddering on the blast, or the faint moan
With which some soul bursts from the frame of clay
Wrapped round its struggling powers.
                                    The gray morn
Dawns on the mournful scene; the sulphurous smoke
Before the icy wind slow rolls away,   60
And the bright beams of frosty morning dance
Along the spangling snow. There tracks of blood
Even to the forest's depth, and scattered arms,
And lifeless warriors, whose hard lineaments
Death's self could change not, mark the dreadful path   65
Of the outsallying victors: far behind,
Black ashes note where their proud city stood.
Within yon forest is a gloomy glen—
Each tree which guards its darkness from the day,
Waves o'er a warrior's tomb.
                                    I see thee shrink,   70
Surpassing Spirit!—wert thou human else?
I see a shade of doubt and horror fleet
Across thy stainless features: yet fear not;

This is no unconnected misery,
Nor stands uncaused, and irretrievable.   75
Man's evil nature, that apology
Which kings who rule, and cowards who crouch, set up
For their unnumbered crimes, sheds not the blood
Which desolates the discord-wasted land.
From kings, and priests, and statesmen, war arose,   80
Whose safety is man's deep unbettered woe,
Whose grandeur his debasement. Let the axe
Strike at the root, the poison-tree will fall;
And where its venomed exhalations spread
Ruin, and death, and woe, where millions lay   85
Quenching the serpent's famine, and their bones
Bleaching unburied in the putrid blast,
A garden shall arise, in loveliness
Surpassing fabled Eden.
                    Hath Nature's soul,
That formed this world so beautiful, that spread   90
Earth's lap with plenty, and life's smallest chord
Strung to unchanging unison, that gave
The happy birds their dwelling in the grove,
That yielded to the wanderers of the deep
The lovely silence of the unfathomed main,   95
And filled the meanest worm that crawls in dust
With spirit, thought, and love; on Man alone,
Partial in causeless malice, wantonly
Heaped ruin, vice, and slavery; his soul
Blasted with withering curses; placed afar   100
The meteor-happiness, that shuns his grasp,
But serving on the frightful gulf to glare,
Rent wide beneath his footsteps?
                       Nature!—no!
Kings, priests, and statesmen, blast the human flower
Even in its tender bud; their influence darts   105
Like subtle poison through the bloodless veins
Of desolate society. The child,
Ere he can lisp his mother's sacred name,
Swells with the unnatural pride of crime, and lifts
His baby-sword even in a hero's mood.   110
This infant-arm becomes the bloodiest scourge

Of devastated earth; whilst specious names,
Learned in soft childhood's unsuspecting hour,
Serve as the sophisms with which manhood dims
Bright Reason's ray, and sanctifies the sword   115
Upraised to shed a brother's innocent blood.
Let priest-led slaves cease to proclaim that man
Inherits vice and misery, when Force
And Falsehood hang even o'er the cradled babe,
Stifling with rudest grasp all natural good.   120
'Ah! to the stranger-soul, when first it peeps
From its new tenement, and looks abroad
For happiness and sympathy, how stern
And desolate a tract is this wide world!
How withered all the buds of natural good!   125
No shade, no shelter from the sweeping storms
Of pitiless power! On its wretched frame,
Poisoned, perchance, by the disease and woe
Heaped on the wretched parent whence it sprung
By morals, law, and custom, the pure winds   130
Of Heaven, that renovate the insect tribes,
May breathe not. The untainting light of day
May visit not its longings. It is bound
Ere it has life: yea, all the chains are forged
Long ere its being: all liberty and love   135
And peace is torn from its defencelessness;
Cursed from its birth, even from its cradle doomed
To abjectness and bondage!

'Throughout this varied and eternal world
Soul is the only element: the block   140
That for uncounted ages has remained
The moveless pillar of a mountain's weight
Is active, living spirit. Every grain
Is sentient both in unity and part,
And the minutest atom comprehends   145
A world of loves and hatreds; these beget
Evil and good: hence truth and falsehood spring;
Hence will and thought and action, all the germs

IV. 140 element: *1904*] element, *1813 and edd.*   141 remained *1904*] remained.
1813 and edd.

Of pain or pleasure, sympathy or hate,
That variegate the eternal universe.   150
Soul is not more polluted than the beams
Of Heaven's pure orb, ere round their rapid lines
The taint of earth-born atmospheres arise.
'Man is of soul and body, formed for deeds
Of high resolve, on fancy's boldest wing   155
To soar unwearied, fearlessly to turn
The keenest pangs to peacefulness, and taste
The joys which mingled sense and spirit yield.
Or he is formed for abjectness and woe,
To grovel on the dunghill of his fears,   160
To shrink at every sound, to quench the flame
Of natural love in sensualism, to know
That hour as blessed when on his worthless days
The frozen hand of Death shall set its seal,
Yet fear the cure, though hating the disease.   165
The one is man that shall hereafter be;
The other, man as vice has made him now.

'War is the statesman's game, the priest's delight,
The lawyer's jest, the hired assassin's trade,
And, to those royal murderers, whose mean thrones   170
Are bought by crimes of treachery and gore,
The bread they eat, the staff on which they lean.
Guards, garbed in blood-red livery, surround
Their palaces, participate the crimes
That force defends, and from a nation's rage   175
Secure the crown, which all the curses reach
That famine, frenzy, woe and penury breathe.
These are the hired bravos who defend
The tyrant's throne—the bullies of his fear:
These are the sinks and channels of worst vice,   180
The refuse of society, the dregs
Of all that is most vile: their cold hearts blend
Deceit with sternness, ignorance with pride,
All that is mean and villainous with rage
Which hopelessness of good, and self-contempt,   185
Alone might kindle; they are decked in wealth,

IV. 176 Secure *1904, 1839*] Secures *1813*   184 villainous [villanous, *edd*.

Honour and power, then are sent abroad
To do their work. The pestilence that stalks
In gloomy triumph through some eastern land
Is less destroying. They cajole with gold,   190
And promises of fame, the thoughtless youth
Already crushed with servitude: he knows
His wretchedness too late, and cherishes
Repentance for his ruin, when his doom
Is sealed in gold and blood!   195
Those too the tyrant serve, who, skilled to snare
The feet of Justice in the toils of law,
Stand, ready to oppress the weaker still;
And right or wrong will vindicate for gold,
Sneering at public virtue, which beneath   200
Their pitiless tread lies torn and trampled, where
Honour sits smiling at the sale of truth.

'Then grave and hoary-headed hypocrites,
Without a hope, a passion, or a love,
Who, through a life of luxury and lies,   205
Have crept by flattery to the seats of power,
Support the system whence their honours flow. . . .
They have three words:—well tyrants know their use,
Well pay them for the loan, with usury
Torn from a bleeding world!—God, Hell, and Heaven. 210
A vengeful, pitiless, and almighty fiend,
Whose mercy is a nickname for the rage
Of tameless tigers hungering for blood.
Hell, a red gulf of everlasting fire,
Where poisonous and undying worms prolong   215
Eternal misery to those hapless slaves
Whose life has been a penance for its crimes.
And Heaven, a meed for those who dare belie
Their human nature, quake, believe, and cringe
Before the mockeries of earthly power.   220

'These tools the tyrant tempers to his work,
Wields in his wrath, and as he wills destroys,
Omnipotent in wickedness: the while

IV. 203–20 *omitted* 1839¹. *See MWS, Note, below, p. 337, § 1.*

Youth springs, age moulders, manhood tamely does
His bidding, bribed by short-lived joys to lend   225
Force to the weakness of his trembling arm.

'They rise, they fall; one generation comes
Yielding its harvest to destruction's scythe.
It fades, another blossoms: yet behold!
Red glows the tyrant's stamp-mark on its bloom,   230
Withering and cankering deep its passive prime.
He has invented lying words and modes,
Empty and vain as his own coreless heart;
Evasive meanings, nothings of much sound,
To lure the heedless victim to the toils   235
Spread round the valley of its paradise.

'Look to thyself, priest, conqueror, or prince!
Whether thy trade is falsehood, and thy lusts
Deep wallow in the earnings of the poor,
With whom thy Master was:—or thou delight'st   240
In numbering o'er the myriads of thy slain,
All misery weighing nothing in the scale
Against thy short-lived fame: or thou dost load
With cowardice and crime the groaning land,
A pomp-fed king. Look to thy wretched self!   245
Ay, art thou not the veriest slave that e'er
Crawled on the loathing earth? Are not thy days
Days of unsatisfying listlessness?
Dost thou not cry, ere night's long rack is o'er,
"When will the morning come?" Is not thy youth   250
A vain and feverish dream of sensualism?
Thy manhood blighted with unripe disease?
Are not thy views of unregretted death
Drear, comfortless, and horrible? Thy mind,
Is it not morbid as thy nerveless frame,   255
Incapable of judgement, hope, or love?
And dost thou wish the errors to survive
That bar thee from all sympathies of good,
After the miserable interest
Thou hold'st in their protraction?
                              When the grave   260

Has swallowed up thy memory and thyself,
Dost thou desire the bane that poisons earth
To twine its roots around thy coffined clay,
Spring from thy bones, and blossom on thy tomb,
That of its fruit thy babes may eat and die?   265

V

'THUS do the generations of the earth
Go to the grave, and issue from the womb,
Surviving still the imperishable change
That renovates the world; even as the leaves
Which the keen frost-wind of the waning year   5
Has scattered on the forest soil, and heaped
For many seasons there—though long they choke,
Loading with loathsome rottenness the land,
All germs of promise, yet when the tall trees
From which they fell, shorn of their lovely shapes,   10
Lie level with the earth to moulder there,
They fertilize the land they long deformed,
Till from the breathing lawn a forest springs
Of youth, integrity, and loveliness,
Like that which gave it life, to spring and die.   15
Thus suicidal selfishness, that blights
The fairest feelings of the opening heart,
Is destined to decay, whilst from the soil
Shall spring all virtue, all delight, all love,
And judgement cease to wage unnatural war   20
With passion's unsubduable array.
Twin-sister of religion, selfishness!
Rival in crime and falsehood, aping all
The wanton horrors of her bloody play;
Yet frozen, unimpassioned, spiritless,   25
Shunning the light, and owning not its name,
Compelled, by its deformity, to screen
With flimsy veil of justice and of right,
Its unattractive lineaments, that scare
All, save the brood of ignorance: at once   30
The cause and the effect of tyranny;
Unblushing, hardened, sensual, and vile;

Dead to all love but of its abjectness,
With heart impassive to more noble powers
Than unshared pleasure, sordid gain, or fame;   35
Despising its own miserable being,
Which still it longs, yet fears to disenthrall.

'Hence commerce springs, the venal interchange
Of all that human art or nature yield;
Which wealth should purchase not, but want demand,   40
And natural kindness hasten to supply
From the full fountain of its boundless love,
For ever stifled, drained, and tainted now.
Commerce! beneath whose poison-breathing shade
No solitary virtue dares to spring,   45
But Poverty and Wealth with equal hand
Scatter their withering curses, and unfold
The doors of premature and violent death,
To pining famine and full-fed disease,
To all that shares the lot of human life,   50
Which poisoned, body and soul, scarce drags the chain,
That lengthens as it goes and clanks behind.

'Commerce has set the mark of selfishness,
The signet of its all-enslaving power
Upon a shining ore, and called it gold: 55
Before whose image bow the vulgar great,
The vainly rich, the miserable proud,
The mob of peasants, nobles, priests, and kings,
And with blind feelings reverence the power
That grinds them to the dust of misery.   60
But in the temple of their hireling hearts
Gold is a living god, and rules in scorn
All earthly things but virtue.

'Since tyrants, by the sale of human life,
Heap luxuries to their sensualism, and fame   65
To their wide-wasting and insatiate pride,
Success has sanctioned to a credulous world
The ruin, the disgrace, the woe of war.

V. 34 to] by *1813 and edd.*

His hosts of blind and unresisting dupes
The despot numbers; from his cabinet   70
These puppets of his schemes he moves at will,
Even as the slaves by force or famine driven,
Beneath a vulgar master, to perform
A task of cold and brutal drudgery;—
Hardened to hope, insensible to fear,   75
Scarce living pulleys of a dead machine,
Mere wheels of work and articles of trade,
That grace the proud and noisy pomp of wealth!

'The harmony and happiness of man
Yields to the wealth of nations; that which lifts   80
His nature to the heaven of its pride,
Is bartered for the poison of his soul;
The weight that drags to earth his towering hopes,
Blighting all prospect but of selfish gain,
Withering all passion but of slavish fear,   85
Extinguishing all free and generous love
Of enterprise and daring, even the pulse
That fancy kindles in the beating heart
To mingle with sensation, it destroys,—
Leaves nothing but the sordid lust of self,   90
The grovelling hope of interest and gold,
Unqualified, unmingled, unredeemed
Even by hypocrisy.   And statesmen boast
Of wealth! The wordy eloquence, that lives
After the ruin of their hearts, can gild   95
The bitter poison of a nation's woe,
Can turn the worship of the servile mob
To their corrupt and glaring idol, Fame,
From Virtue, trampled by its iron tread,
Although its dazzling pedestal be raised   100
Amid the horrors of a limb-strewn field,
With desolated dwellings smoking round.
The man of ease, who, by his warm fireside,
To deeds of charitable intercourse,
And bare fulfilment of the common laws   105
Of decency and prejudice, confines

The struggling nature of his human heart,
Is duped by their cold sophistry; he sheds
A passing tear perchance upon the wreck
Of earthly peace, when near his dwelling's door					110
The frightful waves are driven,—when his son
Is murdered by the tyrant, or religion
Drives his wife raving mad. But the poor man,
Whose life is misery, and fear, and care;
Whom the morn wakens but to fruitless toil;					115
Who ever hears his famished offspring's scream,
Whom their pale mother's uncomplaining gaze
For ever meets, and the proud rich man's eye
Flashing command, and the heart-breaking scene
Of thousands like himself;—he little heeds					120
The rhetoric of tyranny; his hate
Is quenchless as his wrongs; he laughs to scorn
The vain and bitter mockery of words,
Feeling the horror of the tyrant's deeds,
And unrestrained but by the arm of power,					125
That knows and dreads his enmity.

'The iron rod of Penury still compels
Her wretched slave to bow the knee to wealth,
And poison, with unprofitable toil,
A life too void of solace to confirm					130
The very chains that bind him to his doom.
Nature, impartial in munificence,
Has gifted man with all-subduing will.
Matter, with all its transitory shapes,
Lies subjected and plastic at his feet,					135
That, weak from bondage, tremble as they tread.
How many a rustic Milton has passed by,
Stifling the speechless longings of his heart,
In unremitting drudgery and care!
How many a vulgar Cato has compelled					140
His energies, no longer tameless then,
To mould a pin, or fabricate a nail!
How many a Newton, to whose passive ken
Those mighty spheres that gem infinity

V. 116 offspring's *1904, 1839*] offsprings *1813*

Were only specks of tinsel, fixed in Heaven   145
To light the midnights of his native town!

'Yet every heart contains perfection's germ:
The wisest of the sages of the earth,
That ever from the stores of reason drew
Science and truth, and virtue's dreadless tone,   150
Were but a weak and inexperienced boy,
Proud, sensual, unimpassioned, unimbued
With pure desire and universal love,
Compared to that high being, of cloudless brain,
Untainted passion, elevated will,   155
Which Death (who even would linger long in awe
Within his noble presence, and beneath
His changeless eyebeam) might alone subdue.
Him, every slave now dragging through the filth
Of some corrupted city his sad life,   160
Pining with famine, swoln with luxury,
Blunting the keenness of his spiritual sense
With narrow schemings and unworthy cares,
Or madly rushing through all violent crime,
To move the deep stagnation of his soul,—   165
Might imitate and equal.
                  But mean lust
Has bound its chains so tight around the earth,
That all within it but the virtuous man
Is venal: gold or fame will surely reach
The price prefixed by selfishness, to all   170
But him of resolute and unchanging will;
Whom, nor the plaudits of a servile crowd,
Nor the vile joys of tainting luxury,
Can bribe to yield his elevated soul
To Tyranny or Falsehood, though they wield   175
With blood-red hand the sceptre of the world.

'All things are sold: the very light of Heaven
Is venal; earth's unsparing gifts of love,
The smallest amd most despicable things
That lurk in the abysses of the deep,   180
All objects of our life, even life itself,

And the poor pittance which the laws allow
Of liberty, the fellowship of man,
Those duties which his heart of human love
Should urge him to perform instinctively,   185
Are bought and sold as in a public mart
Of undisguising selfishness, that sets
On each its price, the stamp-mark of her reign.
Even love is sold; the solace of all woe
Is turned to deadliest agony, old age   190
Shivers in selfish beauty's loathing arms,
And youth's corrupted impulses prepare
A life of horror from the blighting bane
Of commerce; whilst the pestilence that springs
From unenjoying sensualism, has filled   195
All human life with hydra-headed woes.

'Falsehood demands but gold to pay the pangs
Of outraged conscience; for the slavish priest
Sets no great value on his hireling faith:
A little passing pomp, some servile souls,   200
Whom cowardice itself might safely chain,
Or the spare mite of avarice could bribe
To deck the triumph of their languid zeal,
Can make him minister to tyranny.
More daring crime requires a loftier meed: 205
Without a shudder, the slave-soldier lends
His arm to murderous deeds, and steels his heart,
When the dread eloquence of dying men,
Low mingling on the lonely field of fame,
Assails that nature, whose applause he sells   210
For the gross blessings of a patriot mob,
For the vile gratitude of heartless kings,
And for a cold world's good word,—viler still!

'There is a nobler glory, which survives
Until our being fades, and, solacing   215
All human care, accompanies its change;
Deserts not virtue in the dungeon's gloom,
And, in the precincts of the palace, guides
Its footsteps through that labyrinth of crime;

Imbues his lineaments with dauntlessness,   220
Even when, from Power's avenging hand, he takes
Its sweetest, last and noblest title—death;
—The consciousness of good, which neither gold,
Nor sordid fame, nor hope of heavenly bliss
Can purchase; but a life of resolute good,   225
Unalterable will, quenchless desire
Of universal happiness, the heart
That beats with it in unison, the brain,
Whose ever wakeful wisdom toils to change
Reason's rich stores for its eternal weal.   230

'This commerce of sincerest virtue needs
No mediative signs of selfishness,
No jealous intercourse of wretched gain,
No balancings of prudence, cold and long;
In just and equal measure all is weighed,   235
One scale contains the sum of human weal,
And one, the good man's heart.
                                    How vainly seek
The selfish for that happiness denied
To aught but virtue! Blind and hardened, they,
Who hope for peace amid the storms of care,   240
Who covet power they know not how to use,
And sigh for pleasure they refuse to give,—
Madly they frustrate still their own designs;
And, where they hope that quiet to enjoy
Which virtue pictures, bitterness of soul,   245
Pining regrets, and vain repentances,
Disease, disgust, and lassitude, pervade
Their valueless and miserable lives.

'But hoary-headed Selfishness has felt
Its death-blow, and is tottering to the grave: 250
A brighter morn awaits the human day,
When every transfer of earth's natural gifts
Shall be a commerce of good words and works;
When poverty and wealth, the thirst of fame,
The fear of infamy, disease and woe,   255
War with its million horrors, and fierce hell

Shall live but in the memory of Time,
Who, like a penitent libertine, shall start,
Look back, and shudder at his younger years.'

VI

ALL touch, all eye, all ear,
The Spirit felt the Fairy's burning speech.
O'er the thin texture of its frame,
The varying periods painted changing glows,
    As on a summer even,   5
When soul-enfolding music floats around,
  The stainless mirror of the lake
  Re-images the eastern gloom,
Mingling convulsively its purple hues
    With sunset's burnished gold.   10

    Then thus the Spirit spoke:
'It is a wild and miserable world!
    Thorny, and full of care,
Which every fiend can make his prey at will.
  O Fairy! in the lapse of years,   15
    Is there no hope in store?
    Will yon vast suns roll on
Interminably, still illuming
The night of so many wretched souls,
    And see no hope for them?   20
Will not the universal Spirit e'er
Revivify this withered limb of Heaven?'

    The Fairy calmly smiled
In comfort, and a kindling gleam of hope
  Suffused the Spirit's lineaments.   25
'Oh! rest thee tranquil; chase those fearful doubts,
Which ne'er could rack an everlasting soul,
That sees the chains which bind it to its doom.
Yes! crime and misery are in yonder earth,
    Falsehood, mistake, and lust;   30
    But the eternal world
Contains at once the evil and the cure.

Some eminent in virtue shall start up,
    Even in perversest time:
The truths of their pure lips, that never die,   35
Shall bind the scorpion falsehood with a wreath
    Of ever-living flame,
Until the monster sting itself to death.

  'How sweet a scene will earth become!
Of purest spirits a pure dwelling-place,   40
Symphonious with the planetary spheres;
When man, with changeless Nature coalescing,
Will undertake regeneration's work,
When its ungenial poles no longer point
    To the red and baleful sun   45
    That faintly twinkles there.

  'Spirit! on yonder earth,
  Falsehood now triumphs; deadly power
Has fixed its seal upon the lip of truth!
  Madness and misery are there!   50
The happiest is most wretched! Yet confide,
Until pure health-drops, from the cup of joy,
Fall like a dew of balm upon the world.
Now, to the scene I show, in silence turn,
And read the blood-stained charter of all woe,   55
Which Nature soon, with re-creating hand,
Will blot in mercy from the book of earth.
How bold the flight of Passion's wandering wing,
How swift the step of Reason's firmer tread,
How calm and sweet the victories of life,   60
How terrorless the triumph of the grave!
How powerless were the mightiest monarch's arm,
Vain his loud threat, and impotent his frown!
How ludicrous the priest's dogmatic roar!
The weight of his exterminating curse   65
How light! and his affected charity,
To suit the pressure of the changing times,
What palpable deceit!—but for thy aid,
Religion! but for thee, prolific fiend,

VI. 54–238 *omitted* 1839¹. *See MWS, Note, below, p.* 337,§ *1.*

Who peoplest earth with demons, Hell with men,   70
And Heaven with slaves!

'Thou taintest all thou look'st upon!—the stars,
Which on thy cradle beamed so brightly sweet,
Were gods to the distempered playfulness
Of thy untutored infancy: the trees,   75
The grass, the clouds, the mountains, and the sea,
All living things that walk, swim, creep, or fly,
Were gods: the sun had homage, and the moon
Her worshipper. Then thou becam'st, a boy,
More daring in thy frenzies: every shape,   80
Monstrous or vast, or beautifully wild,
Which, from sensation's relics, fancy culls;
The spirits of the air, the shuddering ghost,
The genii of the elements, the powers
That give a shape to Nature's varied works,   85
Had life and place in the corrupt belief
Of thy blind heart: yet still thy youthful hands
Were pure of human blood. Then manhood gave
Its strength and ardour to thy frenzied brain;
Thine eager gaze scanned the stupendous scene,   90
Whose wonders mocked the knowledge of thy pride:
Their everlasting and unchanging laws
Reproached thine ignorance. Awhile thou stoodst
Baffled and gloomy; then thou didst sum up
The elements of all that thou didst know;   95
The changing seasons, winter's leafless reign,
The budding of the Heaven-breathing trees,
The eternal orbs that beautify the night,
The sunrise, and the setting of the moon,
Earthquakes and wars, and poisons and disease,   100
And all their causes, to an abstract point
Converging, thou didst bend and called it God!
The self-sufficing, the omnipotent,
The merciful, and the avenging God!
Who, prototype of human misrule, sits   105
High in Heaven's realm, upon a golden throne,
Even like an earthly king; and whose dread work,
Hell, gapes for ever for the unhappy slaves

Of fate, whom He created, in his sport,
To triumph in their torments when they fell!   110
Earth heard the name; Earth trembled, as the smoke
Of His revenge ascended up to Heaven,
Blotting the constellations; and the cries
Of millions, butchered in sweet confidence
And unsuspecting peace, even when the bonds   115
Of safety were confirmed by wordy oaths
Sworn in His dreadful name, rung through the land;
Whilst innocent babes writhed on thy stubborn spear,
And thou didst laugh to hear the mother's shriek
Of maniac gladness, as the sacred steel   120
Felt cold in her torn entrails!

'Religion! thou wert then in manhood's prime:
But age crept on: one God would not suffice
For senile puerility; thou framedst
A tale to suit thy dotage, and to glut   125
Thy misery-thirsting soul, that the mad fiend
Thy wickedness had pictured might afford
A plea for sating the unnatural thirst
For murder, rapine, violence, and crime,
That still consumed thy being, even when   130
Thou heardst the step of Fate;—that flames might light
Thy funeral scene, and the shrill horrent shrieks
Of parents dying on the pile that burned
To light their children to thy paths, the roar
Of the encircling flames, the exulting cries   135
Of thine apostles, loud commingling there,
     Might sate thine hungry ear
     Even on the bed of death!

'But now contempt is mocking thy gray hairs;
Thou art descending to the darksome grave,   140
Unhonoured and unpitied, but by those
Whose pride is passing by like thine, and sheds,
Like thine, a glare that fades before the sun
Of truth, and shines but in the dreadful night
That long has lowered above the ruined world.   145

'Throughout these infinite orbs of mingling light,
Of which yon earth is one, is wide diffused
A Spirit of activity and life,
That knows no term, cessation, or decay;
That fades not when the lamp of earthly life,   150
Extinguished in the dampness of the grave,
Awhile there slumbers, more than when the babe
In the dim newness of its being feels
The impulses of sublunary things,
And all is wonder to unpractised sense: 155
But, active, steadfast, and eternal, still
Guides the fierce whirlwind, in the tempest roars,
Cheers in the day, breathes in the balmy groves,
Strengthens in health, and poisons in disease;
And in the storm of change, that ceaselessly   160
Rolls round the eternal universe, and shakes
Its undecaying battlement, presides,
Apportioning with irresistible law
The place each spring of its machine shall fill;
So that when waves on waves tumultuous heap   165
Confusion to the clouds, and fiercely driven
Heaven's lightnings scorch the uprooted ocean-fords,
Whilst, to the eye of shipwrecked mariner,
Lone sitting on the bare and shuddering rock,
All seems unlinked contingency and chance: 170
No atom of this turbulence fulfils
A vague and unnecessitated task,
Or acts but as it must and ought to act.
Even the minutest molecule of light,
That in an April sunbeam's fleeting glow   175
Fulfils its destined, though invisible work,
The universal Spirit guides; nor less,
When merciless ambition, or mad zeal,
Has led two hosts of dupes to battlefield,
That, blind, they there may dig each other's graves,   180
And call the sad work glory, does it rule
All passions: not a thought, a will, an act,
No working of the tyrant's moody mind,
Nor one misgiving of the slaves who boast
Their servitude, to hide the shame they feel,   185

Nor the events enchaining every will,
That from the depths of unrecorded time
Have drawn all-influencing virtue, pass
Unrecognized, or unforeseen by thee,
Soul of the Universe! eternal spring   190
Of life and death, of happiness and woe,
Of all that chequers the phantasmal scene
That floats before our eyes in wavering light,
Which gleams but on the darkness of our prison,
    Whose chains and massy walls   195
    We feel, but cannot see.

'Spirit of Nature! all-sufficing Power,
Necessity! thou mother of the world!
Unlike the God of human error, thou
Requir'st no prayers or praises; the caprice   200
Of man's weak will belongs no more to thee
Than do the changeful passions of his breast
To thy unvarying harmony: the slave,
Whose horrible lusts spread misery o'er the world,
And the good man, who lifts, with virtuous pride,   205
His being, in the sight of happiness,
That springs from his own works; the poison-tree,
Beneath whose shade all life is withered up,
And the fair oak, whose leafy dome affords
A temple where the vows of happy love   210
Are registered, are equal in thy sight:
No love, no hate thou cherishest; revenge
And favouritism, and worst desire of fame
Thou know'st not: all that the wide world contains
Are but thy passive instruments, and thou   215
Regard'st them all with an impartial eye,
Whose joy or pain thy nature cannot feel,
    Because thou hast not human sense,
    Because thou art not human mind.

'Yes! when the sweeping storm of time   220
Has sung its death-dirge o'er the ruined fanes
And broken altars of the almighty Fiend
Whose name usurps thy honours, and the blood

Through centuries clotted there, has floated down
The tainted flood of ages, shalt thou live   225
Unchangeable! A shrine is raised to thee,
    Which, nor the tempest-breath of time,
    Nor the interminable flood,
    Over earth's slight pageant rolling,
      Availeth to destroy,—   230
The sensitive extension of the world.
    That wondrous and eternal fane,
Where pain and pleasure, good and evil join,
To do the will of strong necessity,
    And life, in multitudinous shapes,   235
Still pressing forward where no term can be,
    Like hungry and unresting flame
Curls round the eternal columns of its strength.'

VII

Spirit

'I WAS an infant when my mother went
To see an atheist burned. She took me there:
The dark-robed priests were met around the pile;
The multitude was gazing silently;
And as the culprit passed with dauntless mien,   5
Tempered disdain in his unaltering eye,
Mixed with a quiet smile, shone calmly forth:
The thirsty fire crept round his manly limbs;
His resolute eyes were scorched to blindness soon;
His death-pang rent my heart! the insensate mob   10
Uttered a cry of triumph, and I wept.
"Weep not, child!" cried my mother, "for that man
Has said, 'There is no God.'"'

Fairy

                'There is no God!
Nature confirms the faith his death-groan sealed:
Let heaven and earth, let man's revolving race,   15
His ceaseless generations tell their tale;

VII. 1–end *omitted 1839*[1]. *See MWS, Note, below, p. 337, § 1.*

Let every part depending on the chain
That links it to the whole, point to the hand
That grasps its term! let every seed that falls
In silent eloquence unfold its store   20
Of argument; infinity within,
Infinity without, belie creation;
The exterminable spirit it contains
Is nature's only God; but human pride
Is skilful to invent most serious names   25
To hide its ignorance.
                         The name of God
Has fenced about all crime with holiness,
Himself the creature of His worshippers,
Whose names and attributes and passions change,
Seeva, Buddh, Foh, Jehovah, God, or Lord,   30
Even with the human dupes who build His shrines,
Still serving o'er the war-polluted world
For desolation's watchword; whether hosts
Stain His death-blushing chariot-wheels, as on
Triumphantly they roll, whilst Brahmins raise   35
A sacred hymn to mingle with the groans;
Or countless partners of His power divide
His tyranny to weakness; or the smoke
Of burning towns, the cries of female helplessness,
Unarmed old age, and youth, and infancy,   40
Horribly massacred, ascend to Heaven
In honour of His name; or, last and worst,
Earth groans beneath religion's iron age,
And priests dare babble of a God of peace,
Even whilst their hands are red with guiltless blood,   45
Murdering the while, uprooting every germ
Of truth, exterminating, spoiling all,
Making the earth a slaughter-house!

          'O Spirit! through the sense
By which thy inner nature was apprised   50
     Of outward shows, vague dreams have rolled,
     And varied reminiscences have waked
          Tablets that never fade;

VII. 23 *see n., p. 388*

All things have been imprinted there,
The stars, the sea, the earth, the sky,   55
Even the unshapeliest lineaments
   Of wild and fleeting visions
      Have left a record there
      To testify of earth.

'These are my empire, for to me is given   60
The wonders of the human world to keep,
And Fancy's thin creations to endow
With manner, being, and reality;
Therefore a wondrous phantom, from the dreams
Of human error's dense and purblind faith,   65
I will evoke, to meet thy questioning.
      Ahasuerus, rise!'

      A strange and woe-worn wight
   Arose beside the battlement,
      And stood unmoving there.   70
His inessential figure cast no shade
      Upon the golden floor;
His port and mien bore mark of many years,
And chronicles of untold ancientness
Were legible within his beamless eye: 75
   Yet his cheek bore the mark of youth;
Freshness and vigour knit his manly frame;
The wisdom of old age was mingled there
   With youth's primaeval dauntlessness;
      And inexpressible woe,   80
Chastened by fearless resignation, gave
An awful grace to his all-speaking brow.

Spirit

'Is there a God?'

Ahasuerus

'Is there a God!—ay, an almighty God,
And vengeful as almighty! Once His voice   85
Was heard on earth: earth shuddered at the sound;
The fiery-visaged firmament expressed

Abhorrence, and the grave of Nature yawned
To swallow all the dauntless and the good
That dared to hurl defiance at His throne,   90
Girt as it was with power. None but slaves
Survived,—cold-blooded slaves, who did the work
Of tyrannous omnipotence; whose souls
No honest indignation ever urged
To elevated daring, to one deed   95
Which gross and sensual self did not pollute.
These slaves built temples for the omnipotent Fiend,
Gorgeous and vast: the costly altars smoked
With human blood, and hideous paeans rung
Through all the long-drawn aisles. A murderer heard   100
His voice in Egypt, one whose gifts and arts
Had raised him to his eminence in power,
Accomplice of omnipotence in crime,
And confidant of the all-knowing one.
     These were Jehovah's words:—   105

'From an eternity of idleness
I, God, awoke; in seven days' toil made earth
From nothing; rested, and created man:
I placed him in a Paradise, and there
Planted the tree of evil, so that he   110
Might eat and perish, and My soul procure
Wherewith to sate its malice, and to turn,
Even like a heartless conqueror of the earth,
All misery to My fame. The race of men
Chosen to My honour, with impunity   115
May sate the lusts I planted in their heart.
Here I command thee hence to lead them on,
Until, with hardened feet, their conquering troops
Wade on the promised soil through woman's blood,
And make My name be dreaded through the land.   120
Yet ever-burning flame and ceaseless woe
Shall be the doom of their eternal souls,
With every soul on this ungrateful earth,
Virtuous or vicious, weak or strong,—even all
Shall perish, to fulfil the blind revenge   125
(Which you, to men, call justice) of their God.'

The murderer's brow
Quivered with horror.
'God omnipotent,
Is there no mercy? must our punishment
Be endless? will long ages roll away,   130
And see no term? Oh! wherefore hast Thou made
In mockery and wrath this evil earth?
Mercy becomes the powerful—be but just:
O God! repent and save.'

'One way remains:
I will beget a Son, and He shall bear   135
The sins of all the world; He shall arise
In an unnoticed corner of the earth,
And there shall die upon a cross, and purge
The universal crime; so that the few
On whom My grace descends, those who are marked   140
As vessels to the honour of their God,
May credit this strange sacrifice, and save
Their souls alive: millions shall live and die,
Who ne'er shall call upon their Saviour's name,
But, unredeemed, go to the gaping grave.   145
Thousands shall deem it an old woman's tale,
Such as the nurses frighten babes withal:
These in a gulf of anguish and of flame
Shall curse their reprobation endlessly,
Yet tenfold pangs shall force them to avow,   150
Even on their beds of torment, where they howl,
My honour, and the justice of their doom.
What then avail their virtuous deeds, their thoughts
Of purity, with radiant genius bright,
Or lit with human reason's earthly ray?   155
Many are called, but few will I elect.
Do thou My bidding, Moses!'
Even the murderer's cheek
Was blanched with horror, and his quivering lips
Scarce faintly uttered—'O almighty One,
I tremble and obey!'   160

'O Spirit! centuries have set their seal
On this heart of many wounds, and loaded brain,

Since the Incarnate came: humbly He came,
Veiling His horrible Godhead in the shape
Of man, scorned by the world, His name unheard,   165
Save by the rabble of His native town,
Even as a parish demagogue. He led
The crowd; He taught them justice, truth, and peace,
In semblance; but He lit within their souls
The quenchless flames of zeal, and blessed the sword   170
He brought on earth to satiate with the blood
Of truth and freedom His malignant soul.
At length His mortal frame was led to death.
I stood beside Him: on the torturing cross
No pain assailed His unterrestrial sense;   175
And yet He groaned. Indignantly I summed
The massacres and miseries which His name
Had sanctioned in my country, and I cried,
"Go! Go!" in mockery.
A smile of godlike malice reillumed   180
His fading lineaments.—"I go," He cried,
"But thou shalt wander o'er the unquiet earth
Eternally."——The dampness of the grave
Bathed my imperishable front. I fell,
And long lay tranced upon the charmèd soil.   185
When I awoke Hell burned within my brain,
Which staggered on its seat; for all around
The mouldering relics of my kindred lay,
Even as the Almighty's ire arrested them,
And in their various attitudes of death   190
My murdered children's mute and eyeless skulls
Glared ghastily upon me.
                              But my soul,
From sight and sense of the polluting woe
Of tyranny, had long learned to prefer
Hell's freedom to the servitude of Heaven.   195
Therefore I rose, and dauntlessly began
My lonely and unending pilgrimage,
Resolved to wage unweariable war
With my almighty Tyrant, and to hurl
Defiance at His impotence to harm   200

VII. 180 reillumed *1904, 1839²*] reillumined *1839¹, 1813*

Beyond the curse I bore. The very hand
That barred my passage to the peaceful grave
Has crushed the earth to misery, and given
Its empire to the chosen of His slaves.
These have I seen, even from the earliest dawn   205
Of weak, unstable and precarious power,
Then preaching peace, as now they practise war;
So, when they turned but from the massacre
Of unoffending infidels, to quench
Their thirst for ruin in the very blood   210
That flowed in their own veins, and pitiless zeal
Froze every human feeling, as the wife
Sheathed in her husband's heart the sacred steel,
Even whilst its hopes were dreaming of her love;
And friends to friends, brothers to brothers stood   215
Opposed in bloodiest battlefield, and war,
Scarce satiable by fate's last death-draught, waged,
Drunk from the winepress of the Almighty's wrath;
Whilst the red cross, in mockery of peace,
Pointed to victory! When the fray was done,   220
No remnant of the exterminated faith
Survived to tell its ruin, but the flesh,
With putrid smoke poisoning the atmosphere,
That rotted on the half-extinguished pile.

'Yes! I have seen God's worshippers unsheathe   225
The sword of His revenge, when grace descended,
Confirming all unnatural impulses,
To sanctify their desolating deeds;
And frantic priests waved the ill-omened cross
O'er the unhappy earth: then shone the sun   230
On showers of gore from the upflashing steel
Of safe assassination, and all crime
Made stingless by the Spirits of the Lord,
And blood-red rainbows canopied the land.

'Spirit, no year of my eventful being   235
Has passed unstained by crime and misery,
Which flows from God's own faith. I've marked His slaves

With tongues whose lies are venomous, beguile
The insensate mob, and, whilst one hand was red
With murder, feign to stretch the other out   240
For brotherhood and peace; and that they now
Babble of love and mercy, whilst their deeds
Are marked with all the narrowness and crime
That Freedom's young arm dare not yet chastise,
Reason may claim our gratitude, who now   245
Establishing the imperishable throne
Of truth, and stubborn virtue, maketh vain
The unprevailing malice of my Foe,
Whose bootless rage heaps torments for the brave,
Adds impotent eternities to pain,   250
Whilst keenest disappointment racks His breast
To see the smiles of peace around them play,
To frustrate or to sanctify their doom.

'Thus have I stood,—through a wild waste of years
Struggling with whirlwinds of mad agony,   255
Yet peaceful, and serene, and self-enshrined,
Mocking my powerless Tyrant's horrible curse
With stubborn and unalterable will,
Even as a giant oak, which Heaven's fierce flame
Had scathèd in the wilderness, to stand   260
A monument of fadeless ruin there;
Yet peacefully and movelessly it braves
The midnight conflict of the wintry storm,
    As in the sunlight's calm it spreads
    Its worn and withered arms on high   265
To meet the quiet of a summer's noon.'

      The Fairy waved her wand:
      Ahasuerus fled
Fast as the shapes of mingled shade and mist,
That lurk in the glens of a twilight grove,   270
      Flee from the morning beam:
    The matter of which dreams are made
    Not more endowed with actual life
    Than this phantasmal portraiture
    Of wandering human thought.   275

VIII

The Fairy

'THE Present and the Past thou hast beheld:
It was a desolate sight. Now, Spirit, learn
   The secrets of the Future.—Time!
Unfold the brooding pinion of thy gloom,
Render thou up thy half-devoured babes,   5
And from the cradles of eternity,
Where millions lie lulled to their portioned sleep
By the deep murmuring stream of passing things,
Tear thou that gloomy shroud.—Spirit, behold
   Thy glorious destiny!'   10

   Joy to the Spirit came.
Through the wide rent in Time's eternal veil,
Hope was seen beaming through the mists of fear:
   Earth was no longer Hell;
   Love, freedom, health, had given   15
Their ripeness to the manhood of its prime,
   And all its pulses beat
Symphonious to the planetary spheres:
   Then dulcet music swelled
Concordant with the life-strings of the soul;   20
It throbbed in sweet and languid beatings there,
Catching new life from transitory death,—
Like the vague sighings of a wind at even,
That wakes the wavelets of the slumbering sea
And dies on the creation of its breath,   25
And sinks and rises, fails and swells by fits,
   Was the pure stream of feeling
   That sprung from these sweet notes,
And o'er the Spirit's human sympathies
With mild and gentle motion calmly flowed.   30

   Joy to the Spirit came,—
   Such joy as when a lover sees

VIII. 3–4 Time! / . . . gloom *revised but cancelled as* mighty time / Relentless sire
inexorable King *Fn.*   26 fits,] fits: *edd.*

The chosen of his soul in happiness,
    And witnesses her peace
Whose woe to him were bitterer than death,   35
    Sees her unfaded cheek
Glow mantling in first luxury of health,
    Thrills with her lovely eyes,
Which like two stars amid the heaving main
    Sparkle through liquid bliss.   40

Then in her triumph spoke the Fairy Queen:
'I will not call the ghost of ages gone
To unfold the frightful secrets of its lore;
    The present now is past,
And those events that desolate the earth   45
Have faded from the memory of Time,
Who dares not give reality to that
Whose being I annul. To me is given
The wonders of the human world to keep,
Space, matter, time, and mind. Futurity   50
Exposes now its treasure; let the sight
Renew and strengthen all thy failing hope.
O human Spirit! spur thee to the goal
Where virtue fixes universal peace,
And midst the ebb and flow of human things,   55
Show somewhat stable, somewhat certain still,
A lighthouse o'er the wild of dreary waves.

'The habitable earth is full of bliss;
Those wastes of frozen billows that were hurled
By everlasting snowstorms round the poles,   60
Where matter dared not vegetate or live,
But ceaseless frost round the vast solitude
Bound its broad zone of stillness, are unloosed;
And fragrant zephyrs there from spicy isles
Ruffle the placid ocean-deep, that rolls   65

VIII. 41 Then from the mighty shape a voice came forth *Fn., probably, rejected 1816*
47 give *1904, 1813 and edd.*] lend *Fn., rejected 1816*   52 all thy failing *1904,
1813 and edd.*] thy suspended *Fn., rejected 1816*   61 not vegetate or live, *1904,
1813*] not vegetate nor live, *1839* nor vegetate nor live *1816*

Its broad, bright surges to the sloping sand,
Whose roar is wakened into echoings sweet
To murmur through the Heaven-breathing groves
And melodize with man's blest nature there.

'Those deserts of immeasurable sand,　　　　70
Whose age-collected fervours scarce allowed
A bird to live, a blade of grass to spring,
Where the shrill chirp of the green lizard's love
Broke on the sultry silentness alone,
Now teem with countless rills and shady woods,　　　75
Cornfields and pastures and white cottages;
And—where the startled wilderness beheld
A savage conqueror stained in kindred blood,
A tigress sating with the flesh of lambs
The unnatural famine of her toothless cubs,　　　80
Whilst shouts and howlings through the desert rang—
Sloping and smooth the daisy-spangled lawn,
Offering sweet incense to the sunrise, smiles
To see a babe before his mother's door,
　　Sharing his morning's meal　　　85
　With the green and golden basilisk
　　That comes to lick his feet.

'Those trackless deeps, where many a weary sail
Has seen above the illimitable plain,
Morning on night, and night on morning rise,　　　90
Whilst still no land to greet the wanderer spread
Its shadowy mountains on the sun-bright sea,
Where the loud roarings of the tempest-waves
So long have mingled with the gusty wind
In melancholy loneliness, and swept　　　95
The desert of those ocean solitudes,
But vocal to the sea-bird's harrowing shriek,
The bellowing monster, and the rushing storm,
Now to the sweet and many-mingling sounds
Of kindliest human impulses respond.　　　100
Those lonely realms bright garden-isles begem,
With lightsome clouds and shining seas between,

VIII. 77 And—] And *edd.* 81 Whilst *1904, 1813*] While *1839* rang—], rang, *edd.*

And fertile valleys, resonant with bliss,
Whilst green woods overcanopy the wave,
Which like a toil-worn labourer leaps to shore,   105
To meet the kisses of the flow'rets there.

'All things are recreated, and the flame
Of consentaneous love inspires all life:
The fertile bosom of the earth gives suck
To myriads, who still grow beneath her care,   110
Rewarding her with their pure perfectness:
The balmy breathings of the wind inhale
Her virtues, and diffuse them all abroad:
Health floats amid the gentle atmosphere,
Glows in the fruits, and mantles on the stream: 115
No storms deform the beaming brow of Heaven,
Nor scatter in the freshness of its pride
The foliage of the ever-verdant trees;
But fruits are ever ripe, flowers ever fair,
And Autumn proudly bears her matron grace,   120
Kindling a flush on the fair cheek of Spring,
Whose virgin bloom beneath the ruddy fruit
Reflects its tint, and blushes into love.

'The lion now forgets to thirst for blood:
There might you see him sporting in the sun   125
Beside the dreadless kid; his claws are sheathed,
His teeth are harmless, custom's force has made
His nature as the nature of a lamb.
Like passion's fruit, the nightshade's tempting bane
Poisons no more the pleasure it bestows: 130
All bitterness is past; the cup of joy
Unmingled mantles to the goblet's brim,
And courts the thirsty lips it fled before.

'But chief, ambiguous Man, he that can know
More misery, and dream more joy than all;   135
Whose keen sensations thrill within his breast
To mingle with a loftier instinct there,
Lending their power to pleasure and to pain,
Yet raising, sharpening, and refining each;

Who stands amid the ever-varying world,   140
The burthen or the glory of the earth;
He chief perceives the change, his being notes
The gradual renovation, and defines
Each movement of its progress on his mind.

'Man, where the gloom of the long polar night   145
Lowers o'er the snow-clad rocks and frozen soil,
Where scarce the hardiest herb that braves the frost
Basks in the moonlight's ineffectual glow,
Shrank with the plants, and darkened with the night;
His chilled and narrow energies, his heart,   150
Insensible to courage, truth, or love,
His stunted stature and imbecile frame,
Marked him for some abortion of the earth,
Fit compeer of the bears that roamed around,
Whose habits and enjoyments were his own: 155
His life a feverish dream of stagnant woe,
Whose meagre wants, but scantily fulfilled,
Apprised him ever of the joyless length
Which his short being's wretchedness had reached;
His death a pang which famine, cold and toil   160
Long on the mind, whilst yet the vital spark
Clung to the body stubbornly, had brought:
All was inflicted here that Earth's revenge
Could wreak on the infringers of her law;
One curse alone was spared—the name of God.   165

'Nor where the tropics bound the realms of day
With a broad belt of mingling cloud and flame,
Where blue mists through the unmoving atmosphere
Scattered the seeds of pestilence, and fed
Unnatural vegetation, where the land   170
Teemed with all earthquake, tempest and disease,
Was Man a nobler being; slavery
Had crushed him to his country's blood-stained dust;
Or he was bartered for the fame of power,
Which all internal impulses destroying,   175
Makes human will an article of trade;

VIII. 165 *omitted 1839¹. See MWS, Note, below, p. 337, § 1.*

Or he was changed with Christians for their gold,
And dragged to distant isles, where to the sound
Of the flesh-mangling scourge, he does the work
Of all-polluting luxury and wealth,   180
Which doubly visits on the tyrants' heads
The long-protracted fulness of their woe;
Or he was led to legal butchery,
To turn to worms beneath that burning sun,
Where kings first leagued against the rights of men,   185
And priests first traded with the name of God.

'Even where the milder zone afforded Man
A seeming shelter, yet contagion there,
Blighting his being with unnumbered ills,
Spread like a quenchless fire; nor truth till late   190
Availed to arrest its progress, or create
That peace which first in bloodless victory waved
Her snowy standard o'er this favoured clime:
There man was long the train-bearer of slaves,
The mimic of surrounding misery,   195
The jackal of ambition's lion-rage,
The bloodhound of religion's hungry zeal.

'Here now the human being stands adorning
This loveliest earth with taintless body and mind;
Blessed from his birth with all bland impulses,   200
Which gently in his noble bosom wake
All kindly passions and all pure desires.
Him, still from hope to hope the bliss pursuing
Which from the exhaustless lore of human weal
Dawns on the virtuous mind, the thoughts that rise   205
In time-destroying infiniteness, gift
With self-enshrined eternity, that mocks
The unprevailing hoariness of age,
And man, once fleeting o'er the transient scene

VIII. 177–8   Thier perfidy, thier poisons and thier pride
                               Fn., rejected 1816
184–6 *Cancelled in Fn. in favour of* A banquet for the vultures and the worms, |
Beneath that sun where *which, in turn, is also cancelled*   204 lore *1904, Notes,*
1813] store *text 1813, 1839*   205 Dawns *1904, Notes, 1813*] Draws
text 1813, 1839

Swift as an unremembered vision, stands   210
Immortal upon earth: no longer now
He slays the lamb that looks him in the face,
And horribly devours his mangled flesh,
Which, still avenging Nature's broken law,
Kindled all putrid humours in his frame,   215
All evil passions, and all vain belief,
Hatred, despair, and loathing in his mind,
The germs of misery, death, disease, and crime.
No longer now the wingèd habitants,
That in the woods their sweet lives sing away,   220
Flee from the form of man; but gather round,
And prune their sunny feathers on the hands
Which little children stretch in friendly sport
Towards these dreadless partners of their play.
All things are void of terror: Man has lost   225
His terrible prerogative, and stands
An equal amidst equals: happiness
And science dawn though late upon the earth;
Peace cheers the mind, health renovates the frame;
Disease and pleasure cease to mingle here,   230
Reason and passion cease to combat there;
Whilst each unfettered o'er the earth extends
Its all-subduing energies, and wields
The sceptre of a vast dominion there;
Whilst every shape and mode of matter lends   235
Its force to the omnipotence of mind,
Which from its dark mine drags the gem of truth
To decorate its Paradise of peace.'

IX

'O HAPPY Earth! reality of Heaven!
To which those restless souls that ceaselessly
Throng through the human universe, aspire;
Thou consummation of all mortal hope!
Thou glorious prize of blindly-working will!   5
Whose rays, diffused throughout all space and time,

VIII. 232–3 extends / Its ... wields *1839*] extend / Their . . . wield *1904*, *1813*.
Cf. The Daemon of the World, *465–7*, *where Shelley himself has revised syntax at the cost of sound.*

Verge to one point and blend for ever there:
Of purest spirits thou pure dwelling-place!
Where care and sorrow, impotence and crime,
Languor, disease, and ignorance dare not come: 10
O happy Earth, reality of Heaven!

'Genius has seen thee in her passionate dreams,
And dim forebodings of thy loveliness
Haunting the human heart, have there entwined
Those rooted hopes of some sweet place of bliss   15
Where friends and lovers meet to part no more.
Thou art the end of all desire and will,
The product of all action; and the souls
That by the paths of an aspiring change
Have reached thy haven of perpetual peace,   20
There rest from the eternity of toil
That framed the fabric of thy perfectness.

'Even Time, the conqueror, fled thee in his fear;
That hoary giant, who, in lonely pride,
So long had ruled the world, that nations fell   25
Beneath his silent footstep. Pyramids,
That for millenniums had withstood the tide
Of human things, his storm-breath drove in sand
Across that desert where their stones survived
The name of him whose pride had heaped them there.   30
Yon monarch, in his solitary pomp,
Was but the mushroom of a summer day,
That his light-wingèd footstep pressed to dust:
Time was the king of earth: all things gave way
Before him, but the fixed and virtuous will,   35
The sacred sympathies of soul and sense,
That mocked his fury and prepared his fall.

'Yet slow and gradual dawned the morn of love;
Long lay the clouds of darkness o'er the scene,

    IX. 27 millenniums *italicized in 1813*   withstood the tide *1904, 1813 and edd.*]
withstood the blast *BM^a*   32 summer day, *1904, 1813 and edd.*] winter day *BM^a*
33 that thy light footstep presses into dust *BM^a*

Till from its native Heaven they rolled away: 40
First, Crime triumphant o'er all hope careered
Unblushing, undisguising, bold and strong;
Whilst Falsehood, tricked in Virtue's attributes,
Long sanctified all deeds of vice and woe,
Till done by her own venomous sting to death,   45
She left the moral world without a law,
No longer fettering Passion's fearless wing,
Nor searing Reason with the brand of God.
Then steadily the happy ferment worked;
Reason was free; and wild though Passion went   50
Through tangled glens and wood-embosomed meads,
Gathering a garland of the strangest flowers,
Yet like the bee returning to her queen,
She bound the sweetest on her sister's brow,
Who meek and sober kissed the sportive child,   55
No longer trembling at the broken rod.

'Mild was the slow necessity of death:
The tranquil spirit failed beneath its grasp,
Without a groan, almost without a fear,
Calm as a voyager to some distant land,   60
And full of wonder, full of hope as he.
The deadly germs of languor and disease
Died in the human frame, and Purity
Blessed with all gifts her earthly worshippers.
How vigorous then the athletic form of age!   65
How clear its open and unwrinkled brow!
Where neither avarice, cunning, pride, nor care,
Had stamped the seal of gray deformity
On all the mingling lineaments of time.
How lovely the intrepid front of youth!   70
Which meek-eyed courage decked with freshest grace;
Courage of soul, that dreaded not a name,
And elevated will, that journeyed on
Through life's phantasmal scene in fearlessness,
With virtue, love, and pleasure, hand in hand.   75

IX. 48 *omitted 1839. See MWS, Note, below, p.* 337, § 1.   58 spirit *emended*
in Fn. from Spirit *1813*   67 nor *1904, 1839*] or *1813*

'Then, that sweet bondage which is Freedom's self,
And rivets with sensation's softest tie
The kindred sympathies of human souls,
Needed no fetters of tyrannic law:
Those delicate and timid impulses   80
In Nature's primal modesty arose,
And with undoubted confidence disclosed
The growing longings of its dawning love,
Unchecked by dull and selfish chastity,
That virtue of the cheaply virtuous,   85
Who pride themselves in senselessness and frost.
No longer prostitution's venomed bane
Poisoned the springs of happiness and life;
Woman and man, in confidence and love,
Equal and free and pure together trod   90
The mountain-paths of virtue, which no more
Were stained with blood from many a pilgrim's feet.

'Then, where, through distant ages, long in pride
The palace of the monarch-slave had mocked
Famine's faint groan, and Penury's silent tear,   95
A heap of crumbling ruins stood, and threw
Year after year their stones upon the field,
Wakening a lonely echo; and the leaves
Of the old thorn, that on the topmost tower
Usurped the royal ensign's grandeur, shook   100
In the stern storm that swayed the topmost tower
And whispered strange tales in the Whirlwind's ear.

'Low through the lone cathedral's roofless aisles
The melancholy winds a death-dirge sung:
It were a sight of awfulness to see   105
The works of faith and slavery, so vast,
So sumptuous, yet so perishing withal!
Even as the corpse that rests beneath its wall.
A thousand mourners deck the pomp of death

IX. 76–7   That mental bondage which is freedom's self
                And borrows from sensation's purest tie.   *cancelled Fn.*
83 love] *emended in Fn. to* lore *which better suits the context of the changes made for* The
Daemon of the World   93–102 *cancelled in Fn. Previously* field (97) *changed to*
waste *and that . . . shook (99–100) specifically cancelled*

To-day, the breathing marble glows above   110
To decorate its memory, and tongues
Are busy of its life: to-morrow, worms
In silence and in darkness seize their prey.

'Within the massy prison's mouldering courts,
Fearless and free the ruddy children played,   115
Weaving gay chaplets for their innocent brows
With the green ivy and the red wallflower,
That mock the dungeon's unavailing gloom;
The ponderous chains, and gratings of strong iron,
There rusted amid heaps of broken stone   120
That mingled slowly with their native earth:
There the broad beam of day, which feebly once
Lighted the cheek of lean Captivity
With a pale and sickly glare, then freely shone
On the pure smiles of infant playfulness: 125
No more the shuddering voice of hoarse Despair
Pealed through the echoing vaults, but soothing notes
Of ivy-fingered winds and gladsome birds
And merriment were resonant around.

'These ruins soon left not a rack behind: 130
Their elements, wide scattered o'er the globe,
To happier shapes were moulded, and became
Ministrant to all blissful impulses:
Thus human things were perfected, and earth,
Even as a child beneath its mother's love,   135
Was strengthened in all excellence, and grew
Fairer and nobler with each passing year.

'Now Time his dusky pennons o'er the scene
Closes in steadfast darkness, and the past
Fades from our charmèd sight. My task is done: 140
Thy lore is learned. Earth's wonders are thine own,
With all the fear and all the hope they bring.
My spells are passed: the present now recurs.
Ah me! a pathless wilderness remains
Yet unsubdued by man's reclaiming hand.   145

IX. 130 rack] wreck *all edd. Cf. Shakespeare*, The Tempest, IV. i. 156. *Even if Shelley did write* rack *and not* wrack *the misreading is easy.*

'Yet, human Spirit, bravely hold thy course,
Let virtue teach thee firmly to pursue
The gradual paths of an aspiring change:
For birth and life and death, and that strange state
Before the naked soul has found its home,   150
All tend to perfect happiness, and urge
The restless wheels of being on their way,
Whose flashing spokes, instinct with infinite life,
Bicker and burn to gain their destined goal:
For birth but wakes the spirit to the sense   155
Of outward shows, whose unexperienced shape
New modes of passion to its frame may lend;
Life is its state of action, and the store
Of all events is aggregated there
That variegate the eternal universe;   160
Death is a gate of dreariness and gloom,
That leads to azure isles and beaming skies
And happy regions of eternal hope.
Therefore, O Spirit! fearlessly bear on:
Though storms may break the primrose on its stalk,   165
Though frosts may blight the freshness of its bloom,
Yet Spring's awakening breath will woo the earth
To feed with kindliest dews its favourite flower,
That blooms in mossy banks and darksome glens,
Lighting the greenwood with its sunny smile.   170

'Fear not then, Spirit, Death's disrobing hand,
So welcome when the tyrant is awake,
So welcome when the bigot's hell-torch burns;
'Tis but the voyage of a darksome hour,
The transient gulf-dream of a startling sleep.   175
Death is no foe to Virtue: earth has seen
Love's brightest roses on the scaffold bloom,
Mingling with Freedom's fadeless laurels there,
And presaging the truth of visioned bliss.
Are there not hopes within thee, which this scene   180
Of linked and gradual being has confirmed?
Whose stingings bade thy heart look further still,
When, to the moonlight walk by Henry led,

167 earth] earth, *edd.*

Sweetly and sadly thou didst talk of death?
And wilt thou rudely tear them from thy breast,   185
Listening supinely to a bigot's creed,
Or tamely crouching to the tyrant's rod,
Whose iron thongs are red with human gore?
Never: but bravely bearing on, thy will
Is destined an eternal war to wage   190
With tyranny and falsehood, and uproot
The germs of misery from the human heart.
Thine is the hand whose piety would soothe
The thorny pillow of unhappy crime,
Whose impotence an easy pardon gains,   195
Watching its wanderings as a friend's disease:
Thine is the brow whose mildness would defy
Its fiercest rage, and brave its sternest will,
When fenced by power and master of the world.
Thou art sincere and good; of resolute mind,   200
Free from heart-withering custom's cold control,
Of passion lofty, pure and unsubdued.
Earth's pride and meanness could not vanquish thee,
And therefore art thou worthy of the boon
Which thou hast now received: Virtue shall keep   205
Thy footsteps in the path that thou hast trod,
And many days of beaming hope shall bless
Thy spotless life of sweet and sacred love.
Go, happy one, and give that bosom joy
Whose sleepless spirit waits to catch   210
Light, life and rapture from thy smile.'

The Fairy waves her wand of charm.
Speechless with bliss the Spirit mounts the car,
That rolled beside the battlement,
Bending her beamy eyes in thankfulness.   215
Again the enchanted steeds were yoked,
Again the burning wheels inflame
The steep descent of Heaven's untrodden way.
Fast and far the chariot flew:
The vast and fiery globes that rolled   220
Around the Fairy's palace-gate
Lessened by slow degrees and soon appeared

Such tiny twinklers as the planet orbs
That there attendant on the solar power
With borrowed light pursued their narrower way.   225

Earth floated then below:
  The chariot paused a moment there;
  The Spirit then descended:
The restless coursers pawed the ungenial soil,
Snuffed the gross air, and then, their errand done,   230
Unfurled their pinions to the winds of Heaven.

The Body and the Soul united then,
A gentle start convulsed Ianthe's frame:
Her veiny eyelids quietly unclosed;
Moveless awhile the dark blue orbs remained: 235
She looked around in wonder and beheld
Henry, who kneeled in silence by her couch,
Watching her sleep with looks of speechless love,
      And the bright beaming stars
      That through the casement shone.   240

SHELLEY'S NOTES ON *QUEEN MAB*[1]

Note 1: I. 242, 243

> *The sun's unclouded orb*
> *Rolled through the black concave.*

BEYOND our atmosphere the sun would appear a rayless orb of fire in
the midst of a black concave. The equal diffusion of its light on earth is
owing to the refraction of the rays by the atmosphere, and their reflection
from other bodies. Light consists either of vibrations propagated through
a subtle medium, or of numerous minute particles repelled in all direc-
tions from the luminous body. Its velocity greatly exceeds that of any
substance with which we are acquainted: observations on the eclipses of
Jupiter's satellites have demonstrated that light takes up no more than
8' 7" in passing from the sun to the earth, a distance of 95,000,000
miles.—Some idea may be gained of the immense distance of the fixed
stars when it is computed that many years would elapse before light
could reach this earth from the nearest of them; yet in one year light

---

[1] See General Introduction, pp. xli–xlii.

travels 5,422,400,000,000 miles, which is a distance 5,707,600 times greater than that of the sun from the earth.

Note 2: I. 252, 253

> *Whilst round the chariot's way*
> *Innumerable systems rolled.*

The plurality of worlds,—the indefinite immensity of the universe, is a most awful subject of contemplation. He who rightly feels its mystery and grandeur is in no danger of seduction from the falsehoods of religious systems, or of deifying the principle of the universe. It is impossible to believe that the Spirit that pervades this infinite machine begat a son upon the body of a Jewish woman; or is angered at the consequences of that necessity, which is a synonym of itself. All that miserable tale of the Devil, and Eve, and an Intercessor, with the childish mummeries of the God of the Jews, is irreconcilable with the knowledge of the stars. The works of His fingers have borne witness against Him.

The nearest of the fixed stars is inconceivably distant from the earth, and they are probably proportionably distant from each other. By a calculation of the velocity of light, Sirius is supposed to be at least 54,224,000,000,000 miles from the earth.[1] That which appears only like a thin and silvery cloud streaking the heaven is in effect composed of innumerable clusters of suns, each shining with its own light, and illuminating numbers of planets that revolve around them. Millions and millions of suns are ranged around us, all attended by innumerable worlds, yet calm, regular, and harmonious, all keeping the paths of immutable necessity.

Note 3: IV. 178, 179

> *These are the hired bravos who defend*
> *The tyrant's throne.*

To employ murder as a means of justice is an idea which a man of an enlightened mind will not dwell upon with pleasure. To march forth in rank and file, and all the pomp of streamers and trumpets, for the purpose of shooting at our fellow-men as a mark; to inflict upon them all the variety of wound and anguish; to leave them weltering in their blood; to wander over the field of desolation, and count the number of the dying and the dead,—are employments which in thesis we may maintain to be necessary, but which no good man will contemplate with gratulation and delight. A battle we suppose is won:—thus truth is established, thus the cause of

---

[1] See Nicholson's *British Encyclopedia*, art. Light.

justice is confirmed! It surely requires no common sagacity to discern the connexion between this immense heap of calamities and the assertion of truth or the maintenance of justice.

'Kings, and ministers of state, the real authors of the calamity, sit un-molested in their cabinet, while those against whom the fury of the storm is directed are, for the most part, persons who have been trepanned into the service, or who are dragged unwillingly from their peaceful homes into the field of battle. A soldier is a man whose business it is to kill those who never offended him, and who are the innocent martyrs of other men's iniquities. Whatever may become of the abstract question of the justifiable-ness of war, it seems impossible that the soldier should not be a depraved and unnatural being.

To these more serious and momentous considerations it may be proper to add a recollection of the ridiculousness of the military character. Its first constituent is obedience: a soldier is, of all descriptions of men, the most completely a machine; yet his profession inevitably teaches him something of dogmatism, swaggering, and self-consequence: he is like the puppet of a showman, who, at the very time he is made to strut and swell and display the most farcical airs, we perfectly know cannot assume the most insignificant gesture, advance either to the right or the left, but as he is moved by his exhibitor.'—Godwin's *Enquirer*, Essay v.

I will here subjoin a little poem, so strongly expressive of my abhor-rence of despotism and falsehood, that I fear lest it never again may be depictured so vividly. This opportunity is perhaps the only one that ever will occur of rescuing it from oblivion.

Falsehood and Vice

A DIALOGUE

[*See above, pp. 86-90*]

Note 4: V. 1, 2

> *Thus do the generations of the earth*
> *Go to the grave, and issue from the womb.*

'One generation passeth away, and another generation cometh; but the earth abideth for ever. The sun also ariseth, and the sun goeth down, and hasteth to his place where he arose. The wind goeth toward the south, and turneth about unto the north; it whirleth about continually, and the wind returneth again according to his circuits. All the rivers run into the sea; yet the sea is not full; unto the place from whence the rivers come, thither they return again.'—*Ecclesiastes*, chap. i. vv. 4-7.

Note 5: V. 4–6

Even as the leaves
Which the keen frost-wind of the waning year
Has scattered on the forest soil.

Οἵη περ φύλλων γενεή, τοιήδε καὶ ἀνδρῶν.
Φύλλα τὰ μέν τ᾿ ἄνεμος χαμάδις χέει, ἄλλα δέ θ᾿ ὕλη
Τηλεθόωσα φύει, ἔαρος δ᾿ ἐπιγίγνεται ὥρῃ.
Ὣς ἀνδρῶν γενεή, ἡ μὲν φύει, ἡ δ᾿ ἀπολήγει.

Homer, *Iliad*, vi. 146–9.

Note 6: V. 58

The mob of peasants, nobles, priests, and kings.

Suave mari magno turbantibus aequora ventis
E terra magnum alterius spectare laborem;
Non quia vexari quemquam est iucunda voluptas,
Sed quibus ipse malis careas quia cernere suave est.
Suave etiam belli certamina magna tueri
Per campos instructa, tua sine parte pericli;
Sed nil dulcius est bene quam munita tenere
Edita doctrina sapientum templa serena,
Despicere unde queas alios, passimque videre
Errare atque viam palantis quaerere vitae;
Certare ingenio; contendere nobilitate;
Noctes atque dies niti praestante labore
Ad summas emergere opes, rerumque potiri.
O miseras hominum mentes! O pectora caeca!

Lucretius, *De Rerum Natura*, ii. 1–14.

Note 7: V. 93, 94

And statesmen boast
Of wealth!

There is no real wealth but the labour of man. Were the mountains of
gold and the valleys of silver, the world would not be one grain of corn
the richer; no one comfort would be added to the human race. In con-
sequence of our consideration for the precious metals, one man is enabled
to heap to himself luxuries at the expense of the necessaries of his neigh-
bour; a system admirably fitted to produce all the varieties of disease and
crime, which never fail to characterize the two extremes of opulence and
penury. A speculator takes pride to himself as the promoter of his country's
prosperity, who employs a number of hands in the manufacture of articles

avowedly destitute of use, or subservient only to the unhallowed cravings of luxury and ostentation. The nobleman, who employs the peasants of his neighbourhood in building his palaces, until

> *iam pauca aratro iugera regiae*
> *moles relinquent*

flatters himself that he has gained the title of a patriot by yielding to the impulses of vanity. The show and pomp of courts adduce the same apology for its continuance; and many a fête has been given, many a woman has eclipsed her beauty by her dress, to benefit the labouring poor and to encourage trade. Who does not see that this is a remedy which aggravates whilst it palliates the countless diseases of society? The poor are set to labour,—for what? Not the food for which they famish: not the blankets for want of which their babes are frozen by the cold of their miserable hovels: not those comforts of civilization without which civilized man is far more miserable than the meanest savage; oppressed as he is by all its insidious evils, within the daily and taunting prospect of its innumerable benefits assiduously exhibited before him:—no; for the pride of power, for the miserable isolation of pride, for the false pleasures of the hundredth part of society. No greater evidence is afforded of the wide extended and radical mistakes of civilized man than this fact: those arts which are essential to his very being are held in the greatest contempt; employments are lucrative in an inverse ratio to their usefulness[1]: the jeweller, the toyman, the actor gains fame and wealth by the exercise of his useless and ridiculous art; whilst the cultivator of the earth, he without whom society must cease to subsist, struggles through contempt and penury, and perishes by that famine which but for his unceasing exertions would annihilate the rest of mankind.

I will not insult common sense by insisting on the doctrine of the natural equality of man. The question is not concerning its desirableness, but its practicability: so far as it is practicable, it is desirable. That state of human society which approaches nearer to an equal partition of its benefits and evils should, *caeteris paribus*, be preferred: but so long as we conceive that a wanton expenditure of human labour, not for the necessities, not even for the luxuries of the mass of society, but for the egotism and ostentation of a few of its members, is defensible on the ground of public justice, so long we neglect to approximate to the redemption of the human race.

Labour is required for physical, and leisure for moral improvement: from the former of these advantages the rich, and from the latter the poor, by the inevitable conditions of their respective situations, are precluded.

[1] See Rousseau, *De l'Inégalité parmi les Hommes*, note 7.

A state which should combine the advantages of both would be subjected to the evils of neither. He that is deficient in firm health, or vigorous intellect, is but half a man: hence it follows that to subject the labouring classes to unnecessary labour is wantonly depriving them of any opportunities of intellectual improvement; and that the rich are heaping up for their own mischief the disease, lassitude, and ennui by which their existence is rendered an intolerable burthen.

English reformers exclaim against sinecures,—but the true pension list is the rent-roll of the landed proprietors: wealth is a power usurped by the few, to compel the many to labour for their benefit. The laws which support this system derive their force from the ignorance and credulity of its victims: they are the result of a conspiracy of the few against the many, who are themselves obliged to purchase this pre-eminence by the loss of all real comfort.

'The commodities that substantially contribute to the subsistence of the human species form a very short catalogue: they demand from us but a slender portion of industry. If these only were produced, and sufficiently produced, the species of man would be continued. If the labour necessarily required to produce them were equitably divided among the poor, and, still more, if it were equitably divided among all, each man's share of labour would be light, and his portion of leisure would be ample. There was a time when this leisure would have been of small comparative value: it is to be hoped that the time will come when it will be applied to the most important purposes. Those hours which are not required for the production of the necessaries of life may be devoted to the cultivation of the understanding, the enlarging our stock of knowledge, the refining our taste, and thus opening to us new and more exquisite sources of enjoyment.

.   .   .   .

'It was perhaps necessary that a period of monopoly and oppression should subsist, before a period of cultivated equality could subsist. Savages perhaps would never have been excited to the discovery of truth and the invention of art but by the narrow motives which such a period affords. But surely, after the savage state has ceased, and men have set out in the glorious career of discovery and invention, monopoly and oppression cannot be necessary to prevent them from returning to a state of barbarism.'—Godwin's *Enquirer*, Essay ii. See also *Polit. Just.*, book VIII, chap. ii.

It is a calculation of this admirable author, that all the conveniences of civilized life might be produced, if society would divide the labour equally among its members, by each individual being employed in labour two hours during the day.

Note 8: V. 112, 113

or religion
Drives his wife raving mad.

I am acquainted with a lady of considerable accomplishments, and the mother of a numerous family, whom the Christian religion has goaded to incurable insanity. A parallel case is, I believe, within the experience of every physician.

Nam iam saepe homines patriam, carosque parentes
Prodiderunt, vitare Acherusia templa petentes.
Lucretius, *De Rerum Natura*, iii. 85–6.

Note 9: V. 189

Even love is sold.

Not even the intercourse of the sexes is exempt from the despotism of positive institution. Law pretends even to govern the indisciplinable wanderings of passion, to put fetters on the clearest deductions of reason, and, by appeals to the will, to subdue the involuntary affections of our nature. Love is inevitably consequent upon the perception of loveliness. Love withers under constraint: its very essence is liberty: it is compatible neither with obedience, jealousy, nor fear: it is there most pure, perfect, and unlimited, where its votaries live in confidence, equality, and un-reserve.

How long then ought the sexual connection to last? what law ought to specify the extent of the grievances which should limit its duration? A husband and wife ought to continue so long united as they love each other: any law which should bind them to cohabitation for one moment after the decay of their affection would be a most intolerable tyranny, and the most unworthy of toleration. How odious an usurpation of the right of private judgement should that law be considered which should make the ties of friendship indissoluble, in spite of the caprices, the inconstancy, the fallibility, and capacity for improvement of the human mind. And by so much would the fetters of love be heavier and more unendurable than those of friendship, as love is more vehement and capricious, more dependent on those delicate peculiarities of imagination, and less capable of reduction to the ostensible merits of the object.

The state of society in which we exist is a mixture of feudal savageness and imperfect civilization. The narrow and unenlightened morality of the Christian religion is an aggravation of these evils. It is not even until lately that mankind have admitted that happiness is the sole end of the science of ethics, as of all other sciences; and that the fanatical idea of mortifying the flesh for the love of God has been discarded. I have heard, indeed, an ignorant collegian adduce, in favour of Christianity, its hostility to every worldly feeling![1]

But if happiness be the object of morality, of all human unions and disunions; if the worthiness of every action is to be estimated by the quantity of pleasurable sensation it is calculated to produce, then the connection of the sexes is so long sacred as it contributes to the comfort of the parties, and is naturally dissolved when its evils are greater than its benefits. There is nothing immoral in this separation. Constancy has nothing virtuous in itself, independently of the pleasure it confers, and partakes of the temporizing spirit of vice in proportion as it endures tamely moral defects of magnitude in the object of its indiscreet choice. Love is free: to promise for ever to love the same woman is not less absurd than to promise to believe the same creed: such a vow, in both cases, excludes us from all inquiry. The language of the votarist is this: The woman I now love may be infinitely inferior to many others; the creed I now profess may be a mass of errors and absurdities; but I exclude myself from all future information as to the amiability of the one and the truth of the other, resolving blindly, and in spite of conviction, to adhere to them. Is this the language of delicacy and reason? Is the love of such a frigid heart of more worth than its belief?

The present system of constraint does no more, in the majority of instances, than make hypocrites or open enemies. Persons of delicacy and virtue, unhappily united to one whom they find it impossible to love, spend the loveliest season of their life in unproductive efforts to appear otherwise than they are, for the sake of the feelings of their partner or the welfare of their mutual offspring: those of less generosity and refinement openly avow their disappointment, and linger out the remnant of that union, which only death can dissolve, in a state of incurable bickering and hostility. The early education of their children takes its colour from the squabbles of the parents; they are nursed in a systematic school of ill-humour, violence, and falsehood. Had they been suffered to part at the moment when indifference rendered their union irksome, they would have been spared many years of misery: they would have connected themselves more suitably, and would have found that happiness in the society of more congenial partners which is for ever denied them by the despotism of marriage. They would have been separately useful and happy members of society, who, whilst united, were miserable and rendered

---

[1] The first Christian emperor made a law by which seduction was punished with death; if the female pleaded her own consent, she also was punished with death; if the parents endeavoured to screen the criminals, they were banished and their estates were confiscated; the slaves who might be accessory were burned alive, or forced to swallow melted lead. The very offspring of an illegal love were involved in the consequences of the sentence.—Gibbon's *Decline and Fall*, etc., vol. ii, p. 210. See also, for the hatred of the primitive Christians to love and even marriage, p. 269.

misanthropical by misery. The conviction that wedlock is indissoluble holds out the strongest of all temptations to the perverse: they indulge without restraint in acrimony, and all the little tyrannies of domestic life, when they know that their victim is without appeal. If this connection were put on a rational basis, each would be assured that habitual ill-temper would terminate in separation, and would check this vicious and dangerous propensity.

Prostitution is the legitimate offspring of marriage and its accompanying errors. Women, for no other crime than having followed the dictates of a natural appetite, are driven with fury from the comforts and sympathies of society. It is less venial than murder; and the punishment which is inflicted on her who destroys her child to escape reproach is lighter than the life of agony and disease to which the prostitute is irrecoverably doomed. Has a woman obeyed the impulse of unerring nature;—society declares war against her, pitiless and eternal war: she must be the tame slave, she must make no reprisals; theirs is the right of persecution, hers the duty of endurance. She lives a life of infamy: the loud and bitter laugh of scorn scares her from all return. She dies of long and lingering disease: yet *she* is in fault, *she* is the criminal, *she* the froward and untamable child,—and society, forsooth, the pure and virtuous matron, who casts her as an abortion from her undefiled bosom! Society avenges herself on the criminals of her own creation; she is employed in anathematizing the vice to-day, which yesterday she was the most zealous to teach. Thus is formed one-tenth of the population of London: meanwhile the evil is twofold. Young men, excluded by the fanatical idea of chastity from the society of modest and accomplished women, associate with these vicious and miserable beings, destroying thereby all those exquisite and delicate sensibilities whose existence cold-hearted worldlings have denied; annihilating all genuine passion, and debasing that to a selfish feeling which is the excess of generosity and devotedness. Their body and mind alike crumble into a hideous wreck of humanity; idiocy and disease become perpetuated in their miserable offspring, and distant generations suffer for the bigoted morality of their forefathers. Chastity is a monkish and evangelical superstition, a greater foe to natural temperance even than unintellectual sensuality; it strikes at the root of all domestic happiness, and consigns more than half of the human race to misery, that some few may monopolize according to law. A system could not well have been devised more studiously hostile to human happiness than marriage.

I conceive that from the abolition of marriage, the fit and natural arrangement of sexual connection would result. I by no means assert that the intercourse would be promiscuous: on the contrary, it appears, from the relation of parent to child, that this union is generally of long duration, and marked above all others with generosity and self-devotion. But this is a subject which it is perhaps premature to discuss. That which will result from the abolition of marriage will be natural and right; because choice and change will be exempted from restraint.

In fact, religion and morality, as they now stand, compose a practical code of misery and servitude: the genius of human happiness must tear every leaf from the accursed book of God ere man can read the inscription on his heart. How would morality, dressed up in stiff stays and finery, start from her own disgusting image should she look in the mirror of nature!

Note 10: VI. 45, 46

> *To the red and baleful sun*
> *That faintly twinkles there.*

The north polar star, to which the axis of the earth, in its present state of obliquity, points. It is exceedingly probable, from many considerations, that this obliquity will gradually diminish, until the equator coincides with the ecliptic: the nights and days will then become equal on the earth throughout the year, and probably the seasons also. There is no great extravagance in presuming that the progress of the perpendicularity of the poles may be as rapid as the progress of intellect; or that there should be a perfect identity between the moral and physical improvement of the human species. It is certain that wisdom is not compatible with disease, and that, in the present state of the climates of the earth, health, in the true and comprehensive sense of the word, is out of the reach of civilized man. Astronomy teaches us that the earth is now in its progress, and that the poles are every year becoming more and more perpendicular to the ecliptic. The strong evidence afforded by the history of mythology, and geological researches, that some event of this nature has taken place already, affords a strong presumption that this progress is not merely an oscillation, as has been surmised by some late astronomers[1]. Bones of animals peculiar to the torrid zone have been found in the north of Siberia, and on the banks of the river Ohio. Plants have been found in the fossil state in the interior of Germany, which demand the present climate of Hindostan for their production[2]. The researches of M. Bailly[3] establish the existence of a people who inhabited a tract in Tartary 49° north latitude, of greater antiquity than either the Indians, the Chinese, or the

---

[1] Pierre Simon, Marquis de Laplace, *Exposition du Système du Monde*, Paris, 1796 (2 vols.).

[2] Pierre Jean-Georges Cabanis, *Rapports du Physique et du Moral de l'Homme*, Paris, 1802, vol. ii, p. 406.

[3] Jean Sylvain Bailly, *Lettres sur l'origine des sciences et sur celle des peuples d'Asie, adressées à M. de Voltaire et précédées de quelques lettres de M. de Voltaire à l'auteur*, Paris, 1777.

Chaldeans, from whom these nations derived their sciences and theology. We find, from the testimony of ancient writers, that Britain, Germany, and France were much colder than at present, and that their great rivers were annually frozen over. Astronomy teaches us also that since this period the obliquity of the earth's position has been considerably diminished.

Note 11: VI. 171–173

> *No atom of this turbulence fulfils*
> *A vague and unnecessitated task,*
> *Or acts but as it must and ought to act.*

'Deux exemples serviront à nous rendre plus sensible le principe qui vient d'être posé; nous emprunterons l'un du physique et l'autre du moral. Dans un tourbillon de poussière qu'élève un vent impétueux, quelque confus qu'il paraisse à nos yeux; dans la plus affreuse tempête excitée par des vents opposés qui soulèvent les flots, — il n'y a pas une seule molécule de poussière ou d'eau qui soit placée au *hasard*, qui n'ait sa cause suffisante pour occuper le lieu où elle se trouve, et qui n'agisse rigoureusement de la manière dont elle doit agir. Un géomètre qui connaîtrait exactement les différentes forces qui agissent dans ces deux cas, et les propriétés des molécules qui sont mues, démontrerait que d'après des causes données, chaque molécule agit précisément comme elle doit agir, et ne peut agir autrement qu'elle ne fait.

'Dans les convulsions terribles qui agitent quelquefois les sociétés politiques, et qui produisent souvent le renversement d'un empire, il n'y a pas une seule action, une seule parole, une seule pensée, une seule volonté, une seule passion dans les agents qui concourent à la révolution comme destructeurs ou comme victimes, qui ne soit nécessaire, qui n'agisse comme elle doit agir, qui n'opère infailliblement les effets qu'elle doit opérer, suivant la place qu'occupent ces agents dans ce tourbillon moral. Cela paraîtrait évident pour une intelligence qui sera en état de saisir et d'apprécier toutes les actions et réactions des esprits et des corps de ceux qui contribuent à cette révolution.'—Holbach, *Système de la Nature*, vol. i, p. 44.

Note 12: VI. 198

Necessity! thou mother of the world!

He who asserts the doctrine of Necessity means that, contemplating the events which compose the moral and material universe, he beholds only an immense and uninterrupted chain of causes and effects, no one of which could occupy any other place than it does occupy, or act in any other place than it does act. The idea of necessity is obtained by our experience of the connection between objects, the uniformity of the operations of nature, the constant conjunction of similar events, and the consequent inference of one from the other. Mankind are therefore agreed in the admission of necessity, if they admit that these two circumstances take place in voluntary action. Motive is to voluntary action in the human mind what cause is to effect in the material universe. The word liberty, as applied to mind, is analogous to the word chance as applied to matter: they spring from an ignorance of the certainty of the conjunction of antecedents and consequents.

Every human being is irresistibly impelled to act precisely as he does act: in the eternity which preceded his birth a chain of causes was generated, which, operating under the name of motives, make it impossible that any thought of his mind, or any action of his life, should be otherwise than it is. Were the doctrine of Necessity false, the human mind would no longer be a legitimate object of science; from like causes it would be in vain that we should expect like effects; the strongest motive would no longer be paramount over the conduct; all knowledge would be vague and undeterminate; we could not predict with any certainty that we might not meet as an enemy to-morrow him with whom we have parted in friendship to-night; the most probable inducements and the clearest reasonings would lose the invariable influence they possess. The contrary of this is demonstrably the fact. Similar circumstances produce the same unvariable effects. The precise character and motives of any man on any occasion being given, the moral philosopher could predict his actions with as much certainty as the natural philosopher could predict the effects of the mixture of any particular chemical substances. Why is the aged husbandman more experienced than the young beginner? Because there is a uniform, undeniable necessity in the operations of the material universe. Why is the old statesman more skilful than the raw politician? Because, relying on the necessary conjunction of motive and action, he proceeds to produce moral effects, by the application of those moral causes which experience has shown to be effectual. Some actions may be found to which we can attach no motives, but these are the effects of causes with which we are unacquainted. Hence the relation which motive bears to voluntary action is that of cause to effect; nor, placed in this point of view, is it, or ever has it been, the subject of popular or philosophical dispute. None but the few fanatics who are engaged in the herculean task of reconciling the justice of their God with the misery of man, will longer outrage common sense by the supposition of an event without a cause, a voluntary action without a motive. History, politics, morals, criticism, all grounds of reasonings, all principles of science, alike assume the truth of the doctrine of Necessity. No farmer carrying his corn to market doubts the sale of it at the market price. The master of a manufactory no more doubts that he can purchase the human labour necessary for his purposes than that his machinery will act as they have been accustomed to act.

But, whilst none have scrupled to admit necessity as influencing matter, many have disputed its dominion over mind. Independently of its militating with the received ideas of the justice of God, it is by no means obvious to a superficial inquiry. When the mind observes its own operations, it feels no connection of motive and action: but as we know 'nothing more of causation than the constant conjunction of objects and the consequent inference of one from the other, as we find that these two circumstances are universally allowed to have place in voluntary action, we may be easily led to own that they are subjected to the necessity common to all causes.' The actions of the will have a regular conjunction with circumstances and characters; motive is to voluntary action what cause is to effect. But the only idea we can form of causation is a constant conjunction of similar objects, and the consequent inference of one from the other: wherever this is the case necessity is clearly established.

The idea of liberty, applied metaphorically to the will, has sprung from a misconception of the meaning of the word power. What is power?—*id quod potest*, that which can produce any given effect. To deny power is to say that nothing can or has the power to be or act. In the only true sense of the word power, it applies with equal force to the lodestone as to the human will. Do you think these motives, which I shall present, are powerful enough to rouse him? is a question just as common as, Do you think this lever has the power of raising this weight? The advocates of free-will assert that the will has the power of refusing to be determined by the strongest motive: but the strongest motive is that which, overcoming all others, ultimately prevails; this assertion therefore amounts to a denial of the will being ultimately determined by that motive which does determine it, which is absurd. But it is equally certain that a man cannot resist the strongest motive as that he cannot overcome a physical impossibility.

The doctrine of Necessity tends to introduce a great change into the established notions of morality, and utterly to destroy religion. Reward and punishment must be considered, by the Necessarian, merely as motives which he would employ in order to procure the adoption or abandonment of any given line of conduct. Desert, in the present sense of the word, would no longer have any meaning; and he who should inflict pain upon another for no better reason than that he deserved it, would only gratify his revenge under pretence of satisfying justice. It is not enough, says the advocate of free-will, that a criminal should be prevented from a repetition of his crime: he should feel pain, and his torments, when justly inflicted, ought precisely to be proportioned to his fault. But utility is morality; that which is incapable of producing happiness is useless; and though the crime of Damiens must be condemned, yet the frightful torments which revenge, under the name of justice, inflicted on this unhappy man cannot be supposed to have augmented, even at the long run, the stock of pleasurable sensation in the world. At the same time, the doctrine of Necessity does not in the least diminish our disapprobation of vice. The conviction which all feel that a viper is a poisonous animal, and that a tiger is constrained, by the inevitable condition of his existence, to devour men, does not induce us to avoid them less sedulously, or, even more, to hesitate in destroying them: but he would surely be of a hard heart who, meeting with a serpent on a desert island, or in a situation where it was incapable of injury, should wantonly deprive it of existence. A Necessarian is inconsequent to his own principles if he indulges in hatred or contempt; the compassion which he feels for the criminal is unmixed with a desire of injuring him: he looks with an elevated and dreadless composure upon the links of the universal chain as they pass before his eyes; whilst cowardice, curiosity, and inconsistency only assail him in proportion to the feebleness and indistinctness with which he has perceived and rejected the delusions of free-will.

Religion is the perception of the relation in which we stand to the principle of the universe. But if the principle of the universe be not an organic being, the model and prototype of man, the relation between it and human beings is absolutely none. Without some insight into its will respecting our actions religion is nugatory and vain. But will is only a mode of animal mind; moral qualities also are such as only a human being can possess; to attribute them to the principle of the universe is to annex to it properties incompatible with any possible definition of its nature. It is probable that the word God was originally only an expression denoting the unknown cause of the known events which men perceived in the universe. By the vulgar mistake of a metaphor for a real being, of a word for a thing, it became a man, endowed with human qualities and governing the universe as an earthly monarch governs his kingdom. Their addresses to this imaginary being, indeed, are much in the same style as those of subjects to a king. They acknowledge his benevolence, deprecate his anger, and supplicate his favour.

But the doctrine of Necessity teaches us that in no case could any event have happened otherwise than it did happen, and that, if God is the author of good, He is also the author of evil; that, if He is entitled to our gratitude for the one, He is entitled to our hatred for the other; that, admitting the existence of this hypothetic being, He is also subjected to the dominion of an immutable necessity. It is plain that the same arguments which prove that God is the author of food, light, and life, prove Him also to be the author of poison, darkness, and death. The wide-wasting earthquake, the storm, the battle, and the tyranny, are attributable to this hypothetic being in the same degree as the fairest forms of nature, sunshine, liberty, and peace.

But we are taught, by the doctrine of Necessity, that there is neither good nor evil in the universe, otherwise than as the events to which we apply these epithets have relation to our own peculiar mode of being. Still less than with the hypothesis of a God will the doctrine of Necessity accord with the belief of a future state of punishment. God made man such as he is, and then damned him for being so: for to say that God was the author of all good, and man the author of all evil, is to say that one man made a straight line and a crooked one, and another man made the incongruity.

A Mahometan story, much to the present purpose, is recorded, wherein Adam and Moses are introduced disputing before God in the following manner. Thou, says Moses, art Adam, whom God created, and animated with the breath of life, and caused to be worshipped by the angels, and placed in Paradise, from whence mankind have been expelled for thy fault. Whereto Adam answered, Thou art Moses, whom God chose for His apostle, and entrusted with His word, by giving thee the tables of the law, and whom He vouchsafed to admit to discourse with Himself. How many years dost thou find the law was written before I was created? Says Moses, Forty. And dost thou not find, replied Adam, these words therein, And Adam rebelled against his Lord and transgressed? Which Moses confessing, Dost thou therefore blame me, continued he, for doing that which God wrote of me that I should do, forty years before I was created, nay, for what was decreed concerning me fifty thousand years before the creation of heaven and earth?—Sale's *Preliminary Discourse to the Koran*, p. 164.

Note 13: VII. 13

There is no God.

This negation must be understood solely to affect a creative Deity. The hypothesis of a pervading Spirit co-eternal with the universe remains unshaken.

A close examination of the validity of the proofs adduced to support any proposition is the only secure way of attaining truth, on the advantages of which it is unnecessary to descant: our knowledge of the existence of a Deity is a subject of such importance that it cannot be too minutely investigated; in consequence of this conviction we proceed briefly and impartially to examine the proofs which have been adduced. It is necessary first to consider the nature of belief.

When a proposition is offered to the mind, it perceives the agreement or disagreement of the ideas of which it is composed. A perception of their

agreement is termed *belief*. Many obstacles frequently prevent this per-
ception from being immediate; these the mind attempts to remove in
order that the perception may be distinct. The mind is active in the in-
vestigation in order to perfect the state of perception of the relation which
the component ideas of the proposition bear to each, which is passive: the
investigation being confused with the perception has induced many falsely
to imagine that the mind is active in belief,—that belief is an act of volition,
—in consequence of which it may be regulated by the mind. Pursuing,
continuing this mistake, they have attached a degree of criminality to
disbelief; of which, in its nature, it is incapable: it is equally incapable
of merit.

Belief, then, is a passion, the strength of which, like every other passion,
is in precise proportion to the degrees of excitement.

The degrees of excitement are three.

The senses are the sources of all knowledge to the mind; consequently
their evidence claims the strongest assent.

The decision of the mind, founded upon our own experience, derived
from these sources, claims the next degree.

The experience of others, which addresses itself to the former one,
occupies the lowest degree.

(A graduated scale, on which should be marked the capabilities of pro-
positions to approach to the test of the senses, would be a just barometer
of the belief which ought to be attached to them.)

Consequently no testimony can be admitted which is contrary to reason;
reason is founded on the evidence of our senses.

Every proof may be referred to one of these three divisions: it is to be
considered what arguments we receive from each of them, which should
convince us of the existence of a Deity.

1st, The evidence of the senses. If the Deity should appear to us, if He
should convince our senses of His existence, this revelation would neces-
sarily command belief. Those to whom the Deity has thus appeared have
the strongest possible conviction of His existence. But the God of Theolo-
gians is incapable of local visibility.

2d, Reason. It is urged that man knows that whatever is must either
have had a beginning, or have existed from all eternity: he also knows that
whatever is not eternal must have had a cause. When this reasoning is
applied to the universe, it is necessary to prove that it was created: until
that is clearly demonstrated we may reasonably suppose that it has en-
dured from all eternity. We must prove design before we can infer a
designer. The only idea which we can form of causation is derivable from
the constant conjunction of objects, and the consequent inference of one
from the other. In a case where two propositions are diametrically op-
posite, the mind believes that which is least incomprehensible;—it is

easier to suppose that the universe has existed from all eternity than to conceive a being beyond its limits capable of creating it: if the mind sinks beneath the weight of one, is it an alleviation to increase the intolerability of the burthen?

The other argument, which is founded on a man's knowledge of his own existence, stands thus. A man knows not only that he now is, but that once he was not; consequently there must have been a cause. But our idea of causation is alone derivable from the constant conjunction of objects and the consequent inference of one from the other; and, reasoning experimentally, we can only infer from effects causes exactly adequate to those effects. But there certainly is a generative power which is effected by certain instruments: we cannot prove that it is inherent in these instruments; nor is the contrary hypothesis capable of demonstration: we admit that the generative power is incomprehensible; but to suppose that the same effect is produced by an eternal, omniscient, omnipotent being leaves the cause in the same obscurity, but renders it more incomprehensible.

3d, Testimony. It is required that testimony should not be contrary to reason. The testimony that the Deity convinces the senses of men of His existence can only be admitted by us if our mind considers it less probable that these men should have been deceived than that the Deity should have appeared to them. Our reason can never admit the testimony of men, who not only declare that they were eye-witnesses of miracles, but that the Deity was irrational; for He commanded that He should be believed, He proposed the highest rewards for faith, eternal punishments for disbelief. We can only command voluntary actions; belief is not an act of volition; the mind is even passive, or involuntarily active; from this it is evident that we have no sufficient testimony, or rather that testimony is insufficient to prove the being of a God. It has been before shown that it cannot be deduced from reason. They alone, then, who have been convinced by the evidence of the senses can believe it.

Hence it is evident that, having no proofs from either of the three sources of conviction, the mind *cannot* believe the existence of a creative God: it is also evident that, as belief is a passion of the mind, no degree of criminality is attachable to disbelief; and that they only are reprehensible who neglect to remove the false medium through which their mind views any subject of discussion. Every reflecting mind must acknowledge that there is no proof of the existence of a Deity.

God is an hypothesis, and, as such, stands in need of proof: the *onus probandi* rests on the theist. Sir Isaac Newton says: *Hypotheses non fingo, quicquid enim ex phaenomenis non deducitur hypothesis vocanda est, et hypotheses vel metaphysicae, vel physicae, vel qualitatum occultarum, seu mechanicae, in philosophia locum non habent.* To all proofs of the existence of a creative God apply this valuable rule. We see a variety of bodies possessing a variety of powers: we merely know their effects; we are in a state of ignorance with respect to their essences and causes. These Newton calls the phenomena of things; but the pride of philosophy is unwilling to admit its ignorance of their causes. From the phenomena, which are the objects of our senses, we attempt to infer a cause, which we call God, and gratuitously endow it with all negative and contradictory qualities. From this hypothesis we invent this general name, to conceal our ignorance of causes and essences. The being called God by no means answers with the conditions prescribed by Newton; it bears every mark of a veil woven by philosophical conceit, to hide the ignorance of philosophers even from themselves. They borrow the threads of its texture from the anthropomorphism of the vulgar. Words have been used by sophists for the same purposes, from the occult qualities of the peripatetics to the *effluvium* of Boyle and the *crinities* or *nebulae* of Herschel. God is represented as infinite, eternal, incomprehensible; He is contained under every *predicate in non* that the logic of ignorance could fabricate. Even His worshippers allow that it is impossible to form any idea of Him: they exclaim with the French poet,

> *Pour dire ce qu'il est, il faut être lui-même.*

Lord Bacon says that atheism leaves to man reason, philosophy, natural piety, laws, reputation, and everything that can serve to conduct him to virtue; but superstition destroys all these, and erects itself into a tyranny over the understandings of men: hence atheism never disturbs the government, but renders man more clear-sighted, since he sees nothing beyond the boundaries of the present life.—Bacon's *Moral Essays*.

La première théologie de l'homme lui fit d'abord craindre et adorer les éléments même, des objets matériels et grossiers; il rendit ensuite ses hommages à des agents présidant aux éléments, à des génies inférieurs, à des héros, ou à des hommes doués de grandes qualités. A force de réfléchir il crut simplifier les choses en soumettant la nature entière à un seul agent, à un esprit, à une âme universelle, qui mettait cette nature et ses parties en mouvement. En remontant de causes en causes, les mortels ont fini par ne rien voir; et c'est dans cette obscurité qu'ils ont placé leur Dieu; c'est dans cet abîme ténébreux que leur imagination inquiète travaille toujours à se fabriquer des chimères, qui les affligeront jusqu'à ce que la connaissance de la nature les détrompe des fantômes qu'ils ont toujours si vainement adorés.

Si nous voulons nous rendre compte de nos idées sur la Divinité, nous serons obligés de convenir que, par le mot *Dieu*, les hommes n'ont jamais pu désigner que la cause la plus cachée, la plus éloignée, la plus inconnue des effets qu'ils voyaient: ils ne font usage de ce mot, que lorsque le jeu des causes naturelles et connues cesse d'être visible pour eux; dès qu'ils perdent le fil de ces causes, ou dès que leur esprit ne peut plus en suivre la chaîne, ils tranchent leur difficulté, et terminent leurs recherches en appellant Dieu la dernière des causes, c'est-à-dire celle qui est au-delà de toutes les causes qu'ils connaissent; ainsi ils ne font qu'assigner une dénomination vague à une cause ignorée, à laquelle leur paresse ou les bornes de leurs connaissances les forcent de s'arrêter. Toutes les fois qu'on nous dit que Dieu est l'auteur de quelque phénomène, cela signifie qu'on ignore comment un tel phénomène a pu s'opérer par le secours des forces ou des causes que nous connaissons dans la nature. C'est ainsi que le commun des hommes, dont l'ignorance est le partage, attribue à la Divinité non seulement les effets inusités qui les frappent, mais encore les évènemens les plus simples, dont les causes sont les plus faciles à connaître pour quiconque a pu les méditer. En un mot, l'homme a toujours respecté les causes inconnues des effets surprenans, que son ignorance l'empêchait de démêler. Ce fut sur les débris de la nature que les hommes élevèrent le colosse imaginaire de la Divinité.

Si l'ignorance de la nature donna la naissance aux dieux, la connaissance de la nature est faite pour les détruire. A mesure que l'homme s'instruit, ses forces et ses ressources augmentent avec ses lumières; les sciences, les arts conservateurs, l'industrie, lui fournissent des secours; l'expérience le rassure ou lui procure des moyens de résister aux efforts de bien des causes qui cessent de l'alarmer dès qu'il les a connues. En un mot, ses terreurs se dissipent dans la même proportion que son esprit s'éclaire. L'homme instruit cesse d'être superstitieux.

Ce n'est jamais que sur parole que des peuples entiers adorent le Dieu de leurs pères et de leurs prêtres: l'autorité, la confiance, la soumission, et l'habitude leur tiennent lieu de conviction et de preuves; ils se prosternent et prient, parce que leurs pères leur ont appris à se prosterner et prier: mais pourquoi ceux-ci se sont-ils mis à genoux? C'est que dans les temps éloignés leurs législateurs et leurs guides leur en ont fait un devoir. 'Adorez et croyez,' ont-ils dit, 'des dieux que vous ne pouvez comprendre; rapportez-vous-en à notre sagesse profonde; nous en savons plus que vous sur la divinité.' Mais pourquoi m'en rapporterais-je à vous? C'est que Dieu le veut ainsi, c'est que Dieu vous punira si vous osez résister. Mais ce Dieu n'est-il donc pas la chose en question? Cependant les hommes se sont toujours payés de ce cercle vicieux; la paresse de leur esprit leur fit trouver plus court de s'en rapporter au jugement des autres. Toutes les notions religieuses sont fondées uniquement sur l'autorité; toutes les religions du monde défendent l'examen et ne veulent pas que l'on raisonne; c'est l'autorité qui veut qu'on croie en Dieu; ce Dieu n'est lui-même fondé que sur l'autorité de quelques hommes qui prétendent le connaître, et venir de sa part pour l'annoncer à la terre. Un Dieu fait par les hommes a sans doute besoin des hommes pour se faire connaître aux hommes.

Ne serait-ce donc que pour des prêtres, des inspirés, des métaphysiciens que serait réservée la conviction de l'existence d'un Dieu, que l'on dit néanmoins si nécessaire à tout le genre humain ? Mais trouvons-nous de l'harmonie entre les opinions théologiques des différens inspirés, ou des penseurs répandus sur la terre ? Ceux même qui font profession d'adorer le même Dieu, sont-ils d'accord sur son compte ? Sont-ils contents des preuves que leurs collègues apportent de son existence ? Souscrivent-ils unanimement aux idées qu'ils présentent sur sa nature, sur sa conduite, sur la façon d'entendre ses prétendus oracles ? Est-il une contrée sur la terre où la science de Dieu se soit réellement perfectionnée ? A-t-elle pris quelque part la consistance et l'uniformité que nous voyons prendre aux connaissances humaines, aux arts les plus futiles, aux métiers les plus méprisés ? Ces mots d'*esprit*, d'*immatérialité*, de *création*, de *prédestination*, de *grâce*; cette foule de distinctions subtiles dont la théologie s'est partout remplie dans quelques pays, ces inventions si ingénieuses, imaginées par des penseurs qui se sont succédés depuis tant de siècles, n'ont fait, hélas! qu'embrouiller les choses, et jamais la science la plus nécessaire aux hommes n'a jusqu'ici pu acquérir la moindre fixité. Depuis des milliers d'années ces rêveurs oisifs se sont perpétuellement relayés pour méditer la Divinité, pour deviner ses voies cachées, pour inventer des hypothèses propres à développer cette énigme importante. Leur peu de succès n'a point découragé la vanité théologique; toujours on a parlé de Dieu: on s'est égorgé pour lui, et cet être sublime demeure toujours le plus ignoré et le plus discuté.

Les hommes auraient été trop heureux, si, se bornant aux objets visibles qui les intéressent, ils eussent employé à perfectionner leurs sciences réelles, leurs lois, leur morale, leur éducation, la moitié des efforts qu'ils ont mis dans leurs recherches sur la Divinité. Ils auraient été bien plus sages encore, et plus fortunés, s'ils eussent pu consentir à laisser leurs guides désœuvrés se quereller entre eux, et sonder des profundeurs capables de les étourdir, sans se mêler de leurs disputes insensées. Mais il est de l'essence de l'ignorance d'attacher de l'importance à ce qu'elle ne comprend pas. La vanité humaine fait que l'esprit se roidit contre des difficultés. Plus un objet se dérobe à nos yeux, plus nous faisons d'efforts pour le saisir, parce que dès-lors il aiguillonne notre orgueil, il excite notre curiosité, il nous paraît intéressant. En combattant pour son Dieu chacun ne combattit en effet que pour les intérêts de sa propre vanité, qui de toutes les passions produites par la mal-organisation de la société est la plus prompte à s'alarmer, et la plus propre à produire de très grandes folies.

Si écartant pour un moment les idées fâcheuses que la théologie nous donne d'un Dieu capricieux, dont les décrets partiaux et despotiques décident du sort des humains, nous ne voulons fixer nos yeux que sur la

bonté prétendue, que tous les hommes, même en tremblant devant ce
Dieu, s'accordent à lui donner; si nous lui supposons le projet qu'on lui
prête de n'avoir travaillé que pour sa propre gloire, d'exiger les hommages
des êtres intelligens; de ne chercher dans ses œuvres que le bien-être
du genre humain: comment concilier ces vues et ces dispositions avec
l'ignorance vraiment invincible dans laquelle ce Dieu, si glorieux et si
bon, laisse la plupart des hommes sur son compte? Si Dieu veut être
connu, chéri, remercié, que ne se montre-t-il sous des traits favorables à
tous ces êtres intelligens dont il veut être aimé et adoré? Pourquoi ne
point se manifester à toute la terre d'une façon non équivoque, bien plus
capable de nous convaincre que ces révélations particulières qui semblent
accuser la Divinité d'une partialité fâcheuse pour quelques-unes de ses
créatures? Le tout-puissant n'auroit-il donc pas des moyens plus convain-
quans de se montrer aux hommes que ces métamorphoses ridicules, ces
incarnations prétendues, qui nous sont attestées par des écrivains si peu
d'accord entre eux dans les récits qu'ils en font? Au lieu de tant de miracles,
inventés pour prouver la mission divine de tant de législateurs révérés
par les différens peuples du monde, le souverain des esprits ne pouvait-il
pas convaincre tout d'un coup l'esprit humain des choses qu'il a voulu lui
faire connaître? Au lieu de suspendre un soleil dans la voûte du firma-
ment; au lieu de répandre sans ordre les étoiles et les constellations qui
remplissent l'espace, n'eût-il pas été plus conforme aux vues d'un Dieu si
jaloux de sa gloire et si bien-intentionné pour l'homme d'écrire, d'une
façon non sujette à dispute, son nom, ses attributs, ses volontés per-
manentes en caractères ineffaçables, et lisibles également pour tous les
habitants de la terre? Personne alors n'aurait pu douter de l'existence d'un
Dieu, de ses volontés claires, de ses intentions visibles. Sous les yeux de
ce Dieu si terrible, personne n'aurait eu l'audace de violer ses ordon-
nances; nul mortel n'eût osé se mettre dans le cas d'attirer sa colère: enfin
nul homme n'eût eu le front d'en imposer en son nom, ou d'interpréter
ses volontés suivant ses propres fantaisies.

En effet, quand même on admettrait l'existence du Dieu théologique
et la réalité des attributs si discordans qu'on lui donne, l'on n'en peut
rien conclure, pour autoriser la conduite ou les cultes qu'on prescrit de lui
rendre. La théologie est vraiment *le tonneau des Danaïdes*. A force de
qualités contradictoires et d'assertions hasardées, elle a, pour ainsi dire,
tellement garrotté son Dieu qu'elle l'a mis dans l'impossibilité d'agir. S'il
est infiniment bon, quelle raison aurions-nous de le craindre? S'il est
infiniment sage, de quoi nous inquiéter sur notre sort? S'il sait tout,
pourquoi l'avertir de nos besoins, et le fatiguer de nos prières? S'il est
partout, pourquoi lui élever des temples? S'il est maître de tout, pourquoi
lui faire des sacrifices et des offrandes? S'il est juste, comment croire qu'il
punisse des créatures qu'il a rempli de faiblesses? Si la grâce fait tout en

elles, quelle raison aurait-il de les récompenser? S'il est tout-puissant, comment l'offenser, comment lui résister? S'il est raisonnable, comment se mettrait-il en colère contre des aveugles, à qui il a laissé la liberté de déraisonner? S'il est immuable, de quel droit prétendrions-nous faire changer ses décrets? S'il est inconcevable, pourquoi nous en occuper? S'IL A PARLÉ, POURQUOI L'UNIVERS N'EST-IL PAS CONVAINCU? Si la connaissance d'un Dieu est la plus nécessaire, pourquoi n'est-elle pas la plus évidente et la plus claire?—*Système de la Nature*. London, 1781.

The enlightened and benevolent Pliny thus publicly professes himself an atheist:—Quapropter effigiem Dei formamque quaerere imbecillitatis humanae reor. Quisquis est Deus (si modo est aliquis) et quacunque in parte, totus est sensus, totus est visus, totus auditus, totus animae, totus animi, totus sui. . . . Inperfectae vero in homine naturae praecipua solacia, ne deum quidem posse omnia,—namque nec sibi potest mortem consciscere, si velit, quod homini dedit optimum in tantis vitae poenis, nec mortales aeternitate donare, aut revocare defunctos, nec facere ut qui vixit non vixerit, qui honores gessit non gesserit,—nullumque habere in praeteritum ius praeterquam oblivionis, atque (ut facetis quoque argumentis societas haec cum deo copuletur) ut bis dena viginti non sint, et multa similiter efficere non posse: per quae declaratur haud dubie naturae potentia idque esse quod Deum vocamus.—Pliny, *Nat. Hist.* II. v. 14, 27.

The consistent Newtonian is necessarily an atheist. See Sir W. Drummond's *Academical Questions*, chap. iii.—Sir W. seems to consider the atheism to which it leads as a sufficient presumption of the falsehood of the system of gravitation; but surely it is more consistent with the good faith of philosophy to admit a deduction from facts than an hypothesis incapable of proof, although it might militate with the obstinate preconceptions of the mob. Had this author, instead of inveighing against the guilt and absurdity of atheism, demonstrated its falsehood, his conduct would have been more suited to the modesty of the sceptic and the toleration of the philosopher.

Omnia enim per Dei potentiam facta sunt: immo naturae potentia nulla est nisi ipsa Dei potentia. Certum est nos eatenus Dei potentiam non intelligere, quatenus causas naturales ignoramus; adeoque stulte ad eandem Dei potentiam recurritur, quando rei alicuius causam naturalem, hoc est, ipsam Dei potentiam ignoramus.—Spinoza, *Tract. Theologico-Pol.* chap. i, p. 14.

Note 14. VII. 67

Ahasuerus, rise!

'Ahasuerus the Jew crept forth from the dark cave of Mount Carmel. Near two thousand years have elapsed since he was first goaded by never-ending restlessness to rove the globe from pole to pole. When our Lord was wearied with the burthen of His ponderous cross, and wanted to rest before the door of Ahasuerus, the unfeeling wretch drove Him away with brutality. The Saviour of mankind staggered, sinking under the heavy load, but uttered no complaint. An angel of death appeared before Ahasuerus, and exclaimed indignantly, "Barbarian! thou hast denied rest to the Son of man: be it denied thee also, until He comes to judge the world."

'A black demon, let loose from hell upon Ahasuerus, goads him now from country to country; he is denied the consolation which death affords, and precluded from the rest of the peaceful grave.

'Ahasuerus crept forth from the dark cave of Mount Carmel—he shook the dust from his beard—and taking up one of the skulls heaped there, hurled it down the eminence: it rebounded from the earth in shivered atoms. "This was my father!" roared Ahasuerus. Seven more skulls rolled down from rock to rock; while the infuriate Jew, following them with ghastly looks, exclaimed—"And these were my wives!" He still continued to hurl down skull after skull, roaring in dreadful accents—"And these, and these, and these were my children! They *could die*; but I! reprobate wretch! alas! I cannot die! Dreadful beyond conception is the judgement that hangs over me. Jerusalem fell—I crushed the sucking babe, and precipitated myself into the destructive flames. I cursed the Romans—but, alas! alas! the restless curse held me by the hair,—and I could not die!

' "Rome the giantess fell—I placed myself before the falling statue—she fell and did not crush me. Nations sprang up and disappeared before me; —but I remained and did not die. From cloud-encircled cliffs did I precipitate myself into the ocean; but the foaming billows cast me upon the shore, and the burning arrow of existence pierced my cold heart again. I leaped into Etna's flaming abyss, and roared with the giants for ten long months, polluting with my groans the Mount's sulphureous mouth—ah! ten long months. The volcano fermented, and in a fiery stream of lava cast me up. I lay torn by the torture-snakes of hell amid the glowing cinders, and yet continued to exist.—A forest was on fire: I darted on wings of fury and despair into the crackling wood. Fire dropped upon me from the trees, but the flames only singed my limbs; alas! it could not consume them.—I now mixed with the butchers of mankind, and plunged in the tempest of the raging battle. I roared defiance to the infuriate Gaul, defiance to the victorious German; but arrows and spears rebounded in shivers from my body. The Saracen's flaming sword broke upon my skull: balls in vain hissed upon me: the lightnings of battle glared harmless around my loins: in vain did the elephant trample on me, in vain the iron hoof of the wrathful steed! The mine, big with destructive power, burst under me, and hurled me high in the air—I fell on heaps of smoking limbs, but was only singed. The giant's steel club rebounded from my body; the executioner's hand could not strangle me, the tiger's tooth could not pierce me, nor would the hungry lion in the circus devour me. I cohabited with poisonous snakes, and pinched the red crest of the dragon.—The serpent stung, but could not destroy me. The dragon tormented, but dared not to devour me.—I now provoked the fury of tyrants: I said to Nero, 'Thou art a bloodhound!' I said to Christian, 'Thou art a bloodhound!' I said to Muley Ismail, 'Thou art a bloodhound!'—The tyrants invented cruel torments, but did not kill me.———Ha! not to be able to die—not to be able to die—not to be permitted to rest after the toils of life—to be doomed to be imprisoned for ever in the clay-formed dungeon—to be for ever clogged with this worthless body, its load of diseases and infirmities—to be condemned to [be]hold for millenniums that yawning monster Sameness, and Time, that hungry hyaena, ever bearing children, and ever devouring again her offspring!—Ha! not to be permitted to die! Awful Avenger in Heaven, hast Thou in Thine armoury of wrath a punishment more dreadful? then let it thunder upon me, command a hurricane to sweep me down to the foot of Carmel, that I there may lie extended; may pant, and writhe, and die!" '

This fragment is the translation of part of some German work, whose title I have vainly endeavoured to discover. I picked it up, dirty and torn, some years ago, in Lincoln's-Inn Fields.

Note 15: VII. 135, 136

> *I will beget a Son, and He shall bear*
> *The sins of all the world.*

A book is put into our hands when children, called the Bible, the purport of whose history is briefly this: That God made the earth in six days, and there planted a delightful garden, in which He placed the first pair of human beings. In the midst of the garden He planted a tree, whose fruit, although within their reach, they were forbidden to touch. That the Devil, in the shape of a snake, persuaded them to eat of this fruit; in consequence of which God condemned both them and their posterity yet unborn to satisfy His justice by their eternal misery. That, four thousand years after these events (the human race in the meanwhile having gone unredeemed to perdition), God engendered with the betrothed wife of a carpenter in Judea (whose virginity was nevertheless uninjured), and begat a son, whose name was Jesus Christ; and who was crucified and died, in order that no more men might be devoted to hell-fire, He bearing the burthen of His Father's displeasure by proxy. The book states, in addition, that the soul of whoever disbelieves this sacrifice will be burned with ever-lasting fire.

During many ages of misery and darkness this story gained implicit belief; but at length men arose who suspected that it was a fable and imposture, and that Jesus Christ, so far from being a God, was only a man like themselves. But a numerous set of men, who derived and still derive immense emoluments from this opinion, in the shape of a popular belief, told the vulgar that if they did not believe in the Bible they would be damned to all eternity; and burned, imprisoned, and poisoned all the unbiassed and unconnected inquirers who occasionally arose. They still oppress them, so far as the people, now become more enlightened, will allow.

The belief in all that the Bible contains is called Christianity. A Roman governor of Judea, at the instance of a priest-led mob, crucified a man called Jesus eighteen centuries ago. He was a man of pure life, who desired to rescue his countrymen from the tyranny of their barbarous and degrading superstitions. The common fate of all who desire to benefit mankind awaited him. The rabble, at the instigation of the priests, demanded his death, although his very judge made public acknowledgement of his innocence. Jesus was sacrificed to the honour of that God with whom he was afterwards confounded. It is of importance, therefore, to distinguish between the pretended character of this being as the Son of God and the Saviour of the world, and his real character as a man, who, for a vain attempt to reform the world, paid the forfeit of his life to that overbearing tyranny which has since so long desolated the universe in his name. Whilst the one is a hypocritical Daemon, who announces Himself as the God of compassion and peace, even whilst He stretches forth His blood-red hand with the sword of discord to waste the earth, having confessedly devised this scheme of desolation from eternity; the other stands in the foremost list of those true heroes who have died in the glorious martyrdom of liberty, and have braved torture, contempt, and poverty in the cause of suffering humanity[1].

The vulgar, ever in extremes, became persuaded that the crucifixion of Jesus was a supernatural event. Testimonies of miracles, so frequent in unenlightened ages, were not wanting to prove that he was something divine. This belief, rolling through the lapse of ages, met with the reveries of Plato and the reasonings of Aristotle, and acquired force and extent, until the divinity of Jesus became a dogma, which to dispute was death, which to doubt was infamy.

Christianity is now the established religion: he who attempts to impugn it must be contented to behold murderers and traitors take precedence of him in public opinion; though, if his genius be equal to his courage, and assisted by a peculiar coalition of circumstances, future ages may exalt him to a divinity, and persecute others in his name, as he was persecuted in the name of his predecessor in the homage of the world.

The same means that have supported every other popular belief have

---

[1] Since writing this note I have some reason to suspect that Jesus was an ambitious man, who aspired to the throne of Judea.

supported Christianity. War, imprisonment, assassination, and falsehood; deeds of unexampled and incomparable atrocity have made it what it is. The blood shed by the votaries of the God of mercy and peace, since the establishment of His religion, would probably suffice to drown all other sectaries now on the habitable globe. We derive from our ancestors a faith thus fostered and supported: we quarrel, persecute, and hate for its maintenance. Even under a government which, whilst it infringes the very right of thought and speech, boasts of permitting the liberty of the press, a man is pilloried and imprisoned because he is a deist, and no one raises his voice in the indignation of outraged humanity. But it is ever a proof that the falsehood of a proposition is felt by those who use coercion, not reasoning, to procure its admission; and a dispassionate observer would feel himself more powerfully interested in favour of a man who, depending on the truth of his opinions, simply stated his reasons for entertaining them, than in that of his aggressor who, daringly avowing his unwillingness or incapacity to answer them by argument, proceeded to repress the energies and break the spirit of their promulgator by that torture and imprisonment whose infliction he could command.

Analogy seems to favour the opinion that as, like other systems, Christianity has arisen and augmented, so like them it will decay and perish; that as violence, darkness, and deceit, not reasoning and persuasion, have procured its admission among mankind, so, when enthusiasm has subsided, and time, that infallible controverter of false opinions, has involved its pretended evidences in the darkness of antiquity, it will become obsolete; that Milton's poem alone will give permanency to the remembrance of its absurdities; and that men will laugh as heartily at grace, faith, redemption, and original sin, as they now do at the metamorphoses of Jupiter, the miracles of Romish saints, the efficacy of witchcraft, and the appearance of departed spirits.

Had the Christian religion commenced and continued by the mere force of reasoning and persuasion, the preceding analogy would be inadmissible. We should never speculate on the future obsoleteness of a system perfectly comformable to nature and reason: it would endure so long as they endured; it would be a truth as indisputable as the light of the sun, the criminality of murder, and other facts, whose evidence, depending on our organization and relative situations, must remain acknowledged as satisfactory so long as man is man. It is an incontrovertible fact, the consideration of which ought to repress the hasty conclusions of credulity, or moderate its obstinacy in maintaining them, that, had the Jews not been a fanatical race of men, had even the resolution of Pontius Pilate been equal to his candour, the Christian religion never could have prevailed, it could not even have existed: on so feeble a thread hangs the most cherished opinion of a sixth of the human race!

When will the vulgar learn humility? When will the pride of ignorance blush at having believed before it could comprehend?

Either the Christian religion is true, or it is false: if true, it comes from God, and its authenticity can admit of doubt and dispute no further than its omnipotent author is willing to allow. Either the power or the goodness of God is called in question, if He leaves those doctrines most essential to the well-being of man in doubt and dispute; the only ones which, since their promulgation, have been the subject of unceasing cavil, the cause of irreconcilable hatred. *If God has spoken, why is the universe not convinced?*

There is this passage in the Christian Scriptures: 'Those who obey not God, and believe not the Gospel of his Son, shall be punished with everlasting destruction.' This is the pivot upon which all religions turn: they all assume that it is in our power to believe or not to believe; whereas the mind can only believe that which it thinks true. A human being can only be supposed accountable for those actions which are influenced by his will. But belief is utterly distinct from and unconnected with volition: it is the apprehension of the agreement or disagreement of the ideas that compose any proposition. Belief is a passion, or involuntary operation of the mind, and, like other passions, its intensity is precisely proportionate to the degrees of excitement. Volition is essential to merit or demerit. But the Christian religion attaches the highest possible degrees of merit and demerit to that which is worthy of neither, and which is totally unconnected with the peculiar faculty of the mind, whose presence is essential to their being.

Christianity was intended to reform the world: had an all-wise Being planned it, nothing is more improbable than that it should have failed: omniscience would infallibly have foreseen the inutility of a scheme which experience demonstrates, to this age, to have been utterly unsuccessful.

Christianity inculcates the necessity of supplicating the Deity. Prayer may be considered under two points of view;—as an endeavour to change the intentions of God, or as a formal testimony of our obedience. But the former case supposes that the caprices of a limited intelligence can occasionally instruct the Creator of the world how to regulate the universe; and the latter, a certain degree of servility analogous to the loyalty demanded by earthly tyrants. Obedience indeed is only the pitiful and cowardly egotism of him who thinks that he can do something better than reason.

Christianity, like all other religions, rests upon miracles, prophecies, and martyrdoms. No religion ever existed which had not its prophets, its attested miracles, and, above all, crowds of devotees who would bear patiently the most horrible tortures to prove its authenticity. It should appear that in no case can a discriminating mind subscribe to the genuineness of a miracle. A miracle is an infraction of nature's law, by a supernatural cause; by a cause acting beyond that eternal circle within which all things are included. God breaks through the law of nature, that He may convince mankind of the truth of that revelation which, in spite of His precautions, has been, since its introduction, the subject of unceasing schism and cavil.

Miracles resolve themselves into the following question[1]:—Whether it is more probable the laws of nature, hitherto so immutably harmonious, should have undergone violation, or that a man should have told a lie? Whether it is more probable that we are ignorant of the natural cause of an event, or that we know the supernatural one? That, in old times, when the powers of nature were less known than at present, a certain set of men were themselves deceived, or had some hidden motive for deceiving others; or that God begat a Son, who, in His legislation, measuring merit by belief, evidenced Himself to be totally ignorant of the powers of the human mind—of what is voluntary, and what is the contrary?

We have many instances of men telling lies;—none of an infraction of nature's laws, those laws of whose government alone we have any knowledge or experience. The records of all nations afford innumerable instances of men deceiving others either from vanity or interest, or themselves being deceived by the limitedness of their views and their ignorance of natural causes: but where is the accredited case of God having come upon earth, to give the lie to His own creations? There would be something truly wonderful in the appearance of a ghost; but the assertion of a child that he saw one as he passed through the churchyard is universally admitted to be less miraculous.

But even supposing that a man should raise a dead body to life before our eyes, and on this fact rest his claim to being considered the son of God;—the Humane Society restores drowned persons, and because it makes no mystery of the method it employs, its members are not mistaken for the sons of God. All that we have a right to infer from our ignorance of the cause of any event is that we do not know it: had the Mexicans attended to this simple rule when they heard the cannon of the Spaniards, they would not have considered them as gods: the experiments of modern chemistry would have defied the wisest philosophers of ancient Greece and Rome to have accounted for them on natural principles. An author of strong common sense has observed that 'a miracle is no miracle at second-hand'; he might have added that a miracle is no miracle in any case; for until we are acquainted with all natural causes, we have no reason to imagine others.

There remains to be considered another proof of Christianity—Prophecy. A book is written before a certain event, in which this event is

---

[1] See Hume's *Essay*, vol. ii, p. 121.

foretold; how could the prophet have foreknown it without inspiration? how could he have been inspired without God? The greatest stress is laid on the prophecies of Moses and Hosea on the dispersion of the Jews, and that of Isaiah concerning the coming of the Messiah. The prophecy of Moses is a collection of every possible cursing and blessing; and it is so far from being marvellous that the one of dispersion should have been fulfilled, that it would have been more surprising if, out of all these, none should have taken effect. In Deuteronomy, chap. xxviii. ver. 64, where Moses explicitly foretells the dispersion, he states that they shall there serve gods of wood and stone: 'And the Lord shall scatter thee among all people, from the one end of the earth even to the other; *and there thou shalt serve other gods, which neither thou nor thy fathers have known, even gods of wood and stone.*' The Jews are at this day remarkably tenacious of their religion. Moses also declares that they shall be subjected to these curses for disobedience to his ritual: 'And it shall come to pass, if thou wilt not hearken unto the voice of the Lord thy God, to observe to do all the commandments and statutes which I command thee this day; that all these curses shall come upon thee, and overtake thee.' Is this the real reason? The third, fourth, and fifth chapters of Hosea are a piece of immodest confession. The indelicate type might apply in a hundred senses to a hundred things. The fifty-third chapter of Isaiah is more explicit, yet it does not exceed in clearness the oracles of Delphos. The historical proof that Moses, Isaiah, and Hosea did write when they are said to have written is far from being clear and circumstantial.

But prophecy requires proof in its character as a miracle; we have no right to suppose that a man foreknew future events from God, until it is demonstrated that he neither could know them by his own exertions, nor that the writings which contain the prediction could possibly have been fabricated after the event pretended to be foretold. It is more probable that writings, pretending to divine inspiration, should have been fabricated after the fulfilment of their pretended prediction than that they should have really been divinely inspired, when we consider that the latter supposition makes God at once the creator of the human mind and ignorant of its primary powers, particularly as we have numberless instances of false religions, and forged prophecies of things long past, and no accredited case of God having conversed with men directly or indirectly. It is also possible that the description of an event might have foregone its occurrence; but this is far from being a legitimate proof of a divine revelation, as many men, not pretending to the character of a prophet, have nevertheless, in this sense, prophesied.

Lord Chesterfield was never yet taken for a prophet, even by a bishop, yet he uttered this remarkable prediction: 'The despotic government of France is screwed up to the highest pitch; a revolution is fast approaching;

that revolution, I am convinced, will be radical and sanguinary.' This appeared in the letters of the prophet long before the accomplishment of this wonderful prediction. Now, have these particulars come to pass, or have they not? If they have, how could the Earl have foreknown them without inspiration? If we admit the truth of the Christian religion on testimony such as this, we must admit, on the same strength of evidence, that God has affixed the highest rewards to belief, and the eternal tortures of the never-dying worm to disbelief, both of which have been demonstrated to be involuntary.

The last proof of the Christian religion depends on the influence of the Holy Ghost. Theologians divide the influence of the Holy Ghost into its ordinary and extraordinary modes of operation. The latter is supposed to be that which inspired the Prophets and Apostles; and the former to be the grace of God, which summarily makes known the truth of His revelation to those whose mind is fitted for its reception by a submissive perusal of His word. Persons convinced in this manner can do anything but account for their conviction, describe the time at which it happened, or the manner in which it came upon them. It is supposed to enter the mind by other channels than those of the senses, and therefore professes to be superior to reason founded on their experience.

Admitting, however, the usefulness or possibility of a divine revelation, unless we demolish the foundations of all human knowledge, it is requisite that our reason should previously demonstrate its genuineness; for, before we extinguish the steady ray of reason and common sense, it is fit that we should discover whether we cannot do without their assistance, whether or no there be any other which may suffice to guide us through the labyrinth of life[1]: for, if a man is to be inspired upon all occasions, if he is to be sure of a thing because he is sure, if the ordinary operations of the Spirit are not to be considered very extraordinary modes of demonstration, if enthusiasm is to usurp the place of proof, and madness that of sanity, all reasoning is superfluous. The Mahometan dies fighting for his prophet, the Indian immolates himself at the chariot-wheels of Brahma, the Hottentot worships an insect, the Negro a bunch of feathers, the Mexican sacrifices human victims! Their degree of conviction must certainly be very strong: it cannot arise from reasoning, it must from feelings, the reward of their prayers. If each of these should affirm, in opposition to the strongest possible arguments, that inspiration carried internal evidence, I fear their inspired brethren, the orthodox missionaries, would be so uncharitable as to pronounce them obstinate.

Miracles cannot be received as testimonies of a disputed fact, because all human testimony has ever been insufficient to establish the possibility of

---

[1] See Locke's *Essay Concerning the Human Understanding*, book iv, chap. xix, on Enthusiasm.

miracles. That which is incapable of proof itself is no proof of anything else. Prophecy has also been rejected by the test of reason. Those, then, who have been actually inspired are the only true believers in the Christian religion.

> [Quemque utero inclusum Mariae] mox numine viso
> Virginei tumuere sinus, innuptaque mater
> Arcano stupuit compleri viscera partu,
> Auctorem paritura suum. Mortalia corda
> Artificem texere poli, latuitque sub uno
> Pectore, qui totum late complectitur orbem.
> Claudian, De Salvatore.

Does not so monstrous and disgusting an absurdity carry its own infamy and refutation with itself?

Note 16: VIII. 203–207

> *Him, still from hope to hope the bliss pursuing*
> *Which from the exhaustless lore of human weal*
> *Dawns on the virtuous mind, the thoughts that rise*
> *In time-destroying infiniteness, gift*
> *With self-enshrined eternity, etc.*

Time is our consciousness of the succession of ideas in our mind. Vivid sensation, of either pain or pleasure, makes the time seem long, as the common phrase is, because it renders us more acutely conscious of our ideas. If a mind be conscious of an hundred ideas during one minute, by the clock, and of two hundred during another, the latter of these spaces would actually occupy so much greater extent in the mind as two exceed one in quantity. If, therefore, the human mind, by any future improvement of its sensibility, should become conscious of an infinite number of ideas in a minute, that minute would be eternity. I do not hence infer that the actual space between the birth and death of a man will ever be prolonged; but that his sensibility is perfectible, and that the number of ideas which his mind is capable of receiving is indefinite. One man is stretched on the rack during twelve hours; another sleeps soundly in his bed: the difference of time perceived by these two persons is immense; one hardly will believe that half an hour has elapsed, the other could credit that centuries had flown during his agony. Thus, the life of a man of virtue and talent, who should die in his thirtieth year, is, with regard to his own feelings, longer than that of a miserable priest-ridden slave, who dreams out a century of dulness. The one has perpetually cultivated his mental faculties, has rendered himself master of his thoughts, can abstract and generalize amid the lethargy of every-day business;—the other can slumber over the brightest moments of his being, and is unable to remember the happiest hour of his life. Perhaps the perishing ephemeron enjoys a longer life than the tortoise.

> Dark flood of time!
> Roll as it listeth thee—I measure not
> By months or moments thy ambiguous course.
> Another may stand by me on the brink
> And watch the bubble whirled beyond his ken
> That pauses at my feet. The sense of love,
> The thirst for action, and the impassioned thought
> Prolong my being: if I wake no more,
> My life more actual living will contain
> Than some gray veteran's of the world's cold school,
> Whose listless hours unprofitably roll,
> By one enthusiast feeling unredeemed.

See Godwin's *Polit. Just.* vol. i, p. 411; and Condorcet, *Esquisse d'un Tableau Historique des Progrès de l'Esprit Humain*, époque ix.

Note 17: VIII. 211, 212

> *No longer now*
> *He slays the lamb that looks him in the face.*

I hold that the depravity of the physical and moral nature of man originated in his unnatural habits of life. The origin of man, like that of the universe of which he is a part, is enveloped in impenetrable mystery. His generations either had a beginning, or they had not. The weight of evidence in favour of each of these suppositions seems tolerably equal; and it is perfectly unimportant to the present argument which is assumed. The language spoken, however, by the mythology of nearly all religions seems to prove that at some distant period man forsook the path of nature, and sacrificed the purity and happiness of his being to unnatural appetites. The date of this event seems to have also been that of some great change in the climates of the earth, with which it has an obvious correspondence. The allegory of Adam and Eve eating of the tree of evil, and entailing upon their posterity the wrath of God and the loss of everlasting life, admits of no other explanation than the disease and crime that have flowed from unnatural diet. Milton was so well aware of this that he makes Raphael thus exhibit to Adam the consequence of his disobedience:—

> Immediately a place
> Before his eyes appeared, sad, noisome, dark;
> A lazar-house it seemed; wherein were laid
> Numbers of all diseased—all maladies

Of ghastly spasm, or racking torture, qualms
Of heart-sick agony, all feverous kinds,
Convulsions, epilepsies, fierce catarrhs,
Intestine stone and ulcer, colic pangs,
Demoniac frenzy, moping melancholy,
And moon-struck madness, pining atrophy,
Marasmus, and wide-wasting pestilence,
Dropsies and asthmas, and joint-racking rheums.

And how many thousands more might not be added to this frightful catalogue!

The story of Prometheus is one likewise which, although universally admitted to be allegorical, has never been satisfactorily explained. Prometheus stole fire from heaven, and was chained for this crime to Mount Caucasus, where a vulture continually devoured his liver, that grew to meet its hunger. Hesiod says that, before the time of Prometheus, mankind were exempt from suffering; that they enjoyed a vigorous youth, and that death, when at length it came, approached like sleep, and gently closed their eyes. Again, so general was this opinion that Horace, a poet of the Augustan age, writes—

Audax omnia perpeti,
Gens humana ruit per vetitum nefas;
Audax Iapeti genus
Ignem fraude malâ gentibus intulit:
Post ignem aetheriâ domo
Subductum, macies et nova febrium
Terris incubuit cohors,
Semotique prius tarda necessitas
Lethi corripuit gradum.

How plain a language is spoken by all this! Prometheus (who represents the human race) effected some great change in the condition of his nature, and applied fire to culinary purposes; thus inventing an expedient for screening from his disgust the horrors of the shambles. From this moment his vitals were devoured by the vulture of disease. It consumed his being in every shape of its loathsome and infinite variety, inducing the soul-quelling sinkings of premature and violent death. All vice rose from the ruin of healthful innocence. Tyranny, superstition, commerce, and inequality were then first known, when reason vainly attempted to guide the wanderings of exacerbated passion. I conclude this part of the subject with an extract from Mr. Newton's *Defence of Vegetable Regimen*, from whom I have borrowed this interpretation of the fable of Prometheus.

'Making allowance for such transposition of the events of the allegory as time might produce after the important truths were forgotten, which this portion of the ancient mythology was intended to transmit, the drift of the fable seems to be this:—Man at his creation was endowed with the gift of perpetual youth; that is, he was not formed to be a sickly suffering creature as we now see him, but to enjoy health, and to sink by slow degrees into the bosom of his parent earth without disease or pain. Prometheus first taught the use of animal food (primus bovem occidit Prometheus[1]) and of fire, with which to render it more digestible and pleasing to the taste. Jupiter, and the rest of the gods, foreseeing the consequences of these inventions, were amused or irritated at the short-sighted devices of the newly-formed creature, and left him to experience the sad effects of them. Thirst, the necessary concomitant of a flesh diet' (perhaps of all diet vitiated by culinary preparation), 'ensued; water was resorted to, and man forfeited the inestimable gift of health which he had received from heaven: he became diseased, the partaker of a precarious existence, and no longer descended slowly to his grave[2].'

> But just disease to luxury succeeds,
> And every death its own avenger breeds;
> The fury passions from that blood began,
> And turned on man a fiercer savage—man.

Man, and the animals whom he has infected with his society, or depraved by his dominion, are alone diseased. The wild hog, the mouflon, the bison, and the wolf, are perfectly exempt from malady, and invariably die either from external violence or natural old age. But the domestic hog, the sheep, the cow, and the dog, are subject to an incredible variety of distempers; and, like the corrupters of their nature, have physicians who thrive upon their miseries. The supereminence of man is like Satan's, a supereminence of pain; and the majority of his species, doomed to penury, disease, and crime, have reason to curse the untoward event that, by enabling him to communicate his sensations, raised him above the level of his fellow-animals. But the steps that have been taken are irrevocable. The whole of human science is comprised in one question:—How can the advantages of intellect and civilization be reconciled with the liberty and pure pleasures of natural life? How can we take the benefits and reject the evils of the system, which is now interwoven with all the fibres of our being?—I believe that abstinence from animal food and spirituous liquors would in a great measure capacitate us for the solution of this important question.

It is true that mental and bodily derangement is attributable in part to other deviations from rectitude and nature than those which concern diet. The mistakes cherished by society respecting the connection of the sexes,

---

[1] Pliny, *Nat. Hist.*, lib. vii. sect. 57.
[2] *Return to Nature, or Defence of Vegetable Regimen*, Thomas Cadell, 1811.

whence the misery and diseases of unsatisfied celibacy, unenjoying pros-
titution, and the premature arrival of puberty, necessarily spring; the
putrid atmosphere of crowded cities; the exhalations of chemical processes;
the muffling of our bodies in superfluous apparel; the absurd treatment of
infants:—all these and innumerable other causes contribute their mite to
the mass of human evil.

Comparative anatomy teaches us that man resembles frugivorous ani-
mals in everything, and carnivorous in nothing; he has neither claws
wherewith to seize his prey, nor distinct and pointed teeth to tear the
living fibre. A Mandarin of the first class, with nails two inches long, would
probably find them alone inefficient to hold even a hare. After every sub-
terfuge of gluttony, the bull must be degraded into the ox, and the ram
into the wether, by an unnatural and inhuman operation, that the flaccid
fibre may offer a fainter resistance to rebellious nature. It is only by
softening and disguising dead flesh by culinary preparation that it is ren-
dered susceptible of mastication or digestion; and that the sight of its
bloody juices and raw horror does not excite intolerable loathing and dis-
gust. Let the advocate of animal food force himself to a decisive experi-
ment on its fitness, and, as Plutarch recommends, tear a living lamb with
his teeth, and plunging his head into its vitals slake his thirst with the
steaming blood; when fresh from the deed of horror, let him revert to the
irresistible instincts of nature that would rise in judgement against it, and
say, 'Nature formed me for such work as this.' Then, and then only,
would he be consistent.

Man resembles no carnivorous animal. There is no exception, unless
man be one, to the rule of herbivorous animals having cellulated colons.

The orang-outang perfectly resembles man both in the order and
number of his teeth. The orang-outang is the most anthropomorphous of
the ape tribe, all of which are strictly frugivorous. There is no other
species of animals, which live on different food, in which this analogy
exists[1]. In many frugivorous animals, the canine teeth are more pointed
and distinct than those of man. The resemblance also of the human
stomach to that of the orang-outang is greater than to that of any other
animal.

The intestines are also identical with those of herbivorous animals,
which present a larger surface for absorption and have ample and cellulated
colons. The caecum also, though short, is larger than that of carnivorous
animals; and even here the orang-outang retains its accustomed similarity.

The structure of the human frame, then, is that of one fitted to a pure
vegetable diet, in every essential particular. It is true that the reluctance
to abstain from animal food, in those who have been long accustomed to

---

[1] Cuvier, *Leçons d'Anat. Comp.*, tom. iii, pp. 169, 373, 448, 465, 480. Rees's *Cyclo-
paedia*, art. Man.

its stimulus, is so great in some persons of weak minds as to be scarcely overcome; but this is far from bringing any argument in its favour. A lamb, which was fed for some time on flesh by a ship's crew, refused its natural diet at the end of the voyage. There are numerous instances of horses, sheep, oxen, and even wood-pigeons, having been taught to live upon flesh, until they have loathed their natural aliment. Young children evidently prefer pastry, oranges, apples, and other fruit, to the flesh of animals; until, by the gradual depravation of the digestive organs, the free use of vegetables has for a time produced serious inconveniences; *for a time*, I say, since there never was an instance wherein a change from spirituous liquors and animal food to vegetables and pure water has failed ultimately to invigorate the body, by rendering its juices bland and consentaneous, and to restore to the mind that cheerfulness and elasticity which not one in fifty possesses on the present system. A love of strong liquors is also with difficulty taught to infants. Almost every one remembers the wry faces which the first glass of port produced. Unsophisticated instinct is invariably unerring; but to decide on the fitness of animal food from the perverted appetites which its constrained adoption produces, is to make the criminal a judge in his own cause: it is even worse, it is appealing to the infatuated drunkard in a question of the salubrity of brandy.

What is the cause of morbid action in the animal system? Not the air we breathe, for our fellow-denizens of nature breathe the same uninjured; not the water we drink (if remote from the pollutions of man and his inventions[1]), for the animals drink it too; not the earth we tread upon; not the unobscured sight of glorious nature, in the wood, the field, or the expanse of sky and ocean; nothing that we are or do in common with the undiseased inhabitants of the forest. Something, then, wherein we differ from them: our habit of altering our food by fire, so that our appetite is no longer a just criterion for the fitness of its gratification. Except in children, there remain no traces of that instinct which determines, in all other animals, what aliment is natural or otherwise; and so perfectly obliterated are they in the reasoning adults of our species, that it has become necessary to urge considerations drawn from comparative anatomy to prove that we are naturally frugivorous.

Crime is madness. Madness is disease. Whenever the cause of disease shall be discovered, the root, from which all vice and misery have so long overshadowed the globe, will lie bare to the axe. All the exertions of man, from that moment, may be considered as tending to the clear profit of his species. No sane mind in a sane body resolves upon a real crime. It is a

---

[1] The necessity of resorting to some means of purifying water, and the disease which arises from its adulteration in civilized countries, is sufficiently apparent. See Dr. Lambe's *Reports on Cancer*. I do not assert that the use of water is in itself unnatural, but that the unperverted palate would swallow no liquid capable of occasioning disease.

man of violent passions, bloodshot eyes, and swollen veins, that alone can grasp the knife of murder. The system of a simple diet promises no Utopian advantages. It is no mere reform of legislation, whilst the furious passions and evil propensities of the human heart, in which it had its origin, are still unassuaged. It strikes at the root of all evil, and is an experiment which may be tried with success, not alone by nations, but by small societies, families, and even individuals. In no cases has a return to vegetable diet produced the slightest injury; in most it has been attended with changes undeniably beneficial. Should ever a physician be born with the genius of Locke, I am persuaded that he might trace all bodily and mental derangements to our unnatural habits, as clearly as that philosopher has traced all knowledge to sensation. What prolific sources of disease are not those mineral and vegetable poisons that have been introduced for its extirpation! How many thousands have become murderers and robbers, bigots and domestic tyrants, dissolute and abandoned adventurers, from the use of fermented liquors; who, had they slaked their thirst only with pure water, would have lived but to diffuse the happiness of their own unperverted feelings! How many groundless opinions and absurd institutions have not received a general sanction from the sottishness and intemperance of individuals! Who will assert that, had the populace of Paris satisfied their hunger at the ever-furnished table of vegetable nature, they would have lent their brutal suffrage to the proscription-list of Robespierre? Could a set of men, whose passions were not perverted by unnatural stimuli, look with coolness on an *auto da fé*? Is it to be believed that a being of gentle feelings, rising from his meal of roots, would take delight in sports of blood? Was Nero a man of temperate life? Could you read calm health in his cheek, flushed with ungovernable propensities of hatred for the human race? Did Muley Ismael's pulse beat evenly, was his skin transparent, did his eyes beam with healthfulness, and its invariable concomitants, cheerfulness and benignity? Though history has decided none of these questions, a child could not hesitate to answer in the negative. Surely the bile-suffused cheek of Buonaparte, his wrinkled brow, and yellow eye, the ceaseless inquietude of his nervous system, speak no less plainly the character of his unresting ambition than his murders and his victories. It is impossible, had Buonaparte descended from a race of vegetable feeders, that he could have had either the inclination or the power to ascend the throne of the Bourbons. The desire of tyranny could scarcely be excited in the individual, the power to tyrannize would certainly not be delegated by a society neither frenzied by inebriation nor rendered impotent and irrational by disease. Pregnant indeed with inexhaustible calamity is the renunciation of instinct, as it concerns our physical nature; arithmetic cannot enumerate, nor reason perhaps suspect, the multitudinous sources of disease in civilized life. Even common water, that apparently innoxious pabulum, when corrupted by the filth of populous cities, is a deadly and insidious destroyer[1]. Who can wonder that all the inducements held out by God Himself in the Bible to virtue should have been vainer than a nurse's tale; and that those dogmas, by which He has there excited and justified the most ferocious propensities, should have alone been deemed essential; whilst Christians are in the daily practice of all those habits which have infected with disease and crime, not only the reprobate sons, but these favoured children of the common Father's love? Omnipotence itself could not save them from the consequences of this original and universal sin.

There is no disease, bodily or mental, which adoption of vegetable diet and pure water has not infallibly mitigated, wherever the experiment has been fairly tried. Debility is gradually converted into strength; disease into healthfulness; madness, in all its hideous variety, from the ravings of the fettered maniac to the unaccountable irrationalities of ill-temper, that make a hell of domestic life, into a calm and considerate evenness of temper, that alone might offer a certain pledge of the future moral reformation of society. On a natural system of diet, old age would be our last and our only malady; the term of our existence would be protracted; we should enjoy life, and no longer preclude others from the enjoyment of it; all sensational delights would be infinitely more exquisite and perfect; the very sense of being would then be a continued pleasure, such as we now feel it in some few and favoured moments of our youth. By all that is sacred in our hopes for the human race, I conjure those who love happiness and truth to give a fair trial to the vegetable system. Reasoning is surely superfluous on a subject whose merits an experience of six months would set for ever at rest. But it is only among the enlightened and benevolent that so great a sacrifice of appetite and prejudice can be expected, even though its ultimate excellence should not admit of dispute. It is found easier, by the short-sighted victims of disease, to palliate their torments by medicine than to prevent them by regimen. The vulgar of all ranks are invariably sensual and indocile; yet I cannot but feel myself persuaded that when the benefits of vegetable diet are mathematically proved, when it is as clear that those who live naturally are exempt from premature death as that nine is not one, the most sottish of mankind will feel a preference towards a long and tranquil, contrasted with a short and painful, life. On the average, out of sixty persons four die in three years. Hopes are entertained that, in April, 1814, a statement will be given that sixty persons, all having lived more than three years on vegetables and pure water, are then *in perfect health*. More than two years have now elapsed; *not one of them has died*; no such example will be found in any sixty persons taken at random. Seventeen persons of all ages (the families

---

[1] Lambe's *Reports on Cancer*.

of Dr. Lambe and Mr. Newton) have lived for seven years on this diet without a death, and almost without the slightest illness. Surely, when we consider that some of these were infants, and one a martyr to asthma now nearly subdued, we may challenge any seventeen persons taken at random in this city to exhibit a parallel case. Those who may have been excited to question the rectitude of established habits of diet by these loose remarks, should consult Mr. Newton's luminous and eloquent essay[1].

When these proofs come fairly before the world, and are clearly seen by all who understand arithmetic, it is scarcely possible that abstinence from aliments demonstrably pernicious should not become universal. In proportion to the number of proselytes, so will be the weight of evidence; and when a thousand persons can be produced, living on vegetables and distilled water, who have to dread no disease but old age, the world will be compelled to regard animal flesh and fermented liquors as slow but certain poisons. The change which would be produced by simpler habits on political economy is sufficiently remarkable. The monopolizing eater of animal flesh would no longer destroy his constitution by devouring an acre at a meal, and many loaves of bread would cease to contribute to gout, madness and apoplexy, in the shape of a pint of porter, or a dram of gin, when appeasing the long-protracted famine of the hardworking peasant's hungry babes. The quantity of nutritious vegetable matter, consumed in fattening the carcase of an ox, would afford ten times the sustenance, undepraving indeed, and incapable of generating disease, if gathered immediately from the bosom of the earth. The most fertile districts of the habitable globe are now actually cultivated by men for animals, at a delay and waste of aliment absolutely incapable of calculation. It is only the wealthy that can, to any great degree, even now, indulge the unnatural craving for dead flesh, and they pay for the greater licence of the privilege by subjection to supernumerary diseases. Again, the spirit of the nation that should take the lead in this great reform would insensibly become agricultural; commerce, with all its vice, selfishness, and corruption, would gradually decline; more natural habits would produce gentler manners, and the excessive complication of political relations would be so far simplified that every individual might feel and understand why he loved his country, and took a personal interest in its welfare. How would England, for example, depend on the caprices of foreign rulers if she contained within herself all the necessaries, and despised whatever they possessed of the luxuries, of life? How could they starve her into compliance with their views? Of what consequence would it be that they refused to take her woollen manufactures, when large and fertile tracts of the island ceased to be allotted to the waste of pasturage? On a natural system

---

[1] *Return to Nature, or Defence of Vegetable Regimen*, Thomas Cadell, 1811.

of diet we should require no spices from India; no wines from Portugal, Spain, France, or Madeira; none of those multitudinous articles of luxury, for which every corner of the globe is rifled, and which are the causes of so much individual rivalship, such calamitous and sanguinary national disputes. In the history of modern times, the avarice of commercial mono · poly, no less than the ambition of weak and wicked chiefs, seems to have fomented the universal discord, to have added stubbornness to the mistakes of cabinets, and indocility to the infatuation of the people. Let it ever be remembered that it is the direct influence of commerce to make the interval between the richest and the poorest man wider and more unconquerable. Let it be remembered that it is a foe to everything of real worth and excellence in the human character. The odious and disgusting aristocracy of wealth is built upon the ruins of all that is good in chivalry or republicanism; and luxury is the forerunner of a barbarism scarce capable of cure. Is it impossible to realize a state of society, where all the energies of man shall be directed to the production of his solid happiness? Certainly, if this advantage (the object of all political speculation) be in any degree attainable, it is attainable only by a community which holds out no factitious incentives to the avarice and ambition of the few, and which is internally organized for the liberty, security, and comfort of the many. None must be entrusted with power (and money is the completest species of power) who do not stand pledged to use it exclusively for the general benefit. But the use of animal flesh and fermented liquors directly militates with this equality of the rights of man. The peasant cannot gratify these fashionable cravings without leaving his family to starve. Without disease and war, those sweeping curtailers of population, pasturage would include a waste too great to be afforded. The labour requisite to support a family is far lighter[1] than is usually supposed. The peasantry work, not only for themselves, but for the aristocracy, the army, and the manufacturers.

The advantage of a reform in diet is obviously greater than that of any other. It strikes at the root of the evil. To remedy the abuses of legislation, before we annihilate the propensities by which they are produced, is to suppose that by taking away the effect the cause will cease to operate. But the efficacy of this system depends entirely on the proselytism of individuals, and grounds its merits, as a benefit to the community, upon the total change of the dietetic habits in its members. It proceeds securely from a number of particular cases to one that is universal, and has this

[1] It has come under the author's experience that some of the workmen on an embankment in North Wales, who, in consequence of the inability of the proprietor to pay them, seldom received their wages, have supported large families by cultivating small spots of sterile ground by moonlight. In the notes to Pratt's poem, *Bread, or the Poor*, is an account of an industrious labourer who, by working in a small garden before and after his day's task, attained to an enviable state of independence.

advantage over the contrary mode, that one error does not invalidate all that has gone before.

Let not too much, however, be expected from this system. The healthiest among us is not exempt from hereditary disease. The most symmetrical, athletic, and longlived is a being inexpressibly inferior to what he would have been, had not the unnatural habits of his ancestors accumulated for him a certain portion of malady and deformity. In the most perfect specimen of civilized man, something is still found wanting by the physiological critic. Can a return to nature, then, instantaneously eradicate predispositions that have been slowly taking root in the silence of innumerable ages?—Indubitably not. All that I contend for is, that from the moment of the relinquishing all unnatural habits no new disease is generated; and that the predisposition to hereditary maladies gradually perishes, for want of its accustomed supply. In cases of consumption, cancer, gout, asthma, and scrofula, such is the invariable tendency of a diet of vegetables and pure water.

Those who may be induced by these remarks to give the vegetable system a fair trial, should, in the first place, date the commencement of their practice from the moment of their conviction. All depends upon breaking through a pernicious habit resolutely and at once. Dr. Trotter[1] asserts that no drunkard was ever reformed by gradually relinquishing his dram. Animal flesh, in its effects on the human stomach, is analogous to a dram. It is similar in the kind, though differing in the degree, of its operation. The proselyte to a pure diet must be warned to expect a temporary diminution of muscular strength. The subtraction of a powerful stimulus will suffice to account for this event. But it is only temporary, and is succeeded by an equable capability for exertion, far surpassing his former various and fluctuating strength. Above all, he will acquire an easiness of breathing, by which such exertion is performed, with a remarkable exemption from that painful and difficult panting now felt by almost every one after hastily climbing an ordinary mountain. He will be equally capable of bodily exertion, or mental application, after as before his simple meal. He will feel none of the narcotic effects of ordinary diet. Irritability, the direct consequence of exhausting stimuli, would yield to the power of natural and tranquil impulses. He will no longer pine under the lethargy of ennui, that unconquerable weariness of life, more to be dreaded than death itself. He will escape the epidemic madness, which broods over its own injurious notions of the Deity, and 'realizes the hell that priests and beldams feign.' Every man forms, as it were, his god from his own character; to the divinity of one of simple habits no offering would be more acceptable than the happiness of his creatures. He would be incapable of hating or persecuting others for the love of God. He will find,

---

[1] See Trotter, *A View of the Nervous Temperament.*

moreover, a system of simple diet to be a system of perfect epicurism. He will no longer be incessantly occupied in blunting and destroying those organs from which he expects his gratification. The pleasures of taste to be derived from a dinner of potatoes, beans, peas, turnips, lettuces, with a dessert of apples, gooseberries, strawberries, currants, raspberries, and in winter, oranges, apples and pears, is far greater than is supposed. Those who wait until they can eat this plain fare with the sauce of appetite will scarcely join with the hypocritical sensualist at a lord-mayor's feast, who declaims against the pleasures of the table. Solomon kept a thousand concubines, and owned in despair that all was vanity. The man whose happiness is constituted by the society of one amiable woman would find some difficulty in sympathizing with the disappointment of this venerable debauchee.

I address myself not only to the young enthusiast, the ardent devotee of truth and virtue, the pure and passionate moralist, yet unvitiated by the contagion of the world. He will embrace a pure system, from its abstract truth, its beauty, its simplicity, and its promise of wide-extended benefit; unless custom has turned poison into food, he will hate the brutal pleasures of the chase by instinct; it will be a contemplation full of horror, and disappointment to his mind, that beings capable of the gentlest and most admirable sympathies should take delight in the death-pangs and last convulsions of dying animals. The elderly man, whose youth has been poisoned by intemperance, or who has lived with apparent moderation, and is afflicted with a variety of painful maladies, would find his account in a beneficial change produced without the risk of poisonous medicines. The mother, to whom the perpetual restlessness of disease and unaccountable deaths incident to her children are the causes of incurable unhappiness, would on this diet experience the satisfaction of beholding their perpetual healths and natural playfulness[1]. The most valuable lives are daily destroyed by diseases that it is dangerous to palliate and impossible to cure by medicine. How much longer will man continue to pimp for the gluttony of Death, his most insidious, implacable, and eternal foe?

Ἀλλὰ δράκοντας ἀγρίους καλεῖτε καὶ παρδάλεις καὶ λέοντας, αὐτοὶ δὲ μιαιφονεῖτε εἰς ὠμότητα καταλιπόντες ἐκείνοις οὐδέν· ἐκείνοις μὲν γὰρ ὁ φόνος τροφή, ὑμῖν δὲ ὄψον ἐστίν. . . . Ὅτι γὰρ οὐκ ἔστιν ἀνθρώπῳ

---

[1] See Mr. Newton's book. His children are the most beautiful and healthy creatures it is possible to conceive; the girls are perfect models for a sculptor; their dispositions are also the most gentle and conciliating; the judicious treatment, which they experience in other points, may be a correlative cause of this. In the first five years of their life, of 18,000 children that are born, 7,500 die of various diseases; and how many more of those that survive are not rendered miserable by maladies not immediately mortal? The quality and quantity of a woman's milk are materially injured by the use of dead flesh. In an island near Iceland, where no vegetables are to be got, the children invariably die of tetanus before they are three weeks old, and the population is supplied from the mainland.—Sir G. Mackenzie's *Hist. of Iceland*. See also *Émile*, chap. i, pp. 53, 54, 56.

κατὰ φύσιν τὸ σαρκοφαγεῖν, πρῶτον μὲν ἀπὸ τῶν σωμάτων δηλοῦται τῆς κατασκευῆς. Οὐδενὶ γὰρ ἔοικε τὸ ἀνθρώπου σῶμα τῶν ἐπὶ σαρκοφαγίᾳ γεγονότων, οὐ γρυπότης χείλους, οὐκ ὀξύτης ὄνυχος, οὐ τραχύτης ὀδόντος πρόσεστιν, οὐ κοιλίας εὐτονία καὶ πνεύματος θερμότης, πέψαι καὶ κατεργάσασθαι δυνατὴ τὸ βαρὺ καὶ κρεῶδες· ἀλλ᾽ αὐτόθεν ἡ φύσις τῇ λειότητι τῶν ὀδόντων καὶ τῇ σμικρότητι τοῦ στόματος καὶ τῇ μαλακότητι τῆς γλώσσης καὶ τῇ πρὸς πέψιν ἀμβλύτητι τοῦ πνεύματος, ἐξόμνυται τὴν σαρκοφαγίαν. Εἰ δὲ λέγεις πεφυκέναι σεαυτὸν ἐπὶ τοιαύτην ἐδωδήν, ὃ βούλει φαγεῖν πρῶτον αὐτὸς ἀπόκτεινον, ἀλλ᾽ αὐτὸς διὰ σεαυτοῦ, μὴ χρησάμενος κοπίδι μηδὲ τυμπάνῳ τινὶ μηδὲ πελέκει· ἀλλά, ὡς λύκοι καὶ ἄρκτοι καὶ λέοντες αὐτοὶ ὅσα ἐσθίουσι φονεύουσιν, ἄνελε δήγματι βοῦν ἢ στόματι σῦν, ἢ ἄρνα ἢ λαγωὸν διάρρηξον καὶ φάγε προσπεσὼν ἔτι ζῶντος, ὡς ἐκεῖνα. . . . Ἡμεῖς δ᾽ οὕτως ἐν τῷ μιαιφόνῳ τρυφῶμεν, ὥστ᾽ ὄψον τὸ κρέας προσαγορεύομεν, εἶτ᾽ ὄψων πρὸς αὐτὸ τὸ κρέας δεόμεθα, ἀναμιγνύντες ἔλαιον οἶνον μέλι γάρον ὄξος ἡδύσμασι Συριακοῖς Ἀραβικοῖς, ὥσπερ ὄντως νεκρὸν ἐνταφιάζοντες. Καὶ γὰρ οὕτως αὐτῶν διαλυθέντων καὶ μαλαχθέντων καὶ τρόπον τινὰ προσαπέντων ἔργον ἐστὶ τὴν πέψιν κρατῆσαι, καὶ διακρατηθείσης [δὲ] δεινὰς βαρύτητας ἐμποιεῖ καὶ νοσώδεις ἀπεψίας. . . . Οὕτω τὸ πρῶτον ἄγριόν τι ζῷον ἐβρώθη καὶ κακοῦργον, εἶτ᾽ ὄρνις τις ἢ ἰχθὺς ὃς εἵλκυστο· καὶ γευσάμενον οὕτω καὶ προμελετῆσαν ἐν ἐκείνοις τὸ φονικὸν ἐπὶ βοῦν ἐργάτην ἦλθε καὶ τὸ κόσμιον πρόβατον καὶ τὸν οἰκουρὸν ἀλεκτρυόνα· καὶ κατὰ μικρὸν οὕτω τὴν ἀπληστίαν στομώσαντες ἐπὶ σφαγὰς ἀνθρώπων καὶ πολέμους καὶ φόνους προήλθομεν.— Πλούτ. περὶ τῆς Σαρκοφαγίας.

NOTE ON *QUEEN MAB*, BY MARY SHELLEY

[1] SHELLEY was eighteen when he wrote *Queen Mab*; he never published it. When it was written, he had come to the decision that he was too young to be a 'judge of controversies'; and he was desirous of acquiring 'that sobriety of spirit which is the characteristic of true heroism.' But he never doubted the truth or utility of his opinions; and, in printing and privately distributing *Queen Mab*, he believed that he should further their dissemination, without occasioning the mischief either to others or himself that might arise from publication. It is doubtful whether he would himself have admitted it into a collection of his works. His severe classical taste, refined by the constant study of the Greek poets, might have discovered defects that escape the ordinary reader; and the change his opinions underwent in many points would have prevented him from putting forth the speculations of his boyish days. But the poem is too beautiful in itself, and far too remarkable as the production of a boy of eighteen, to allow of

its being passed over: besides that, having been frequently reprinted, the omission would be vain. In the former edition certain portions were left out, as shocking the general reader from the violence of their attack on religion. I myself had a painful feeling that such erasures might be looked upon as a mark of disrespect towards the author, and am glad to have the opportunity of restoring them. The notes also are reprinted entire—not because they are models of reasoning or lessons of truth, but because Shelley wrote them, and that all that a man at once so distinguished and so excellent ever did deserves to be preserved. The alterations his opinions underwent ought to be recorded, for they form his history.

[2] A series of articles was published in the *New Monthly Magazine* during the autumn of the year 1832, written by a man of great talent, a fellow-collegian and warm friend of Shelley: they describe admirably the state of his mind during his collegiate life. Inspired with ardour for the acquisition of knowledge, endowed with the keenest sensibility and with the fortitude of a martyr, Shelley came among his fellow-creatures, congregated for the purposes of education, like a spirit from another sphere; too delicately organized for the rough treatment man uses towards man, especially in the season of youth, and too resolute in carrying out his own sense of good and justice, not to become a victim. To a devoted attachment to those he loved he added a determined resistance to oppression. Refusing to fag at Eton, he was treated with revolting cruelty by masters and boys: this roused instead of taming his spirit, and he rejected the duty of obedience when it was enforced by menaces and punishment. To aversion to the society of his fellow-creatures, such as he found them when collected together in societies, where one egged-on the other to acts of tyranny, was joined the deepest sympathy and compassion; while the attachment he felt for individuals, and the admiration with which he regarded their powers and their virtues, led him to entertain a high opinion of the perfectibility of human nature; and he believed that all could reach the highest grade of moral improvement, did not the customs and prejudices of society foster evil passions and excuse evil actions.

[3] The oppression which, trembling at every nerve yet resolute to heroism, it was his ill-fortune to encounter at school and at college, led him to dissent in all things from those whose arguments were blows, whose faith appeared to engender blame and hatred. 'During my existence,' he wrote to a friend in 1812, 'I have incessantly speculated, thought, and read.' His readings were not always well chosen; among them were the works of the French philosophers: as far as metaphysical argument went, he temporarily became a convert. At the same time, it was the cardinal article of his faith that, if men were but taught and induced to treat their fellows with love, charity, and equal rights, this earth would realize

paradise. He looked upon religion, as it is professed, and above all practised, as hostile instead of friendly to the cultivation of those virtues which would make men brothers.

[4] Can this be wondered at? At the age of seventeen, fragile in health and frame, of the purest habits in morals, full of devoted generosity and universal kindness, glowing with ardour to attain wisdom, resolved at every personal sacrifice to do right, burning with a desire for affection and sympathy,—he was treated as a reprobate, cast forth as a criminal.

[5] The cause was that he was sincere; that he believed the opinions which he entertained to be true. And he loved truth with a martyr's love; he was ready to sacrifice station and fortune, and his dearest affections, at its shrine. The sacrifice was demanded from, and made by, a youth of seventeen. It is a singular fact in the history of society in the civilized nations of modern times that no false step is so irretrievable as one made in early youth. Older men, it is true, when they oppose their fellows and transgress ordinary rules, carry a certain prudence or hypocrisy as a shield along with them. But youth is rash; nor can it imagine, while asserting what it believes to be true, and doing what it believes to be right, that it should be denounced as vicious, and pursued as a criminal.

[6] Shelley possessed a quality of mind which experience has shown me to be of the rarest occurrence among human beings: this was his *unworldliness*. The usual motives that rule men, prospects of present or future advantage, the rank and fortune of those around, the taunts and censures, or the praise, of those who were hostile to him, had no influence whatever over his actions, and apparently none over his thoughts. It is difficult even to express the simplicity and directness of purpose that adorned him. Some few might be found in the history of mankind, and some one at least among his own friends, equally disinterested and scornful, even to severe personal sacrifices, of every baser motive. But no one, I believe, ever joined this noble but passive virtue to equal active endeavours for the benefit of his friends and mankind in general, and to equal power to produce the advantages he desired. The world's brightest gauds and its most solid advantages were of no worth in his eyes, when compared to the cause of what he considered truth, and the good of his fellow-creatures. Born in a position which, to his inexperienced mind, afforded the greatest facilities to practise the tenets he espoused, he boldly declared the use he would make of fortune and station, and enjoyed the belief that he should materially benefit his fellow-creatures by his actions; while, conscious of surpassing powers of reason and imagination, it is not strange that he should, even while so young, have believed that his written thoughts would tend to disseminate opinions which he believed conducive to the happiness of the human race.

[7] If man were a creature devoid of passion, he might have said and done all this with quietness. But he was too enthusiastic, and too full of hatred of all the ills he witnessed, not to scorn danger. Various disappointments tortured, but could not tame, his soul. The more enmity he met, the more earnestly he became attached to his peculiar views, and hostile to those of the men who persecuted him.

[8] He was animated to greater zeal by compassion for his fellow-creatures. His sympathy was excited by the misery with which the world is burning. He witnessed the sufferings of the poor, and was aware of the evils of ignorance. He desired to induce every rich man to despoil himself of superfluity, and to create a brotherhood of property and service, and was ready to be the first to lay down the advantages of his birth. He was of too uncompromising a disposition to join any party. He did not in his youth look forward to gradual improvement: nay, in those days of intolerance, now almost forgotten, it seemed as easy to look forward to the sort of millennium of freedom and brotherhood which he thought the proper state of mankind as to the present reign of moderation and improvement. Ill-health made him believe that his race would soon be run; that a year or two was all he had of life. He desired that these years should be useful and illustrious. He saw, in a fervent call on his fellow-creatures to share alike the blessings of the creation, to love and serve each other, the noblest work that life and time permitted him. In this spirit he composed *Queen Mab*.

[9] He was a lover of the wonderful and wild in literature, but had not fostered these tastes at their genuine sources—the romances and chivalry of the middle ages—but in the perusal of such German works as were current in those days. Under the influence of these he, at the age of fifteen, wrote two short prose romances of slender merit. The sentiments and language were exaggerated, the composition imitative and poor. He wrote also a poem on the subject of Ahasuerus—being led to it by a German fragment he picked up, dirty and torn, in Lincoln's Inn Fields. This fell afterwards into other hands, and was considerably altered before it was printed. Our earlier English poetry was almost unknown to him. The love and knowledge of Nature developed by Wordsworth—the lofty melody and mysterious beauty of Coleridge's poetry—and the wild fantastic machinery and gorgeous scenery adopted by Southey—composed his favourite reading; the rhythm of *Queen Mab* was founded on that of *Thalaba*, and the first few lines bear a striking resemblance in spirit, though not in idea, to the opening of that poem. His fertile imagination, and ear tuned to the finest sense of harmony, preserved him from imitation. Another of his favourite books was the poem of *Gebir* by Walter Savage Landor. From his boyhood he had a wonderful facility of versifica-

tion, which he carried into another language; and his Latin school-verses
were composed with an ease and correctness that procured for him prizes,
and caused him to be resorted to by all his friends for help. He was, at the
period of writing *Queen Mab*, a great traveller within the limits of England,
Scotland, and Ireland. His time was spent among the loveliest scenes of
these countries. Mountain and lake and forest were his home; the phe-
nomena of Nature were his favourite study. He loved to inquire into their
causes, and was addicted to pursuits of natural philosophy and chemistry,
as far as they could be carried on as an amusement. These tastes gave
truth and vivacity to his descriptions, and warmed his soul with that deep
admiration for the wonders of Nature which constant association with
her inspired.

[10] He never intended to publish *Queen Mab* as it stands; but a few years
after, when printing *Alastor*, he extracted a small portion which he
entitled *The Daemon of the World*. In this he changed somewhat the versi-
fication, and made other alterations scarcely to be called improvements.
The invocation of Queen Mab to the Soul of Ianthe,[1] as altered in *The
Daemon of the World*, might be taken as a specimen of the alterations
made. It well characterises his own state of mind.

[11] Some years after, when in Italy, a bookseller published an edition of
Queen Mab as it originally stood. Shelley was hastily written to by his
friends, under the idea that, deeply injurious as the mere distribution of
the poem had proved, the publication might awaken fresh persecutions.
At the suggestion of these friends he wrote a letter on the subject, printed
in the *Examiner* newspaper—with which I close this history of his earliest
work.

To the Editor of the 'Examiner.'

'Sir,

'Having heard that a poem entitled *Queen Mab* has been surreptitiously
published in London, and that legal proceedings have been instituted
against the publisher, I request the favour of your insertion of the follow-
ing explanation of the affair, as it relates to me.

'A poem entitled *Queen Mab* was written by me at the age of eighteen,
I daresay in a sufficiently intemperate spirit—but even then was not
intended for publication, and a few copies only were struck off, to be dis-
tributed among my personal friends. I have not seen this production for
several years. I doubt not but that it is perfectly worthless in point of
literary composition; and that, in all that concerns moral and political
speculation, as well as in the subtler discriminations of metaphysical and
religious doctrine, it is still more crude and immature. I am a devoted

_____
[1] *The Daemon of the World*, 78–107.

enemy to religious, political, and domestic oppression; and I regret this publication, not so much from literary vanity, as because I fear it is better fitted to injure than to serve the sacred cause of freedom. I have directed my solicitor to apply to Chancery for an injunction to restrain the sale; but, after the precedent of Mr. Southey's *Wat Tyler* (a poem written, I believe, at the same age, and with the same unreflecting enthusiasm), with little hope of success.

'Whilst I exonerate myself from all share in having divulged opinions hostile to existing sanctions, under the form, whatever it may be, which they assume in this poem, it is scarcely necessary for me to protest against the system of inculcating the truth of Christianity or the excellence of Monarchy, however true or however excellent they may be, by such equivocal arguments as confiscation and imprisonment, and invective and slander, and the insolent violation of the most sacred ties of Nature and society.

'SIR,

'I am your obliged and obedient servant,

'PERCY B. SHELLEY.

'*Pisa, June* 22, 1821.'

APPENDIX

ESDAILE POEMS NOT BY SHELLEY OR OF DOUBTFUL AUTHORSHIP

43. *Fragment of a Poem*

The Original Idea of which was Suggested
by the Cowardly and Infamous Bombardment of Copenhagen

Before January 1811

THE ice-mountains echo, the Baltic, the Ocean,
  Where cold sits enthroned on its solium of snow;
Even Spitzbergen perceives the terrific commotion,
  The roar floats on the whirlwinds of sleet as they blow;
  Blood clots with the streams as half-frozen they flow,   5
Lurid flame o'er the cities the meteors of war,
And mix their deep gleam with the bright polar glare.

AUTHORSHIP: *Elizabeth Shelley, but perhaps helped by Shelley; see nn., p. 359.*
AUTOGRAPH: *PBS, Esd.; Pf., letter to Hogg, 11 Jan. 1811. See n., p. 401.*   TITLE, *Esd.*
DATE: *See n., p. 401.*   PRINTED: *From Pf., Hogg, 1858/from Esd., Rog. 1966.*   TEXT:
1966/Esd.
    The Pf. version consists of 4 stanzas of which the first and third correspond, apart from
a few variations, with stanzas II and I respectively of the Esdaile version. Its second and
fourth stanzas are as follows

> Old Ocean to shrieks of Despair is resounding
>   It washes the terror-struck nations with gore
> Wild horror the fear-palsied Earth is astounding
>   And murmurs of fate fright the dread-convulsed shore.
>   The Andes in Sympathy start at the roar
> Vast Etna alarmed leans his flame-glowing brow
> And huge Teneriffe stoops with his pinnacled snow.

> All are Bretheren,—   the African bending
>   To the stroke of the hard hearted Englishmans rod,
> The courtier at Luxury's Palace attending,
>   The Senator trembling at Tyranny's nod
>   Each nation wch kneels at the footstool of God
> All are Bretheren; then banish Distinction afar
> Let concord & Love heal the miseries of War!

For a complete, literal transcript of Pf. see Kenneth Neill Cameron, Shelley and his
Circle, ii. 701–3.

Yes! the arms of Britannia victorious are bearing
    Fame, triumph, and terror wherever they spread;
Her Lion his crest o'er the nations is rearing,—   10
    Ruin follows—it tramples the dying and dead.
    But her countrymen fall—the blood-reeking bed
Of the battle-slain sends a complaint-breathing sigh:
It is mixed with the shoutings of victory.

I see the lone female,—the sun is descending,   15
    Dank carnage-smoke sheds an ensanguining glare,—
Night its shades in the orient earlier is blending,
    Yet the light faintly marks a wild maniac's stare,—
    She lists to the death shrieks that came on the air,
The pride of her heart to her bosom she prest,   20
Then sunk on his form in the sleep of the blest.

45. 'Cold are the Blasts...'

1808

COLD are the blasts when December is howling,
    Chill are the damps on a dying friend's brow,—
Stern is the Ocean when tempests are rolling,
    Sad is the grave where a brother lies low;
But chillier is scorn from the false one that loved thee,   5
More stern is the sneer from the friend that has proved thee,
More sad are the tears when these sorrows have moved thee,
    That envenomed by wildest delirium flow.

And alas! thou, Louisa, hast felt all this horror,—
    Full long the fallen victim contended with fate,   10
Till, a destitute outcast, abandoned to sorrow,
    She sought her babe's food at her ruiner's gate.

AUTHORSHIP: *Elizabeth Shelley. See nn., p. 359.*   AUTOGRAPH: *PBS, Esd., Pf.*
DATE: *Esd.*   PRINTED: *from Pf., Hogg, 1858/from Esd., Rog. 1966.*   TEXT: *1966/Esd.*
   The Esd. version of this poem is a variant of the third poem in Original Poetry by Victor
and Cazire, *the joint work of Shelley and his sister, Elizabeth; see above, pp. 37–63.
The Pf. version represents an attempt by Shelley to write out from memory, for Hogg's
benefit, some samples of Elizabeth's composition. It consists of the 5 Esdaile stanzas together
with broken passages, adding up to some 14 lines, taken from* Victor and Cazire, XII *and*
XIII; *there are considerable verbal variants. For a literal transcription see Kenneth Neill
Cameron,* Shelley and his Circle, ii. 625–7.

Another had charmed the remorseless betrayer,
He turned laughing away from her anguish-fraught prayer,—
She spoke not but, wringing the rain from her hair,   15
    Took the rough mountain path though the hour was late.

On the cloud-shrouded summit of dark Penmanmawr
    The form of the wasted Louisa reclined;
She shrieked to the ravens loud-croaking afar,
    She sighed to the gusts of the wild-sweeping wind:—   20
'Ye storms o'er the peak of the lone mountain soaring,
Ye clouds with the thunder-winged tempest-shafts lowering,
Thou wrath of black Heaven, I blame not thy pouring,
    But thee, cruel Henry, I call thee unkind!'

Then she wreathed a wild crown from the flowers of the
      mountain,   25
    And deliriously laughing the heath-twigs entwined,
She bedewed it with tear drops, then leaned o'er the fountain,
    And cast it a prey to the wild-sweeping wind.
'Ah, go!' she exclaimed, 'where the tempest is yelling,
'Tis unkind to be cast on the sea that is swelling,   30
But I left, a pitiless outcast, my dwelling;
    My garments are torn—so, they say, is my mind.'

Not long lived Louisa, and over her grave
    Wave the desolate limbs of a storm-blasted yew;
Around it no demon or ghosts dare to rave,   35
    But spirits of love steep her slumbers in dew.
Then stay thy swift steps 'mid the dark mountain heather,
Though bleak be the scene and severe be the weather,
For perfidy, traveller, cannot bereave her
    Of the tears to the tombs of the innocent due.   40

55. 'Full Many a Mind . . .'

1815

FULL many a mind with radiant genius fraught
    Is taught the dark scowl of misery to bear,—
How many a great soul has often sought
    To stem the sad torrent of wild despair!

AUTHORSHIP: [?] *Harriet Shelley.*   TRANSCRIPT: *H. Shelley,* in *Esd.*   DATE: *Esd.*
PRINTED: *Louise S. Boas,* Harriet Shelley, *1962/Rog. 1966*   TEXT: *1966/Esd.*

It would not be Earth's laws were given   5
   To stand between Man, God and Heaven,—
To teach him where to seek and truly find
   That lasting comfort, peace of mind.

57. 'Late was the Night . . .'

Undated

LATE was the night, the moon shone bright;
   It tinted the walls with a silver light,
And threw its wide, uncertain beam
   Upon ⟨?the⟩ rolling mountain stream.

That stream so swift that rushes along   5
   Has oft been ⟨?dyed⟩ by the murderers' song,
It oft has heard the exulting wave
   Of one who oft the murderers braved.

The Alpine summits which, raised on high,
   Peacefully frown on the valley beneath   10
And lift their huge forms to the sky
   Oft have heard the voices of death.

Now not a murmur floats on the air,
   Save the distant sounds of the torrent's tide,
Not a cloud obscures the moon so fair,   15
   Not a shade is seen on the rocks to glide.

See, that fair form that [?none] ⟨?can save⟩;
   Her garments are tattered her bosom so bare,—
She shrinks from the yawning, watery grave,
   And, shivering, around her enwraps her dark hair.   20

Poor Emma has toiled o'er many a mile,
   The victim of misery's own sad child,
Pale is her cheek, all trembling awhile,
   She totters and falls on the cold-stricken wild.

⋀ *Under line 8 Harriet has written* Stanmore *1815.*

⋁ AUTHORSHIP: [?] *Harriet Shelley.*   TRANSCRIPT: *H. Shelley, in Esd.*   DATE: *See
n., p. 401.*   PRINTED: *Rog. 1966.*   TEXT: *1966/Esd.*
   4 ⟨?the⟩] its *Esd.*   6 murderers'] murderes *Esd.*   8 murderers] murderes *Esd.*
5–8, 17 *See nn., p. 401.*

NOTES ON MARY SHELLEY'S
PREFACES

p. xlix, para. 1: *Obstacles* ...: After the publication, in 1824, of her edition of *Posthumous Poems*, Sir Timothy Shelley had threatened to withdraw the funds on which she and her son depended unless she undertook to hand over all unsold copies and to publish nothing further about Shelley without his permission. In 1839 she obtained permission to publish the Poetical Works, provided no biography were attached. This condition she cleverly circumvented by interlarding the text with her Notes.

p. l, para. 2: ... *the workings of passion on general and unselfish subjects*: The word 'passion', which recurs three or four times in this Preface, had a high significance for Shelley. Writing to Hogg on 2 June 1811 (Jones, *Letters of Shelley*, i. 95) he defined it as 'an incapacity for action, otherwise than in unison with its dictates'. In relation to his poetry it means 'a capacity for giving himself up body and soul to what he believed to be good and beautiful'. Cf. the reference, in Mary's Note on *Queen Mab*, to his 'unworldliness'. Cf., also, Esdaile Poem No. 4 and n., p. 362.

p. l, para. 4: ... *the purely imaginative* means his poetry of ideas, mostly Platonically coloured. Mary's second category covers those minor, much anthologized, lyrics so long thought the measure of his achievement.

p. li, para. 6: *few of us understand or sympathize* ... *Plato his study*: For the three levels of Shelley's Platonism, natural, indirect, and direct, see, *passim*, the Notes in this edition. In J. A. Notopoulos's *The Platonism of Shelley*, chapters II, III, and IV, each of these Platonic strands is, in turn, explained and illustrated; for the many today who are unable to study, at first hand, 'the good and beautiful of the Socratic philosophers', Chapter I, 'Platonism and the Platonic Mind', is a valuable introduction.

p. lii, para. 7: *A wise friend* ... refers to Godwin's letter of 4 March 1812 (Jones *Letters*, i. 260–2).

The epigraphs:

Like Shelley's epigraphs these Italian quotations have an illuminating aptness that has usually been overlooked. The quotation here given at the head of her Preface to 1839[1] was originally on the title-page. It is from Petrarch, *Sonetti e canzoni in morte di Madonna Laura*, in the edition of Carducci and Ferrari, Sansoni, 1916, No. CCCVI, 12–14, pp. 420–1. The poet, accompanied by Love, mournfully looks around all the places where he had been accustomed to find Laura. With the feminine *Lei* adapted to *Lui* Mary's meaning is

Him do I not find, but I see his sacred footprints, all leading to heaven above, and away from the waters of Avernus and Styx.

His 'footprints' are the trail of poetry she has been following through his manuscripts, and 'Avernus and Styx' signify 'the hell of my widowhood here below'. The quotation which concludes her 1839 Preface is from the same group of poems, No. CCXCVII, 12–14, the sonnet beginning 'Due gran nemiche...' in the Carducci–Ferrari edition, p. 410. Once again Mary adapts the genders, changing *tardo* to the feminine *tarda*. Petrarch's language on the death of Laura is most subtly invoked to express her grief on Shelley's death and her Petrarchian dedication to his memory. The Platonic love which is a driving force through Shelley's thought and poetry finds for his widow a microcosm in the *fino amore* of the *Duecento*; it had had a nineteenth-century renewal in their life together and now her edition of her poet's work will crown, she hopes, the dedication of her life to his. The 'questa stanca penna' is a brave reference to the weary struggles of her life between Shelley's death in 1822 and the moment in 1839 when, having at last overcome his father's opposition, she is able to give his poetry its *envoi*:

If I am slow to follow [him], perhaps it may come about that I shall consecrate his fair good name with this weary pen of mine.

Fifteen years earlier, introducing the *Posthumous Poems* (see p. liv), Mary had similarly invoked, and identified, Petrarch: see, in the Carducci–Ferrari edition, p. 308, CCXV, 1–4, the lines being taken this time from *Sonetti e canzoni in vita di Madonna Laura*. Shelley's death being less distant the thoughts of the *life* of the lost one are more apposite:

With noble birth went a quiet, simple way of life; with his lofty mind went a pure heart; from the flower of youth grew the fruit of maturity, and in his grave demeanour lurked a spirit of delight.

In one of Mary Shelley's fair-copy books, Bodleian MS., Shelley adds. d. 9, is noted a third Petrarch quotation, which she did not print. It is from *Sonetti e canzoni in morte di Madonna Laura*, No. CCCXXXIII:

> ma, ricogliendo le sue sparte fronde,
> dietro lo vo pur così passo passo.

But in gathering up his scattered leaves, I follow after him, in that way, step by step.

NOTES ON THE POEMS

EARLY SHORTER POEMS AND TRANSLATIONS

p. 3, VERSES ON A CAT. *Text*: For a description of the manuscript see Cameron, *Shelley and his Circle*, iv. 813–19. It bears no title but is headed by a drawing of a cat. On the verso is a note in another hand: 'Percy Bysshe Shelley, written at ten years of age to his sister at school.' Mr. Cameron thinks this date, 1802, may be a little too early, but places it before 1805. I have emended the unmetrical seventh line, which may be due to faulty memory or miscopying.

p. 4, OMENS. *Date*: Written, says Medwin, when Shelley was 'about fifteen . . .' Chatterton was then one of his greatest 'favourites'. Cf. the dirge in *Aella*:

> Harke! the raven flappes his winge
> In the briered delle belowe;
> Harke! the dethe-owle loude dothe synge,
> To the nyghte-mares as heie goe . . .

Medwin suggests also some influence from a translation of Bürger's *Leonore* in the translation of W. R. Spencer, 1796. See nn. on *Poems from St. Irvyne*, III. 1.

p. 4, EPITAPHIUM. Medwin adduces this and the following poem as proofs that at Eton, 'Shelley had attained great skill in the art of versification', but this must be viewed in relation to the freedom and diffuseness held permissible by teachers in 1808–9. Words and phrases could be misused—'recepit' (14), 'Longius fuge' (17), weakened the more by the repetition of 'fuge' (18, 19), 'suspicari' (18), or misplaced—'quod' (13), '-que' (24)—and incorrect, inferior, or doubtful forms passed over, e.g. 'Cespitis' (2), 'despicata' (6), 'moestis' (13). As a classical exercise the verses are rhythmically rough, e.g. the concatenated dissyllables in line 19, and too much coloured by suggestion of late or Christian Latin, such as the use of 'coelum' (12) and 'coelo' (15) and the whole conception of 'laudes' (18) and 'virtutes' (22) as things *lying* on the bosom of their Father and their God. The general sense of Latinity is inadequate and faltering— 'caespes' would hardly be equipped in the Roman mind with a 'gremium', nor, were this conceivable, could the idea of 'Patris sedes' have very well followed; again 'tristis . . . Sollicitudo' poorly conveys the difficult 'Melancholy', and to a reasonably educated Roman the whole phrase 'recepit . . . pectus amici' might have been unintelligibile. Again, 'genus natum' and, in the sense intended, 'velle tractas' read oddly.

p. 6, IN HOROLOGIUM. A translation of an epigram 'On Seeing a French Watch round the Neck of a Beautiful Young Woman', published in the *Oxford University and City Herald*, 16 Sept. 1809:

> Mark what we gain from foreign lands,
> Time cannot now be said to linger,—
> Allowed to lay his two rude hands
> Where others dare not lay a finger.

The Latinity is comparable to that of the preceding poem. The gender 'marmoreas', here corrected, may be a copying error; nevertheless the use of 'colles' to mean 'breasts' is without classical authority; 'horas', ending a pentameter, is a false quantity; and 'insensa' is a *vox nihili*.

The *Herald* at that time was published by Munday and Slatter (see below, n. on 'Four Epigrams').

p. 6, FOUR EPIGRAMS. For Shelley's publications in *The Oxford Herald* in 1811 see D. F. MacCarthy, *Shelley's Early Life*, London, 1872. Nos. 1 and 2 were signed 'S' and Nos. 3 and 4 'Versificator'. These versions have the character of eighteenth-century exercises. But, though Shelley had yet to develop the inspiration and skill of his later translating, they show a *Sprachgefühl* which demands interest. The originals are as follows:

1. *Anth. Pal.* ix. 375, Anonymous:

> Τίς ποτ' ἀκηδέστως οἰνοτρόφον ὄμφακα Βάκχου
> ἀνὴρ ἀμπελίνου κλήματος ἐξέταμεν,
> χείλεα δὲ στυφθεὶς ἀπό μιν βάλεν, ὡς ἂν ὁδίταις
> εἴη νισσομένοις ἡμιδακὲς σκύβαλον;
> εἴη οἱ Διόνυσος ἀνάρσιος, οἷα Λυκοῦργος   5
> ὅττι †μιν αὐξομέναν ἔσβεσεν εὐφροσύναν.
> τοῦδε γὰρ ἂν τάχα τις διὰ πώματος ἢ πρὸς ἀοιδὰς
> ἤλυθεν, ἢ γοερού κάδεος ἔσχε λύσιν.

2. *Anth. Pal.* vi. 345, Crinagoras:

> Εἴαρος ἤνθει μὲν τὸ πρὶν ῥόδα, νῦν δ' ἐνὶ μέσσῳ
> χείματι πορφυρέας ἐσχάσαμεν κάλυκας,
> σῇ ἐπιμειδήσαντα γενεθλίῃ ἄσμενα τῇδε
> ἠοῖ, νυμφιδίων ἀσσοτάτῃ λεχέων.
> καλλίστης ὀφθῆναι ἐπὶ κροτάφοισι γυναικὸς   5
> λώϊον ἢ μίμνειν ἠρινὸν ἠέλιον.

3. *Anth. Pal.* ix. 54, Menecrates:

> Γῆρας ἐπὰν μὲν ἀπῇ, πᾶς εὔχεται· ἢν δέ ποτ' ἔλθῃ,
> μέμφεται· ἔστι δ' ἀεὶ κρεῖσσον ὀφειλόμενον.

4. *Anth. Pal.* ix. 39. Musicius, though ascribed by Diogenes Laertius, Shelley's frequent source, to Plato:

> Ἁ Κύπρις Μούσαισι· "Κοράσια, τὰν Ἀφροδίταν
> τιμᾶτ', ἢ τὸν Ἔρων ὑμμιν ἐφοπλίσομαι."
> χαὶ Μοῦσαι ποτὶ Κύπριν· "Ἄρει τὰ στωμύλα ταῦτα·
> ἡμῖν δ' οὐ πέτεται τοῦτο τὸ παιδάριον."

In the 5 January number of the *Herald*, over the signature 'T', and entitled 'The Rose', appeared a paraphrase of Anacreon v and vi, the second stanza of which suggests that it may have been intended as a companion piece:

> And thou, my friend, our lays improve,
>   With me in concert join
> To praise those sweets which mortals love,
>   The breath of power divine.

Possibly Hogg could have been the author.

Shelley's connection with the *Herald* seems to have been quite a close one. On 2 March 1811, under the heading 'Liberty of the Press', appeared an appeal for the Irish journalist Peter Finnerty, 'Mr. P. B. Shelley' being among the subscribers listed. On 9 February the *Herald* announced his forthcoming publication of *The Necessity of Atheism*. Its items of news, its commentary on news, and the satirical poems which it published on the hypocrisy of churchmen and the administration of the University were all very much in line with his thinking. The files from April 1810 to the end of 1813 have been carefully scanned, in the Bodleian by my colleague Dr. James R. Thompson, and in the British Museum by my colleague Dr. Frank B. Fieler, and their researches reveal an interesting relationship between the pattern of its contents and the pattern of Shelley's life at Oxford. I quote from a note by Dr. Fieler:

After the middle of March 1811, when Shelley was expelled, there is a definite falling off in the amount of poetry printed in the *Herald*. What does appear is more or less limited to variant forms of traditional local poems or examples of little-known older poets, chiefly of the 16th and 17th centuries, and printed from MSS in the Bodleian: in addition to these some original humorous verse shows up in early 1812. The flurry of poetry in January, February and March 1811 does seem to suggest the existence of a little clique of poetasters who, led by the young Shelley, persuaded the editors to print their poems and/or translations; it would further seem that when Shelley was expelled, either the clique broke up or the editors, fearful of association with such notoriety, decided to exclude them from their columns.

When Shelley's poem 'to Constantia Singing' appeared in the *Herald* on 31 January 1818 it was over the signature 'Pleyel', which they may have failed to associate with the 'S' and the 'Versificator' of 1811. It is to be noted that the paper was published by Munday and Slatter, the Oxford booksellers whom Sir Timothy Shelley had requested to indulge his son's 'printing freaks'; they it was who published the *Posthumous Fragments of Margaret Nicholson* and who, for twenty minutes, exposed for sale the fatal *Necessity of Atheism*.

p. 7, TRANSLATION ... VINCENT BOURNE. Of Vincent Bourne (1695–1747) the *Cambridge Bibliography of English Literature* records that he edited *Carmina Comitialia Cantabrigensia*, 1721, and published *Poemata, Latine partim reddita, partim scripta*, 1734. The vogue of the latter is attested by the fact that an eighth edition, the one Shelley probably knew, since it was brought out by his publisher, Slatter and Munday, appeared in 1808. Cowper admired his poems, and translated some of them. The original of Shelley's piece is headed 'SI PROPIUS STES, TE CAPIET MINUS' and runs, as follows:

> LONDINI ad pontem prono cum labimur amne,
>   Quam tua dat turris dulce, Maria, melos!

Ut servat justum quaevis campana tenorem!
Pulsata ut variis contremit aura sonis!
Nec mora, nec requies; ripas concentibus implet,   5
Alternans hilares ingeminansque vices.
Quo magis abscedis, tentat numerosior aurem
Musica; laetantur corda, salitque jecur.
Talis ab harmonia surgit distante voluptas;
Sin turrim introëas, omnia clangor erit.   10

The translation is signed 'Versificator'.

p. 8, To MARY WHO DIED, ETC. *Date*: On 23 November 1811 Shelley wrote to
Miss Hitchener, 'I transcribe a little Poem I found this morning; it was written
some time ago, but as it appears to show what I then thought of eternal life
I send it.' (Jones, *Letters of Shelley*, i. 189–90.) This Mary may be presumed
identical with the Mary who inspired four poems in the Esdaile Notebook; see
above, pp. 139–43, and below, p. 369. Since the first of these poems is dated
'November 1810' one may interpret 'some time ago' as probably representing
the same date, and certainly some time between it and the writing of the letter.
By 'this opinion' Shelley means 'the conviction of an eternal life in which she
would meet her lover'—the earliest example, I think, in Shelley's poetry of the
notion of the immortality of the soul: possibly a reminiscence from the *Phaedo*,
but more probably a piece of what Notopoulos (14–28) calls 'natural Platonism'.
For a different 'opinion' see Shelley's footnote to Esdaile Poem No. 33, p. 134.

p. 9, LOVE. *Date*: The poem seems contemporary in feeling with the letter
to Hogg.

p. 10, ON A FÊTE, ETC. Taken down by Garnett from the mouth of Shelley's
cousin, the Revd. Charles Grove; all he could remember of a 50-line poem
inspired by an extravagant fête given by the Prince Regent in June 1811. It is
said that Shelley amused himself by throwing copies into the carriages of the
guests. Cf. (Jones, i. 105) the letter to Graham which begins with a description
of the fête and ends with part of the translation of the Marseillaise (Esdaile
Poem No. 47, p. 160); which is as if a modern student should pass from
describing a state ceremony to a verse from 'The Red Flag'.

p. 10, LETTER TO EDWARD FERGUS GRAHAM. Edward Fergus Graham (? 1787–
1852) remains a somewhat shadowy figure, but he is prominent in Shelley's
early correspondence: see the index to Jones, *Letters*. It is thought that his
father was in Sir Timothy Shelley's employment and that the latter had him
trained as a music master; he certainly was brought up at Field Place and in
some way attached to the Shelleys. He had a residence at 29 Vine St., Piccadilly,
which was a great convenience to Shelley as a London stopping-place, and he
was useful for carrying out small commissions. It may be that he was Lady
Shelley's protégé rather than her husband's. Shelley's idea that his mother was
casting amorous eyes on the young man seems to have begun as a coarse Regency
joke and then developed into a serious suspicion. In his letter to her of 22 October
1811 (see Jones, i. 155) he resents her odd plan for marrying Graham to his
sister Elizabeth, suggesting that this may be merely intended to divert scandal;

the letter, however, remains unanswered because, like other letters of Shelley's, it was sent unopened by Sir Timothy to his lawyer, Whitton.

3: *Killjoy's frank*: The signature of Sir Timothy who, as a Member of Parliament, was entitled to send letters post-free.

7: Thomas Graham, Lord Lynedoch (1788–1843), was a general prominent in Wellington's Peninsular Campaign of 1808–14.

36: Perhaps Shelley's knowledge of the stories concerning Ninon de Lenclos, the famous wit and beauty, may derive from an interest in her early encouragement of Voltaire. Larousse gives her dates as 1620–1705. Other authorities vary, though none suggest that she attained her ninetieth year. Shelley, however, would be less concerned with biographical niceties than with an analogy requiring her to have an age roughly twice his mother's at the time of writing.

42: *cornuting*: A pun involving the idea of Shelley's father (*a*) wearing the horns of a cuckold, (*b*) caught on the horns of a dilemma, the second notion deriving, perhaps, from experience of baiting Sir Timothy in argument.

56: *little Jack*: Shelley's five-year-old brother, John.

p. 13, THE DEVIL'S WALK. *Date*: Of the two versions the first is thought to be the earlier. In the summer of 1812, when Shelley was in Devonshire, he and his servant, Daniel Hill, distributed it together with the *Declaration of Rights*. With this distribution on land went the libertarian messages consigned to the air in balloons and to the sea in bottles—see the poems on pp. 118, 119, and, below, nn. p. 368. Both versions may be regarded less as original verses than as variations on old ones. Shelley does not disguise his imitation of 'The Devil's Thoughts' published by Coleridge in the *Morning Post* of 6 September 1799. Then there is a poem by Southey entitled *The Devil's Walk*, the two being to a large extent identical. The joint authorship has been much discussed and some have asserted that Porson had a hand in it. The references to the lunacy of George III, to the comical vanity of the Prince Regent, and to the horrors of the Peninsular War need no comment. Such early verses are forerunners of *The Mask of Anarchy* and *Swellfoot the Tyrant*.

ll. 7–8: A somewhat forced piece of punning involving the French expressions *faire les beaux bras* (= to play the man-of-fashion) and *chapeau à cornes* (= cocked hat, literally 'horned hat').

p. 19, TO IRELAND. *Date*: Lines 26–end are written out as verse in Shelley's letter to Miss Hitchener. Lines 1–25, which occur earlier in the letter, are written out as rhapsodic prose. Recent editors have attached the two passages. Jones, i. 254, considers this a mistake, and his view must command respect. I have, however, favoured the arrangement because it aptly illustrates, in Shelley's creative process, the tendency of emotion, as it gains intensity, to elevate language from everyday prose-rhythms to a verse measure. *Martin Chuzzlewit*, ch. xxxvi, is a good illustration of this tendency. It is common in prose translations of verse, in sermons, and in political rhetoric.

19–21: Cf. *Queen Mab*, IX. 31–2, and 'The Monarch's Funeral', 57–8. Mr. Desmond King-Hele has reminded me that both passages look back to *The*

Temple of Nature, IV. 383, where Erasmus Darwin describes how, 'when a Monarch or a mushroom dies', the apparently dead mass soon teems with life. For the notion, in a slightly different key, one might compare Hamlet's remarks in the churchyard about King Alexander (*Hamlet*, v. i).

22–5: Another early example in Shelley's poetry of the notion of the immortality of the soul. Cf. above, n. on 'To Mary Who Died in this Opinion'.

p. 20, SADAK THE WANDERER. *Text*: The contents of *The Keepsake for 1828* were anonymous; there existed, however, a volume of the original manuscripts, complete with an index showing the fifth item to be 'Sadak the Wanderer by Percy B. Shelley'. The volume was owned by Dawson Turner and later by Davidson Cook, though in the meantime Shelley's manuscript had been removed (see Cook's article in *TLS*, May 1936). Also in the volume was a prose piece, 'The Deev Alfakir'. The accompanying illustration, 'Sadak by the Waters of Oblivion', was the first picture (1812) of the once famous artist John Martin. Martin's picture is reproduced by Ian Jack in *Keats and the Mirror of Art* (Clarendon Press, 1967), p. 173. It probably influenced *Hyperion* and it may have suggested to Shelley the idea of writing a poem on 'Sadak'. Internal evidence, however, including his use of the name Kalasrade, proves that the poet's inspiration was chiefly derived from the parent source, which was one of the 'Tales of the Genii, or the delightful lessons of Horam the son of Asmar . . . translated from the Persian manuscript . . . by Sir Charles Morell'. The work was originally issued in shilling parts, and reprinted in two octavo volumes in 1764. 'Tales of the Genii', though purporting to be a translation by Sir Charles Morell, Ambassador from the British Settlements in India to the Great Mogul, were entirely the work of James Ridley (1736–65). The tale which inspired Shelley's poem is Number IX in the second volume, where it is entitled 'Sadak and Kalasrade'.

The character of 'Sadak the Wanderer' as portrayed in Ridley's tale and Shelley's poem, is very much akin to that of 'The Wandering Jew'.

p. 25, POEMS FROM ST. IRVYNE

Date: St. Irvyne; or, The Rosicrucian: a Romance, By a Gentleman of the University of Oxford appeared in late 1810, though the title-page is dated '1811'. Medwin says that some of the poems were written a year or two earlier. No. I, on its appearance in *Victor and Cazire*, is dated 1810. The general date 1808–10 seems a reasonable conjecture. Shelley's verse-writing at this time was probably subject to infection from the jingle of metres then popular. Scott's 'Helvellyn' and Byron's 'Hours of Idleness' are traceable. III. 1 is to be compared with a line from Spencer's translation of Bürger's *Leonore*. Cf. n. on 'Omens', above. Medwin says that this poem, with the illustrations of Lady Diana Beauclerk, had a powerful effect on Shelley. For Shelley's sensitivity to illustrations cf. the letter to John Gisborne, 12 January 1822, where he described the effect of the illustrations to Goethe's *Faust*, Part I, by Moritz Retzsch (Jones, ii. 376).

Text: Manuscript b is described by Forman in *The Athenaeum*, 5 June 1909, and in Medwin's *Life*, ed. Forman, pp. 452–4; see also Jones, i. 8–9. It is my belief that manuscript c, the document once described in the Pierpont Library as a forgery, is an authentic Shelley letter, though the process of silking and repair does, certainly, give a strange appearance to the texture of the paper. I believe furthermore that b and c are identical. As will be seen from my textual collation on pp. 31–2, the points at which they vary from manuscript a, used by Shelley for his 1811 printing, are the same, with one single exception that in c, the Morgan manuscript, line 14, of the Additional Stanzas, though it does occur, as Forman says, 'at the foot of the leaf', is not, as he says 'cut away'. I have wondered whether his access to the document was somehow limited, e.g. through seeing it under glass, so that what appeared to be 'cut away' was, in fact, merely *folded*. Again since line 15 is a rhetorical repetition of line 14, varied only in the last two words, a restricted examination might suggest that the repetition of the second line was an accident, displacing a new line.

p. 37, ORIGINAL POETRY BY VICTOR AND CAZIRE

Authorship, Date: This was the combined work of 'Victor' (Shelley) and 'Cazire' (his sister Elizabeth); the period of composition is fixed by the dates appended to the poems. Shelley had the poems printed in Worthing and around August 1810 asked the London publisher, Stockdale, to issue them. Fourteen hundred copies had been delivered to him when Stockdale noticed that No. XIV was not, in fact, 'original'; it was the work of M. G. Lewis, and had been copied by Elizabeth Shelley out of those *Tales of Terror* so beloved by Jane Austen's youngest heroine. Shelley instantly ordered all copies to be destroyed and the book was forgotten till Richard Garnett discovered a reference to it in *Stockdale's Budget* and made known his discovery in *Macmillan's Magazine* for 1860. In 1898 a copy was found in the library of V. E. G. Hussey, great-nephew of the Harriet Grove who was Shelley's first cousin and first love, and who is commemorated in the verses. A facsimile edition was brought out by Richard Garnett, who classified the poems as follows: (1) Familiar poems in the style of Anstey's *Bath Guide*: the first two, (2) a cycle of little poems, evidently addressed to Harriet Grove in the summer of 1810 (III–VII, XII, XIII), (3) Tales of Terror, in the manner of 'Monk' Lewis (XIV–XVII), (4) a few miscellaneous pieces (VIII–XI). I follow Garnett's attributions of authorship, apart from No. III, which he gives to Shelley, but which, according to Shelley's statement to Hogg at Oxford (*Life*, ed. Humbert Wolfe, i. 126), was written by Elizabeth; it has to be remembered, however, that as he was anxious, just then, to foster a relationship between his friend and his sister, he may have been exaggerating her accomplishments.

I. 20: *Entick*, John, *c.* 1703–73, was an English schoolmaster who wrote a number of widely used books on spelling and grammar, among them the *Spelling Dictionary* of 1764, of which a new edition had appeared in 1807. *Murray*, Lindley, 1745–1826: the Anglo-American grammarian whose *Grammar of the English Language* was, till well into the nineteenth century, a standard textbook on both sides of the Atlantic.

I. 35: *Junius*: The name assumed by the anonymous writer of the famous letters which, in 1769 and the following years, assailed the conduct and character of King George III and members of his government; they were reputed to be the work of Sir Philip Francis, 1740–1818.

Plato: The first mention in Shelley's verse of the writer who was to prove the most lasting influence on him: possibly a recollection of the Eton days in which he had been introduced to the *Symposium* by Dr. Lind. (See 'Prince Athanase', 125 foll., Mary Shelley's Note on *Laon and Cythna*, and Medwin's revised *Life*, p. 33.)

I. 55: *Grub-street*: The name of a street near Moorfields in London (now Milton Street) much inhabited by writers of small histories, dictionaries, and temporary poems; hence signifying 'the tribe of literary hacks' (*OED*).

II: Harriet Grove wrote in her journal on 17 September 1810 (Cameron, *Shelley and his Circle*, ii. 590), 'Received the Poetry of Victor & Cazire, Charlotte offended & with reason as I think they have done very wrong in publishing what they have of her.' It was this poem which gave offence because in it (cf. lines 14–15) Elizabeth makes fun of her sister's interest in Colonel Sergison of Cuckfield.

II. 9: *Burdett*, Sir Francis, 1770–1844, M.P. for Westminster, was very prominent in 1810 because of his imprisonment in the cause of free speech. Shelley dedicated *The Wandering Jew* to him. (See p. 181.)

II. 40: Cf. Harriet Grove's journal, 21 April 1810 (Cameron, *Shelley and his Circle*, ii. 576), 'Got to John's; found him and his cat perfectly well & happy to see us as we are to see him.' John Grove, a medical man, lived in Lincoln's Inn.

III. 12: Cf. the similar episode in Shelley's political verses of 1819, hitherto known as 'Young Parson Richards'; re-edited and discussed by William J. McTaggart in *England in 1819: Church, State and Poverty*, Keats–Shelley Memorial Association, 1970.

There are two other versions of this poem, the first among the Esdaile Poems (see above, Appendix, p. 344), the second printed by Hogg (*Life*, ed. Wolfe, i. 125–6), taken from a version which Shelley wrote out from memory for him at Oxford, attaching to it some 14 lines from Nos. XII and XIII.

XIV–XVII: These ephemeral 'Gothic' pieces are the record of a phase of sensibility that Shelley never lost: cf. 'Hymn to Intellectual Beauty', 49–60. No. XVII was used, with variations, with the prose romance, *The Rosicrucian*, see above, p. 25.

p. 67, POSTHUMOUS FRAGMENTS OF
MARGARET NICHOLSON

Our knowledge of how these strange pieces originated derives from Hogg and is slightly coloured by his usual desire to show how Shelley depended on his advice. They were in proof, he says (see *Life*, i. 158–63), when he first saw them and he at once perceived that what was unpresentable as serious verse might easily be remoulded into amusing burlesque. The title was an afterthought. Margaret Nicholson was a mad washerwoman who had attempted the life of George III in 1786, and had been sent to an asylum. In 1810 she was still living. Plausibility and actuality were adduced by the pretence that they were edited by her nephew, and the 'nephew's' name 'John Fitzvictor' (meaning 'son of Victor') was designed to let the initiate see an association with the co-author of *Original Poetry by Victor and Cazire*. John Munday, the Oxford printer, was sufficiently impressed to publish the work at his own expense, and in Oxford, for a while, says Hogg, 'it was indeed a kind of fashion to be seen reading it in public . . . the thing passed off as the genuine production of the would-be regicide'. Later readers have found it dismal enough. Perhaps the nearest approach to imaginative or intellectual fun is to be found in the 'Epithalamium', cast in the form of a dialogue between two successful French tyrannicides, François Ravaillac, who was torn to pieces by horses in 1610 for murdering Henri IV, and Charlotte Corday, who was guillotined in 1793 for assassinating the revolutionary demagogue Jean-Paul Marat. Shelley himself denied authorship of this (see Jones, i. 21–3), saying that it was 'the production of a friend's mistress', possibly a cloak for Hogg, and it was omitted from a copy intended for Shelley's mother. 'Of course to my Father', he wrote, 'Peg is a profound secret.' Shelley's relish for a practical joke attains perspective if we remember the three Sitwells a century later. Political and religious prejudice apart, he had to face the ambivalent attitude of the English 'ruling classes' towards a creative artist: works of art might be collected and artists and writers generously assisted, nevertheless, within the family, all leanings toward art and letters as a *profession* had to be watched and discouraged. According to a family tradition, related to the present editor by Sir John Shelley-Rolls, a few days before his death in 1951, Sir Timothy once said to his second son, 'My boy, never read a book if you can avoid it. Your poor brother used to write them, and that is a thing no gentleman should do.'

In lines 26–30 of the 'Epithalamium' the notion of the music of the spheres (*Republic*, 616 d–617 c) is probably an example of the Platonism which came to Shelley indirectly; among the more obvious of possible sources are *The Merchant of Venice*, v. i. 55–65, and *Twelfth Night*, iii. i. 118–20.

More interesting is the early appearance, in lines 42–5 of this same crude little piece, of Shelley's Platonic faith in something permanent amid the transient. What is here an expression of natural Platonism was to be developed, from later study of the *Symposium* and the *Republic*, into his all-permeating symbolism of the Veil, the Cave, and the Dream. Blended with this faith is the idea of kindred souls seeking immortality through love, which was to be the kernel of *Epipsychidion*. This naturally Platonic touch of imagination had appeared as early as the poem (Esd. No. 58) addressed to Harriet Grove and dated '28 Feb. 1805': see note below, p. 373. Shelley's own commentary on the idea may be found in his letter to Miss Hitchener of 24 November 1811. Underlying the development of this feeling in his letter is the concept of ἀφιλαυτία which he had absorbed in translating a passage of Aristotle's *Nichomachean Ethics*: ἀφιλαυτία comes very close to the ἀγάπη of Plato's *Symposium*, so many threads of which were to run through his mature work. The kinship of these concepts is interesting in view of the antithesis between Plato and Aristotle which he drew during his *Queen Mab* phase; see below, p. 396, n. on No. 15 of his Notes on that poem.

p. 81, THE ESDAILE POEMS

History of Shelley's Early Minor Poems and their manuscripts: What Shelley thought about his early minor poems is plain from passages in letters to Miss Hitchener written about the beginning of the year 1812. Since 'liberty' was their main theme they were 'not wholly useless'; nevertheless they were 'inferior productions . . . only valuable to philosophical and reflecting minds who love to trace the early state of human feelings and opinions . . .' (Jones, i. 214, 239). He hoped that the libertarian theme might move men's minds a little, and that their sale among the rich might produce profits which he could devote to the poor; herein he was thinking, more especially, of helping the lot of the Irish. The poems mark the early stages in which the energetic prose-pamphleteer became merged in the poet. Thanks to the survival of the notebook into which they were transcribed 'the history of Shelley's imagination from the days at Oxford to the days at Tremadoc is no longer a blank' (Dowden, *Life*, i. 345).

One reason why Shelley's plans for his little volume were not fulfilled was that they were displaced by the writing of *Queen Mab*. They had been delayed, in the meanwhile, by the misadventures of the manuscript. R. and J. Stockdale, the Dublin printers to whom Shelley and Harriet consigned it in February 1812, would seem to have set up part of it in print, but by August they were refusing to continue the work until they were paid. The correspondence of the two Shelleys in 1812 bears witness to their concern with the recovery of the manuscript. The common assumption that they did, eventually, recover it has usually been bound up with a second assumption, namely that the Stockdale manuscript is identical with the Esdaile Notebook. This Notebook, into which Shelley and Harriet transcribed the poems printed here, has always been so called because, until its sale at Sotheby's in May 1962, it was preserved at Cothelstone House, near Taunton, Somerset, by the Esdaile family, into which Ianthe Shelley, Harriet's daughter, was married after the death of her parents. Since 1962 it has been the property of the Carl H. Pforzheimer Library.

Until quite recently almost everything printed from or about the Esdaile Notebook derived from Dowden, who was allowed to examine it in the eighteen-eighties and to print selected lines. Dowden noticed that, if we exclude the two sonnets, dated 1813, and the five poems written in later by Harriet, the preceding fifty-one pieces correspond more or less to a line-count which he made in the manuscript (Dowden, *Life*, i. 345. Cf. Commentary on No. 51, p. 174, above), and that this line-count corresponds roughly with an estimate concerning his 'other poems' made in a letter to Hookham (Jones, i. 350). This has usually been accepted as clinching the identification. Oddly enough neither Dowden nor anybody else seems to have noticed that among the Esdaile poems dated by Shelley are two (Nos. 25 and 32) composed in August 1812—within the very period when he and Harriet were trying to recover the Stockdale manuscript. Dowden (*Life*, i. 283–4, 293–5, 404) not only dated those poems but rightly observed that two other poems (Nos. 26 and 27) must, from their subject-matter, also belong to August 1812. Quite clearly, if there is a correspondence between the two manuscripts, it cannot be a complete one.

The possibility of a partial correspondence must be considered. It is not necessary to suppose that when Shelley wrote out the Esdaile poems he had the Stockdale manuscript with him. He could have made use of other documents, of memory, or of both. Some have supposed that he received the papers from Stockdale at Tremadoc in the winter of 1812–13. Good arguments against this have been advanced by Professor Kenneth Neill Cameron (*The Young Shelley*, pp. 381–2), who suggests instead that he may have recovered it on his second expedition to Dublin, in 1813. Failing definite evidence, however, one might doubt whether the alarms and discursions of that period would have allowed the necessary time or mood: for the biographical background see Newman Ivey White, *Shelley*, vol. i, ch. x, and Dowden, *Life*, vol. i, ch. vii. We shall be safe in regarding the recovery of the Stockdale manuscript as 'not proven' and the Esdaile Notebook as being, in any case, the somewhat divergent record of his early, minor poems with which Shelley intended to replace it.

The Esdaile Notebook: The Notebook contains eighty-eight pages of writing, followed by pages left blank. There are fifty-eight poems, unnumbered. (The numbering in the present edition has been supplied for convenience of reference.) Nos. 1–53 are in Shelley's handwriting, Nos. 54–8 in the hand of Harriet Shelley. That the Notebook was intended as a gift to Harriet is suggested by the insertion of the first poem before the original heading, 'Poems', and the addition of the two sonnets, Nos. 52 and 53, after Shelley's final line-count. All the contents have the character of intermediate fair copies, written out for the preservation of the poems rather than for the use of the printer. The penmanship is mainly good and often beautiful, though it sometimes lapses through fatigue. Doubtful readings and passages where meaning has been distorted by probable miscopying have been indicated in the text. (See p. xlvii, 'Signs used'.)

Authorship: Of the fifty-three poems written out by Shelley, fifty-one are his own: the others may be assumed, on good grounds, to be by his sister Elizabeth. Regarding the authorship of No. 43 we have his own statement to Hogg (Jones, *Letters*, i. 43) and, though we may not wholly discount either the possibility of some form of joint authorship or the possibility that he was talking to impress Hogg with her talents, I feel bound to accept it, and likewise his statement, made to Hogg (*Life*, ed. Wolfe, i. 126), about No. 45. Of the five in Harriet Shelley's handwriting No. 54 must, surely, be taken, as Dowden (*Life*, i. 413) took it, to be by Shelley. Nor need we doubt that Nos. 56 and 58, though crude and immature, are authentically his. Nos. 55 and 57 are on an altogether lower level of accomplishment and seem, more likely than anything else, to be pathetic effusions by Harriet herself. Nos. 43, 45, 55, and 57 have here been printed in an Appendix.

Other manuscripts: For eleven out of the fifty-eight poems in the Esdaile Notebook other manuscripts can be identified. They are now distributed between the British Museum, the New York Public Library, the Pforzheimer Library, Texas Christian University, and Trinity College, Cambridge. The location of each, together with conflicts of dating and divergences in form, is best shown by tabular comparison:

Esd.	Date	Other MSS.	Date	Divergence
14	1811	BM, letter to E. Hitchener	7 Jan. 1812	Shorter by 3 stanzas, 4 lines
17		BM, letter to E. Hitchener	14 Feb. 1812	Shorter by 1 stanza
19		Pf., loose sheet given to Hogg (*Life*, i. 126)	1810	Shorter by 20 lines
33	1809	Trin., Camb., loose sheets given to Hogg		Stanzas 1 and 3 each shorter by 2 lines
35	1810	Pf., letter to Hogg	*c.* 19 June 1811	3rd stanza replaced by variant stanza from Esd. No. 34
36	23 Sept. 1809	Pf., letter to Hogg	17 May 1811	
41	1810	TCU, letter to Hogg	28 Apr. 1811	
43		Pf., letter to Hogg	11 Jan. 1811	1 stanza more than the 3 stanzas of Esd.
44	1809	Pf., letter to Hogg	6 Jan. 1811	2 stanzas more than the 3 stanzas of Esd.
45	1808	Pf., loose sheets given to Hogg		14 lines more than the 5 stanzas of Esd.
47		NYPL, letter to E. F. Graham	*c.* 19 June 1811	1 stanza only against Esd. 6 stanzas plus refrain

We may look in vain among the divergences of these manuscripts for indications of a 'superior' text. The letter dates are unreliable and possibly the Esdaile dates too. Nor can we assume that a later date, even if provable, is evidence of Shelley's considered revision. Changes in a later manuscript may be due, no less probably, to miscopying, spontaneous adaptation, or the vagaries of memory (see *Dating*, below). The manuscripts have been collated in my Commentary.

Printed authority: Shelley printed versions of four of the Esdaile poems—Nos. 1, 6, 21, and 45—and 11½ lines from a fifth, No. 24. Textually the later version of No. 1, printed as the Dedication with *Queen Mab*, must claim preference. I have, however, printed both versions, one here and one with *Queen Mab*, and I hope that I have thus respected both Shelley's original intentions and the just claims of Harriet. For No. 6 I have used Shelley's text of 1813, printed among the Notes on *Queen Mab*, and for No. 21 the considerably revised version he printed in the *Alastor* volume in 1816. His text of the lines from No. 24, printed among the Notes on *Queen Mab*, is collated in my Commentary.

With a few minor adjustments the present text follows my edition of *The Esdaile Poems* (Clarendon Press, 1966) in which my text was that of the Esdaile Notebook except where I preferred Shelley's own printed authority. No notice has been taken of the text published in 1964 by the Carl H. Pforzheimer Library (see above, pp. xxxi–xxxii).

Headings and titles: Of the fifty-three poems transcribed by Shelley in the Notebook, forty-four are printed here with the titles that appear in his manuscript; one of these, that of No. 4, he left incomplete, but the name of the plant he had forgotten is unimportant. For No. 1 I have printed the title added by Harriet to Shelley's transcription, and for Nos. 54, 56, and 58 the titles which head her own transcriptions. For No. 34 I have used the simple and obvious title printed by Rossetti in 1870. 'Bigotry's Victim', his time-honoured title for No. 41, was a euphemism adapted to Hogg's doctored text: since, however, it is faithful to the poem as a whole and to Shelley's Lucretian use of the word 'Religion' I have preserved it. Six poems which lack manuscript headings— Nos. 20, 22, 35, 45, 55, 57—have been headed by quotation of the opening line. My comprehensive title for Nos. 37–40 does not appear in the manuscript. I have resorted to invention only twice: with No. 21, where neither the opening line nor Mary Shelley's title in 1839 would catch the Platonic purport significant in Shelley's development; and with No. 42, where I hope that my title is inoffensively descriptive and more apt than a heading from the first line would be.

Dating: If we may trust Harriet Shelley's dating for Nos. 58 and 54 the period of Shelley's composition covered by the Esdaile poems ranges from 28 February 1805 to May 1814; about the second of these dates, at any rate, we may believe her personal witness and, though Dowden (*Life*, i. 48) seems unduly sceptical about the first, I see no reason to suppose her to have invented anything so circumstantial. (It has been suggested that the first date would require improbable precocity—but not, I think, in an early reader of romances.) For present purposes the dates given in the manuscript must, in the main, be accepted, but as we do not know how far they came from reliable documents and how far from memory they cannot be regarded as final. Sometimes a date in the Notebook is in conflict with the date of a letter wherein Shelley transcribed the poem, or some version of it. But the letter dates too are unreliable guides, since even where Shelley is presenting a poem to a friend as a new one it may have been merely something he had rummaged up from papers or memory. No. 41, for example, for which I have accepted the Esdaile dating, 1810, is described in the letter to Hogg of 28 April 1811 as 'a mad effusion of this morning'. For Shelley's reliance on memory see Hogg, *Life*, i. 126. An example of its vagaries was his quotation in a letter of two stanzas of No. 35, supplemented by a stanza from No. 34 in place of the third stanza which he could not remember. See Cameron, *Shelley and his Circle*, ii. 809–12.

The dating of poems in my text falls into five approximate categories:

(i) twenty-five poems dated from the manuscript, namely Nos. 14, 15, 16, 18, 25, 32, 33, 34, 35, 36, 37, 38, 39, 40, 41, 42, 44, 45, 46, 50, 52, 53, 54, 55, 58;

(ii) two poems dated from Shelley's correspondence: Nos. 17 and 47;

(iii) five poems arising out of Shelley's devotion to his wife Harriet which may be ascribed to 1811–12: Nos. 1, 5, 8, 24, 29;

(iv) twenty-four poems datable, with varying degrees of certainty, from biographical, internal, or other evidence: Nos. 2, 3, 4, 6, 7, 9, 10, 11, 12, 13, 19, 20, 21, 22, 23, 26, 27, 28, 30, 31, 43, 48, 49, 51;

(v) two poems which cannot be dated: No. 57, of which the authorship is uncertain, and No. 56 where the manuscript date is improbable and other evidence is lacking.

Points arising from this dating are referred to above in the Commentary accompanying my text and in the Notes below.

p. 81, No. 1, To HARRIET [SHELLEY], Version I. *Title*: As given by Shelley in 1813, 'To Harriet'. Omitted by Mary in 1839[1], Shelley having been glad about its omission in 1821 by a piratical publisher; restored in 1839[2] as 'To Harriet * * * * *'. Cf. Version II, given here with *Queen Mab*, and n. below, p. 381. Though in 1821 the memory of Harriet may have been the reverse of inspiring, the Dedication, in both contexts, is the true expression of a personal and humanitarian love inseparable from the verse.

p. 81, No. 2, A SABBATH WALK. *Date*: The 'winter's day' (l. 28) and the 'mountain labyrinth' (l. 5) suggest Shelley's stay at Keswick, November 1811 to February 1812. The Tremadoc period, a year later, is a possibility, but fits less with the mood and the events. The poem seems to recall Southey's 'Written on Sunday Morning' (1795).

9: Shelley's social and religious resistance was always of the kind deriving from thwarted 'devotedness', the antithesis of natural anarchy or atheism. For the early conflict of 'devotedness' with unattractive forms of worship cf. Rimbaud, 'Les Premières Communions'. For Shelley's habit of alternative recourse to 'the wilds' cf., in 1819, the 'Ode to the West Wind'. See Rogers, *Shelley at Work*, pp. 211–29.

p. 83, No. 3, THE CRISIS. *Date*: Possibly the period of strong Godwinian influence following Shelley's expulsion from Oxford.

These Sapphic stanzas are so arranged in the Notebook as to be both preceded and followed by a pair of poems in loose unrhymed Southeyan stanzas. The dactylic kick in its fourth line made the Sapphic stanza a lively one for political verse-writing, cf. Canning's 'Needy Knife-Grinder', published in *The Anti-Jacobin*, 1798. For its use in eighteenth-century prophecies of doom, cf. Cowper's 'Lines Written During a Period of Insanity' and Isaac Watts's 'The Day of Judgment'.

13: *the consummating hour*, meaning here the fulfilment of the processes of Necessity, is to be compared and contrasted with the Hour in *Prometheus Unbound*, III. iv, a symbolic character representing the era of love and beauty brought round by the operation of the power of Platonic love. This small comparison well illustrates the movement of the young Shelley from Godwinian gloom to mature poetry. For the doctrine of Necessity see below, nn. on *Queen Mab*.

p. 84, No. 4, PASSION. *Title*: Incomplete in Esd. In a memorandum owned by Lord Abinger, Dowden comments: 'Some flower whose name Shelley had forgotten or did not know.' The poem, however, does not hang on identification of the flower. What matters is the meaning of 'Passion'. For Shelley, and many of his period, this frequently meant something like 'enthusiasm together with driving power': something like the *Tätigkeit* or *Wirksamkeit* which is the concern of characters in Goethe. With this goes a notion of devotedness, cf. above, 'A Sabbath Walk'. The important thing was to control 'passion', and not be controlled by it: otherwise the 'Essence of Virtue' would become a poison. This fits with Godwin's tenet that crime and goodness spring from like causes. Cf Hamlet's praise of Horatio (*Hamlet*, III. ii. 76–80). Sexual passion is relevant only in so far as it affects the driving power of the creative artist, philosopher, or reformer: cf. 'The Triumph of Life', 275, and No. 50, 'The Retrospect', below, lines 93 and 147. Cf. Shelley's letter to Hogg, 2 June 1811 (Jones, i. 94–5) where he clearly explains his concept of 'passion', ending with a significant reference to Goethe's *Werther*, a character who fatally fails to control his 'passion'. *Date*: See the following n., and n. on No. 2, above.

6–10: Cf. Wordsworth, 'A Poet's Epitaph', 5–8, which had appeared in *Lyrical Ballads*, 1798. Shelley's interest in Wordsworth was stimulated by Southey at Keswick. See n. on No. 2, above.

p. 85, No. 5, To Harriet [Shelley].

15–20: The remembrance of Harriet and her death haunted Shelley as long as he lived, and Mary even afterwards. In these lines, written while he loved her, there is pathos, irony, and a reminder both of his sea-visions at Lerici and of the preoccupation with drowning which appears in, e.g., 'Stanzas Written in Dejection near Naples', the 'Ode to Liberty', and *Adonais*.

p. 86, No. 6, Falsehood and Vice. *Date*: Possibly the period of *Posthumous Fragments of Margaret Nicholson*, where the macabre humour suggests a kinship; the missed opportunities for Necessitarian treatment seem to place the poem before the Godwinian impetus (cf. No. 3, above). C. D. Locock suggests that an impetus came from 'Fire, Famine and Slaughter', Coleridge's 'War Eclogue'. The general terminology of monarchs, tyrants, superstition, luxury, fetters, liberty, slavery, and war-mongering owes much to Erasmus Darwin, poet of *The Botanic Garden*, *The Temple of Nature*, &c., which Shelley enjoyed, and in which his interest was aroused by Darwin's close associate Dr. Lind, his Platonic mentor at Eton. The following lines (*T. of Nature*, IV. 84–5, 507–8) are typical:

> There the curst spells of Superstition blind,
> And fix her fetters on the tortured mind . . .
> Fierce furies drag to pains and realms unknown
> The blood-stain'd tyrant from his tottering throne.

Like Praed and other Etonians Shelley had early fluency with the octosyllabic couplet; with these cruder beginnings cf. the ease and beauty of, e.g., 'Lines Written among the Euganean Hills'.

40: GOLD, MONARCHY, AND MURDER: Shelley's capitalization is a reminder of the phrase 'blood and gold' of which he later made symbolic use. Cf. *The Mask of Anarchy*, 65; 'Charles I', i. 61; 'Lines on Hearing of the Death of Napoleon Bonaparte', 35; and see Rogers, *Shelley at Work*, pp. 280 foll.

p. 90, No. 7, To the Emperors, Etc. *Date*: Between the battle of Austerlitz and the Godwinian impetus (see nn. on Nos. 3 and 6, above): once again Shelley misses Necessitarian openings in his subject. For the influence of Erasmus Darwin see n. on No. 6.

1: *Coward Chiefs . . .*: Cf. Lucretius, *De Rerum Natura*, ii. 5–6:

> Suave etiam belli certamina magna tueri
> Per campos instructa, tua sine parte pericli . . .

which Shelley quoted among the Notes on *Queen Mab*, V. 58 (see pp. 298 and 391). In line 19 *secure* is probably the Lucretian *securus*.

p. 91, No. 8, To NOVEMBER. Shelley's association of Harriet with Nature is a reminder of his feeling in *Queen Mab* that

> the flame
> Of consentaneous love inspires all life (VIII. 107–8).

It was this feeling, partly Lucretian but also instinctive, which later combined with his intellectual revulsion to free him from the doctrine of Necessity.

p. 92, No. 9, WRITTEN ON A BEAUTIFUL DAY IN SPRING. *Title*: The title and idea may connect with Wordsworth's 'Lines Written in Early Spring', but the manner is eighteenth century, with the variations of line-length then loosely thought 'Pindaric'. *Date*: See nn. on Nos. 2 and 4.

18: The bathetic last line contains an idea better expressed later in the 'Ode to the West Wind': 'If Winter comes, can Spring be far behind?' As a step from these early crudities towards the Ode may be noted the quotation among the Notes on *Queen Mab* (V. 4–6) from *Iliad*, vi. 146 foll., Οἵη περ φύλλων γενεή, τοιήδε καὶ ἀνδρῶν . . . .

p. 93, No. 10, ON LEAVING LONDON FOR WALES. *Date*: The reference to Snowdon, and the poem generally, seem to fit the autumn of 1812 better than Shelley's visit to Cwm Elan in the previous year. For the influence of Erasmus Darwin see n. on No. 6.

19: *Hail to thee . . .*: Shelley is here the disciple of Rousseau, seeking virtue among unspoiled people and places. There would seem to have been psychological repetition in his excursion to Switzerland with Mary in 1816. See Rogers, *Shelley at Work*, 40 foll. Cf. nn. on No. 50, below.

p. 95, No. 11, A WINTER'S DAY. *Date*: The 'cascades' (l. 4) and the 'moor' (l. 12) again suggest the winter at Keswick, 1811–12, though Tremadoc, in the following winter, is also a possibility.

8 foll.: For Shelley's reactions to Nature see notes on Nos. 2, 4, 8, 10, above, and cf. his remark to Peacock in a kindred connection (letter of 6 November 1818): 'I always seek in what I see the manifestation of something beyond the present and tangible object.'

26–7: Syntactically unrelated to what precedes: probably miscopied or mis-remembered. An inversion of subject and verb seems unlikely.

p. 96, No. 12, TO LIBERTY. *Date*: Conjecturable as falling within the period of Godwinian influence (see n. on No. 3, above), and having some relation to the note of Nos. 31 and 32. For the influence of Erasmus Darwin see n. on No. 6.

11–14: There seems to be a note from Bunyan's hymn, 'He who would valiant be . . .'.

26 foll.: Dowden noticed the influence of Campbell's 'Ye Mariners of England' and 'The Battle of the Baltic'. The Shelleyan victory, however, will be achieved not by Nelson's cheerful sailors but by the operation of Necessity in the Universe.

46: Necessity, again, rather than love and Intellectual Beauty, as later, will bring about this Shelleyan paradise.

p. 98, No. 13, ON ROBERT EMMET'S TOMB. *Title*: Printed by Dowden and others as 'On Robert Emmet's Grave'. *Date*: From the visit of Shelley and Harriet to Dublin, February–March 1812. See Shelley's letter to Miss Hitchener, [?] 16 April 1812 (Jones, i. 281–3).
    Robert Emmet (1778–1803) was executed by the British after the failure of his attempt to revive the 'United Irishmen' movement. He could have escaped to America but stayed to await an answer from Sarah Curran, to whom he had proposed marriage. Thomas Moore wrote of the incident in his well-known laments, 'She is far from the land' and 'O breathe not his name'. Shelley writes in the metre made popular by Moore, a forgotten merit of which is that when used, as Moore often used it, for the composition of words to fit tunes it loses its jingle and is wonderfully adaptable alike to 4/4, 3/4, or 6/8 time. Sarah Curran was the daughter of J. P. Curran, and sister of Amelia Curran, who painted the unfinished portrait of Shelley now in the National Portrait Gallery.

12: Syntax demands 'and silently weeping as he passes'. Metre prevents emendation.

p. 99, No. 14, A TALE OF SOCIETY, ETC. *Date*: Esd. has '1811', but in Shelley's letter to Elizabeth Hitchener of 7 January 1812 (BM) the poem is described as 'the overflowings of the mind this morning'. This may be just an attempt to give actuality. See n. on line 37. The comparatively hopeless outlook of the poem is in accordance with Godwin's doctrine in *Political Justice* that the best life the peasant can lead is that of virtue. If he achieves it he 'is in a certain sense happy . . . he is happier than a stone'. Once again something is owed to Wordsworth. For the influence of Erasmus Darwin see n. on No. 6.

15: *Lingering from/to*: Either preposition both fuses and extends two *OED* meanings of the verb, 'to stay on in a place, esp. from reluctance to leave it' and 'to continue barely alive'.

19: Here and in line 26 I have preferred the BM reading as giving a better sense and possibly correcting memory.

37: The row of crosses might be taken as suggesting that BM, in turn, has suffered from a lapse of memory.

p. 103, No. 15, THE SOLITARY. *Text*: Mr. Cameron (*Shelley and his Circle*, iv. 919–20) has mildly taken me to task on the subject of the first printings of this poem and Nos. 24 and 34. I did, indeed, fail to notice (*The Esdaile Poems*, 1966) that some 7–8 lines of No. 24 were first printed by Forman in 1876. Forman states that they were given to him by Rossetti who possessed a transcript made by

Garnett 'from one of the Boscombe MSS.' and Mr. Cameron believes that it was from the same source that Garnett transcribed No. 15 and the fragment of No. 34 which Rossetti had printed in 1870. I find this hard to believe, both because of the close correspondence of all three printings to the Esdaile text and because no other manuscripts of Shelley's early verse are known to have existed at Boscombe. In 1883 Garnett sent Dowden a couple of sonnets copied from the Esdaile manuscript by a former governess of the Esdaile family. As Mr. Cameron notes, his reference to this lady does not make clear how much else she copied. But this is hardly surprising: nor would it be surprising if he wished to disguise the surreptitious provenance of the material by having it supposed to have come from Boscombe.

p. 103, No. 16, THE MONARCH'S FUNERAL.

6: Probably refers to George III, who became ill and incapable late in 1810; cf. Shelley's sonnet of 1819, 'An old mad, blind, despised and dying king . . .'. A Regency Act was passed in January 1811.

45–52: Since the vocative 'Pride' must go with the imperative 'restore' it has seemed best to bring it closer in effect by treating Shelley's exclamation mark as one of his anticipatory ones (see General Introduction, p. xl). The syntactical extension of this same abstract noun to provide a vocative for 'feel' (lines 49, 52) is awkward, but has been helped, I hope, by my forward-pointing dash after the exclamation mark (45).

57–8: Cf. *Queen Mab*, IX. 31–2. Both passages look back to Darwin's *Temple of Nature*, IV. 383; cf. above, 'To Ireland', 19–21, and n., p. 353, and see n. on No. 6. See also D. King-Hele, 'Erasmus Darwin's Influence on Shelley's Early Poems', *Keats–Shelley Memorial Bulletin*, XVI, 1965.

p. 106, No. 17, TO THE REPUBLICANS OF NORTH AMERICA. *Title/Date*: Shelley (Esd.) wrote 'South' and changed this to 'North'; there is more accuracy in Rossetti's 1870 title, 'The Mexican Revolution', taken from BM, where (14 Feb. 1813) Shelley sends Miss Hitchener his 'tribute' to the insurrection of the priest Miguel Hidalgo. This had happened in 1810, but the news seems fresh to him.

p. 108, No. 18, WRITTEN AT CWM ELAN, 1811. *Date*: Shelley's correspondence shows he was at Cwm Elan from *c.* 9 July to *c.* 4 August. The unusual metre is suggestive of 'Stanzas—April, 1814', 12–24, and *Prometheus Unbound*, I. 774 foll.

15: *tangèd*: See *OED*, s.v. *tang*, *sb.*¹ and *v.*². The resonance of woods is a poetic commonplace: cf. Virg., *Ecl.*, i. 5, 'Formosam resonare doces Amaryllida silvas'. It is, however, possible that Shelley meant to write 'tangled' and his pen slipped.

p. 108, No. 19, TO DEATH. *Date*: See Hogg, *Life*, i. 124. The Pf. manuscript was given to Hogg by Shelley at Oxford. The poem has a certain metrical interest. Out of such beginnings in what the eighteenth century called 'Pindarics' grew Shelley's later ode-forms and chorus-forms. See n. on No. 9.

$\left.\begin{smallmatrix}1\\5\end{smallmatrix}\right\}$ Cf. 1 Corinthians 15: 55.

29: Cf. 'Hymn to Intellectual Beauty', 35–6.

63–8: The conclusion is somewhat marred by the point that the 'victory' is won not by a victor but by a process, Necessity, to which the poet seems to offer submission and defiance at the same time.

p. 111, No. 20, 'DARK SPIRIT OF THE DESERT RUDE . . .'. *Date*: The gloomy tone and the Necessitarian note seem to fit Shelley's 1811 visit to Cwm Elan better than his return there with Harriet in 1812. See n. on No. 18.

45–6: Syntax requires 'Suck'st . . . decay'st' or 'To suck . . . to decay'. Rhyme, sound, and metre prevent emendation. Line 46 is underlined, denoting Shelley's intention to revise. In 1966 I mistook this for italicization.

p. 112, No. 21, REALITY. *Title/Date*: The poem marks a movement towards Platonism and away from both Godwinian and 'Gothic' gloom, an indication that it must be of late date among the Esdaile pieces. Shelley rehandled it for his *Alastor* volume of 1816. 'On Death', Mary Shelley's title, 1839, just misses the Platonic point.

Epigraph: Unlike most of Shelley's epigraphs this asserts something which the poem challenges rather than something he is himself asserting.

10: *light*: Shelley's revision of 10–12 and the light-and-darkness imagery of 25–30 anticipate the Platonic symbolism found in *Prometheus Unbound*, *Adonais*, and in his maturer poetry *passim*. Besides the Platonic concept of the immortality of thought, which Shelley substituted for Christian immortality, we have (l. 7) the faith in Man's endurance which is also a keynote in *Prometheus Unbound*.

p. 113, No. 22, 'DEATH-SPURNING ROCKS . . .'. *Date*: Possibly deducible from Shelley's visit to the Valley of Rocks, Lynton, when he was in Devonshire: see letter to Godwin, 5 July 1812. If, however, Cwm Elan was the scenic background the mood of the poem seems fitted to his 1811 visit rather than to his 1812 one.

p. 114, No. 23, THE TOMBS. *Date*: From Shelley's visit to Dublin in 1812.

21–5: Defective sense is probably due to memory or copying. The reference is to such rebels as the supporters of Emmet (see No. 13) or Wolfe Tone.

p. 115, No. 24, TO HARRIET [SHELLEY]. *Text*: See n. on No. 15.

25 foll.: In this, the most mature of the Harriet poems, Shelley approaches the language and ideas both of Shakespeare's Sonnets and of his own *Epipsychidion*.

32–52: The syntax is distorted by punctuation in Esd., 1886 and edd.

40: *Sc.* 'bringing out all the fire . . .'.

42: *holy friendship*: Shelley's mood here is working its way towards the Platonic idea of a purified feeling, beyond Ἔρως. This eighteenth-century usage, perhaps coloured from German Hellenism, did not lack warmth. Nelson wrote to Lady Hamilton as 'My dear friend . . .', and Benjamin Franklin, as a widower, dreamed of 'my friend the former Mrs. Franklin'. Cf. No. 50. 158, where on the warmth of 'ardent friendship' hangs the meaning of the poem, from its title to its climax.

61–5: The language has some affinity with *Hellas*, 197–200 and 795–6.

p. 118, No. 25, SONNET: TO HARRIET [SHELLEY], ON HER BIRTHDAY.

2: *somewhat*: See *OED* for instances of the substantival usage.

p. 118, No. 26, SONNET: TO A BALLOON LADEN WITH *KNOWLEDGE*. *Title*: Shelley's underlining of the last word makes plain that it means 'political instruction'. This and the following poem anticipate whimsically his later plans for a steam-boat service as a means of carrying enlightenment. He has been described as a 'propagandist' during this period, but at no time was he that. All his life he was an inquirer for *knowledge* and a disseminator of it. Knowledge, he hoped, would lead to the will for improvement, but that is not the same thing as 'propaganda'. See Rogers, *Shelley at Work*, pp. 93 foll. *Date*: From Shelley's visit to Devonshire and his dating in Esd. of No. 32.

p. 119, No. 27, SONNET: ON LAUNCHING SOME BOTTLES, ETC. *Title/Date*: See n. on No. 26.

8: *her West*: The United States, thought of by Shelley as a land of Liberty. Hutchinson's capital neatly makes the point.

p. 120, No. 28, SONNET: ON WAITING FOR A WIND, ETC. *Date*: See n. on No. 26.

p. 120, No. 29, TO HARRIET [SHELLEY].

25–9: See n. on No. 1. 5–8.

p. 121, No. 30, MARY TO THE SEA-WIND. *Title*: Not necessarily connected with the Mary of Nos. 37–40. *Date*: Uncertain, but the unusual metre and movement suggest that it belongs to a late part of the period covered by the Esdaile Poems, and the 'Sea Wind' suggests Shelley's period in Devonshire.

p. 122, No. 31, A RETROSPECT OF TIMES OF OLD. *Date*: From its Necessitarian kinship with *Queen Mab* and with the next poem, which is dated in Esd.

Once again a poem falls flat from the dullness of a triumph over tyranny which is due to a process rather than human effort; even the high-sounding names in lines 71–2 do not help this, and the last two lines must represent the climax in Shelley of Godwin's 'happier-than-a-stone' philosophy. See above, n. on No. 14. In 'Ozymandias' the feeling is similar, but it is humanized by the triumphant dramatization.

1–13: Syntax unpointed in manuscript, apart from the absurdities in 11–12.

8, 25: Cf. Erasmus Darwin, *Economy of Vegetation*, IV. 67–8:

> . . . [the Simoom] rides the tainted air,
> Points his keen eye, and waves his whistling hair.

Cf. Coleridge, 'Religious Musings', 268, which comes closer to Darwin than Shelley does, and which Shelley could have known: 'through the tainted noon / The simoom sails'. See n. on No. 6. *OED* (Simoom) cites also 'simoon'.

p. 125, No. 32, THE VOYAGE. Metre probably influenced by Southey's *Thalaba*. The Necessitarian motif of the poem is grafted on to the enthusiasm of contemporary writers for archaeological discovery. Shelley had read Volney's *Les Ruines*, and its information about Palmyra appears in *Queen Mab*.

2: *horrent*: Lat. *horrentem*, 'bristling with fear', but also 'fear-inspiring'. Cf. *Queen Mab*, VI. 132; *Hellas*, 283; also Milton, *P.L.*, II. 513.

68: The nautical superstition that whistling could bring a wind appears in a manuscript of 'The Boat on the Serchio'. See Rogers, 'Shelley's Text', in the *Times Literary Supplement*, 10 August 1951. Cf. M. R. James's famous ghost-story 'Oh, whistle! And I'll come to you my Lad'.

p. 134, No. 33, A DIALOGUE. Shelley's *Note*: the quotation is from *Queen Mab*, III. 80–3.

p. 135, No. 34, EYES. *Text*: See n. on No. 15.

p. 137, No. 35, 'HOPES THAT BUD . . .'.

5: *blossoms*: Perhaps it was because of 'flowers' in the next line that, in Pf., Shelley preferred the pretty eighteenth-century Latinism 'honours', printed by Hogg. Cf. Virgil, *Georgics*, ii. 404, and Jebb's beautiful version of Tennyson, 'Tithonus', 1: 'Marcescunt nemorum, nemorum labuntur honores.'

15–20: Shelley's row of crosses in Pf. seems an acknowledgement that his memory was merely substituting something. Cf. n. on No. 14. 37.

p. 139, Nos. 37–40, FOUR POEMS TO MARY. *Advertisement*: by Shelley. The 'many [poems] written' may not include No. 30, above, but probably include 'To Mary Who Died in This Opinion'. The 'friend' is Hogg; 'Leonora' was the title of a novel which he and Shelley planned. The quotation from St. Augustine ('I was not yet in love and wanted to be in love: I was seeking something to love, liking [the idea of] loving') was used later as an epigraph for *Alastor*. The passage well sums up the kind of sensitivity that Professor Notopoulos (*The Platonism of Shelley*, 14–15) has called 'natural Platonism'.

37. 21–4: The 'voyage symbol', frequently used for escape by travel (cf. No. 10) or the exportation of knowledge and enlightenment (cf. Nos. 26, 27, 28), could also stand for death (cf. *Adonais*, 487–95). Frequently the last involved suicide; cf. Southey's thought, expressed in 1793 to Horace Bedford, of 'seeking happiness in France, America or the grave'. Though these three forms of emigration were more commonly talked of than practised, the fashion may have left some impression on Harriet Shelley and Fanny Imlay.

The reference in Shelley's cancelled footnote to 'Romances of Leadenhall St.' concerns the trashy novels published by the Minerva Press.

p. 143, No. 41, BIGOTRY'S VICTIM.

10: *desert/desart*: With this interesting evidence that two holographs can differ in the same passage cf. the not uncommon belief that Shelley's misspellings have significance, more especially the attempts of H. Buxton Forman to argue that he used *desart* as noun and *desert* as adjective. See Rogers, 'Shelley's Spelling: Theory and Practice', *Keats–Shelley Memorial Bulletin*, XVI, 1965

p. 145, No. 42, LOVE AND TYRANNY. Probably concerned with Shelley's feelings for Harriet Grove.

p. 148, No. 46, HENRY AND LOUISA.

21–2: The gaps seem to indicate that something is lacking in Shelley's memory or his documents.

140–3: In 1966 I could make little sense of these lines, though I suggested that *That* ought to be *Tho*. Mr. King-Hele now points out that by adding a comma at the end of l. 139 we get sense, even if not very good sense.

153–4: Syntax uncertain, but the aposiopesis seems dramatically likely.

159: *mixed ... urge*: Virgil's *immixti* or *commixti ... urgent*; 'urge' here meaning 'continue to press on with'.

166–75: Esd.'s only punctuation is the comma in l. 166. Mr. King-Hele's suggestion of a full stop at the end of l. 170 helps the syntax of the stanza, but even so stanzas I–III do not cohere very well.

166: *the Genius of the South*: An echo probably of Southey, 'To the Genius of Africa'.

168–70: Cf. Erasmus Darwin, *Loves of the Plants*, III. 441–4:

> E'en now in Afric's groves with hideous yell
> Fierce SLAVERY stalks, and slips the dogs of hell;
> From vale to vale the gathering cries rebound,
> And sable nations tremble at the sound.

172: *varied*: Used in the sense of the Latin *varius* = 'many-coloured' involving the idea of 'ever-changing': cf. No. 16. 10, and No. 50. 128. Cameron, *Shelley and his Circle*, iv. 1030, has *veined*, a word which hardly seems apt for the bosom of the earth. Mr. King-Hele suggests that Shelley meant to write *veiled*, in the sense of 'cloudy'; he compares Erasmus Darwin, *Economy of Vegetation*, IV. 323:

> No more shall hoary Boreas, issuing forth
> With Eurus, lead the tempests of the north;
> Rime the pale dawn, or veiled in flaky showers
> Chill the sweet bosoms of the smiling hours.

189: Cf. n. on No. 49. 68.

214 foll.: Cf. Darwin's account (*Loves of the Plants*, III.) of a distraught lady named Eliza seeking her husband on the battlefield of Minden: with l. 233 cf. Darwin (l. 263) 'So wings the wounded deer her headlong flight'.

260: In a note to Book X of *Thalaba the Destroyer* Southey mentions a statue 'like that of Memnon, from which proceeded a small sound and a pleasant noise when the rising sun came, by his heat, to rarify and force out, by certain small conduits, the air which in the cool of the night was condensed within it'. Memnon, son of Eos and Tithonus, was a mythical king of Ethiopia. In *Econ. of Veg.*, I. 183–4, Darwin refers to Memnon's lyre and attaches a long note.

p. 160, No. 47, A TRANSLATION OF THE MARSEILLAISE HYMN. *Date*: Shelley's letter to Graham of *c*. 19 June 1811 seems integrated with the stanza there quoted. See above, p. 352, n. on 'On a Fête at Carlton House'.

Though Shelley had yet to attain his full excellence as a translator this version is remarkable for its insensitiveness both to the original words and to the tune. Possibly it is a versifying, or re-versifying, of some other English version.

5. 6: Bouillé was a royalist general.

p. 162, No. 48, WRITTEN IN VERY EARLY YOUTH. *Date*: Perhaps fifteen might mark the beginning of 'very early youth'; perhaps certain reminders of Gray's *Elegy Written in a Country Churchyard* might be a reason for connecting the poem with Shelley's version in Latin Sapphics, ascribed by Medwin to 1808–9.

p. 163, No. 49, ZEINAB AND KATHEMA. *Date*: In June 1811 Shelley read and was much impressed by Miss Owenson's *The Missionary*, of which the influence is noticeable in this poem.

13–24: The syntax, running across the stanzas, is awkward and hard to improve by punctuation. The stops ending lines 17 and 18 are what appear to be Shelley's.

68: An early example of Shelley's occasionally abrupt metrical variety. The missing foot and the ellipsis of 'of gold' require a pause suggesting 'heap [*sc.*] of dirt'. He is seldom *un*metrical, though cf. No. 46. 189.

163 foll.: With the change of one word this could be summarized as Godwin summarized the ground-plot of his novel *Caleb Williams*: '. . . atrocious crime, committed by a [woman] previously of exemplary habits.'

164–6: 'Shriven', in Esd., must be a miscopying. Otherwise the meaning is clear, despite a syntactical fusion, which leaves 'habits' without its second verb and 'was driven' without a subject.

p. 169, No. 50, THE RETROSPECT, ETC. *Date*: Part of manuscript title. See frontispiece. Shelley put a full stop after 'Retrospect', but to notice this would be to prefer a point in the manuscript to the point of the poem, which is a looking-backward in terms of place and time. *Metre*: Here, better than elsewhere in the Esdaile poems, Shelley foreshadows his mastery of the octosyllabic couplet.

1–3: Cf. Letter to Miss Hitchener, 26 November 1811 (Jones, i. 194), 'were I the charioteer of Time, his burning wheels . . .'.

1–10: The syntax is loose but just intelligible if treated as exclamatory rhetoric ending in an aposiopesis; the latter may be marked by the preservation, for once, of Shelley's three-dot stop, strengthened by an exclamation mark. If preserved at line 4 it would halt the rhetoric, which needed, instead, to be speeded by a comma plus dash. Cf. frontispiece.

11–22: 'It' (line 11) refers to 'to compare' (line 14); 'asks' has three objects, 'An eye . . .', 'a hand . . .', 'Thoughts . . .'. The object of 'compare' is 'A scene' (line 15). The comparison 'With that same scene' (line 17), which is the whole point of the 'Retrospect', would disappear if we allowed Shelley's semicolon after line 14. Cf. frontispiece.

57–63: An example of the direct Platonism derived from Shelley's Oxford studies (Hogg, *Life*, ed. Wolfe, i. 73 foll.). For the idea of the body as the prison of the soul cf. *Phaedo*, 62 b, 67 d, 81 b, 82 e, *Cratylus*, 400 b–c. Cf. *Q. Mab*, I. 135, 188 and n., also the letter to Miss Hitchener referred to in n. on lines 1–3 above.

79: *name*: i.e. the question-begging name of 'atheist'.

153–68: A good example of the long, complex periods which Shelley left others to clarify by punctuation, cf. General Introduction, pp. xxxviii–xli. In lines 153–4 he seems to have telescoped two constructions, 'O thou . . . [who] claim'st . . .' and 'O thou! whose virtues . . . [claim] . . .'; cf. his syntactical confusion in No. 20. 45–6. But the comma placed by Dowden at the end of line 153 indicates that 'whose virtues latest known' is an absolute, participial construction on the model of the Genitive Absolute in Greek and the Ablative Absolute in Latin. The meaning is 'O thou! who, thy virtues being latest known' (i.e. 'more recently than those of Harriet Grove'). The difficulty, smoothed out by Dowden's judicious comma, arises from the brachylogy whereby Shelley leaves his reader to deduce out of the genitive 'whose' a subject for the verb 'claim'st'.

Taken as a whole the sixteen lines construct as follows:

A. The vocative, 'O thou!', invoking Harriet Shelley.
B. Two subordinate clauses qualifying A:
   1. 'whose . . . throne'.
   2. 'Whose . . . sceptre . . . shall . . . share / The sway . . . there'.
C. A reiteration of the vocative 'Thou', picked up from A, and strengthened by the qualifying phrases 'fair . . . mind'.
D. A third subordinate clause, 'whose . . . band', qualifying C.
E. A fourth subordinate clause, picking up the word 'band' from D and qualifying it. (N.B. 'our fates that bind' is an inversion for 'that our fates bind'.)
F. A fifth subordinate clause, 'Which . . . last', again picking up and qualifying 'band' in D.
G. A sixth subordinate clause, 'When . . . soul', picking up the verb 'last' from F and qualifying it.
H. First subject of the main sentence, 'The . . . retrospects'.
I. A seventh subordinate clause, 'that bind . . . mind', qualifying H.
J. Second subject of the main sentence, 'The prospects', asyndetonically co-ordinated with H and qualified by the phrase 'of . . . hue'.
K. An eighth subordinate clause, 'That . . . view', qualifying the co-ordinated subjects, H and J, of the main sentence.
L. The verb of the main sentence, 'Are', required by the co-ordinated subjects H and J.
M. The complement, 'gilt', required by L.
N. A phrase, 'by . . . ray', qualifying M.
O. A ninth subordinate clause, picking up 'ray' from N and qualifying it.

The hinge comes at lines 162–3, where the preliminary concatenation of subordinate clauses is joined to the beginning of the main sentence. Dowden put a semicolon here; Hutchinson's comma plus dash, which seems to look both backward and forward, was a great improvement. The effect in Hutchinson's edition is spoiled, however, by a comma plus dash after 'view' at the end of line 166. This has two effects. First it separates the co-ordinated subjects, 'retrospects' and 'prospects', from their verb and its complement, 'Are gilt'. Secondly, the words between these two strong stops are turned by them into a compartment which upsets the whole meaning of the passage. Hutchinson, who did not have the manuscript before him, is not to be blamed; here too Dowden had put a semicolon, so, allowing for the possibility of some parallelism justified by the manuscript, he repeated his own stop at the end of line 162. To make the passage finally clear we must allow lines 165–8 to run unstopped to their end.

As often elsewhere, the whole point of the poem lies in the force of what the syntax has to convey, which is that in Harriet Shelley's love ('ardent friendship', 158), her husband's 'gloomiest retrospects' and his 'most doubtful prospects' are turned alike to warmth and gold.

For Shelley's use of 'friendship', cf. n. on No. 24. 42.

p. 174, No. 51, THE WANDERING JEW'S SOLILOQUY. Medwin gives, divergently, '1808' and '1809' as the date when Shelley was first drawn to this subject. The style suggests a later date. For Shelley's four-canto poem on the Jew see above, pp. 183 foll., and nn., below, pp. 374 foll.

16: Shelley seems to fuse recollection of the pestilence in 1 Chronicles 21 with the language of Psalm 91: 6.

20: Cf. Byron, 'The Destruction of Sennacherib', and 2 Kings 18–19.

22: Cf. Numbers 16.

28–9: The whole poem depends on a rhetorical pause of some sort between the prayer contained in the three final imperatives and the clause indicating the consummation so devoutly wished by the Jew. The confused meaning of line 29, as hitherto printed, is partly due to Dobell's reading, 'this', and partly due to uncritical acceptance of a manuscript punctuation destructive of the syntax in which the meaning has to be sought.

p. 175, No. 53, SONNET, EVENING, Etc. *Date*: At head of manuscript, 'Sep. 1813'; underneath, 'July 31, 1813'. Probably composed on the earlier date and, with the preceding poem, copied out on the later one.

p. 177, No. 56, TO HARRIET [? GROVE]. *Title/Date*: The manuscript date, 'May 1813', probably represents Harriet Shelley's transcription. Shelley is quite unlikely to have written anything so immature that year. The verses are so far below his standards of 1810–13 that the question arises whether they date from an early time when the 'Harriet' was Harriet Grove. The words added below need not link them with either of Shelley's visits to Cwm Elan; it is not impossible that they could have been left there by Harriet Grove when visiting her relatives, found by Harriet Shelley, and transcribed by her—speculation might further consider whether this could have been under a belief that she herself was their 'Harriet'. The 'my Harriet' of line 18 is, of course, merely a common extension of the 'ethical' usage, and not, as has been suggested to me, an indication that Shelley's wife is referred to.

Perhaps there has been a conflation of two poems, the first ending at line 10.

p. 179, No. 58, TO ST. IRVYNE, ETC. *Title*: St. Irvyne: an estate in the neighbourhood of Field Place. Strood (22) is a near-by village.

17–20: Another example of 'natural' Platonism. From this crude stanza to *Epipsychidion* is a far cry, yet already we have the germ of the 'Soul of my Soul' idea. Cf. *Epips.* 236–8, where the turrets and the gloom seem to reappear in the imagery.

p. 183, THE WANDERING JEW

Textual history: Because Medwin made claims to a share in the authorship this poem has usually been denied acceptance in the Shelley canon. Against the slightness of Medwin's claims must be set considerable evidence that Shelley wrote it. Much of this comes from correspondence: see Jones, *Letters*, i. 17–18, 20, 22, 23. In 1810 Shelley sent a manuscript to the firm of Ballantyne and Co. of Edinburgh. Their letter, declining publication, is dated 24 September of that year. On 28 September he proceeded to offer a second manuscript of the poem to Stockdale, of London, subsequently the publisher of *St. Irvyne*, whose statement that he never received it is doubted by Dobell. Shelley wrote three more letters to Stockdale on the subject. On 14 November he says that he will doubtless be receiving it soon from Ballantyne. On 19 November he says that, alternatively, he would send a copy he possessed. Then, on 2 December, he seems to think that Stockdale may now have two copies; if so he would like to have one of them returned to him for correction. That two copies existed is clear. Shelley himself made quotations from *The Wandering Jew*: see nn. on lines 435, 780; again in his Note on *Queen Mab*, VII. 67, he quotes a passage about Ahasuerus translated from a 'German work' picked up, 'dirty and torn, . . . in Lincoln's-Inn Fields': see above, pp. 316–18. This last incident, and Shelley's poem on Ahasuerus, are referred to by Mary Shelley in her Note on *Queen Mab* (see above, p. 340). Finally, in No. 32 of *The Edinburgh Literary Journal*, 20 June 1829, appears a notice of the forthcoming publication of *The Wandering Jew*, 'a poem in four cantos by the late poet Shelley, and entirely written in his hand'. The manuscript is described as having been brought by the poet to Edinburgh some twenty years before and having 'lain in the custody of a literary gentleman of this town to whom it was offered for publication'. From information gathered by Newman Ivey White (*Shelley*, i. 580) it would seem that the manuscript was received by the editor of the *Literary Journal* from James Ballantyne, brother of the Ballantyne (John) referred to by Shelley in his letter to Stockdale of 19 November 1810. His reference, on 2 December, to 'two copies' suggests a hope either that John's copy had eventually been forwarded, as requested, or that the first manuscript, which he had himself sent to Stockdale, had somehow emerged.

These points are consistent with the fact that the 1829 version, published in the *Edinburgh Literary Journal*, contains a number of passages omitted in, or amplified from, the version which was published in *Fraser's Magazine* in 1831 and which may be presumed to derive from the Stockdale manuscript. It may be noted that Medwin is nowhere mentioned by those who printed the poem. His claims to have participated in the composition (revised *Life*, 39–43) have no independent substantiation and his quotations are not based on an independent text; again he says that seven or eight cantos were written, and there is no evidence that the extant four-canto version is incomplete. It seems to me suspicious too that, while he is at pains to state that Mary Shelley was mistaken about the Lincoln's Inn Fields fragment, picked up in reality, he says, not by

Shelley but by himself, he has failed to notice that her evidence is supported
by Shelley's own statement in the Notes on *Queen Mab*. Dobell's text of 1887
is necessarily based on the *Fraser's* text of 1831, since this is a complete one,
whereas the amplified version printed in the *Literary Journal* in 1829 inter-
sperses quotation with summary. Exclusion of the poem by editors began with
Mary Shelley. This does not mean that she doubted Shelley's authorship; over
and above her reference to it in her Note on *Queen Mab* is the fact that its
publication in *Fraser's*, in 1831, was by her consent. In the last paragraph of
the Preface to her 1839 edition of Shelley's poetry she refers to the loss of material
relating to his early life. It may not be guessing too much to suppose that, with
the world awaiting a collection of poems worthy of the poet, she was not alto-
gether unhappy at having a good reason to exclude some of the less impressive
ones. Whatever may have been her reasons in relation to *The Wandering Jew*
they can have nothing to do with Medwin, for she is not known to have mentioned
him in the context.

The only numbers of the *Literary Journal* named by Dobell as the sources of
his text are Nos. 33 and 34, and, since neither of these numbers includes lines
1171–1420, a temporary puzzle arose to which I could find no answer in the
Bodleian or the British Museum. Fortunately I happened to examine the copy
in the Keats–Shelley Memorial, Rome, where, thanks to somebody's helpfully
pencilled reference, I was able to discover that, although he omitted to say so,
he had taken the 1829 version of these lines from No. 59.

Date: Though the foregoing evidence shows 1810 as the date of composition,
Shelley has dated his Preface '1811': this, however, would be consistent with
the possibility that it was added when he visited Edinburgh with Harriet, and
that it was among the amplifications in the manuscript he then handed to
Ballantyne. Both Dedication and Preface are missing from the 1829 version.

Title: according to the article in *The Edinburgh Literary Journal*, No. 32,
Shelley was in doubt whether to call his poem *The Wandering Jew* or *The Victim
of the Eternal Avenger*, both titles being found in the manuscript.

The Present Text: I have followed Dobell's arrangement of printing from
1831 but substituting in italics, where they occur, the corresponding, amplified
passages from 1829; the rejected, non-amplified passages are given in my
Textual Commentary. Such a text is, necessarily, somewhat arbitrary, but its
design is consistent with what we can learn from the textual history of the poem
about Shelley's intentions. The original editors, both in 1829 and 1831, followed
the usual practice of regularizing accidentals. Between the work of these editors
and that of Dobell, who continued it, Shelley's meaning has been brought out
remarkably well, though here and there, as my Commentary will show, I have
ventured an amendment. In 105, for example, I have inserted a full stop,
accidentally omitted by Dobell from the 1831 text, and in lines 222–37 I
have made one verbal and three punctual changes which the previously
chaotic syntax seemed to demand. A common problem is the distinction
between Shelley's careless, all-purpose dashes and the dashes which serve a
useful purpose in pointing rhetoric; an example of the former may be found in
1026–7, which I have emended, and of the latter in 672–5 which I have allowed
to stand. 1071–81 and 1437–51 are examples of passages where the sense has
required a radical repointing. Shelley had a fondness for double-barrelled nouns

and adjectives, which he used to give something of the effect of Greek compounds. Where it seemed necessary I have silently hyphenated these: e.g. 'tempest-clouds' (343), 'silver-winged' (895). Shelley's indifference to orthographical consistency may be illustrated in 8 by the 'Tipt' of 1831, the 'Tipp'd' of 1829: beside this may be set (42) the 'blossomed' of 1831 and the 'blossom'd' of 1829; different first editions have followed different manuscripts, and I have followed Dobell's acceptance of these unimportant differences.

Dedication: Sir Francis Burdett (1770–1844), M.P. for Westminster, was prominent in 1810 by reason of his great stand for Parliamentary reform and for freedom of discussion. For this he was committed to the Tower. By the Dedication Shelley was associating himself with a new and active form of Whig creed and action. In 1812 his habit of sending letters to Burdett did much to bring him under surveillance by government agents. See the indexes to Jones, *Letters*, and to Kenneth Neill Cameron, *The Young Shelley*.

Preface: Ballantyne had given as his reason for declining to publish Shelley's poem the bigoted attitude of the Scottish public, who had detected atheism even in *The Lady of the Lake*. His hit at the superstitions of the battle of Armageddon, the personal reign of J—— C——, etc., can hardly have acted as a new recommendation. Hardly more tactful is the reference to the absence of annotation and antiquarian research, a side-blow at the practice of Scott, popular among romantically minded readers, which, as Dobell notes, is rather an unfair one in view of the indebtedness to Scott which is plain throughout the poem.

94: The rhythmical clumsiness suggests a possible misreading of Shelley's manuscript.

108–9: Dobell compares Pope, 'The Dying Christian to his Soul':

> Trembling, hoping, ling'ring, flying,
> Oh, the pain, the bliss of dying!

which, presumably, may be traced through Flatman

> Fainting, gasping, trembling, crying,
> Panting, groaning, speechless, dying,

to the Emperor Hadrian's

> Animula, vagula, blandula, etc.

261: Shelley has a comparable passage in *St. Irvyne*, ch. III:

'Never, never shall it end!' enthusiastically exclaimed Wolfstein. 'Never!—What can break the bond joined by congeniality of sentiment, cemented by a union of soul which must endure till the intellectual particles which compose it become annihilated! Oh! never shall it end; for when, convulsed by nature's latest ruin, sinks the fabric of this perishable globe; when the earth is dissolved away, and the face of heaven is rolled from before our eyes like a scroll; then will we seek each other, and in eternal, indivisible, although immaterial union, shall we exist to all eternity.'

Cf. also, from *Zastrozzi*:

'Shall I then call him mine for ever!' mentally inquired Matilda; 'will the passion which now consumes me, possess my soul to all eternity! Ah! well I know it will; and when emancipated from this terrestrial form, my soul departs; still its fervent energies unrepressed, will remain; and in the union of soul to soul, it will taste celestial transports.'

276–7: Apparently a reminiscence from M. G. Lewis, *The Monk*, ch. IX:

> 'Agnes!' said I, while I pressed her to my bosom,
> 'Agnes! Agnes! thou art mine!
> Agnes! Agnes! I am thine!
> In my veins while blood shall roll,
> Thou art mine!
> I am thine!
> Thine my body! thine my soul!

341: According to the article in *The Edinburgh Literary Journal*, No. 32, which preceded the numbers in which the poem appeared, Shelley's manuscript bears a line from Aeschylus, noted between Cantos I and II. Together with the line which follows I give it as it appears among the Fragmenta Adespota in Nauck's *Tragicorum Graecorum Fragmenta*. These lines were a much-quoted tag among the ancients, and Shelley could have come across them in one of several places. (In place of πυρί Dobell prints πόζι, which is a *vox nihili*.)

> ἐμοῦ θανόντος γαῖα μιχθήτω πυρί·
> οὐδὲν μέλει μοι· τἀμὰ γὰρ καλῶς ἔχει.

The meaning is: 'When I am dead let earth be mingled with fire. It matters nothing to me. For my part all is well.' The writer comments that it has reference to something said by Paulo: presumably in lines 296 foll. He notices at the same time how applicable this is to Shelley's own fate. This seems to be the first hint of the prescience which culminated in *Adonais*, 487–95. Cf. above, p. 363, n. on No. 5 of the Esdaile Poems.

459: probably a reminiscence of Scott, *Marmion*, Canto VI, Stanza 30:

> O Woman! in our hours of ease
> Uncertain, coy and hard to please . . .
> When pain and anguish rend the brow,
> A ministering angel thou!

which, in turn, seems to derive from Laertes, in *Hamlet*, v. i:

> A ministering angel shall my sister be,
> When thou liest howling.

435, 443–51: Adapted by Shelley as an epigraph for *St. Irvyne*, ch. VIII.

553–4: *drops . . . chill*: probably objects of *feel*. Syntax doubtful.

569: Medwin makes two statements about this canto the evidence for which is worth examining, since it serves as one measure of his credibility: see revised *Life*, p. 39. The first is that 'the vision is taken from Lewis's *Monk*'. If this refers, as is presumed, to the vision of Don Lorenzo in ch. I, the only passage which bears any positive resemblance to Shelley's poem is the following:

At the same moment the roof of the cathedral opened; harmonious voices pealed along the vaults; and the glory into which Antonia was received, was composed of rays of such dazzling brightness, that Lorenzo was unable to sustain the gaze. His sight failed, and he sank upon the ground.

No less remote from exactitude is the second statement, namely that 'the Cruci-fixion scene [is] altogether a plagiarism from a volume of Cambridge Prize Poems'. The following extracts, from Thomas Zouch's poem 'The Crucifixion', are all that can be adduced in its support:

> 'Memory bids the scene,
> Th' important scene, arise, when dread dismay
> Alarm'd the nations. Melt, thou heart of brass:
> Death triumph'd o'er its victor. Wild amaze
> Seiz'd all the host of heaven, moaning their God
> In agony transfixt, his every sense
> A window to affliction: sorrow fill'd
> Their tide of tragic woe, and chang'd the note
> From fervent rapture to the gloomy strain
> Of deepest lamentation.

> Ye young, ye gay,
> Listen with patient ear the strains of truth:
> Ye who in dissipation waste your days,
> From pleasure's giddy train O steal an hour,
> With sage reflection, nor disdain to gaze
> The solemn scene on Calv'ry's guilty mount,
> Where frighted nature shakes her trembling frame,
> And shudders at the complicated crime
> Of deicide.—The thorn-encircled head
> All pale and languid on the bleeding cross,
> The nail-empierced hand, the mangled feet,
> The perforated side, the heaving sigh
> Of gushing anguish, the deep groan of death,
> The day of darkness, terror and distress:
> Ah! shall not these awake one serious thought!'

> 'See Israel's humble King, mild as the lamb
> Beneath the murdering knife, amidst the sneer,
> The taunt of mad reproach, led to the cross,
> To shame and bitter death. Him late they rais'd
> To fame's bright summit, when they sung his name
> With loud hosannas, or with silent ardor
> Dwelt on his tongue, list'ning the happy lore
> Of evangelic joy. Ye ruffian tribe,
> Ah! check the ruthless rage, that drowns the voice,
> The faithful voice of reason, to your God
> Prefers sedition's son, whom foul with crimes,
> Ripe vengeance waits, and awful justice calls.'

668: Cf. 844.

697: Cf. 850.

716–17: Apparently an absolute construction.

764: Shelley's footnote is to be compared with his Note no. 14 on *Queen Mab*; see above, p. 316, and the n. on this, below, p. 396.

780 foll: Used, with some variations, as the epigraph for *St. Irvyne*, ch. X.

805: For Shelley's concern with present, past, and future cf. the Esdaile Poem 'A Retrospect of Times of Old' (p. 122, above). It runs through his writings: cf. the historical arguments in *A Philosophical View of Reform* and 'A Defence of Poetry': cf. also the reappearance of this theme, in relation to the Wandering Jew, in *Hellas*, 745 foll., and my discussion in *Shelley at Work*, pp. 293 foll. In *Queen Mab* it provides the main design of the poem. For this and for Shelley's indebtedness to Condorcet and Volney see below, pp. 381–2.

861–2: Cf., among the Esdaile Poems, 'To the Republicans of North America', 41–50, especially the hurled/world rhyme. See above, p. 107.

Epigraph (Canto IV): Though Shelley used a text of the *Eumenides* which would not now be acceptable to classical scholars I have accepted it here with two small emendations; what matters is the meaning the passage held for him: 'No! Gorgons, not women I call them. And yet I cannot really say they're like Gorgon-types—black and altogether loathsome, puffing out foul blasts of breath and dropping powerful, poisonous rheum from their eyes.'

1023–59: Dobell comments on the apparent irrelevancy of this passage to the rest of the poem, and raises the question whether it originally formed part of a plan to write a poem in which two speakers would discuss man's relation with the Deity. My guess is that the passage just happened to find its way into the poem because it represented something uppermost in Shelley's mind at the time of writing. The feeling of 'God in Nature' appears in 'A Sabbath Walk' (see above, p. 81) which probably dates from the end of 1811 or the beginning of 1812. There seems to be a Miltonic ring: the feeling is reminiscent of *Paradise Lost* and the language of 'Psalm 136'; with lines 1031–2 cf.

> That by his all-commanding might,
> Did fill the new-made world with light . . .
>
> The horned Moon to shine by night,
> Among her spangled sisters bright.

Relevant here is Shelley's comment to Hogg in July 1816 that 'Rousseau is indeed in my mind the greatest man the world has produced since Milton': see Jones, *Letters*, i. 494. The hyperbole grows out of the context of this letter where Shelley is recording his emotional reaction to Swiss scenery in its relation to Rousseau and his writings; his mind then passes to Milton as another exponent of natural beauties. Herein one may perceive a pointer in *The Wandering Jew* towards the thought and feeling of 'Mont Blanc' and the 'Hymn to Intellectual Beauty'. Cf. the letter to Godwin of 24 February 1812, where once again Shelley passes to Milton from thoughts of man in relation to nature; therea s here there is inconsistency about religion; cf. below, nn. on *Queen Mab*, and my discussion in *Shelley at Work*, pp. 211–29.

1421–37: I give these lines unitalicized since, despite what Dobell says to the contrary, the differences in the *Fraser* version are immaterial.

1437–51: The climax needed heightening by punctuation. Shelley's dashes in 1438 are, for once, helpful, giving pace and pause, but the exclamation at the end of 1440 needed to be marked; then nothing less than a second exclamation mark would do for the last line. This being added I considered changing the old-fashioned 'Come!' to 'Come,'—I hope, however, that an additional exclamation mark may not be excessive..1443 and 1446 then needed attention; the old-fashioned practice of using an exclamation mark with a question that is purely rhetorical is not always effective with modern eyes and here, to distinguish it from the exclamatory sentences between which it stands, a mark of interrogation seemed unavoidable.

The subject of the Wandering Jew: Cf. Esdaile Poem No. 51, *Queen Mab*, VII. 67 foll., and *Hellas*, 132 foll. Over and above Shelley's interest in a rebel and a questioner of religion was his deep concern with man in relation to past, present, and future time: see Rogers, *Shelley at Work*, pp. 291 foll.

p. 231, QUEEN MAB

Date: On 20 December 1810 Shelley mentions a 'Poem on L'infame': cf. the epigraphs. This may well be a clue to the early conception: see below, p. 399. It was begun in April 1812. By 15 February 1813 it was 'finished and transcribed'. By 21 May it was in the press. (Jones, i. 28, 29, 35, 324, 354, 368.)

Text: Shelley had 250 copies printed, of which he circulated some seventy in the summer of 1813. In 1821 he was annoyed by the pirating of both text and Notes by William Clark, a London bookseller. (Jones, ii. 304.) He regarded the poem as immature and foresaw that it could become a false measure of his life's work. In *The Daemon of the World*, the abbreviated version published in 1816 with *Alastor*, he had given all that he wished to have preserved. In her first edition of 1839 Mary Shelley made certain revisions and omissions: see Commentary. This was wise, because she risked prosecution for printing what was then regarded as revolutionary and atheistical material. In her second edition of 1839–40 she printed the text and Notes in full, and her publisher Moxon was prosecuted for a 'libel' on religion, the Scriptures, and God. No sentence was imposed and the case proved to be the last of its kind. (See White, *Shelley*, ii. 407–8.) The poem has continued, however, to be treated by editors as a piece of juvenile imprudence, best relegated to a small-type position at the end of the Poetical Works, and Shelley's Notes have been unduly neglected.

Queen Mab today: The poem is now commonly accepted as Shelley's first major work, and important as such. But his fears continue to be justified. In the place of those who, in the nineteenth century, condemned him as a propagandist have come those who exalt him as such and represent his poetry as growing out of the atheistical and revolutionary doctrine it contains. What the poem marks is not a point in his development but a phase. What he sought to spread was not propaganda but knowledge. With knowledge, he felt, went beauty, and with beauty love. Such is the essence of what Notopoulos has called his 'natural' Platonism. His expressed abhorrence of didactic poetry has seemed paradoxical in a man who seldom stopped teaching. But his teaching methods are the reverse of didactic; they follow the Platonic method of observation, examination, and analysis, illustrated by analogy and allegory. Thus it is that, in *Queen Mab*, the eighteenth-century materialism of Shelley's day can exist side by side with a Platonic idealism, part inborn, part derived from the Renaissance tradition encountered in his studies. The resultant unity, more aesthetic than logical, becomes easier to understand if we remember that even in those eighteenth-century philosophers most opposed to Plato there are to be found such threads of Platonism as are required by any system of coherent thought; many of them are found in Godwin and in the *philosophes* who deprecated Plato. Godwin knew that he had neglected 'the empire of feeling'. His great mistake was to believe that that would not affect his conclusions. Shelley spent years in trying to repair the flaw. In *Queen Mab* he finally failed. Out of the failure he emerged a true poet. This, as he foresaw, is what people have found difficult to understand. Mary Shelley has the point: 'The alterations his opinions underwent ought to be recorded, for they form his history.' The present Notes are an attempt to record them.

The epigraphs:

Crush the monster!—*Correspondence of Voltaire.*

I wander along the by-paths of the Muses, trodden by none before. I love to find fresh springs and to drink from them. I love to gather new garlands . . . wherewith no man's brows were crowned before. And, first of all, do I tell of great matters, and I shall go on to free men's minds from the crippling bonds of superstitions.—Lucretius, Book IV.

Give me a place to stand on, and I will move the Universe.—Archimedes.

Though they have usually been ignored, Shelley's epigraphs are useful road signs, carefully placed. Taken in conjunction with the Dedication, these three show all the main paths of his thought and feeling at the time: love, beauty, freedom, and improvement in human life, and his own ambition to serve these things. For the Voltaire motto cf. Jones, i. 28, 29, 35. For Lucretius cf. Hughes's fine chapter, No. XIII, in *The Nascent Mind of Shelley*, and Shelley's quotation in his Notes, No. 6. This poet with his discussions of Man in the Universe, blending scientific speculation with grand poetry, was a formative influence on Shelley; *religionum . . . nodis*—the word *religio* signifies the ties of institutional religion, its superstitions, etc., to which Shelley objected. In the quotation from Archimedes Shelley seems to be thinking of the power of thought and poetry to move institutions, opinions, and the lives of men; his thought of the poet's need for a fulcrum is not unrelated to his constant concern for effectuality: e.g. his prayer to the West Wind, symbol of a driving force.

Dedication: Writing on 11 June 1821 (Jones, ii. 298) Shelley referred to this as 'foolish'. On this account Mary Shelley omitted it in 1839[1]. Her restoration of it in 1839[2] was more than an act of justice to Harriet. In 1812 Shelley's love for her was a fulfilment of the natural Platonism inherent in the tag from St. Augustine (see above, p. 139, and n., p. 369) which he attached to the early Mary-poems, and again to *Alastor*. The extension of his love for her to a love for mankind is an extension of Platonic love to social concerns which, in *Queen Mab*, begins to humanize the Godwinian influence.

Design/Sources: Shelley's general plan comes from Condorcet's *Esquisse d'un tableau historique des progrès de l'esprit humain*, which examines the potential future of man in the light of the past and the present and considers means of accelerating the process of man's perfectibility. Shelley's 'grand and comprehensive topic' was not exhausted in one poem. He returned to it in *Laon and Cythna*, five years later. In his prose works too, e.g. *A Philosophical View of Reform* and 'A Defence of Poetry', a kindred historical approach is discernible.

As a poetical basis of his plot he borrows from Volney's *Les Ruines* the device of a mystically conducted tour through time and space; in place, however, of Volney's narrator and Genius he gives us a sleeping girl, Ianthe, and Mab, Queen of the Fairies, later to be renamed 'The Daemon of the World': a semi-divine spirit, one of the δαίμονες from Plato's *Symposium* (see Rogers, *Shelley at Work*, ch. 5). Ianthe owes something also to Maia, the heroine of Sir William Jones's *Palace of Fortune*. The structure of the poem is as follows:

I–II. 96   Introductory narrative.
II. 97–end The Past (a review of dead civilizations).
III–VII   The Present (III, evils of monarchy; IV, political tyranny; V, economic corruption; VI, VII, religion).
VIII, IX   A vision of the Future; the heroine is exhorted to strive for its perfectibility.

p. 232, *Canto I.*

1–2: A conjunction of the opening line of Southey's *Thalaba the Destroyer*, 'How beautiful is night!', with Homer, *Iliad*, xvi. 672, Ὕπνῳ καὶ Θανάτῳ διδυμάοσιν.

23–6: Dreams were to become one of Shelley's favourite symbols for the philosophic problem of reality. See Rogers, *Shelley at Work*, ch. 10.

55–6: Cf. Erasmus Darwin, *Loves of the Plants*, III. 23: 'As through the coloured glass the moon-beam falls'.

105: In Jones's *The Palace of Fortune* the heroine Maia is similarly approached by the goddess Fortune, riding in a golden car drawn by peacocks.

181: Throughout Shelley's poetry the Veil is a symbol closely related to, and frequently combined with, the Dream; both are notable in Plato. The Veil signifies something that divides life from death, the world of 'mutability' from the unchanging world of eternity, and it represents the problem of distinguishing the one from the other.

187: Shelley delights in spiritual journeys in space-vehicles. Sometimes they are boats and sometimes chariots, etc.; the distinction is unimportant. They symbolize the freedom of the human soul to get away from a world of mutable things (including tyranny, and all human miseries) towards a world of eternal values—truth, beauty, goodness, liberty. See Rogers, *Shelley at Work*, ch. 6.

188: With 'earth's immurement' cf., above, l. 135, 'Each stain of earthliness'. We have here a poetic echo of Plato, *Phaedo*, 81 b, where the soul of the philosopher is freed from the bonds of the body by the practice of philosophy. Plato's emphasis on dialectic and the pursuit of ideal forms is, of course, vastly different from the romantic, natural Platonism of Shelley into which it has merged. Cf. *Esdaile* Poem No. 50. 1–3, 57–63, and nn.

200–19: Cf. Erasmus Darwin, *Loves of the Plants*, III. 161–4.

249 foll. 'The journey through space . . . shows a more scientific and imaginative comprehension of the universe than do most such accounts (for instance in Jones or Volney), and reveals, too, a sense of the universe as flow and beauty absent from the usual Newtonian picture (as in Pope's *Essay on Man*, or [Eras-

mus] Darwin's *Temple of Nature*, or such standard accounts of the time as those in Rees's Cyclopaedia).' (Kenneth Neill Cameron, *The Young Shelley*, p. 245.)

265–77: Cameron reinforces the previous point by comparing and contrasting this passage with Darwin's mechanical description in *The Temple of Nature*, I. 65–8, which was probably Shelley's model:

> Here, high in air, unconscious of the storm
> Thy temple, NATURE, rears its mystic form;
> From earth to heav'n, unwrought by mortal toil,
> Towers the vast fabric on the desert soil . . .

For Shelley's sensitiveness to the 'Spirit of Nature' see above, p. 362, n. on Esdaile Poem No. 2, 'A Sabbath Walk', and the Esdaile Poems *passim*. Desmond King-Hele, *Shelley: His Thought and Work*, p. 37, comments:

> In short, the Spirit, Shelley's substitute for God and one that needs 'no prayers or praises', pervades every link in the Great Chain of Being. The Spirit is akin to the 'Universal Soul' or 'Sovereign Spirit of the World' to be found in poems like Thomson's *Seasons*, Akenside's *Pleasures of the Imagination* or Young's *Night Thoughts*. Shelley has also made use of Wordsworth's 'something far more deeply interfused', and of the popular eighteenth-century concept of a physical 'subtle fluid' filling up the interstices of matter, though his Spirit is more active than any of these. Shelley never decides whether the Spirit has free-will or not.

The idea of the 'World Spirit', deriving probably from Plato, *Timaeus*, 48 a, has appealed to poets from the Renaissance down to Yeats.

p. 240, *Canto II.*

70–82: J. A. Notopoulos, *The Platonism of Shelley*, p. 181, observes that 'These lines are an expression of Shelley's own cosmic imagination with a distant echo, perhaps, of the Platonic cosmology in *Republic*, 616 c–617 c, or such sources as Psalm 19 and the words from Addison's *Ode*:

> What though, in solemn Silence, all
> Move round the dark terrestrial Ball? . . .'

109 foll.: Although Shelley was acquainted with the idea of biological evolution through Erasmus Darwin's *Temple of Nature*, his survey gives no indication that he accepted the idea. On the contrary, he treats man as biologically static, even on the long time-scale required for geological processes.

Cameron rightly contrasts the emphasis of Shelley, the sociologist, with the nostalgic, romantic emphasis of Volney on the mouldering of ruins, which inspired Peacock's *Palmyra*.

231–43: King-Hele, *Shelley: His Thought and Work*, p. 38, notes the similarity of the modern view: '. . . each particle is allowed a small range of uncertainty, its behaviour being governed by probability laws which degenerate into the macroscopic laws of Nature when the numbers of particles are large.' Though Shelley may have had the idea of sentient atoms straight from Lucretius, his interest was probably aroused by the eighteenth-century vogue for microbes, which he would have met in Thomson's *Seasons*, 'Summer', 289–311. The very small had come into the limelight again in the seventeenth century, after the invention of the microscope, the infinitesimal calculus of Newton and Leibnitz, and the actual observations of animalcules by Leeuwenhoek. Cameron, p. 392, quotes pertinently from two of Shelley's sources: Lord Monboddo's *Antient Metaphysics*, and Sir William Drummond's *Academical Questions*. Erasmus Darwin is another likely source.

252 foll.: Cf. I. 265 and n.

p. 247, *Canto III*.

22 foll.: Shelley's castigation of the monarchy comes partly from the militant republicanism of such writers as Tom Paine, partly from the polemical writings of his contemporaries, e.g. Byron, Hazlitt, Hunt, Coleridge, and Southey, and partly from his sympathy for social suffering in the Napoleonic period in which misery was general and wealth in the hands of the aristocracy and the Court. Much of the feeling of this canto is revealed in the Esdaile Poems; see above, Nos. 12, 16, 19, 31.

143–6: Perhaps a reference to the savage treatment of the Luddites.

150 foll.: Godwinian 'virtuous man' is the central figure in Esdaile Poems Nos. 14 and 32.

176 foll.: Another essentially Godwinian passage, though as usual Shelley's ingredients are mixed. In 199–200 'He fabricates / The sword which stabs his peace', a striking expression for one contemporary exploitation of labour, is echoed from Thomson, *The Seasons*, 'Summer', 746; and, with the substitution of the 'Spirit of Nature' for God, lines 226–40 resemble in feeling the end of the First Epistle of Pope's *Essay on Man*.

p. 254, *Canto IV*.

1 foll.: The opening lines seem to show Shelley enjoying the peaceful beauty of a winter's night in England, while his thoughts (33 foll.) rush off to the Russian winter in which Napoleon's soldiers are perishing. Lines 58 foll. refer, of course, to the burning of Moscow in that year, 1812. With the battle scene described in 41 foll., cf. Esdaile Poem No. 7, about the battle of Austerlitz; there too the central thought is the exploitation of soldiers by monarchs.

89 foll.: *Hath Nature's soul . . .*: The contrast between the perfection of Nature and the corrupting power of man, more especially the rulers among mankind, is the common Rousseau-notion of the day; '. . . life's smallest chord / Strung to unchanging unison' derives from the Platonic tradition of 'the concord of a single harmony' in *Republic*, 617 b.

112–15: Cf. Plato, *Republic*, 377 foll.

139–53: 'The conception of the universe as a sentient organism is one of the most influential contributions of Plato to the poetic mind, for its ultimate re-expression in poetry as the Spirit of Nature gives the poet's soul an appropriate realm for the exercise of imagination.' (Notopoulos, p. 176.) The conception of macrocosm and microcosm which makes it possible for the poet to commune with the Spirit of Nature grew out of certain notions in the *Timaeus* (cf. 30 d and 44 d). Shelley may have picked it up from Paracelsus, whom he read at Eton; in Elizabethan literature it had commonly been applied to the soul of man, which thus becomes a microcosm of the soul of the world. The immortality of the soul is a necessary concomitant of the concept, for, if the world soul is eternal, the soul of man, which is a miniature of it, must be eternal likewise. Hogg, who was Shelley's fellow Platonist at Oxford, says that 'if the great master of the academy could read *Queen Mab* he would at once acknowledge the author for a disciple'. (*Life*, ed. Wolfe, i. 45.) The natural Platonism of Shelley is evident from the moment of the flight of the soul of Ianthe to ascend from the body to heights of clearer vision. The direct Platonism comes from reminiscences of thought, not the least interesting being the conception of the immortality of the soul which is common to the *Phaedo* and to Christianity. For all the materialism and professed atheism something in Shelley too takes flight from this point in the poem. See above, p. 309, Shelley's Note 13, and n. on this, p. 394.

187 foll.: Though the wording is applied to tyrants generally, Shelley is, in effect, violently denouncing the Prince Regent. The wording connects closely with what he wrote to Miss Hitchener on 10 August 1811: see Jones, i. 132.

p. 261, *Canto V.*

1–6: Cf. the alternation of life and death as conceived in Plato, *Phaedo*, 70 c–72 e and *Symposium*, 207 d. It is not necessary to assume that Shelley had these passages in mind: this may be another expression of his 'natural Platonism', arising out of his poetic observation of phenomena. Cf. the letter to Miss Hitchener of 19 October 1811 (Jones, i. 152) where he passes from a similar observation to the Godwinian notion of 'the eventual omnipotence of mind over matter'. He had observed too how 'natural Platonism' can operate in other writers: cf. in his Notes, Nos. 4 and 5, the passages quoted from Ecclesiastes and from Homer. The idea of the regeneration of nature, found in the Homeric passage, recurs in another letter to Miss Hitchener of 24 November 1811 (Jones, i. 192), where the language looks ahead to the 'Ode to the West Wind'. Natural Platonism, from the time of Shelley's friendship with Peacock, in 1812, began to be more and more reinforced by direct study of the Platonic dialogues.

Coming at the beginning of a canto of which the subject is economic corruption, the language is a signpost on the path by which the Godwinian disciple passed into the poet. Meanwhile the attack is a powerful one, the work of an intelligent inquirer and not of a youthful fanatic, as has sometimes been held. Commercial wealth, he believed, was the source of inequality, exploitation, national ambition, and war. The picture, on the whole, was a true one. The year 1812 was a time of war and dictatorship, corruption, vice, crime, poverty, hypocrisy and hatred.

38–41: The 'venal interchange' and 'natural kindness' are an ironic reminder of the way in which Shelley's own 'natural kindness' was exploited by Godwin's insatiable demands for money.

83: A Platonic phrase analogous to, and possibly derived from, *Phaedrus*, 248 c, *Phaedo*, 80 e, 81 c–d, *Republic*, 515 c.

132–5: For the endowment of man with will and power over matter cf. n. on V. 1–6, above; here, however, the Platonism, as shown by the word 'plastic', is less natural than indirectly derived. For Plato's general beliefs on this see

Republic, 617 e, and *Laws*, 897 a–b. Probably the most famous of Shelley's expressions of the concept of a plastic Nature comes in *Adonais*, 379–85; for its origin in the *Timaeus* see Notopoulos, pp. 115–18. Its elaboration by Cudworth influenced Pope, Coleridge, and Wordsworth besides Shelley. Cudworth does not appear in Shelley's reading, but the doctrine could have reached him through these poets or through his reading of Monboddo's *Antient Metaphysics*.

137–45: The reminiscence of Gray's *Elegy*, 57–68, proceeds out of Godwinian perfectibility-notions which a more experienced educationist than Shelley might regard as over-optimistic: cf. Shelley's description to Godwin of the Dublin poor as 'beings capable of soaring to the heights of science, with Newton and Locke'.

p. 268, *Canto VI*.

44: See Shelley's Note 10, p. 304, on the perpendicularity of the poles, and n. on this, p. 393.

71–102: In the *Alastor* volume of 1816 Shelley printed these lines as a separate poem, entitled 'Superstition'. Line 102 was replaced by two lines:

> Converging thou didst give it name, and form,
> Intelligence, and unity, and power.

190–6: No single passage in Plato, or any other author, was to colour Shelley's thought and language more than the famous Allegory of the Cave, in *Republic*, 514 a: see Rogers, *Shelley at Work*, ch. 9. I think, however, that here, at the *Queen Mab* stage, the concept is just a piece of natural Platonism.

197: In this and the following section Shelley attacks Religion. The main attack on Christianity comes in Canto VII; Canto VI is mainly an exposition of the doctrine of Necessity, based on Holbach's *Système de la nature*. In origin it was a fusion of two Platonic concepts, Necessity and the World Soul. In the *Republic*, 616 c–617 c, Necessity is the Mother of the Fates on whose spindle turn the orbits of the Universe. Shelley saw it as an impersonal, impartial power, unlimited and outlasting decay; all actions and thoughts in the Universe were subject to it; all actions were predestined and had always been so. Like Rousseau, Montesquieu, and others Shelley believed that man is naturally virtuous and happy but artificially corrupted by false sophistication and false civilization; in *Queen Mab*, Cantos VIII–IX, he adds, and elaborates, his own peculiar belief in the evils engendered by an animal diet. God, tyranny, and war, and all the evils castigated in the poem, appeared to Shelley as mere creations of the corrupted human mind; in time they would all perish, destroyed by their own corruption. Such was the operation of 'Necessity'—for those who believed in it it was all-sufficing, the 'mother of the world'. In times when biological and psychological thinking were undeveloped and the mechanist outlook had glibly confused the laws governing living matter and dead matter it could make an easy appeal. For Shelley, when he was writing the poem, the Necessitarian doctrine seemed to offer the means of an approach to scientific developments on a social basis. In the end his instincts rebelled against its cold, unrelieved gloom (so disastrously felt throughout the Esdaile Poems) while his intellect rebelled against the weak point underlying all Necessitarian reasoning: this was the strange combination with the belief in predestination, which such a doctrine must obviously postulate, of a limited allowance for human will. Shelley's respect for human beings could not indefinitely tolerate the Necessitarian notion that what held back the general restoration of virtue and happiness was that 'man's all-subduing will', corrupted itself by the selfishness, superstition, and lust which produced the evils of the world, was weak enough to tolerate their existence. See nn. above on V. 1–6 and V. 132–5; also the discussion in *Shelley at Work*, ch. 3.

Lines 197–8 are a turning-point in Shelley's *Queen Mab* phase. The unpoetical concept of Necessity was ill-married with the concept of the Universe as a sentient organism: see Notopoulos, p. 176, quoted above in n. on IV. 139–53. Notopoulos goes on to discuss the Platonic origins of that favourite Shelleyan theme, the union of the poet's soul with the soul of nature. One example of Shelley's contact with this notion will be sufficient here: the reference of Sir William Drummond (*Academical Questions*, p. 237) to 'the ancient dogma of the world's being a sentient and animated being (κόσμος οὐσία ἔμψυχος καὶ αἰσθητική)'. As the poem proceeds Shelley sees further and further into the 'appropriate realm for the exercise of the imagination'. *Prometheus Unbound* is already on the horizon. See n. on VIII. 107–8.

p. 274, Canto VII.

1–13: Shelley is thought to have been indebted to Volney for the scene of the burning of an atheist. Possibly he had seen, as a child, Foxe's *Acts and Monuments*, published about 1564, a horrifying book with plates showing the tortures inflicted on martyrs, which well into Victorian times was considered suitable reading for English children.

13: Shelley's attitude towards Christ was in constant evolution and he died before it became fixed. His much-publicized Oxford pamphlet, *The Necessity of Atheism*, asks questions rather than assumes their answers, an attitude for which there was no name in 1810—not till 1870 did T. H. Huxley coin the word 'agnostic'. (Cf. Ἀγνώστῳ Θεῷ, Acts, 17: 23.) Alike in Shelley's day, among the Victorians, and in our own time, atheists and Christians have combined in isolating the words 'There is no God' from the general context of Shelley's thought and treating them as the mature conclusion of a mature thinker. The whole subject has been less examined in the light of judgement than subjected, from two sides, to a heat of advocacy. A wider inquiry shows that the only consistent thing about his sayings on religion is his inconsistency. As he grew older Platonism brought him closer to Christian feeling, and he was attracted to the person of Christ, as a persecuted reformer, though he never lost his distrust of institutional religion as a political and social force. In *Shelley at Work*, pp. 275 foll., I have attempted an examination of his maturer views, expressed in *Hellas*. (Cf., as important evidence, his Notes on the Choruses which start at line 197 and line 1090.)

17: Shelley is using the 'Vast chain of being' idea, which runs through the eighteenth century from Pope, *Essay on Man*, ll. 237 foll. Cameron notes the relevance to this passage of what Shelley wrote to Miss Hitchener, 2 January 1812, following his discussion of atheism with Southey. In fact the whole of this letter (see Jones, i. 214–19) is full of thought-material for *Queen Mab*. From Southey he passes to Moses, to Newton, and to James Montgomery, son of martyred missionaries, whose religious views vacillated as Shelley's did. From this he passes to Wordsworth and quotes 'A Poet's Epitaph' from *Lyrical Ballads*; cf. above, p. 363, n. on Esdaile Poem No. 4, 'Passion', 6–10.

23: Shelley has started his canto with a dramatic attack: he now reverts to Godwinian Reason, with its substitution of Necessitarian beliefs for Christian ones. *OED*, following Hutchinson on this passage, gives 'exterminable: illimitable (SHELLEY, *rare*)'. Rossetti suggested 'interminable' or 'inexterminable'.

30: The attack on the history of religion is a condensation from Volney; cf. n. on VII. 1–13, above.

67: *Ahasuerus*: This character is a subject recurrent in Shelley's work: see the poems on pp. 174, 183–228, and nn., pp. 374 foll.

161 foll.: This attitude, that Christ taught men truth and peace only in order to rouse their bigotry, gives an alignment with the Lucretian epigraph attached to *Queen Mab*.

177 foll.: Shelley's use of the legend seems to show the Jew less as an unbeliever, punished for his blasphemy, than as a questioner, like Shelley, punished for his analysis of cause and effect.

180: *reillumed*: A good example of Mary Shelley's intelligent textual improvements: see General Introduction, pp. xx, xxiii.

234: Cf. *The Wandering Jew*, 780 foll., *passim*.

p. 282, *Canto VIII.*

1 foll.: Both philosophically and in his own life Shelley was haunted by a profound consciousness of time; cf., in particular, *Hellas*, 137–48, 766–85, 792–806, 841–60, and his remark in a letter to John Gisborne, 18 June 1822, some three weeks before he was drowned: 'If the past and the future could be obliterated . . . I could say with Faust to the passing moment "Remain thou, thou art so beautiful." ' (Jones, ii. 435–6.)

At this point the poem passes to the Future. First of all, in this canto, it is seen as a vision of perfectibility. Then, finally, in the last canto of all, Ianthe's spirit is returned to earth with the exhortation to do everything possible to bring that perfectibility about.

12: For 'the veil' cf. above, n. on I. 181. Cf. also *Prometheus Unbound*, I. 538, where, likewise, the tearing of the Veil symbolizes the destruction of what separates the world of Good from the nearer world of Evil. There is, however, a difference. When the Fury in *Prometheus Unbound* says 'Tear the veil!' this implies recognition of the power of Prometheus' will, actuated by love. Here, however, in *Queen Mab*, it is not love but the process of Necessity that opens up the world of the Good.

58 foll.: Here then is the Godwinian Utopia, the 'bliss' brought about by the process of Necessity. But, as everywhere in Shelley's poetry, the ingredients are mixed. There is much of pastoral feeling, some from Thomson's *Seasons*, some from Milton's Eden. Not least noticeable is the Platonic element which begins

to creep into this canto. In Canto VII, the spearhead of Shelley's attack on religion, the Platonic element is negligible. From here onwards it is like something which Shelley had tried to hold back and which now rushes in despite all his efforts. One of the first things to burst through the rent veil is the Platonic notion of the 'music of the spheres' (cf. *Republic*, 616 c–617 d) which appears in lines 17–20, faintly anticipating the

Music,
Itself the echo of the heart, and all
That tempers or improves man's life, now free

which (III. iii. 46–8) is among the joys awaiting Asia and Prometheus in their Platonic cave where the Good and the Beautiful are one.

107–8: At VI. 197–8 (see n., above) came the turning-point in Shelley's *Queen Mab* phase. These lines are another landmark. By now the Necessitarian, in the midst of his Godwinian Utopia, is well on his way towards the Shelleyan concept of Platonic love, led towards it through the chink in logic caused by the difficulty of reconciling Necessity, a process requiring no exercise of free will, with the notion of 'the eventual omnipotence of mind over matter'. How flat a poem can fall which celebrates freedom or happiness derived from a *process* is illustrated throughout the Esdaile Poems: cf. Nos. 3, 12, 19, 31. Now, throughout the moral universe, the 'Spirit of Nature', originally identified with Necessity, has become identified with love, and love is seen as a cosmic force, based on principles in the *Symposium*.

211: See above, p. 326, Shelley's Note 17 and below, nn., p. 398.

p. 288, *Canto IX.*

1–37: In the previous canto we have had the picture of a transformed society. Now Shelley shows the movement of society towards the transformation. The opening lines give an impression of his own age.

31–2: An echo from Erasmus Darwin, *Temple of Nature*, IV. 383; cf. above, p. 105, Esdaile Poem No. 16, 'The Monarch's Funeral', lines 57–8; also 'To Ireland', 19–21, p. 19, and n., p. 353.

38: Here starts the 'morn of love', i.e. the new condition of affairs, Platonically derived. Cf. 'the daystar dawn of love', etc., in Esdaile Poem No. 17, 'To the Republicans of North America', 41–50, above, p. 107.

57 foll.: There was a good deal of eighteenth-century speculation about the possibility of discovering the 'Panacea', a comprehensive scientific remedy for all ills of the human body. Medwin (p. 50) tells how Shelley used to quote Franklin and Condorcet on the subject. It links up with that Rosicrucian 'secret of eternal life' which appears in *St. Irvyne*, written before Shelley went to Oxford and, no doubt, appealed to his imagination in the same way as the story of the Wandering Jew. Its relevance here is its relationship to the Godwinian belief in 'the eventual omnipotence of mind over matter'. It is, of course, characteristic of Shelley in his *Queen Mab* phase to support the beliefs of materialistic philosophy with points drawn from contemporary scientific beliefs, and equally characteristic to combine these materialist notions with the Platonism developing as his poem proceeds.

130: *rack*: nowadays the preferred reading in *The Tempest*, IV. i. 156: this I prefer to *wreck*, which Shelley may have had from Malone, because the latter obscures the Shakespearian source.

146 foll.: The Fairy's exhortation to Ianthe is Shelley's exhortation to the soul of man. It is pertinent to remember that he gave the name of his heroine to the daughter born in 1813. In his belief in a spiritual universe, and in his exhortation to the soul to pursue through virtue 'the gradual paths of an aspiring change' Shelley's natural Platonism brings the poem to a climax indicative of the phase through which he has been passing. With the natural Platonism of the conception go threads of direct and indirect Platonism that run through the language. The lines on birth and death (149–50, 155–6) are echoes of the *Phaedo*, reminiscent of Wordsworth's *Intimations of Immortality*, and they look ahead to the climax of *Prometheus Unbound*, II. v., cf. lines 98–103:

> We have passed Age's icy caves,
> And Manhood's dark and tossing waves,
> And Youth's smooth ocean, smiling to betray:
> Beyond the glassy gulfs we flee
> Of shadow-peopled Infancy,
> Through Death and Birth, to a diviner day . . .

The *voyage*, the *isles*, the *gulfs* (cf. 175) are all there: for the Platonic symbolism see Rogers, *Shelley at Work*, ch. 6. From 229,

> The restless coursers pawed the ungenial soil

it is not a very far cry to *Prometheus Unbound*, II. v. 1:

> On the brink of the night and the morning
> My coursers are wont to respire . . .

The Spirits in both contexts are accompanied by the Platonic symbolism of *darkness* and *light*. *Queen Mab* might fittingly be regarded as the phase in which Shelley, after he had restlessly 'pawed the ungenial soil' of too unmitigated Godwinism, escaped, as Wordsworth did, into the light.

NOTES ON SHELLEY'S NOTES ON *QUEEN MAB*

These Notes have been commonly passed over as no more than an indigestible adjunct of the poem. But, no less than the poem itself, they form a remarkable record of a remarkable phase. For convenience of reference they have here been numbered from 1 to 17. Eleven—Nos. 1, 2, 3, 4, 5, 6, 8, 10, 11, 14, 16—are comparatively short glosses. Six—Nos. 7, 9, 12, 13, 15, 17—amount to an appendix of essays. The Godwinian disciple is trying to support by reasoning what the poet has said through allegory. The threads are drawn from a tangle of ideas. Next to Godwin the authors he most relies on are Holbach, the French materialist, and J. F. Newton, the vegetarian. His supporting cast, 'bewildering in its variety', as Mr. King-Hele remarks, is headed by Lucretius, Pliny, Bacon, Milton, and Spinoza. He has an appetite for detail that might almost satisfy modern 'Ph.D. requirements'. Yet he does not allow himself to degenerate into a mere collector of points. Despite lapses of judgement and an inexperience which makes him liable to bracket the crank with the thinker, he shows, at an undergraduate's age, the scholar's instinct for picking the significant point and reasoning from it.

pp. 295–6, *Shelley's Note 1, Note 2*: King-Hele notes (pp. 38–9) that the astronomy is correct, apart from an arithmetical lapse or two (one light-year is actually 5,900,000,000,000 miles, which is 63,000 times the distance from the sun to the earth). On one point, the distance of the earth from Sirius, he is, by luck, ahead of the professional astronomers of his day. The fact of the insignificance of the earth in the Universe has, King-Hele notes, been slightly over-exploited for atheistic purposes. Shelley, no doubt, took it from Holbach's *Système de la nature*, 'the Bible of all materialism', where Newtonian science is given a bias towards the doctrine of Necessity. One wonders how Shelley forgot its use by those enemies of science who persecuted Galileo.

Footnote 1: Nicholson's *British Encyclopedia*, 6 vols., 1807–9, was ordered by Shelley from Hookham on 17 December 1812. (Jones, i. 343.)

p. 296, *Shelley's Note 3*: 'To employ murder as a means of justice' is a question-begging phrase, not without parallel in later times, which fails to distinguish between offensive and defensive action. Wars in defence of liberty were later to provide Shelley with major poetical motifs: cf. 'Ode to Liberty', 1820, and *Hellas*, 1821. At this time, however, quite apart from Godwinian theory there was much to stimulate his hatred of the fighting service: the Press Gang (cf. above, pp. 131–3, Esdaile Poem No. 32, 'The Voyage', 221 foll.), the flogging of soldiers, against which the Hunts were campaigning, and the constant sight of starving war-veterans, frequently mutilated by wounds: cf. above, p. 99, Esdaile Poem No. 14, 'A Tale of Society as it is'. 'Falsehood and Vice', which he here quotes from the Esdaile Poems, is 'A Tale of Society' allegorized.

p. 298, *Shelley's Note 5*: οἵη περ φύλλων . . .: 'As with the generation of leaves, so is it with that of men. Some leaves are flung to earth by the wind, while others spring up in the rich woodland, and grow afresh in the spring. So is it with men: one generation grows up, while another wastes away'. [tr. N. R.] Some editions of the *Iliad* read τηλεθόωντα . . . ὥρη.

p. 298, *Shelley's Note 6*: *Suave mari magno* . . .: In the magnificent translation of Charles Stuart Calverley (1831–84):

> Sweet, when the great sea's water is stirred to his depths
>   by the storm-winds,
> Standing ashore to descry one afar-off mightily struggling:
> Not that a neighbour's sorrow to you yields dulcet enjoyment;
> But that the sight hath a sweetness, of ills ourselves are exempt
>   from.
> Sweet 'tis too to behold, on a broad plain mustering, war-hosts
> Arm them for some great battle, one's self unscathed by the
>   danger:—
> Yet still happier this:—To possess, impregnably guarded,
> Those calm heights of the sages, which have for an origin Wisdom;

> Thence to survey our fellows, observe them this way and that way
> Wander amidst Life's paths, poor stragglers seeking a highway:
> Watch mind battle with mind, and escutcheon rival escutcheon;
> Gaze on that untold strife, which is waged 'neath the sun and the starlight,
> Up as they toil on the surface whereon rest Riches and Empire.
>   O race born unto trouble! O minds all lacking of eyesight!

Cf. above, p. 364, n. on Esdaile Poem No. 7.

p. 298, *Shelley's Note 7*: The first paragraph is an adaptation from the essay 'Of Avarice and Profusion' in Godwin's *Enquirer*. Shelley's letters to Miss Hitchener of 25 and 26 July 1811 (Jones, i. 124–8) form a useful commentary on this Note. The quotation from the opening of Horace's *Ode*, II. xv, is apt: 'Nowadays the princely mansions will spare very few acres to the plough'. It relates the short-sighted effects of Regency magnificence to the situation in Italy around 27 B.C., when the number of small holdings had declined and the yeoman class, which had formed the strength of the Roman legions, was threatened with extinction.

Footnotes: Cameron (p. 403) notices that note 7 in Rousseau's essay *De l'inégalité parmi les hommes* is wide of Shelley's point and that he probably accepted Rousseau as his source through a misreading of something in Godwin's essay. For Godwin in Shelley's correspondence see the index to Jones, *Letters*. *Political Justice*, at this time, was the most formative book Shelley had read.

p. 301, *Shelley's Note 8*: *Nam iam saepe* . . .: 'For often men have betrayed their country and their dear parents in trying to avoid the halls of Acheron.' In the vein of bantering classical allusion which runs through his letters to Hogg and Peacock, Shelley refers, with this Lucretian tag, to the disrupting effect of evangelical religion with its gloomy insistence on original sin and the efforts that were necessary to avoid an eternity of hell-fire. Perhaps there is a side-glance at his own family troubles. Cf. the ending of the letter to his father, 6 February 1810 (Jones, i. 51). Shelley may or may not have read *Zoonomia*, IV. 83–4: in this medical text-book Erasmus Darwin gives examples of people driven mad by fear of hell. He includes *Orci timor* and *spes religiosa* as diseases.

p. 301, *Shelley's Note 9*: This youthful Note was to create lasting and unfortunate misapprehension. From the theme of economic corruption a mention of prostitution follows quite naturally. What came less naturally in the poem was the development, among the comments, of a young man's personal preoccupation with the general subject of sex relationships. He is, in the main, recapitulating from Godwin the celebrated free-love passage which in later editions of *Political Justice* was to be considerably modified. A psychologist might, perhaps, see in Shelley's reverence for Godwin a substitute both for religion and for his father. It seems odd that the intolerance at times displayed towards both should accompany a tolerance that saw no irony in the acceptance of a twice-married philosopher who had described marriage as 'a system of fraud', and who, later, while unceasingly demanding money, should ostracize him for living with his daughter in an unmarried state. The reverence for Godwin extended to his late wife, Mary Wollstonecraft, whose *Vindication of the Rights of Woman* is another source of Note 9. Writing to Sir James Lawrence on 17 August 1812 (Jones, i.

323) he says that by then he had 'no doubt of the evils of marriage—Mrs. Wollstonecraft reasons too well for that'. In fact she does nothing of the sort: she approves of marriage, though she does say much of the unhappiness of woman, having been educated to become helpless under its yoke. If it was Godwin who gave the impulse for this lucubration of Shelley's it was Sir James Lawrence who, with his romance *The Empire of the Nairs*, provided the *point d'appui*. Many of Shelley's troubles grew out of the single fact that his ideas and reading were quite disproportionately ahead of his experience. Thus it was that, from a romance based on social abuses in the Far East, he was able to pick on a connection between marriage and prostitution and to generalize it into the most poignant of pleas against marriage. He is, he tells Lawrence, 'a perfect convert'. Such is the basis of the ascription to Shelley of a 'doctrine of free love'. How far he really was from being a convert to such a doctrine may be seen in his review of Hogg's *Prince Alexy Haimatoff* in 1814, when he described it as 'pernicious and disgusting'. Not yet had his direct study evolved the Platonic mould in which his mature poetry was to be shaped, but already his naturally Platonic feeling was all against such a notion. We need look no farther than the Dedication to *Queen Mab* and to the poem addressed to his wife Harriet (Esdaile Poem No. 24, p. 115 above) from which he quoted in Note No. 16. But the harm was done. Even the *fino amore* of *Epipsychidion* has yielded passages which have been interpreted as 'propaganda' for 'free love'.

For a finely penetrating discussion of the foregoing see Hughes, pp. 206–20.

Footnote: Shelley's reference to Gibbon, as a subsidiary source, connects with his letter to Hookham of 17 December 1812, in which he orders, among other books, the 6-volume edition of *Decline and Fall of the Roman Empire*, published in London in 1776–88.

p. 304, *Shelley's Note 10*: Shelley is unfortunate in his attempt to support the doctrine of Necessity by contemporary science. For his anxiety for information on 'the position of the Earth on its poles' see Jones, i. 349, Letter No. 221, probably written to Hookham early in 1813. He wrongly concluded that the obliquity of the ecliptic would decrease, instead of oscillating about the mean value, near 23½ degrees, according to which hypothesis the seasons would become identical and seasonal change be replaced, he hoped, by universal mildness; cf. IX. 57 foll. However, he was correct, Mr. King-Hele tells me, in deducing from the fossil record that the position of the poles has changed, relative to the earth's land mass, a fact usually explained today in terms of continental drift.

Footnotes: Shelley's study of Laplace, [*Exposition du*] *système du monde*, 1796, is mentioned to Hogg on 26 November 1813 (Jones, i. 380). On 17 December 1812 he had ordered from Hookham 'a work by a French physician, Cabanis' (Jones, i. 342).

p. 305, *Shelley's Note 11*: Holbach gives two examples in illustration of the operation of Necessity. The first is taken from the physical Universe. In a storm, he says, there is no grain of dust or drop of water that falls by accident: a geometrician could show exactly why each must fall precisely where it does. Similarly with the upheavals which take place in society: actions, words, and thoughts must produce certain inevitable effects. This too can be appreciated by a specially trained intelligence.

Footnote: Shelley's original footnote does not name the author of the *Système de la nature*, 1781. In two letters to Godwin, of 3 June and 29 July 1812 (Jones, i. 303, 315), he shows a common contemporary ignorance of the author's identity. In the first he refers to him by his pseudonym, as 'M. Mirabaud', and in the second ascribes the book, as many then did, to Helvétius. Cameron (p. 409) thinks that Shelley first encountered Holbach, like other authors, at second hand, possibly through Barruel's *Memoirs Illustrating the History of Jacobinism* which, according to Hogg, was popular at Oxford.

p. 305, *Shelley's Note 12*: Shelley follows up the preceding Note by expanding examples of the effect of Necessity on human behaviour. This note is a re-statement from Godwin and Hume, the Hume influence being partly direct and partly through Godwin. (See n. on VI. 197 foll.) Robert François Damiens, referred to in the fifth paragraph, made an attempt on the life of Louis XV in 1757, and for this, after hours of torture, he was publicly torn to pieces by horses.

p. 309, *Shelley's Note 13*: Shelley repeats the inquiries of *The Necessity of Atheism*, which are mainly based on Locke, extending them by others, taken mainly from Holbach and Hume. For these arguments see Cameron, pp. 257–9. In 1814 much of this ground and more was covered in *A Refutation of Deism*. For a specialized discussion of this see Cameron, pp. 275–87: Cameron, however, takes no account of the advance this essay represents upon the *Queen Mab* phase. For this see Notopoulos, pp. 323–5. See also, above, n. on VI. 197 foll. and below, p. 395, n. on Sir William Drummond.

p. 311, the quotation from Sir Isaac Newton: 'I do not invent hypotheses, for whatever is not derived from phenomena must be called a hypothesis, and hypotheses, whether they concern metaphysics, physics, unknown properties or mechanics, do not have a place in philosophy'. [tr. N. R.]

p. 312, *the French poet*: 'To say just what he is we'd need to be himself'. I owe the tracing of the line to Bodley's Librarian, Dr. R. Shackleton, who discovered in Paris a copy of Sylvain Maréchal's rare volume, published in 1779, *Le Livre de tous les âges, ou le Pibrac moderne, quatrains moraux*. These quatrains are an imitation of the celebrated sixteenth-century quatrains of Pibrac. With *dire* for *scavoir* Shelley is quoting from the last of Maréchal's couplets (but see Corrigendum, below, p. 400):

De Dieu

Loin de rien décider de cet Etre Suprême,
Gardons en l'adorant un silence profond;
Le mystère est immense et l'esprit s'y confond:
Pour scavoir ce qu'il est, il faut être lui-même.

The Holbach passage, summarized: 'Primitive man first worships the ele-ments and local, material objects, sometimes extending his veneration to out-standing human beings; then he thinks that he can simplify the object of his worship by electing one single presiding spirit, a First Cause. Thus does he create chimeras which plague him till his knowledge of nature rids him of them. God is the name given to the First Cause—something we do not know. In God man worships the unknown cause of effects which ignorance prevents him from explaining. Ignorance created gods. Education can destroy them. Gods are accepted for worship on hearsay alone. Men allow authority and the habit of submission to replace conviction and proof. It is the zealots, priests, and metaphysicians who are insistent. But they themselves disagree. And we slit each other's throats for the sake of a god who remains unknown. It is of the very nature of ignorance to attach importance to the unknown, and to harden itself against difficulties. The unknown excites curiosity, and speculation involves pride. Its conclusions are vanity, and when we contend for God we are really contending in the interests of our vanity, the most susceptible and the most foolish of our passions.

'Let us put aside the theologians' God, the capricious despot who dictates our destinies. Let us fix our eyes, for the moment, on his much-vaunted goodness. If it is his glory to work for the well-being of humanity, why does he leave us in ignorance of his glorious self? Why does he not have convincing ways of revealing himself? Why, instead of the equivocal evidence of miracles and of the wonders of the Universe, does he not write his name more clearly and make his will known, so that nobody dares to violate his commandments or to misinterpret his will? As things are, even if we do admit the existence of the God of the theologians, with all attendant contradictions, we still cannot reach any conclusions to authorize what religion demands of us in conduct or worship. Objections can be stated to all the alleged qualities of God—goodness, wisdom, knowledge, omnipresence, justice, grace, reasonableness, and immortality. The stating of these leads to the question "If he has spoken why is the Universe not convinced?" '

With the above might be compared the many passages where Shelley, though in a different way from Pope and others of the eighteenth century, sees God in Nature: cf., for instance, in *Queen Mab*, I. 264 foll., and Canto VIII, *passim*.

p. 316, *Quapropter effigiem* . . .: Translated by H. Rackham in the Loeb Classical Library, from which text Shelley's is here emended: 'For this reason I deem it a mark of human weakness to seek to discover the shape and form of God. Whoever God is—provided there is a God—and in whatever region he is, he consists wholly of sense, sight and hearing, wholly of soul, wholly of mind, wholly of himself. . . . But the chief consolations for nature's imperfection in the case of man are that not even for God are all things possible—for he cannot, even if he wishes, commit suicide, the supreme boon that he has bestowed on man among all the penalties of life, nor bestow eternity on mortals or recall the deceased, nor cause a man that has lived not to have lived or one that has held high office not to have held it—and that he has no power over what is past save to forget it, and (to link our fellowship with God by means of frivolous arguments as well) that he cannot cause twice ten not to be twenty or do many things on similar lines: which facts unquestionably demonstrate the power of nature, and prove that it is this that we mean by the word "God".'

p. 316, Sir William Drummond's *Academical Questions*, 1805, comes second only to *Political Justice* among the contemporary books which influenced Shelley in his early years. See Cameron, pp. 392–3. Shelley's debt to Drummond must not be estimated by a comment, made during his *Queen Mab* phase, upon a single point. In the 'Essay on Life' (Julian edn., vi. 194–5), commonly dated 1812–14, he praises Drummond as one of those who had helped him away from the materialist philosophy—'a seducing system to young and superficial minds. It allows its disciples to talk and dispenses them from thinking.' For a manuscript memorandum of Shelley's, relating to Drummond, for Drummond's visit to Shelley in Rome, and for the relation of both to the Platonic content of *Prometheus Unbound*, see Rogers, *Shelley at Work*, pp. 64–7. For the field of reading, and ideas, mainly Platonic, which Drummond opened up for Shelley, see Notopoulos, pp. 147–51.

p. 316, *Omnia enim per Dei potentiam* . . . : 'For all things have taken place through the power of God. Indeed the power of nature is nothing but just the power of God. It is certain that our lack of understanding of the power of God is proportionate to our ignorance of natural causes; and it is particularly foolish to have recourse to that same power of God when we are ignorant of its natural cause—i.e. of just the power of God.' [tr. N. R.]

p. 316, *Shelley's Note 14*: See above, nn. on Shelley's poem *The Wandering Jew*. Byron and Hogg were both sceptical about the story of the scrap of paper, 'dirty and torn'. It was a common literary device to add to the interest of a piece of writing by a romantic story about its origin: in presenting *Epipsychidion* he made a similar use of the device. The 'translation' seems not to have been Shelley's, as was supposed by Mary Shelley and others: what he discovered was not the German original but a translation already made. Newman Ivey White (*Shelley*, i. 580) thinks that he came across it in *La Belle Assemblée, or Bell's Court and Fashionable Magazine*, for 1809. He gave a transcript to Hogg, who printed part of it, and himself attached a part of it as a footnote to line 764 of *The Wandering Jew*: see above, p. 207.

The tyrants joined in the note with Nero are Christian II of Denmark (1481–1559) and Muley Ismael, Sultan of Morocco (1646–1727). Christian (misprinted as *Christiern* in previous editions) fought to gain the throne of Sweden and celebrated his coronation by 'the Stockholm blood-bath' in which eighty-two of his enemies were executed. Muley Ismael is said to have followed up a military victory by sending back to his capital, Fez, 10,000 heads of the vanquished.

p. 318, *Shelley's Note 15*: The examination of Biblical and Christian history follows up the passage from Holbach, quoted in Note 13. Other sources are Hume, Godwin, and Locke. Shelley's case against Christianity is marshalled with great skill.

The antithesis in the fourth paragraph between 'the reveries of Plato and the reasonings of Aristotle' is an idea that seems to have come to England from Voltaire, Diderot, and others of the *philosophes*, though it dates back through the Renaissance to the Middle Ages. Plato's close reasoning, which they were untrained to follow, was dismissed as 'dazzling sophisms'; Shelley's phrase 'puerile sophisms', used in the preface to his translation of the *Symposium*, is his variant of the formula. Shelley's first reaction, even when he came to the direct study of Plato, was to admire him principally as a poetic dreamer: such extremely Platonic poems as 'Prince Athanase' and *Alastor* are little more than reveries. As Shelley's studies proceeded, the intellectual appeal of Plato became no less than the emotional; his memoranda reveal the quickness of his response to subtly reasoned thought. Something of this ability, paradoxically, came to him at second hand from the *philosophes*, for, despite their reductive, stereotyped notions of Plato, their own thinking is permeated by that current of Socratic reasoning which has always been vital to systematic minds. What is unique in Shelley's *Queen Mab* phase is the strange way in which he blends the Platonism and the anti-Platonism of the *philosophes*. Qua philosopher and Godwinian disciple he uses their anti-Platonism in his Notes and in the versified philosophy of *Queen Mab*. Qua poet he uses, side by side with his materialist arguments, such poetical themes from Plato as the immortality of the soul, the music of the spheres, and the World Soul. The *Queen Mab* phase was a phase of uncertainty, the culmination of the mood of disenchantment and rebellion which succeeded the Oxford disaster. Not till his friendship with Peacock had ripened and he had attained with Mary the serenity underlying his Dedication of *Laon and Cythna* did the tension relax so that he could follow instinct: for the moment Plato and the classics in general were affected by his condemnation of the whole system under which he had been reared.

The reference, in the preceding paragraph, to Jesus as a Daemon is interesting. In the *Symposium* δαίμονες are intermediate deities, existing in the area between gods and mortal men, capable of exerting an influence on either. There were δαίμονες proper and κακοδαίμονες, evil spirits. At times it could be difficult to distinguish between them. Here Shelley seems to be identifying Jesus with the class of κακοδαίμονες. Love, in the *Symposium*, is the most powerful of the δαίμονες and, as the Shelleyan conception of love develops, it gets closer to the spirit of Christianity as expounded by St. Paul; in view of the Platonism which came into Christianity with that apostle the coincidence is not remarkable. This is not to say that the label 'Christian' or the label 'Platonist' would ever have been exact or adequate for Shelley. Of recent years, since his memoranda on the *Symposium* have been analysed, his maturer attitude can be deduced. There is, says Diotima, the wise prophetess who tutored Socrates, 'a state of mind called "right opinion or conjecture" that occupies the same ground between understanding and ignorance that Love holds between gods and men'. Here stood Shelley in 1816, and here he stood in the Notes to *Hellas* which are, in many respects, the far end of the path which began with the Notes to *Queen Mab*. (For Shelley's memoranda on the *Symposium* see Rogers, *Shelley at Work*, ch. 4; for Daemons see ibid., ch. 5.) In the converted version of *Queen Mab*, published in 1816, the Fairy becomes 'The Daemon of the World'.

p. 325, [*Quemque utero inclusum Mariae*] . . .: Translated by M. Plattnauer in the Loeb Classical Library:

The swelling womb of the Virgin Mary conceived thee after that she had been visited by the angel, and the unwed mother, destined to give birth to her own creator, was astonished at the unborn child that grew within her body. A mortal womb hid the artificer of the heavens: the creator of the world became a part of human nature. In one body was conceived the God who embraces the whole wide world, . . . (Claudian, *De Salvatore*).

Shelley's Latin text has been emended here. He gives as the title of the poem '*Carmen Paschale*'. His quotation starts at the seventh line, omitting the first four words, added here to complete a translatable sense; *quemque* follows a *quem*, in line 2, the antecedent, in line 1, being *Christe potens rerum*, 'Christ, lord of the world . . .'.

Footnotes: Hume's *Essays* were ordered by Shelley from Hookham on 17 December 1812 (Jones, i. 342), and Locke's *Essay Concerning the Human Understanding* from Graham, on 11 August 1810 (Jones, i. 13).

p. 325, *Shelley's Note 16*: For Shelley's concern with Time see n. above on the text of VIII. 1 foll. His Note is an interesting example of the fusion in his mind of eighteenth-century philosophy and Platonism. Together with the debt to Godwin and Condorcet, which he acknowledges, we have in the lines he quotes an expression, in terms of the *Phaedo*, of his increasing conviction of the immortality of the soul, together with the conception, from the *Symposium*, of Earthly and Heavenly Love. The development of these notions may be traced through his letters to Elizabeth Hitchener, e.g. those of 20 June and 24 November 1811 (Jones, i. 109–10, 191–2). His quotation is from his own poem 'To Harriet', Esdaile Poem No. 24, lines 58–69: see above, p. 117. The feeling is one with the feeling of the Dedication to *Queen Mab*. In the letter of 24 November comes much about 'self-love' and 'lack of self-love'. The concept of ἀφιλαυτία, 'lack of self-love', had impressed Shelley, it seems, in a passage from Aristotle's *Nichomachean Ethics*, which he had translated between early December 1810 and late January 1811. (See Cameron, *Shelley and his Circle*, ii. 659–62.) The concept, and sometimes the Greek word, recurs through letters to Hogg and Miss Hitchener in the period preceding *Queen Mab*. Its kinship with the ἀγάπη love of the *Symposium*, the personal-cum-social implications of which Shelley was already developing, constitutes a significant comment on the odd antithesis between Aristotle and Plato noticed in my n. on Shelley's Note 15, and a still more interesting point is the use of this word by St. Paul in 1 Corinthians 13, whereby the famous expression of Christian love is seen to be not altogether remote. Shelley's estimate of the value of 'a man of virtue and talent who should die in his thirtieth year' seems curiously applicable to himself.

p. 326, *Shelley's Note 17*: Shelley's zeal may seem to have run away with him, but in his day there was originality even in his attention to matters of health in their social implications. His concern may have proceeded from a natural sympathy with animals, stimulated, perhaps, by a distaste, comparable with that of the Sitwells in our own day, for those sections of English society whose whole life seems dedicated to the killing of birds or animals. This subject appears soon to have faded from his life and thoughts. I have wondered whether his vegetarianism affected his health and whether it became a source of domestic trouble. Perhaps he abandoned it when he left Harriet for Mary.

p. 326, *Immediately a place* . . .: quoted from *Paradise Lost*, XI. 477–88. The speaker is, in fact, not Raphael but Michael.

p. 327, *Audax omnia* . . .: *Od*. I. iii. 25 foll. 'Daring to endure all things humanity plunges to ruin through crime; [Prometheus], the bold son of Iapetus, by a trick, defiantly brought down fire to men; once fire had been stolen from its heavenly home, disease and a whole new host of infections fell on the world, and the slow necessity of death began to quicken its approach.' In *fraude malâ* there is a reminiscence of the legal phrase 'dolus malus', 'of malice prepense'. [tr. N. R.]

p. 336, Ἀλλὰ δράκοντας . . .: 'But you call snakes, panthers, and lions "wild beasts", though you have murderous habits of your own that are every bit as bad as theirs . . . That man is not naturally carnivorous is obvious from his equipment. For a man's body in no way resembles the body of any of the creatures who were born carnivorous, not having a hooked beak, sharp talons, or jagged teeth, a strong stomach or a calorific digestive system, able to take in or assimilate a heavy meat diet. It is precisely on account of our even teeth, small mouths, tender tongues, and dulled digestive system that our nature disowns flesh-eating. If you claim that you *were* designed for that sort of diet, then start killing what you intend to eat; but do it with your own personal resources, don't use a knife, or a club, or an axe, get hold of an ox in your teeth or a boar in your jaws. . . . Or tear a lamb or hare to pieces, then fall on it and eat it alive, as animals do. . . . But we go about our murdering in such a gentlemanly manner that we call meat an "extra"; next we start wanting "extras" with the meat itself, and we mix oil, wine, honey, fish sauce, and vinegar with Syrian and Arabian seasonings, just as if we were really embalming a corpse for burial. The fact is that when meat is so softened and seasoned and, in a way, predigested, it is quite a job for the digestive system to work, and, if it is unsuccessful in doing so, the result is severe pain and a stomach disorder that endangers health. . . . So, to start with, it was some dangerous wild beast that got eaten, then a bird or fish that got torn to pieces. And then when our murder-lust had given us a taste of blood and had first exercised itself on these [creatures], it was extended to the hard-working ox, the respectable sheep, and the cock that guards our homes. In this way, gradually putting an edge to our appetite, we progressed to the slaughter of human beings and to the carnage of war.' [tr. N. R.]

I have made one or two minor emendations of Shelley's text from that of the Loeb Classical Library. The word ὄψων which I have translated 'extras' is explained by Liddell and Scott as 'cooked or otherwise prepared food, a made dish, eaten with bread and wine'.

Footnotes: Rees's *Encyclopaedia* did not appear till 1819. Shelley probably used his edition of Chambers's *Encyclopaedia*. On 26 November 1813 he wrote to Hogg commending Plutarch's essay.

NOTES ON MARY SHELLEY'S NOTE ON *QUEEN MAB*

p. 337, *Note on* Queen Mab, *by Mary Shelley*: [1] *Shelley was eighteen*...: Despite this, and despite his own statement in the letter from which Mary quotes, he was, in fact, twenty when he wrote *Queen Mab*. Yet I venture to suggest a sense in which these statements are neither as exaggerated nor untruthful as they might appear. Writing to Hogg on 20 December 1810 Shelley says, 'I am composing a *Satiricial* [*sic*] *Poem* on L'infame . . .'. Jones (i. 28) comments: 'There has been much speculation on this poem, but it has never been identified.' Myself I cannot doubt that the poem referred to is *Queen Mab*. 'L'infame' not only appears as his first epigraph, but is repeated at the end of the letter as if it were the motto around which Shelley was building his ideas when he wrote; a comparison of letter and poem will show the kinship between the two. If the poem was written in 1812 it therefore seems likely that it was conceived two years earlier: consequently in wishing to present it as the *conception* of an eighteen-year-old boy neither Shelley nor Mary may have been far wide of the essential truth. That Shelley should have had a notion in 1810 and worked it over for two years, reading and making memoranda, is quite consistent with all we know of his working methods: see Rogers, *Shelley at Work*, *passim*: it is equally consistent that, during the long period of gestation of a major poem, ideas for it should have found their way, as they did in the Esdaile Notebook, and elsewhere, into a number of minor pieces, not to mention his correspondence.

[6] . . . *his unworldliness*: Mary refers, I think, to the quality in Shelley which he himself describes as 'lack of self interest' and ἀφιλαυτία (Jones, i. 77, 173). But she may be thinking also of the point that, his ideas and his intellect being usually far ahead of his experience, he was apt to seem a little naïve, and to frustrate his own endeavours thereby. This would be particularly applicable to *Queen Mab*. Cf. n. on Shelley's Note 9, p. 392 above.

Corrigendum to note on Shelley's Note 13 on *Queen Mab*
(See above, p. 394, n. on p. 312.)

While this volume was in the press Dr. Shackleton was kind enough to send me the following additional note:

'My friend R. A. Leigh, of Cambridge, tells me that the quatrain in full is quoted in a letter to Rousseau dated August 1763 and attributed to "un savant professeur". Silvain Maréchal was then thirteen years of age. A further point is that the last line in Leigh's manuscript begins "Pour dire ce qu'il est". This suggests that there is another published text, prior to Maréchal and modified by him, and that this is probably what Shelley saw.'

NOTES ON THE APPENDIX

p. 343, No. 43, FRAGMENT OF A POEM, ETC. *Date*: Pf., a letter to Hogg, is dated '11 Jan. 1811'. With lines 1–2 of its fourth stanza cf. No. 17, *passim*, and No. 27. 5–8, and n. Softer hearts and rods might be accessible in the Land of Liberty, though the problem of the African, like that of Shelley's bottles, might be to survive the voyage.

p. 344, No. 45, 'COLD ARE THE BLASTS . . .'. Versifying of this kind, traceable to 'Gothic' romances and translations, may be due partially to the influence, often circuitous, of 'Ossian'. There are affinities between these lines and the passages of 'Ossian' translated into German by Werther, just before his suicide.

12: *She sought her babe's food at her ruiner's gate*: An anticipation of 'A Ballad', written by Shelley in 1819. See General Introduction, p. xxix n. The poem was first printed in the Julian edn., where, through a misreading of the manuscript, it is entitled 'Young Parson Richards'.

p. 346, No. 57, 'LATE WAS THE NIGHT. . .'. *Date*: Esd. has '1815', but this must refer to the date of the transcription by Harriet Shelley. If, as seems likely, she was the author, no date can be conjectured.

5–8: If, as might be, the rhyme words in 6–7 have been reversed, perhaps the first 'murderes' in Esd. is a miscopying for 'murderous'; perhaps 'wave' should be 'waves' and 'braved' 'braves'; perhaps the second 'murderes' should be 'murderer'. Even so, the sense would seem to defy conjecture.

17: The last two words are just yielded by Esd. if we assume that the first letter is a capital, that the last has lost its ink, and that some such subject for the verb as 'none' has been omitted.

INDEX OF TITLES

INDEX OF FIRST LINES